AHAB'S TRADE

Other books by this author

Fast Company: The Lively Times and Untimely End of the Clipper Ship 'Walter Hood'

Most Perfectly Safe: The Convict Shipwreck Disasters of 1833–42

AHAB'S TRADE

The Saga of South Seas Whaling

Granville Allen Mawer

St. Martin's Press
New York

For Elizabeth

AHAB'S TRADE

Copyright © 1999 Granville Allen Mawer. All rights reserved. Printed by South Wind Production, Singapore. No part of this book may be used or reproduced in any manner whatsoever without written permission except in the case of brief quotations embodied in critical articles or reviews. For information, address St. Martin's Press, Scholarly and Reference Division, 175 Fifth Avenue, New York, N.Y. 10010.

ISBN 0–312–22809–0

Library of Congress Cataloging-in-Publication Data to be found at the Library of Congress.

Jacket image: Coloured engraving by Thomas Sutherland after William John Huggins *South Sea Whale Fishery. A Representation of the Ships* Amelia *and* Castor *off the Island of Bouro—with their Boats and Crew in Various Process of Fishing, Shewing the Spermacetti* (Australian National Maritime Museum)
Jacket design: Juliet Cohen

First published by St. Martin's Press: 1999

10 9 8 7 6 5 4 3 2 1

CONTENTS

Maps and Illustrations

Maps

Illustrations

PREFACE

If I have sought in this book to evoke the past as much as to explain it, it is because in foreign parts it is useful to have some grasp of the language when trying to make sense of the customs and history. And South Sea whaling, although its death is so recent, is already foreign to our experience. The collective attitude of humankind to its object, the whales, has reversed itself within a lifetime, and if our partisanship is engaged at all today it is for the victims of the trade rather than the exploiters. It would be as simple a matter these days to demonise the latter as it was to lionise them a century ago, but playing to the gallery, now as then, would serve no useful purpose. Better to accept that reality is often more complex and ambiguous than most of us would prefer it to be.

Complexity and ambiguity have left their marks on the structure of this book as much as on its contents, for the story of an industry is not like that of a person, who can be relied on to call an author back to the path no matter how far he or she may have strayed into the woods. My chapters, identified by the whale-bent harpoon (from the collection of the Australian National Maritime Museum), as above, take the reader chronologically from origins, through rise, to decline and fall, but the thread of that narrative is self-indulgent. It cannot be trusted at any particular point in time to be discussing the most important matters in the industry, but I hope that it will always be attending to the most interesting and revealing.

Interleaved with the chapters are what, for want of a better word, I have called tailpieces, identified by the logbook stamps with which the whalemen accounted for their catch. These take aspects of the trade or factors in it and explore them free of the tyranny of chronological narrative. They will often relate to some matter in the chapter that precedes them, but that too should not be relied on. If they, or the shorter breakouts identified by a ship-sighting stamp, are a distraction, they may safely be left for later attention without fear that they contain something vital to the plot.

Herman Melville haunts the pages of this book much as Ahab stalks the pages of his, but more important is the influence of another long-dead American, Alexander Starbuck, and a very lively Englishman, A G E Jones. Their exhaustive researches into the southern fisheries of their respective nations are the ballast of this book and, I hope, have been taken on board well enough to keep it on an even keel. All honour too, to the memory of Edouard Stackpole, who was the first to write of South Sea whaling as an industry that transcended national boundaries.

Closer to home, I am indebted to Averil Edwards and the staff of the Petherick Room in the National Library of Australia for their untiring pursuit of obscure texts, and to Patricia Miles and the Australian National Maritime Museum for their generous assistance with the illustrations. Dale Chatwin kindly allowed me access to his MA thesis on the later British trade, and Captain Merv Palmer was a most tolerant source of advice on seamanship. Such virtue as this book has is due in no small part to their efforts and those of many others who know how much I have appreciated their assistance; its vices, I am afraid, are all my own work.

Granville Allen Mawer
February 1999

INTRODUCTION:
LOITERING WITH
INTENT

In the late summer afternoon of 3 February 1998 a nursery school of 66 sperm whales, females and juveniles, approached the west coast of Tasmania in the vicinity of Macquarie Harbour. The sandy bottom shelved too gradually to give a good return to the sonar pulses of the whales' navigation system, and the school stranded. In a scene that is repeated many times each year around the world, concerned humans gathered at the isolated spot in a futile effort to assist their fellow mammals. Stranded sperm whales die relatively quickly. Like all large whales, their internal organs are crushed by the immense weight of the animal when unsupported by water, but they also have a unique disability; if they topple to the left, the single assymetrical blowhole will fill with sand, suffocating them. Only three of the 66 could be manhandled off the beach and dissuaded from returning. These were found washed up dead within a few days. The Parks and Wildlife Service, which had overseen the rescue attempt, dragged all the corpses beyond the high-water mark and buried them. They were careful to bury the adults at the bottom of the pit to discourage human scavenging for teeth and jawbones, the makings of scrimshaw. Respect and exploitation: it was ever thus.

Once upon a time—but not a lifetime ago—there was a way of life as foreign to our experience as that of a gladiator or a galley slave. It was, in the view of its humbler practitioners, as dangerous as the former and as oppressive, brutal, back-breaking and tedious as the latter. They called it whaling, but it was not the whaling of steam catchers and floating factories. It was whaling from small oaken ships and fragile cedar boats, and it survived far longer than it had any right to, into an age when iron and steam, which had somehow passed it by, were giving way in their turn to steel and internal combustion. Long before it finally expired as a deep-sea occupation in the early years of our century it had become as anachronistic as the trident and the trireme. By then it was an industrial fossil with equipment and methods that had been largely unchanged for 200 years, but in those centuries whalemen had pushed outwards from the coasts of the far North Atlantic until there was not a corner of the world ocean they had not searched in pursuit of leviathan. If the Industrial Revolution seemed to have bypassed the wooden whalers it might have been because they were so seldom at home.

Such conservatism can be an indication that the participants are conscious that there is something special about their trade. This is particularly true when some see themselves as an elite, and whaling did have a distinct pecking order. Lowest of the low were the sealers. The objects of their 'skinning business' were considered easy prey, albeit pursued in impossibly remote and inaccessible places. Next up the scale were the shore whalers, who rowed out to intercept the coastal migrations of right and humpback whales. Higher still were the ship-based right whalers, who patrolled the breeding bays and ice pack refuges. At the pinnacle of this hierarchy were the sperm whalers, lords of the open ocean, the South Seamen. There were even distinctions between these brahmins; Nantucketers called New London and Sag Harbour whalers 'outlandishmen' because they stooped to taking 'right whale glue' as well as sperm oil. This book is the story of the brahmins, although it cannot be told without admitting the lower castes in their rightful places. The sperm whalers' claim to our special attention is not because their prey was the most dangerous and most valuable (although both of these things were true), nor because they were great if unconscious self-publicists (although the whaling literature of the nineteenth century is ample testimony that they were), but because it was they who broke whaling out of the ice of the North Atlantic and led it south to become the first truly global industry.

It was also they who defined whaling in our collective consciousness. Ask any child today to draw a whale and you will get the unique and unmistakeable outline of a sperm whale. Ask the same child to illustrate the hazards of whaling and the odds are that you will get a picture of a whale chewing a boat, an experience unique to the sperm fishery. These images come from the romance of whaling, but there are others that more properly belong to its mystique. Most potent of these is the figure of Ahab, Herman Melville's profoundest descent into the human psyche. Ahab is a man whose mind has been diseased by too much opportunity, year after year at sea, to dwell on the mutilation of his body. He is free to indulge his obsession with the white whale that crippled him because of the isolation of command and the lack of any limit to his authority. It is a climate for dysfunction. There is evidence in the structure of *Moby Dick* that Melville originally intended Ishmael's whaling experiences to be a semi-fictional instalment of the author's own adventures in the South Pacific, a follow-up to *Typee* and *Omoo*. He initially conceived of the novel as a romance, and in the character of Bulkington he appears to be introducing a conventional hero, only to discard him in a perfunctory apotheosis. Ahab, the anti-hero, appropriates the book and does it so completely that, whereas *Typee* and *Omoo* had both been critically acclaimed, *Moby Dick* was initially a failure in America. Readers found themselves drawn, without fair warning, into the recesses of the human mind. They did not like what they were shown there.

There is more than one Ahab in this book. Many of the stories that passed into whaling folklore can only be understood as dysfunctional behaviour in response to stress. It will become apparent that, in Ahab's trade, a life of extremes was the norm—

salt pork one day and tropical fruit the next, weeks of enervating inactivity succeeded by episodes of sheer terror, and months without alcohol relieved by binges that could incapacitate for days. As far as possible these men and the wives who accompanied some of them will be allowed to speak for themselves. Their stories have been drawn from media as diverse as experience-based fiction, published reminiscences, journals, and laconic, sometimes semi-literate, logbook entries. Outsiders' voices will also be heard but even these are nearly all those of engaged observers. One of the striking features of whaling literature is the relative paucity of purely imaginative fiction of any quality. The whaling experience seems to have been so extreme, and therefore such a strain on the credulity of ordinary readers, that only writers who could lay claim to having been there were likely to have credibility. And even they, after all, were only a species of sailor, and everyone knew about sailors' stories. The truth was so much like fiction that there was little room for the real thing.

A sperm whaling cruise had a number of characteristics that set it apart from other whaling voyages. Duration and distance were the most significant of these. By the 1840s four-year voyages were common. The record is held by the *Nile*, which returned to New London, Connecticut, in April 1869 after eleven years out. We will do even better, starting from Long Island in 1650 and unshipping in New Bedford in 1925. As to course and distance, we will take our cue from those captains who believed that owners' instructions invariably directed them to grounds which were past their best by the time it took for the news to get to New England. We will therefore be following our own inclination, and as the sperm whale can be found anywhere in tropical or temperate seas, there also might we be found. Indeed, should we wish to top up with right whale oil in the season, braving the disgust of the Nantucketers, we might have to cruise in polar seas during the summer months. And as, like the sperm whaler, we will be loitering with intent, it should not surprise if occasionally we divert or even reverse course for the chance of 'greasy luck'.

SOUTH FOR SPERMACETI

The Southern Fishery may be said to embrace, with the exception of the seas constituting what is properly called the Northern or Greenland Fishery, the whole expanse of ocean.

Charles Enderby

By 1650 Europeans had already been whaling for the better part of a thousand years. Like the littoral dwellers of other continents, the Basques had long pursued the whales that ventured near their coasts. Rowing boats carried the hunters close enough to fix their prey with spears or arrows attached to lines, floats or drogues. Harassment to exhaustion was their hunting technique. As the target species, the Biscay whale (*Eubalaena glacialis*), became scarcer and more timid, it became necessary to venture further from shore in pursuit. Small sea-going vessels came into use and they carried the whaling boats ever deeper into the cold northern seas. The Basques were whaling off Newfoundland within a few years of its discovery by John Cabot.

Others also were interested in the commercial possibilities of whaling. In the seventeenth century Britain and Holland jostled for maritime supremacy in the northern seas. Both employed Basques and Friesians in the ships they sent to take the whales found off Spitsbergen and Greenland. Like the Biscay whale these were baleen (whalebone) whales, but the body of *Balaena mysticetus* yielded larger quantities of oil and longer mouth bone. Like its Biscay cousin, the Greenland whale was slow and relatively docile, and could usually be relied upon to stay afloat after being killed. From every point of view the Biscay and Greenland whales were 'the right whales' to catch, and so they were called.

The seventeenth century also saw the start of British colonisation of North America, and it was not long before the New Englanders began to exploit the whales that each year appeared on their coasts. As early as 1650 a company was licenced at Southampton on Long Island. In a prophetic clause, their licence was 'to kill whales upon the South sea'. This might have been a reference to right whales migrating along the south coast of Long Island but it is tempting to believe that the company had grander ambitions, the more so as a map illustration of the 1670s shows what is unmistakably a sperm whale (*Physeter catodon*) being pursued by three boats to the south of the Island.[1]

The Americans were not the first to exploit the species. A Portuguese document of 1643 records that inhabitants of the Indonesian island of Lembata traded 'fish oil', and it is reasonable to infer that this was sperm oil because the men of the village of Lamalera continue to catch sperm whales to this day, beyond the ambit of the International Whaling Commission. They use a traditional harpoon, line and boat method sufficiently unlike its 'primitive' North American equivalent to stamp it as an indigenous development.[2]

In 1666 a correspondent reported to the Royal Society

> that about two years since, there stranded upon the Coast of New-England a dead Whale, of that sort, which they call Trumpo, having Teeth resembling those of a Mill, and its mouth at a good distance from, and under the Nose or Trunk, and several boxes or partitions in the Nose, like those of the Tailes in Lobsters; and that being open'd there run out of it a thin oily substance, which would candy in time; after which, the remainder, being a thick fatty substance, was taken out of the same part, with a scoop. And this

substance he affirmed to be the Sperma Ceti; adding further, that the Blubber, as they call it, it self, of the same sort of (Right) Whales, when stewed, yields on the top a creamy substance, which taken off, and thrown upon white wine, lets off a dirty heterogeneous sediment, but what remains aloft, affords a Sperma-Ceti-like matter.[3]

The correspondent added that this type of whale 'might be' caught on the coast eight or nine months in the year. Two years later, Richard Stafford of Bermuda wrote to the society that he had seen drift sperm whales at the Bahamas:

Myself with about 20 more have agreed to try, whether we can master and kill them, for I could never hear of any of that sort, that were kill'd by any man; such is their fierceness and swiftness. One such whale would be worth many hundred pounds.[4]

Others followed. In 1688 a Dutch resident of New York sought permission to hunt sperm whales off the Bahamas and the coast of Florida. Their success or failure is unrecorded. It was clearly ship-based whaling that Stafford and the others had in mind but, like the Basques, the colonists had begun as shore whalers, sending boats to pursue whales seen from observation points along the coast. Once captured, the whales were towed ashore, 'cut in' and boiled down. Many communities participated, but the inhabitants of a small island south of Cape Cod quickly became noted for their skill and determination in the business.

Nantucket is little more than a crescent-shaped sandbank, 22 kilometres long and 5.5 across at its widest point. Its soil is poor, and it was flight from religious persecution rather than economic opportunity that prompted its first proprietors to cross from the mainland in 1659. They started with four boats around 1690, each operating from its own designated stretch of shore, but by 1715 they were venturing into the deep, as they called it, in sloops of as little as 12 tons towing a single whaleboat. The Nattick Indians proved to be adept at the white man's way of hunting what was one of their traditional food sources. They were recruited to the ships according to a formula that appears to be an attempt to ration their skills and cheap labour throughout the

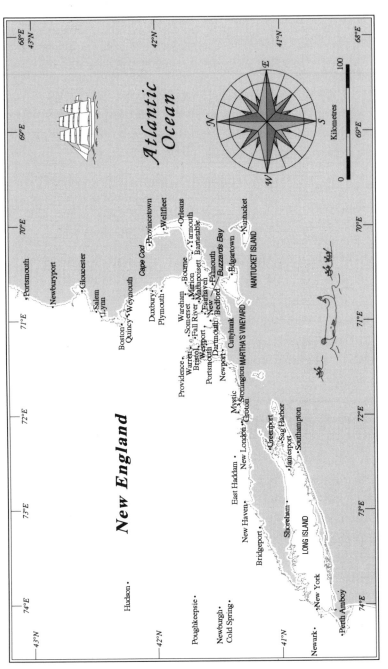

Hornet's Nest—the principal whaling ports of the US eastern seaboard

fleet: a two-boat ship, for example, had a crew of thirteen of whom five were Indians—two for each boat plus a shipkeeper. The whales were brought alongside the ship and stripped of their blubber, which was then casked and carried back to the island for rendering down, or 'trying out' as the term was. Voyages were short: a single whale would fill the hogsheads.

The original prey of the islanders were Atlantic right whales, the North American population of the Biscay whale. It was not until some time around the turn of the century that the sperm whale, on which the wealth and fame of Nantucket would be built, came to their attention. A large specimen was washed ashore. There was a heated local debate about ownership, and by the time it was resolved someone had made off with the large teeth that lined its lower jaw. When the blubber was tryed out the oil contained a white waxy substance. When the huge head was opened there was a large reservoir of the same matter in its upper part. It was found that the merchants of Boston were willing to pay a substantial premium for this head matter. From it they manufactured fine candles that were not inferior to those of beeswax for clarity of light and absence of smoke and odour. They were also cheaper.

Exactly when the islanders began systematically to pursue the sperm whale is shrouded in the obscurity appropriate to such a legendary and epoch-making event. Nantucket's first historian, Obed Macy, writing in 1835, ascribed it to the year 1712 when, so the story went, Christopher Hussey was blown well out into the Atlantic in a storm. Although he was looking for right whales, he struck a sperm whale when one presented. Intentional or not, it was a bold stroke; the armament of the great toothed whale and its disposition when attacked are quite different from that of the right whale. The sperm whale is dangerous at both ends. Its flukes are as powerful and nearly as flexible as those of the right whale, but its mouth is a unique hazard for boat whalers. The lower jaw can be 5 metres in length, with 15-centimetre teeth.

The sturdiest of wooden boats could not resist its bite, much less the light, slender cedarwork of the whaleboat.

And sperm whales can be ugly. Most whales when harpooned are only concerned with escape. This is also true for the majority of sperm whales but the exceptions, and there were many, tended to stick in whalemen's memories. If a sperm whale fought, its attackers would count themelves lucky to escape without a stove boat. The death of a crewman was by no means a rare occurrence. Hussey seems to have been lucky on two counts: he did not experience the disappointment of many before him who had seen their irons and hundreds of fathoms of whale line being trailed into the distance by a type of whale too deep-diving, too strong and too fast to be held using the techniques of the day; and his sperm whale appears to have rolled fin out without offering any more resistance than would have been expected from a right whale.

Unfortunately, the folk history of whalers is not always reliable. In 1712 Macy's hero, a grandson of one of Nantucket's original proprietors, was only six years old. But Nantucket had six whalers in the deep as early as 1715, so the date of the exploit is not as unlikely as the attribution. We are on firmer ground with Judge Paul Dudley's 1725 *Essay upon the Natural History of Whales*, in which he tells us that an informant named Atkins, ten or twelve years in the trade, was one of the first to fish for the sperm whale, an event that he dated around 1720.[5] By 1730 there were 25 vessels in the offshore fleet, ranging in size from 38 to 50 tons.[6] The significance of Hussey's whale is difficult to assess. It is clear that there was already a well-established premium market for sperm whale products: George Ripley's *Compound of Alchemy* (1471) advised the use of 'Sperma cete ana with redd Wyne when ye wax old'. Unless this need was entirely met from drift whales and by-catch from the right whale fishery, Stafford and the other early venturers must have enjoyed some success.

Be that as it may, the Nantucketers were confident that their expertise would allow them to dominate the market. 'Time and experience,' noted an observer, 'gave them advantages which made it difficult to rival them.' The bounty for which they became eligible by an Act of Parliament in 1748, introduced to support the struggling British industry, was, to the efficient islanders, a gift. Pursuing their comparative advantage, however, had other implications. The sperm whale was pelagic, monarch of the deep ocean 'off soundings'. It was also mainly a creature of the temperate zones and tropics. The waters in which it was chiefly encountered were the ocean deeps to the south and east of Nantucket.

Bermuda and the Bahamas excepted, European and colonial whaling had hitherto looked and sailed north, the direction in which the right whales travelled to reach their summer feeding grounds. During the summer months it was possible to follow them into the Arctic, the more easily after the expulsion of the French from Canada during the Seven Years War, which also opened up the Gulf of St Lawrence and the Straits of Belle Isle to the New England whalers. It seemed to the Nantucketers that they could have the best of both worlds; south into the Atlantic for sperm in the spring and then north along the American littoral during the summer, following the migrating right whales. Ships and crews could be employed for a larger part of each year without the need to extend the distance or duration of individual voyages. Nothing would have been further from the thoughts of the islanders than whaling the South Seas, even though at that time the term would have been understood to mean no further afield than the coasts of South America. The phrase had come into common use in connection with the great financial speculation of 1720, the South Sea Bubble, but to English-speaking peoples the wastes beyond the Cape of Good Hope and Cape Horn, other than the routes to India and China, were still a great unknown. The islanders could have had no idea that they were on the verge of redirecting their trade in a way that would take them and their competitors to the ends of the earth. They would find, as did the citizens of Southampton, that the South Seas started at their own south shore.

These New Englanders were businessmen, not explorers. They ventured no further in pursuit of the sperm whale than it took to fill their ships. In the earliest days this meant no further than the Gulf Stream or the Bermuda Triangle, and the sloops that had sufficed for right whale fishing were adequate. But the inexorable dynamic of whaling meant that filling the ships, one year to the next, required ever more distant and hence longer voyages. Whaling on any known ground reduced its population and 'gallied' (frightened) the survivors. These might abandon the ground or, even if they remained, become so difficult to approach that looking for an undisturbed population could be a better investment of a whaleman's time and effort. Ship size and fitout reflected this development. In 1756, when Bermuda was still a long voyage, the average size of a Nantucket vessel was 75 tons; by 1775, when they could be found as far away as the Falkland Islands, the size range was 90 to 180 tons.

From this era come the earliest of surviving American whaling logbooks. One, dated 1756, records a voyage by the sloop *Manufactor*, master John Taber, out of Dartmouth, Massachusetts. In 1756 the place that would become New Bedford, the most famous of whaling ports, was the farm of Joseph Russell. From his waterfront he traded to the West Indies and sent out whalers, and he also payed a Captain Chaffee, late of the business in Lisbon, the large salary of £100 a year to supervise the manufacture of spermaceti candles. John Taber's account of his 3½-week cruise reveals in their earliest state many arrangements that were still features of wooden ship whaling a century and a half later.[7]

> *9 April 1756* weigh'd anchor in Acushnet River Bound to Nantucket and from thence on a whale Voyage.
>
> *11 April* went to meeting [at Nantucket, where Quakers were a large part of the population]
>
> *12 April* got up our Rigging and Shipd Zecheas Gardner on a 19th [share, or lay] of the whale Clear of all charges Except Small Stores

[New Bedford was learning sperm whaling from the Nantucket experts]

16 April Spoke with Jonathon Coffen [master of another whaler] the wind Shifting to Eastward after some debate put to sea off of the maneland we lay by and caught Codfish this day we had fresh winds and rain until night got under Short Sail, my Self very unwell

17 April At evening Brought to under trysail [As whalers were looking for whales rather than making a passage they carried minimal sail at night.]

19 April Found a Dead Whale with one iron [harpoon] in her; But not worth cutting [too far decomposed]

20 April was fresh NNW winds we saw plenty of Sparmecitys and struck four but could not get one N 37° 40'

21 April Saw many whales and I struck one and got in a 2nd [two harpoons were attached to each whale line] and tow-yron [harpoon attached to a drogue] after which Z Gardner Lanc'd her [ie Taber harpooned the whale from the bow and then changed positions with Gardner, the expert who knew how best to kill it—but the whale had other ideas]

She Stove and over-Set our Boat but did not hurt a man afterwards we got her but left her head [The most valuable part of the whale and a serious but common loss—when a sperm whale was cut in its head was first severed from the body and towed astern until the blubber was all aboard.]

22 April was Rough SSW Winds so that we could neither mend our Boat [probably the only one aboard] nor cut our whale on Deack. Saw Whales

23 April was moderate wind at SW this Day we mended our Boat and Cutt our whale on Deak after wards we found a [drift] whale which we cutt

24 April the fore part was moderate we Cutt our whale on Deack the latter part rough we saw whales but could not try for them

27 April was Rough whale weather we Killd a whale and took her on Board and saw one dead which we did not Cutt

28 April we Cutt our whale on Deack and now have our Hogsheads full and are very Desiorus to fill our Small Casks. Spoke with Jonathon Macy and one Freeman [As there is no mention of trying out, the casks would contain blubber and head matter rather than oil. Three whales have filled the ship.]

2 May was Rough weather and a very Large Sea from the SW last night was very Squally with Showers of Rain at 12 o'clock of noon we

put up our helm for home to Gratifie the Crew wind SW Course N
b(y) E

3 May We continued our Course N b E till noon were in Lat 40 2
then Souned had 29 fathom Course gravel which I Supose to be off
the western shore then bore away NE

Taber included a memorandum of the expenses of the voyage.

¾ bushel peas	£1/7/-	1 gallon rum	£1/2/6
¼ quintle codfish	£1/9/-	2 lb tobacco	5/-
1 bushel corn	£1/-/-	½ lb chocolate	
port charges	£3/3/9	½ lb tobacco	5/-

For an outlay of £8 12s 3d, some depreciation of the ship and
gear, and less than a month's work, he and his crew of six or
seven had won for themselves and the owners a cargo probably
worth about £270 (3 whales by 3 tuns by £30). Gardner's 19th lay
(net of the small stores) would have come to more than £14. An
agricultural labourer would have earned £1 over the same period.

The cruise of the *Manufactor* had taken her an unknown
distance along the 37th parallel eastwards of Chesapeake Bay.
Taber lacked a reliable method of fixing longitude and trusted
the lead to tell him when he was near land again, but this did
not matter if it was known that whales could be found in a certain
latitude. When competition thinned out the whales near the
American coast, the whalers were drawn further out along the
parallel, a siren call that by the mid-1760s had led them to
the Azores, or Western Islands, in much the same latitude but
two-thirds of the way across the ocean. This stretch of the Atlantic
became known as the 36° north ground.

The years before the outbreak of the American Revolution
were the piping days of Nantucket. Its population grew rapidly,
although from such a small base that it was only five or six
thousand in 1775. Of these, 2025 manned a fleet of 150 whalers
and others were employed as fishermen. It was a community in
which most of the employment was generated by the whale

fishery. Hector St John de Crèvecoeur, a French American who visited Nantucket in the early 1770s on Quaker business, recorded how the industry structured whole working lives.

> At schools they learn to read, and to write a good hand, until they are twelve years old; they are then in general put apprentices to the cooper's trade, which is the second essential branch of business followed here; at fourteen they are sent to sea, where in their leisure hours their companions teach them the art of navigation . . . Then they go gradually through every station of rowers, steersmen, and harpooners; thus they learn to attack, to pursue, to overtake, to cut, to dress their huge game: and having performed several such voyages, and perfected themselves in this business, they are fit either for the counting house or the chase [as a whaling captain].[8]

A lad would ship as a greenhand as soon as his mother would let him, and he would sail as likely as not in a vessel that had his father or an older brother for an officer. More than professional advancement hung on success as a whaleman. It was alleged that the girls of Nantucket were all bound by a secret oath not to entertain the advances of any suitor who had not killed his first whale. A boatsteerer ashore wore in his lapel, as a badge of office, the chock pin that channeled the whaleline through the bows of his boat. In Nantucket, horizontal integration of the industry was almost complete, and vertical integration began in about 1745 when Joseph Rotch and others began shipping oil to London in ships usually co-owned with British merchants, thus cutting out the Boston middlemen. They needed only the secret of spermaceti candle manufacture to complete the picture.

One of the lads who followed Nantucket's *cursus honorum*, as he might have called it, was the Quaker Peleg Folger, who is known to us as a whaler from his journals. From the age of eighteen, in 1751, he served on a succession of vessels until 1760. A sampling of his observations, which in the original are liberally sprinkled with Latin, leaves an impression that the education of which de Crèvecoeur thought so highly might have over-qualified him for the whaling.

On Journal-Keeping Many People who keep Journals at Sea fill them up with some trifles or other. My part I purpose in the following sheets, not to keep overstrict history of every trifling occurrence that happens, only now and then of Some particular affair; and to fill up the rest with subjects either mathematical, theological, Historical, Philosophical, or poetical, or anything else that best suits mine inclination.

On Man A Dunghill Blanched with Snow, a May-Game of Fortune, a Mark for Malice, a Butt for Envy! If Poor dispised, if Rich flatter'd; He is born crying; lives laughing, & Dies groaning.

On Manners In the morning we Spyed a Sail and Drew up with her but the Clown would not Speak with us.

On the Chase . . . we row'd about a mile and a Half from the Vessel, and then a whale came up under us, & stove our boat very much, and threw us every man overboard Save one. And we all came up and Got Hold of the Boat & Held to her until the other boat (which was a mile and a half off) came up and took us in, all Safe, and not one man Hurt, which was remarkable, the boat being threshed to pieces very much.

On Navigation Nothing very remarkable these 24 hours, only I like a Dunce forgot myself and rubbed out my Knots, Courses and Winds off the Logbook before I had set them down on my Reckoning. However, I had cast up my Difference of Lat and [significantly] Long, so I have not lost my reckoning, yet this was a very careless trick.

On Mortality Death Summons all Men to the Silent Grave [a recurrent theme].

On Nantucket Girls if the weather is So Pleasant at home it is a charming day for the Young Ladies to go to Meeting & if they do but Get any Good by it it will be very well.

On Ennui This 24 hours Very Shuffling and unsettled air Nothing Else very much worth While to Set down as I can find but Let me See first our Job has got his hair cut off and he Looks quite Strangely; And our Hog, Sheep & Dog all messed together.

A Toast So Remembering all at Home both Male & Female Mother, Brothers, Sisters, Friends & acquaintance & all others without Exception & wishing them all well & a happy & prosperous Meeting in the Royal Assembly while we are Drinking Flip & Chasing Whales & wishing them all Well till we once more meet together which I hope will not be Long first (by the Blessing of God) I Conclude the Remarks of this 24 hours Being in the vast Atlantick Ocean & how

far to Eastward of the Grand Bank of Newfoundland We know not
nor Greatly Care for we are all in health & all merry together.

Some of his shipmates seem to have thought that young Folger
was a bit too full of himself. 'Peleg Folger is a Rum Soull for
writing Latin', scribbled Nathaniel Worth at the foot of one page
but, lest Peleg should take offence at this liberty, added that he
would 'intercede with Anna Pitts in his behalf for Retaliation for
the same'.[9]

Folger sailed no further than 'offshore' and to the Grand Banks
of Newfoundland, but his years afloat coincided with the collapse
of shore whaling from Nantucket. The great year had been 1726,
when 86 whales were taken. By about 1760 whales had become
scarce and gradually the shore stations were abandoned. At
the same time the British authorities began restricting New
Englander access to the Newfoundland and Labrador coasts. It
was alleged that they were damaging the cod and seal fisheries
and taking advantage of the Indians, which was very likely true,
but this was an excuse rather than a reason. As early as 1732 the
Americans had come into contact and competition with British
whalers in the Davis Strait west of Greenland, and there was little
love lost. Among the ships the Americans might have encountered
there, irony of ironies, were those of the South Sea Company,
whose charter gave it exclusive whaling rights in South American
waters, but whose whalers, in their brief and unsuccessful careers,
never sailed those tropical seas. As the British whalemen felt
American competition intensifying, *de facto* was succeeded by
de jure discrimination. In 1766 a duty was placed on colonial
whalebone and oil imported into Britain and, as British producers
continued to be paid a bounty from which colonials were now
excluded, the Americans were doubly disadvantaged.

The British restrictions created an even greater incentive to
look for more profitable grounds and so commenced a parallel
movement southwards on both sides of the Atlantic. From the
Bahamas the Americans swept through the West Indies to the

Leeward Islands and then on to the Brazil Banks, which were probably pioneered by the *Leviathan* of Rhode Island in 1772. From the Azores they island-hopped past Madeira and the Canaries to the Cape Verde Islands and thence to the coast of Guinea, although Macy claimed that Nantucket whalers had been there as early as 1763, two years earlier than their first visit to the Azores. Working down the African coast they came to Walvis Bay. Perversely, the Americans sometimes corrupted this to Woolwich Bay, not recognising the Dutch word for whale-fish.

On voyages of such duration it was no longer practicable to cask the blubber for shipment home. It was not an efficient use of space, and in warm climates the fat quickly went rancid, reducing its value as well as making shipboard life intolerable. The solution was to try out on board and Peleg Folger gives us one of the earliest references to the practice, recording that as the *Greyhound* turned for home on 30 July 1753, 'the tryworks [were] set a-going by a flaming torch under our caboose'. By the 1770s the practice was general. Another consequence of longer voyages was that it was no longer possible to undertake a northern and a southern cruise in the same year. On the eve of the revolution a majority of the Massachusetts whalers still fitted for the shorter northern cruises.

Nantucket was the exception: of its 150 whalers, 85 went south. The average annual yields for the colony as a whole strongly suggest that Nantucket's priority was sound; with half of the fleet it produced two-thirds of the oil. It is significant however that even the northern fleet took more sperm oil than right whale oil. New Bedford was still learning; each of its ships, which were only slightly smaller than those of Nantucket, took on average only half as much oil.[10] But there were those in Nantucket who appreciated the advantages of a mainland deep-water port and an established manufactory. In 1765 Joseph Rotch bought 10 acres from Joseph Russell and took up residence, leaving his son William to conduct family affairs in Nantucket. The business and dwelling houses that Joseph Rotch built became the nucleus of

The Secret of the Candle

The process for refining sperm oil, or more particularly for separating from it the more valuable spermaceti, was a closely guarded secret in the eighteenth century. The secret was too valuable to keep. Those who could afford to, like Joseph Russell of New Bedford, bought an expert. Others, like William Rotch, simply kept their eyes open. In 1792 Nantucket alone had ten candle factories. By the 1850s Lewis Holmes was able to persuade Charles Barney, the foreman of Daniel Fisher's factory at Edgartown, that there was no commercial disadvantage in disclosing the process publicly.

> The first step in the process of manufacture, is to take the oil in its crude state, and put it into large kettles, or boilers, and subject it to a heat of 180 to 200 degrees, and then all the water which happened to become mixed with the oil, either on shipboard or since, will evaporate.
>
> *Winter Strained Sperm Oil* In the fall, or autumn, the oil is boiled for the purpose of granulation during the approaching cold weather. The oil thus passes from a purely liquid into a solid state, or one in which it is in grains, or masses. When the temperature of the atmosphere rises, or the weather slackens during the winter, the oil which has been frozen, but is now somewhat softened, is shovelled out of the casks and put into strong bags that will hold half a bushel or more, in order to be pressed . . .
>
> *Spring Sperm Oil* What remains in the bags after the first pressing, is again heated by being put into boilers, after which it is baled into casks again, and upon cooling, it becomes more compact and solid than it was before. During the month of April, when the temperature is about 50 degrees, the oil becomes softened; it is then put into bags, and goes through a second process of pressing . . .
>
> *Tight Pressed Oil* That which is left in the bags after the second pressing, is again melted, and put into tin pans or tubs which will hold about 40 pounds each. When this liquid is thoroughly cooled, as each pressing makes what is

left harder . . . the cakes taken from the tubs are then carried into a room heated to about 90 degrees; and as they begin to yield to the influence of this high temperature, or the remaining oil begins to soften the cakes, they are taken and shaved into very fine pieces, or ground up in some instances, deposited in bags as hitherto, and put into the hydraulic press . . . the bags subjected to a powerful pressure of 300 tons or more, all the oil is extracted from them, and what is left is perfectly dry, free from any oily matter, and brittle . . .

Spermaceti What remains after the several pressings, and the removal of all the oil, is called stearine, or spermaceti . . . the spermaceti from the head oil is quite different from that of the body oil; the former presents fine, bright, transparent scales like small particles of isinglass, while the latter is more compact, something like dough. In cooling, one exhibits a sparry, crystalline structure, the other that of clay. Head oil or matter is usually manufactured with the body oil of the whale, and mixed in proportion to one-third of the former to two-thirds of the latter.

Spermaceti Candles . . . The oil, it is supposed, is wholly extracted, and nothing now remains but the spermaceti. Its color, however, is not white, but interspersed with grayish streaks, bordering on the yellow. The spermaceti is put into large boilers adapted for the purpose, and heated to the temperature of 210 degrees. It is refined and cleared of all foreign ingredients by the application of alkali. Afterwards water is added, which, with a temperature of 240 degrees, throws off the alkali in the form of vapor. The liquid which remains is as pure and clear as the crystal water, and ready to be made into the finest spermaceti candles. [*The Arctic Whaleman*, Thayer & Eldridge, Boston, 1861, pp 288–92]

The process had much in common with that for extracting olive oil, but the value of its products was inverted, for with spermaceti the best came last.

New Bedford. Seven years later the Nantucketers began manufacturing spermaceti candles. They put it about that they had learned the secret from Rhode Island.

In little more than half a century Nantucket's production had risen thirty-fold. Even more impressive was an eighty-fold increase in income thanks to the premium on sperm oil and a rising price for right whale oil that took it from £7 per tun at the beginning of the period to £17–18 at its close. William Rotch claimed that just before the revolution he was getting £30 for sperm. In 1715 six sloops took 600 barrels of oil and 11,000 pounds of whalebone, value £1100 ($5500). In 1769, 119 vessels produced 19,140 barrels worth $462,996. By that date as much again would have been earned by the other whaling ports, eight in Massachusetts plus Providence, Warren, Sag Harbour, New London and New York.[11] American whaling was now a signficant industry by European as well as by local standards and it was in competition with British producers. It was time, thought the British government, for it to start paying its way, and whaling too became subject to the taxation without representation that was so agitating the colonists.

The duty on American whale products introduced in 1766 was supposed, among other things, to pay for upkeep of the Royal Navy frigates that allegedly provided whalers at sea with protection against pirates and French privateers. It was of a piece with the Stamp Act and the Tea Act as far as the whalemen were concerned, but their indignation was tinged with apprehension. In the event of a rupture with Britain, no American industry was more vulnerable than that of the whalemen. Far from looking after them, the frigates would be looking for them and the London market would be closed. Gestures were all very well— Joseph Russell called one of his whaling brigs *No Duty on Tea*—but few would have been prepared to go further. Most nervous of all were the Nantucketers; if blockaded they would starve in a matter of months.

It was a particularly malicious turn of events, therefore, that embroiled the oilmen in the Boston Tea Party. The sons of Joseph Rotch, William and Francis, had back-loaded two of the family's oil carriers from London with the East India Company's tea. When the Bostonians refused to let the tea land and the Governor denied the ships customs clearance to sail, the *Beaver* and the *Dartmouth* were left in limbo. The negotiations that Francis Rotch conducted with both parties in search of a compromise that would release his ships foreshadowed in miniature the efforts that the whalemen would make in succeeding years to stand aside from a conflict that threatened to destroy their all. The precipitate action of the Sons of Liberty on the night of 16 December 1773 resolved Rotch's immediate dilemma but created a much larger one for him and for all other colonial whalemen.

The event that seems to have brought the American industry to the attention of the general public in Britain was the news that the Yankees were whaling off the Falkland Islands. In 1757 Edmund Burke could write two volumes on the history of the European settlements in America without once mentioning whaling. By 1774 the territorial dispute over the Falklands, pursued by Argentina to this day, was already souring relations between Britain and Spain. That there was British commercial activity around the islands gave substance to the claim of sovereignty. And it gave Burke a peg on which to hang one of the most famous passages of his speech of 22 March 1775 to the House of Commons, in which he urged conciliation with the rebellious American colonies.

> As to the wealth which the colonies have drawn from the sea by their fisheries . . . you surely thought these acquisitions of value, for they seemed even to excite your envy; and yet the spirit by which that enterprising employment has been exercised ought rather, in my opinion, to have raised your esteem and admiration. And pray, Sir, what in the world is equal to it? Pass by the other parts, and look at the manner in which the people of New England have of late carried on the whale fishery. Whilst we follow them among the tumbling mountains of ice, and behold them penetrating into the deepest frozen recesses of Hudson's Bay and Davis's Straits, whilst we are

looking for them beneath the arctic circle, we hear that they have
pierced into the opposite region of polar cold, that they are at the
antipodes, and engaged under the frozen serpent of the south.
Falkland Island, which seemed too remote and romantic an object for
the grasp of national ambition, is but a stage and resting-place in the
progress of their victorious industry. Nor is the equinoctial heat more
discouraging to them than the accumulated winter of both the poles.
We know that whilst some of them draw the line and strike the
harpoon on the coast of Africa, others run the longitude and pursue
their gigantic game along the coast of Brazil. No sea but what is
vexed by their fisheries. No climate that is not witness to their toils.
Neither the perseverence of Holland, nor the captivity of France, nor
the dexterous and firm sagacity of English enterprise ever carried this
most perilous mode of hard industry to the extent to which it has
been pushed by this recent people—a people who are still, as it were,
but in the gristle, and not yet hardened into the bone of manhood
. . . when I see how profitable they have been to us, I feel all pride
of power sink, and all wisdom in the wisdom of human contrivances
melt and die away within me. My rigour relents. I pardon something
to the spirit of liberty.[12]

The bill to which Burke spoke was one in a series of increasingly
coercive measures by which Lord North's administration hoped
to bring the colonies to heel. Among other things it proposed to
exclude American whalers from the Newfoundland Banks. In vain
did the colonials argue against the Restraining Act as a whole,
but at least Nantucket's peculiar vulnerability was recognised. It
was exempted from some of the provisions. Burke's reference to
British envy of the American whalemen's success was fair comment, but misleading. The British owners had not ventured into
the southern fishery at all. Their Greenland fishery was moribund
in spite of the government bounty and produced less than a
quarter of the oil that Britain imported. Most of the remainder
came from the American colonies, and mutually profitable
arrangements were in place. William Rotch, for example, owned
at least one vessel in partnership with Champion and Dickason
of London. The British firm of Samuel Enderby may have had
an interest in the Rotch ships embroiled in the Boston Tea Party.
   The profit came mainly from tax avoidance. Oil imported in

'English' vessels attracted duty of only three shillings per tun while oil imported in a colonial vessel paid six shillings. The arrangements also kept the colonial ships properly employed on the whaling grounds instead of wasting their time freighting. So complementary were tax avoidance and transport efficiency that ship-to-ship transfer of oil sometimes occurred on the whaling grounds.[13] The British whaling interests believed that their government's policy would disrupt activities profitable to them and they petitioned against the Restraining Act accordingly.

In the early hours of 20 April 1775 British troops marched out of Boston to their appointment with history at Lexington and Concord. In Nantucket it was business as usual but when the ships returned from their cruises to the Azores, Guinea and Brazil, now taking as long as a year, there were great reservations about sending them out again. The islanders were used to risk, but they were not foolhardy. It seemed that there might be safety in distance. The further south they were, the more likely they would be out of harm's way, although the trick would then be to get their oil to market.

Trumpo
or What's in a Name?

*A Spermaceti is a Large whale; they will make from ten
to a hundred barrels of oyl: They have no bone in their
head and their brains is all oyl: They have a hump on
the after part of their back: one Spouthole:—their under
jaw is full of hard ivory teeth: and tongue very Small.*

Peleg Folger

In Folger's day and throughout the nineteenth century the
preferred scientific name of the Great Toothed Whale was
Physeter (from the Greek for blowing) *macrocephalus* (Latin for
great head). Our century has decreed, to the disadvantage of those
of us with a little Latin but less Greek, that it should be *Physeter
catodon*—the spouter with teeth in its under jaw. Linnaeus gave
us both names, thinking that he was describing different animals,
but his more detailed description of *macrocephalus* and the inferior
size of his *catodon* (probably derived from immature specimens)
meant that the whale was 'great head' until the zoologists
invented their Law of Priority and began arguing over the earliest
unambiguous description. If priority is the touchstone it might be
asked why the whale is not *Physeter trumpo*. That name was
recognised by Baron Cuvier, acknowledged by him to be synony-
mous with *P. macrocephalus*, and current at least as far back as

1666. It is possibly of Azorean origin, from the Portuguese *tromba d'àgua*, a water spout. Unfortunately it predates the Linnaean Creation, which occurred in 1758, and therefore does not exist. *Trumpo* might not tell us anything about dentition, a useful prompt in archetypal classification, but the name would be inoffensive to post-Darwinian nomenclature. Were he alive today, Linneaus would undoubtedly tell us to stop being silly. The irony is that trumpo is now acknowledged to be the only member of the genus *Physeter* and in logic, if not in taxonomy, there is no need for a specific name at all.

It was not, however, necessary for Folger to use any of the scientific names then contending in order to satisfy his fondness for Latin. The common name current among English speakers in his day was also Latin—*sperma cetus*—the spermaceti whale. It acquired this name from a perceived similarity between semen and the white liquid found in its head cavity. Folger thought that spermaceti was oil (in fact, it is more like a wax) and knew it had nothing to do with reproduction but, like many other writers, he assumed from its location that it must be brain matter. The French managed to avoid the issue by calling this whale *cachalot*, from the Bayonnaise word for toothed.

Spermaceti is in fact a far more mysterious substance than either brains or semen. It is found confined in other parts of the whale's head and body as well as in a free state in the case. It is also found dispersed throughout the coat of blubber at least as far back as the hump, though the concentration diminishes the farther aft one goes. The best-informed opinion about its purpose (the animal's size and environment making close study of its physiology in action difficult, to say the least) is that it has a hydrostatic function, enabling the whale to neutralise buoyancy in a dive by cooling its head wax with water admitted to the nasal passages. As the spermaceti solidifies and shrinks, it increases the density of the head. In this hardened state it may also function as an acoustic lens for echo location purposes.

The earliest uses to which it was put by humans were medicinal. It was not until 1787 that internal use was debunked by the anatomist and surgeon John Hunter, but for many years thereafter it continued to form the basis for *unguentum cetacei*, an ointment for external application to bruises and the like. Another use that dated back at least to the seventeenth century was in the combing of wool, but the focus of demand was its luminous qualities. Sperm oil itself, stated Brande's *Manual of Chemistry* (1819), 'is more pure, and burns more brilliantly in lamps than common whale oil', but in addition

> . . . it deposits, as it cools after the death of the animal, a crystalline, fatty substance, called spermaceti, which is purified by pressure and boiling in weak solutions of potassa; it is then washed, fused in boiling water, and cast into blocks and cakes . . . [1]

And it made superb candles which burned so brilliantly that they were adopted as the standard measure of artificial light. One candle-power is the light from a pure spermaceti candle of one-sixth of a pound weight burning at a rate of 120 grains per hour.

Another product of the sperm whale, more valuable even than spermaceti, was ambergris, which also had its secrets.

In appearance the sperm whale is quite unlike any of the other large whales. The massive blunt head accounts for fully one-third of its length. The single blowhole is located on the upper left side of the head, well forward. The spout is low and bushy in appearance, and is projected forward at an angle of 45°. The fins are short and play no part in propulsion, which is provided by the tail. The tail is horizontal, unlike that of a fish, and usually moves up and down to provide forward motion although a sculling half-rotation, first to one side then to the other, has been observed. The ear is tiny, having no external part, and its aperture is about the diameter of a human finger. The eyes are also disproportionate, most often being likened to those of an ox in size. They are located so far back and so low on either side of the head that stereoscopic vision is impossible. Offsetting this,

Grey Amber

Ambergris was known and prized long before sperm
whales were hunted. It was initially found as flotsam, and
many stories were invented to account for its occurrence.
Like amber, it was found on the seashore, and one school
of thought associated the two substances as the resinous
product of trees, whence its French name. Its association
with the sperm whale was known by the mid-sixteenth
century, but not necessarily from its discovery in the
intestines. Some authors believed that it was the congealed
sperm of the whale. With such uncertainty about its
provenance, and the unpalatability of most of the theories,
Charles II would have to rank for bravery alongside Swift's
man that first ate an oyster—his favorite dish was said to
be 'eggs and ambergrease'.

Ambergris was thought to have aphrodisiacal, laxative
and other medicinal properties, but by the early nineteenth
century its main use was in cosmetics, where it was known
to enhance the scent of perfume, particularly attar of roses.
European perfumers added it to scented pastilles, candles,
bottles, gloves and hair powder. Frederick Bennett, noting
that it was of infrequent occurrence, declared it to be 'a
morbid concretion in the intestines of the Cachalot'.
Thomas Beale was blunter, ignoring its rarity: '[it] appears
to be nothing but the hardened faeces of the spermaceti
whale'. His evidence was the squid beaks usually found in
it, and Charles Enderby had shown him a specimen which
bore 'very evident marks of having been moulded by the
lower portion of the rectum of the whale'. Beale had also
observed that the semi-fluid faeces of the sperm whale,
when dried out, 'bore all the properties of ambergris'.
Some experimented further.

> Mr Homberg found that a vessel in which he had made a
> long digestion of human faeces, acquired a very strong and
> perfect smell of ambergris, inasmuch that any one would
> have thought that a great quantity of essence of ambergris

had been made in it, the perfume was so strong and
offensive that the vessel had to be removed from the
laboratory. [Brande's *Manual of Chemistry*, first edition, p 594]

Brande warned against imitations, as well he might. The
genuine article could be identified by inserting a hot pin,
which would produce a fragrant scent and melt the
substance 'like fat of a uniform consistence'. A counterfeit
would not smell so, nor would its texture be fatty. The
French chemist Chevreul found that the fat, which was up
to 60 per cent of total weight, resembled cholesterol. The
concretions were black, grey and yellow, or ash-coloured,
with yellow and black mottling. All had some value, but
the most valuable was the grey, which retailed for 25
shillings an ounce in the 1790s and for £5–10 an ounce a
century later. Few whales suffered so acutely from their
peptic ulcers as to contain ambergris; from those that did,
the yield could range from a few ounces up to several
hundred pounds.

The clue to the true nature of ambergris lay in the
observation by whalemen that it was most often found in
emaciated animals that had yielded little oil. It seems that
over-indulgence in their favourite food, squid, leaves an
indigestible mass of horny beaks lodged in the whale's
intestines. The intestines become ulcerated and the pain
of digestion inhibits feeding, leading to a loss of condition.
The ambergris appears to be a fatty secretion that forms
around the beaks and reduces their abrasive effect.

A significant proportion of the ambergris found by
whalemen was, at least until the end of the eighteenth
century, not declared to owners. Whalemen saw it as
windfall, and there are many stories of individuals making
fortunes from the oversight or inattention of others.

DE PISCIB. MONSTRO.

De ſpermate Ceti, quod Ambra dicitur, & eius Medicinis.

By the sixteenth century, ambergris was known to be somehow associated with the sperm whale (Historia de Gentibus Septentrionalibus, *1555*)

the whale can see through almost 360° with one eye or the other without turning its head, the only blind spots being dead ahead and dead aft. Teeth, usually 40–50 in number, are found only in the lower jaw, which is a long narrow cylinder and can be opened nearly 90°. Inside, the mouth is very white and it is believed that in the watery darkness where the whale feeds it serves as a lure. The gullet would have been about large enough to admit Jonah.

There is a considerable disparity in size between the sexes, the male usually growing to 15–18 metres while the female will reach only 11–12 metres. Individual males up to 25 metres have been recorded. The gestation period for these mammals is $14\frac{1}{2}$–$16\frac{1}{2}$ months and as lactation can last for up to two years a female will reproduce only once in every four or five years. Twins are rare. The species is polygynous, with two or three mature males maintaining a harem, or school, of up to 40 individuals including females, their calves and juveniles. The dominance of the males is apparently hard won, as many are extensively deformed and scarred from battles to maintain their position. The surplus bulls associate when young but become increasingly unsociable as they age and in their later years are usually solitary. The breeding schools are usually found no further north or south than 40° but unattached males are also encountered at the Arctic and Antarctic circles. Sperm whales live as long as humans, females reaching sexual maturity in ten years and males in twenty. A male is socially mature at 25 but does not reach full size until 30. A female will have finished growing at 25.

Their preferred food is squid, in search of which they are capable of diving to depths of at least 1100 metres and remaining submerged for an hour and more. In 1972 the dives of two bulls were timed off South Africa at 53 minutes and 112 minutes. One was caught with two small sharks, believed to be bottom-dwellers, in its stomach. The bottom there sounded at about 3200 metres. Surface cruising speed is 3–4 knots with a sprint capability of 20 knots. Underwater escape speed at constant depth has been calculated at 11–12 knots but it is the dive speeds that are truly phenomenal. The average rate of descent is a modest 4 knots, but an ascent at 21.9 knots and a descent at 24.6 knots have been recorded.[2]

Such information has been hard won, and largely through the use of modern technologies like sonar. The natural scientists of the eighteenth and early nineteenth centuries laboured under severe disadvantages in their attempts to describe, much less classify, whales. It took no less brave a scientist than Baron Cuvier to suggest that there was only one type of large toothed whale, but even he had to rely on fanciful accounts for information on its behaviour. Some of his informants may have been whalemen. If so, they spun him some yarn: among other things, he solemnly recorded that sperm whales are attacked from the left because their eye on that side is smaller.

> The terrible armament, the powerful and numerous teeth with which nature has provided the cachalot, renders it a terrific adversary to all the inhabitants of the deep, even those that are more dangerous to

others, such as the Phocae, the Balenoptera, the Dolphins, the Sharks, and Squalae. So terrified are all these animals at the sight of the cachalot, that they hurry to conceal themselves from him in the sand or mud, and often, in the precipitancy of their flight, dash themselves against the rocks with such violence as to cause instantaneous death. It is not, therefore, surprising if the myriads of fishes on which this tyrant preys are struck with the most lively terror at his presence. So powerful is this feeling, that the multitudes of fish which seek with avidity the dead carcasses of the other cetacea to devour, dare not approach the body of the cachalot when it is floating lifeless on the surface of the water . . . this animal ejects . . . water to a considerable height . . . Spring is the time of rut, when desperate combats take place between the males, accompanied by loud and piercing cries.

Cuvier was aware of the limitations of his information. He pointed out that some scientists did not pretend to have seen the whale at all,

. . . having only observed the animal cast ashore on its back, and not finding it too easy to turn a carcass sixty or seventy feet long, and twenty feet thick. Scarcely does such an occurrence take place, but the populace rush to the spot and speedily dismember the body. Fortunate if the naturalist can find but a few bones remaining.[3]

He was frustrated by the lack of what he could accept as reliable observations. Were there cachalots with a dorsal fin? With a central spout? Without a cylindrical lower jaw? 'All this remains to be proved, and to be proved otherwise than by figures drawn by common sailors', he complained. There was in fact a very fair representation of a sperm whale available to him. It had been drawn to scale by Captain James Colnett, RN, in August 1793 when a 5-metre calf had been hoisted aboard his ship *Rattler* during an exploratory whaling cruise. Colnett carried a whaling master to manage the fishing. His remarks, therefore, are those of an interested and intelligent observer, although one who was neither scientifically nor practically expert about sperm whales.

The Ear . . . is remarkably small in proportion to the body, as is also the Eye from which a hollow or concave line runs to the fore part of the head the Eyes being prominent enables them to pursue their Prey in a direct line, and by inclining the head a little either to

the right or to the left to see their enemy astern, they have only one
row of Teeth, which are in the lower Jaw with sockets in the upper
one to receive them, the number depends on the age of the Fish, the
lower Jaw is a solid bone that narrows nearly to a point and closes
under the upper, when they spout, they throw the water forwards and
not upwards like other Whales except when they are enraged, they
also spout more regular and stay longer under water the larger the
Fish the more frequently they spout and continue longer under water.
The Tail is horizontal with which he does much mischief in
defending himself. Their food, from all the observations I have had
an oppertunity [sic] of making, has been the Sepia or middle Cuttle
Fish.[4]

Perhaps the Baron put Colnett among the common sailors on the
strength of the captain's own disclaimer about literary qualifications, which, he believed, were 'only to be obtained in the calm
of life, while so many of my years have been passed amid the
winds and waves, in various climes and different oceans'. Cuvier

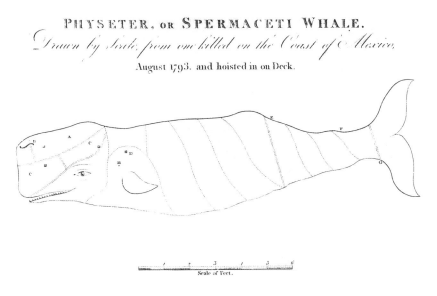

PHYSETER, or SPERMACETI WHALE.
Drawn by Jode, from one killed on the Coast of Mexico,
August 1793. and hoisted in on Deck.

Scale of Feet.

James Colnett's whale (from A Voyage to the South Atlantic and
Round Cape Horn into the Pacific Ocean, *National Library
of Australia)*

would have done well to inform himself about those years: Colnett had sailed with Cook.

It was not until the 1830s that people who would have been acceptable to Cuvier as scientifically trained observers began describing the sperm whale in its element. They were not naturalists but surgeons, and they signed on for whaling voyages in their professional capacity. The first was Thomas Beale, demonstrator of anatomy to the Eclectic Society of London, who sailed in the *Kent* in 1830 and returned, after falling out with the *Kent*'s captain, in the *Sarah and Elizabeth* two and a half years later. Beale reviewed all of the scientific literature on the sperm whale and compared it with his own observations. He found himself demolishing a house of straw. The sperm whale, he asserted, looked very little like the illustration Cuvier's brother had published in his *Natural History of Whales*; Colnett was more reliable. As to the whale spouting water,

> I have seen them at a distance, and I have been within a few yards of several hundreds of them, and I never saw water pass from the spout-hole. But the column of thick and dense vapour which is certainly ejected, is exceedingly likely to mislead the judgement of the casual observer in these matters; and this column does indeed appear very much like a jet of water, when seen at a distance of one or two miles on a clear day, because the condensation of the vapour, which takes place the moment it escapes from the nostril, and its consequent opacity, which makes it appear of a white colour, and which is not observed when the whale is close to the spectator, and it then appears only like a jet of white steam . . .[5]

Far from being the terror of the deep, Beale wrote, the sperm whale is timid and inoffensive, and indeed the formation of its teeth and the size of its gullet alone are sufficient evidence of its incapacity to prey on anything as large as another whale. The sperm whale was hardly ever seen near sand, mud or rocks so it was unlikely that its alleged prey would encounter them while escaping. Whalemen lost large amounts of blubber to sharks feeding on dead sperm whales alongside. The species had no voice, nor did it mate only in the spring. And so on.

While Beale seems to have embarked with no intention of doing more than duty as a doctor, Frederick Debell Bennett FRCS had a larger agenda when he joined the *Tuscan* in October 1833. He called his voyage an adventure and declared his principal object to be an investigation of the anatomy and habits of southern whales and the conduct of the sperm fishery. In the book he later published recounting his adventures he was less focused than Beale, for he devoted much space to other anthropological, zoological and botanical matter, but he too was able to contribute to the demystification of the sperm whale. A particularly valuable opportunity, which Beale envied, came in January 1835 when the *Tuscan* took a cow that was only a few hours short of giving birth. The 4½-metre male foetus was taken aboard and Bennett performed a dissection that, even with a small whale, was more like an excavation. Concentrating on the soft tissues, which were the least accessible to naturalists, he found that the stomach was complex, with four chambers, and that the intestines could be extended nearly 63 metres around the deck of the ship. The left lung had a single bronchial tube but the right lung had two, one smaller than the other. Bennett's description of the eye was particularly detailed and he presented a paper on the subject to the Zoological Society of London. A comparison with Colnett's description of the same organ shows that the naturalist and the whaleman were interested in quite different aspects of it.

> The eyes are placed far back in the head, above and between the pectoral fin and angle of the mouth: their situation being chiefly denoted by a prominence of the surrounding integuments. The aperture for vision is not larger than two inches in its longitudinal, and one in its vertical, diameter . . . The eyeball is not a perfect sphere: its anterior and posterior surfaces being much flattened. It is deeply set within the lids, and chiefly lodged in the soft parts; but little if any of its substance occupying the bony orbit . . .[6]

Bennett also recorded, without comment, that the position of the foetus in the womb was that of a bent bow, 'the head and tail being approximated, and the back arched'. In the second edition of his *Natural History of the Sperm Whale*, Beale turned this singular into a plural, thus misrepresenting Bennett as saying that all sperm foetuses were found in this position. As a scientist, Beale should have known better than to generalise from the particular, but in any case a moment's reflection should have suggested to him that the position of the young whale was likely to be the terminus of its struggle to escape suffocation in the womb after the death of its dam. Common sailors were not the only source of misinformation that the learned might encounter while studying the whale.

The whaleman's interest in his prey was much more limited than that of the naturalist, amateur or professional. Beale sternly observed that in over half a century not one whaleman had 'stepped forward to vindicate its history from the absurd and fabulous accounts with which it has been loaded'. One man who tried was Joel Polack who, as a trader in New Zealand's Bay of Islands in the 1830s, was well placed to watch and interrogate the visiting sperm whalers. His descriptions are a strange blend of scientific jargon and vivid behavioural observation, as in his account of the whale's hearing.

> The auricular organs of the Sperm whale are curiously concealed by the gelabrous appearance of the body, only perceivable on removing the skin, under which they lie in a cubiculary position. The animal, it would be supposed, is particularly dull in its perception, had we not ocular proof, as well as many credible anecdotes evidencing to the contrary. These fish, after being once alarmed, dive under the ocean, and are seen to rise slowly in a perpendicular position, with their blunt heads more or less above the surface of the water, in apparently a listening attitude, remaining in that position for a full half hour, scarcely moving. An electrical feeling is also at times perceivable among them. A shoal of upwards of a hundred of these fish, have been seen spreading themseves over the ocean, disporting as far as the human eye could reach around, from the ship's masthead; presently a whaleman throws a lance at one of these marine monsters, who no sooner feels the wound, than an instantaneous disappearance ensues of the shoal; a simultaneous feeling appears to pervade them all, however distant from each other, diving with their utmost celerity . . . It is difficult to what cause to attribute this feeling, as the

auriculary powers of the whale are not disturbed by a boat being
propelled in front of the fish . . . [7]

Polack also remarked on their lack of uniformity in colour, 'the
outer skin of many being quite white, others are black, brown,
and an ocrous dingy red, or mottled, not a few partake of a dark
atramentous appearance'. Where Beale was moved to complain
about the whalemen's reticence or lack of curiosity about the
natural history of the whale, Polack found that he faced Cuvier's
problem; the tales he was told were 'fish stories'. And even when
not invented to confound landsmen, the observations of the
whalemen, though often acute, seldom extended beyond what
was relevant in the conversion of whales into dollars and cents.
Captain H W Seabury was eminently well qualified on that score.
He was master of the *Coral* of New Bedford on her highly
profitable 1846–50 cruise, returning with 3350 barrels which sold
for $126 630.

The largest sperm whale that I have seen taken was 120 barrels
(15 tuns); though I have heard of one that made 148 barrels. The
male or bull, when full grown, varies from 70 to 110 barrels, very
seldom going beyond the latter amount, and is from 50 to 70 feet
long. Female or cow sperm whales have been caught that made 50
barrels, though they do not often yield more than 35 barrels. They
vary much in size in different places. In the Caribbean Sea, Gulf of
Mexico, and along the Gulf Stream through the Atlantic, they run
small, and full-grown cows will not average over 15 barrels. Those
caught in the Pacific Ocean near the equator as far as longitude 135°
west, average about 25 barrels while those caught farther west and in
most parts of the Indian Ocean run smaller. The cows with their
young give from nothing up to 35 barrels, and seem to go in schools
together, and we frequently see from 25 to 50 and sometimes 100 or
more in a school, with occasionally a large bull among them, and at
times, though seldom, we find all sizes together. The male or bull
whales seem to separate from the cows and calves when about the
size of 35 barrels, as we seldom get them in the schools of the
mother and its young to make oil more than that, and we find the
young bulls in pods or schools beyond that size; we find them in
what we call 40-barrel bulls, where they generally go in larger
numbers than they do as they increase in size; we find them again in
smaller schools of about the size of 50 barrels, and again about 60

barrels, where we sometimes see eight or ten together, and 70 barrels four or five, and beyond that one, two, and three, except on New Zealand Ground, where the large whales go in larger bodies; many times we raise a large sperm whale alone, or sometimes two within a short distance of each other going their regular course from three to six miles per hour; they will make their course as straight as we can steer a ship, and make their distances very regular during the time they are up and down; a large whale will usually stay down when not disturbed from 40 to 50 minutes; have known them to stay down one hour; their time on the top of the water about 15 minutes—spouting during that time say 45 times, or three times to the minute.[8]

The observation about spouting conforms to the whaleman's rule of thumb that for every foot of its length a surfacing sperm whale will spout once and at the next sounding remain submerged for one minute. Regularity of respiration also made it possible to calculate to a nicety how much time there was for an attack. The reference to New Zealand suggests that the Polack observation cited earlier relates to bull whales. The reaction of females under attack was different. Far from running when one of their number was struck, they would surround and support her, tails outward, in the daisy formation known as a marguerite. This was very convenient for the attacking whalemen but sometimes, infrequently, the protective circle would form facing outwards, a development that could give pause to all but the most determined. The solicitude of cows for their calves also made them vulnerable, and few whalemen would scruple to fasten to the youngster to bring its mother within range, a practice which some had the grace to acknowledge was not only cruel but in the long run self-defeating for the industry.

Before the middle of the nineteenth century the whalemen had long known all they needed to know about the sperm whale. They had even found him in miniature.

May there not also be more than one kind of sperm whale? We discovered a remarkable difference between the whales we caught in the Sooloo Sea, and those taken elsewhere; they were more deeply covered with deep wrinkles, and the head was differently proportioned; but the distinctive difference was in the size and the motion . . . During the voyage we took fifty of them, which made us only four hundred barrels, thus averaging, male and female, only eight barrels apiece; while the common sperm *cows* average at least fifteen barrels.[9]

It was the pygmy sperm whale. Many years later the naturalists would decide that it was of a different genus and name it *Kogia breviceps*. Brief in form and briefly exploited, its value to the sperm whalers and its inoffensive size quickly made it one of the rarer whales. This one the naturalists were in danger of missing altogether. The Japanese knew of an even smaller relative, the dwarf sperm whale (*Kogia sima*), all of 2 metres long, but these were beneath the notice of South Seamen.

THE BRITISH
ARE COMING

*The American . . . are the only people who
kill the Sperm Whale.*

Francis Rotch

The British merchants who imported colonial whale oil were as dismayed as their trading partners at the growing political crisis in North America. They too began planning to deal with the consequences of rupture. If South Sea whaling in colonial vessels became too hazardous, why not continue the business in British-owned and -registered ships? Some of the Nantucketers agreed, seeing the continued employment of their men, if not their capital, as better than nothing. In the summer of 1775 a number of vessels, some of them American-built oil carriers from the Nantucket–London run, were fitted out for whaling on the American pattern by a number of firms, notably those of Champion, Enderby, Buxton and Mather. Most of the masters, mates and boatsteerers were from Nantucket.

The Champions and others who began to look south were initially concerned to make arrangements that would tide them over what they hoped would be a temporary unpleasantness. As the unpleasantness went on, year after year, it gradually locked them into the trade. For one family firm, the Enderbys, it became a magnificent obsession that absorbed the ambition, energy and fortune of three generations. As the history of British South Sea whaling was coeval with Enderby participation, and ended with the ruin of both, it will be as well to understand how the firm came to be involved.

Samuel Enderby was born in humble circumstances in 1720. He was apprenticed as a cooper and established his own firm in London in 1753. In 1763 he married the daughter of the oil cooper Charles Buxton and, by natural extension, became at first an oil merchant and then, in the 1760s, a shipowner with the whaler *Weymouth* in the struggling Greenland fishery. By 1775 he owned three Greenland whalers but, in association with the Buxtons, also sent the *Union*, *Rockingham* and *Neptune* off to the Brazil Banks. The firm was keen to exploit the opportunity further and Samuel wrote to an associate in America urging him to recruit 31 whalemen and bring them to Britain 'as I have a grand scheme in view'. Whether Samuel would have entered the southern fishery of his own volition is uncertain; family tradition ascribed the interest in this new venture to his son, Samuel junior, then in his early twenties. The son may have been his father's representative in Massachusetts at the time of the Boston Tea Party.

Not all of the New Englanders were prepared to see their business appropriated by British firms. In August 1775 Francis Rotch assembled his ships and those of his associates at Martha's Vineyard, gave bonds of £2000 each against their return, as ordered by the General Court of Massachusetts, and then sent them off with instructions to rendezvous at the Falklands. It was rumoured that his real intention was to take the catch to England. Rotch himself proceeded to London and arrived to hear that five of his ships had been seized by British frigates off the Azores. The memorials that he presented to the government seeking release of the ships made it clear that the rumour was correct. Rotch wanted to relocate his business in its entirety.

> . . . your petitioners came to London with the Intention of residing
> here and fitting out such Vessels for the whale fishery as proper men
> could be obtained for . . . all the oil and other produce of the Fishery
> will be shipped . . . Immediately for London; this will be as agreeable
> to their Interest as to their Inclination, no other market calling for the
> quantity or affording so good a price for the proceeds of the Sperm
> Fishery.[1]

Anticipating objections from British shipping interests about
admitting colonial vessels, Rotch went on to explain that he had
no choice. Having fitted out his present fleet in America, he had
then, like Enderby, tried to recruit American whalers to come to
London to man ships that were to be purchased and outfitted in
the capital, 'but from the Public Clamour very few would be
prevailed with'. As a further inducement to the government he
held out the promise of manufacturing spermaceti candles in
London, 'a branch which is become of considerable consequence
in America, though very little known & but imperfectly executed
here'. The ships were released, but not before all their whalemen
were lost. Whether it was to the Royal Navy or to British whalers
Rotch does not say, but he did seek for his men the Admiralty's
protection certificates that exempted British whalemen from
impressment.

These were a curiosity of public policy. The theory was that the
whale fishery was a 'nursery of seamen', providing a reservoir of
manpower for the navy in time of war. Adam Smith accepted it as
an argument in favour of bounties which, although inefficient, he
thought might be a cheaper way of maintaining ships and sailors
for defence than keeping a standing navy. Regrettably, the
theory did not translate into practice. When war came, with a hot
press to man His Majesty's ships, the protections were not withdrawn. If anything they increased in number as shipowners
agitated with the politicians for preferential treatment. Enderby
and others also agitated for extension of the Greenland bounties
to the British ships now participating in the South Seas trade,
as they called it. This was too much for the long-suffering

Commissioners of Customs, who would have agreed with Adam Smith's other view that

> The usual effect of such bounties [for whaling and fishing] is to encourage rash undertakers to adventure in a business which they do not understand, and what they lose by their own negligence and ignorance, more than compensates all that they can gain by the utmost liberality of government.[2]

The Commissioners were able to persuade the government to restrict support for the southern industry to premiums of £500, £400, £300, £200 and £100 for the five most successful of the ships that returned each year. Their task had probably been made easier by Francis Rotch who, in laying his plans before the government, had pointed out that he was attempting to establish the sperm fishery in Britain 'without any previous requisition from Government for support'.

While Rotch and the British firms were sending their ships into the South Atlantic, the worst fears of the Nantucketers were being realised. Blockaded, and raided from time to time by both sides, the Quakers tried to endure an ordeal that was as offensive to their beliefs as to their interests. Their greatest anxiety was for returning ships. If intercepted by a British frigate the entire crew, officers and men, could be impressed under the provisions of the Restraining Act. Fortunate was the Quaker who was given the option of prison. In taking it, some were motivated as much by patriotism as by pacifism: Peleg Folger's cousin Nathaniel refused to be pressed, declaring 'hang me if you will to the yardarm of your ship, but do not ask me to be a traitor to my country'. The British imprisoned him on a hulk instead, as they did hundreds of his fellow islanders in Halifax and New York. Many died there. Upwards of 30 Nantucket whaleships were captured and sold into Britain's Greenland and southern fleets.

The Rotch family was far too canny to put all of its oil into the one cask. William remained on Nantucket for the duration, negotiating with both sides for licences to sail and return without

From Wall.   A WHALING SCENE OF 1763.   Britton & Rey lith.

Joseph Russell's New Bedford in 1763 (engraving in Scammon's Marine
Mammals, *from a nineteenth-century painting by William Wall, National
Library of Australia)*

fear of seizure. This was claiming a neutrality that neither side
could accept. For years his efforts and those of the selectmen of
Nantucket were unsuccessful and the fleet dwindled. Some of
the young men of New England turned to privateering along the
coast, with such success that in September 1778 the British
command in New York was stung into mounting a large-scale
punitive expedition. Its first port of call was New Bedford, which
was burned to the ground. Twenty-eight vessels were destroyed
or confiscated. A week later the British descended on Martha's
Vineyard. They stripped the island of sheep, cattle and arms, and
demanded payment of a sum equal to that levied in tax by the
Continental Congress. By 11 September it was Nantucket's turn,
but for three days in succession the promising morning breeze
turned to disappointment by midday and the turn of the tide

then forced the expedition back to the Vineyard. At this extremity word came from New York that the expedition was recalled. 'Nothing short of the interposition of Divine Providence', wrote William Rotch, 'preserved us from apparent ruin'.[3]

The absence of the New Englanders from the southern fishery gave the British a chance to establish themselves. Their South American venture thrived and so did Francis Rotch. It did not escape the notice of Benjamin Franklin (the son of Peleg Folger's great-aunt) and John Adams, then the American Commissioners at the French court, that here was an opportunity to strike a blow at British commerce. In October 1778 they urged the French to destroy the British whale fleet and liberate its American crewmen.

> The English last year carried on a very valuable whale fishery on the coast of Brazil off the River Plate, in South America, in latitude 35° south and from thence to 40°, just on the edge of soundings, off and on, about the longitude 65 from London. They have this year about seventeen vessels in this fishery which have all sailed in the months of September and October. All the officers and almost all the men . . . are Americans . . . For the destruction or captivity of a fishery so entirely defenceless (for not one of the vessels has any arms) a single frigate or privateer . . . would be quite sufficient. The beginning of December would be the best time to proceed from hence, because they would then find the whale vessels nearly loaded . . . at least 450 of the best kind of seamen would be taken out of the hands of the English, and might be gained into the American service to act against the enemy. Most of the officers and men wish well to their country, and would gladly be in its service if they could be delivered from that they are engaged in. But whenever the English . . . have taken an American vessel they have given to the whalemen among the crews their choice, either to go aboard a man-of-war and fight against their country, or to go into the whale fishery . . . We thought it proper to communicate this intelligence to your Excellency . . . to take from the British at once so profitable a branch of commerce and so valuable a nursery of seamen . . .[4]

The French might have been wondering how unwilling the whalemen really were, or have been deterred by the alleged presence of a British frigate with the fleet, but in the end they did nothing. In America the following September, Adams urged the same course on his home state, Massachusetts, 'as almost the whole fleet belongs to it'. As it happened, the matter was already in hand but largely through the initiative of American privateers. Even as Adams wrote, a Danish ship was reporting that the *Reward*, probably a Rotch ship, had been taken by the American privateer *Black Prince* and ransomed for 150 guineas. The *Egmont* had also been taken, by the privateer *Hornet*, and sent with her 150 tons of oil to Salem to be sold as a prize. The scale of these depredations did not become clear until December, when Lloyd's List published the names of a further nine British whalers that had been intercepted on their way home from the southern fishery and carried into New England.[5] It dampened the enthusiasm of the British owners somewhat: only four of their whalers went south in 1779, compared with nineteen the year before.

Nantucket's escape from the British raid in 1778 proved to be only a temporary relief. Loyalist refugees raided the island in April 1779 and removed goods worth more than $50,000. William Rotch and two others were deputed to ask the British to desist. They were successful and an order was issued forbidding British ships to interfere with Nantucket Harbour. Even more precious was a number of permits to whale. The concession immediately aroused the ire of the American military command, which accused the Nantucketers of treasonably seeking a separate peace. Nantucket was forbidden to treat with the enemy but the severity of the winter of 1779–80 reduced the islanders to desperation. In October 1780 Rotch and others were again commissioned to approach the British authorities, and this time Admiral Digby raised the number of permits to 24. They were not a complete solution, as Rotch acknowledged. 'It was necessary to secrete these Documents from American Cruisers, but such was the difficulty of distinguishing them [from British cruisers], that two were presented to American armed vessels, who immediately took the vessels as prizes.'[6]

What was needed was similar documentation from the rebels (and captains sharp enough to know which papers to use when boarded). Without double papers, the risks remained great, but the islanders persevered, sending out seventeen whalers in 1782. By then it was clear to all that the war had run its course and the time seemed propitious for an approach to the American authorities for permits. A memorial was presented to the General Court of Massachusetts which passed it to Congress. Rotch lobbied hard and effectively, his most telling argument being that with Nantucket out of commission America was in danger of losing the whaling trade to Britain. The islanders got their permits. In effect, Nantucket had finally gained the only kind of neutrality that mattered to it. It lasted one day. On 23 March 1783 a vessel brought news from London that a provisional treaty of peace had been signed and Nantucket was now part of a United States of America. Rotch was well ahead of these events. A month earlier his ship the *Bedford* had entered the Thames with a load of oil and an unfamiliar flag at the mizzen gaff. It was the first time that the Stars and Stripes had been seen in Britain.

The continuing access of the United States to British fisheries was a major sticking point in the negotiations that led to peace. The Americans found that their erstwhile allies, the French and the Spanish, could as often be at odds with them, and with each other, as all three might be with the British. Count Vergennes, the French foreign minister, narrowed the ambit of contention by declaring that 'the fishery on the high seas is as free as the sea itself, and it is superfluous to discuss the right of the Americans to it'. British acceptance of this dictum settled the sperm fishery, but a larger issue for the American whalemen was whether they could continue to pursue right whales off the coasts of Nova Scotia, Canada and Newfoundland. It was ultimately resolved in their favour, but not before a French negotiator had been moved to tell John Jay that Louis XVI was not about to risk his Spanish alliance 'only to secure an increase of fortune to a few shipmasters of New England'.[7]

If peace had simply restored pre-war arrangements in the whaling trade, there can be little doubt that New England would quickly have reasserted its dominance. In less than a year Nantucket alone could muster a fleet of 60 vessels in place of the 200 that they had lost. In the meantime however, Old England had become quite attached to the profits that could be made by combining British capital with American expertise. The dog-in-the-manger mercantilism that had cost Britain an empire now claimed an industry as compensation: American oil, as foreign produce, was subjected to a duty of £18/3/- per ton. Many Nantucketers talked of leaving the island, and a number of whalemen removed to the Hudson River. Others led by Samuel Starbuck and Timothy Folger, Peleg's cousin, were induced by the British provincial authorities to go to Nova Scotia. William Rotch was dismayed. He had lost property to the value of $60,000 in the revolution. How could he do business, much less recoup his losses, when oil that fetched only £17 in Nantucket cost £25 to produce? It was true that the market price of sperm oil, which had reached £95 per tun during the war and was still three times the price of common oil, still allowed a profit, but for how long? It could only be a matter of time before the British whalers, supported by government premiums and protected by duty, would be able to supply their domestic market at a price that the Americans could not hope to match.

Both the American and Massachusetts governments were sensible of the danger to one of their few export industries, but the economic defences of the infant republic were frail. In 1785 Massachusetts, having rejected Nantucket's renewed request for neutrality, tried to match the European subsidies by granting bounties of £5 per ton for white spermaceti oil ('head matter'), £3 for brown or yellow spermaceti oil (sperm oil) and £2 for right whale oil. The ensuing boom quickly faded as over-production began forcing down prices. The domestic market was too small. John Adams, sent as Minister to Britain in 1785 with the task of negotiating a commercial treaty, found that the younger Pitt, then Chancellor of the Exchequer, was not disposed to make concessions on whale oil, or much else, but he did want to know if the

Americans had found any foreign market other than France. Adams could only point to Bremen, but he had no doubt that

> . . . spermaceti oil might find a market in most of the great cities of Europe which were illuminated in the night, as it is so much better and cheaper than the vegetable oil that is commonly used. The fat of the spermaceti whale gives the clearest and most beautiful flame of any substance that is known in nature, and we are all surprised that you prefer darkness, and in consequence robberies, burglaries, and murders in your streets, to the receiving, as a remittance [in payment for British goods] our spermaceti oil. The lamps around Grosvenor Square, I know, and in Downing Street, too, I suppose, are dim by midnight, and extinguished by two o'clock; whereas our oil would burn bright till nine o'clock in the morning, and chase away, before the watchman, all the villains, and save you the trouble and danger of introducing a new police into the city.[8]

Pitt might have been impressed by the vigorous advocacy for this wondrous substance, but he gave Adams no encouragement. If he could get American whalemen for his British merchants, the efforts of Enderby and the others would keep both robbers and policemen at bay. In the upshot, there was no commercial treaty and Adams would spend much of his time in London seeking the release of American seamen pressed from American ships. So far as the Royal Navy was concerned, if they spoke English that was British enough.

For two years of peace William Rotch had struggled against the reality that Britain was 'the only market of any consequence for Sperm oil', but in 1785 he reluctantly decided that he would have to relocate. Contrariwise, Francis decided that he could afford to return to New Bedford. It was clear which of the brothers had been doing business on the right side of the Atlantic during the war years. It says much for the tough-mindedness of William that he went to London to bargain, not to plead. He took it for granted that Britain would wish to secure as many American whalemen as could be persuaded to emigrate. He put it to Pitt that the determining factor would be the amount of 'encourage-ment' Britain could offer. Pitt referred the matter to the Privy

Council, which kept Rotch cooling his heels for four months
before nominating Charles Jenkinson, Lord Hawkesbury to negotiate. The Quaker stated Nantucket's terms: £20,000 for 100
families, and 30 American ships to be admitted to the British
register. Hawkesbury was prepared to offer £87/10/- for each
family, but the ships were another matter. These would deny
work to British shipbuilders and, as he said, 'tis seamen we want'.
He nevertheless indicated that the ship question could be
addressed in a forthcoming Fisheries Bill. Rotch was unimpressed
and hinted at the French interest. Hawkesbury was sure he knew
a bluff when he saw one. 'Quakers go to France?', he queried.
'Yes', said Rotch, 'but with regret'. Within days he had sent
proposals to the French government, which were just as expedi-
tiously accepted.[9]

Hawkesbury had been too clever by half, but he had been
honest about Britain's objective. On his arrival in England Rotch
had written home that 'The spirit of whaling seems almost running
to a degree of madness, they intend if men can be got to send out
30 ships, but at present there appears no possibility of getting
men'.[10] In its attempts to get those men the British government
had even tried to discourage its own governor in Nova Scotia, who
was told that the Nantucketers should be emigrating to Britain
rather than to his province. This was at the urging of the British
whaling firms, who were playing a complicated game. They were
keen to have access to the seamen and, like the government, would
reluctantly accept that admission of American ships might be a
price worth paying. What they feared was American competition
for their premiums. Their solution to this dilemma was to propose
replacing the premiums with a tonnage bounty, to be initially on
the same terms as the Greenland bounty. They knew how to dress
it up for government consumption.

> . . . your memorialists have proposed the bounty of forty shillings per
> ton for three years, as they know it will be an inducement to the
> Americans to settle in England, and it will be a means of establishing
> the fishery here in preference to Nova Scotia, where it will be out of

the power of [British] Government to prevent American oil from
coming here free of duty, and from its near situation to the
Massachusetts, will be a cover to a great deal of American property
and whaling vessels, besides the disadvantage of the nursery of
seamen being in America, from whence it will be difficult to get them
in case of a war.[11]

Hawkesbury saw no need to subsidise the American whalers at
all, and his bill simply made them ineligible for the premiums,
but he quadrupled the number available and reserved five of
them, at higher rates of £700 down to £300, for British whalers
proceeding south of the old limit of 36° south. With these exclusive incentives in their pockets the British merchants were happy
to write to Rotch in Paris telling him that the Fisheries Bill now
made provision for 40 American ships. Rotch also reported to
Nantucket that the Enderbys, old business associates, had offered
to assist him, an offer that he had reason to believe was genuine.
It was; not until 1788 did Samuel Enderby junior 'despair of
getting that Family from Nantucket to this Country'.[12] The
attempt was misconceived, as were all the British dealings with
Rotch. His interest was in free access to a substantial market for
Nantucket oil. If one could be found, there would be no need
for the efficient Nantucketers to move at all, and for this blessing
he would gladly forgo premium, subsidy or protection. Arrangements with men and ships were merely counters on the board.
This the French understood. Their main objective was to deny
the British five or six thousand trained seamen, although they
aimed to get the American whalemen for their own fishery if they
could.

In Paris Rotch was given assurances about freedom of religion
and exemption from military service. The French government's
business terms were extremely generous; they would pay a bounty
of 50 livres per ton (42 shillings, slightly more than that paid by
the British to their Greenland whalers) for each ship of 20 tons or
more. In return, the ships must fit out in France. Also, if Monsieur
Rotch should find business difficult in the interim, perhaps this

year he and the other Nantucket merchants might wish to bring into Dunkirk say, 250 tuns duty-free? Having done so much for the common good thus far, Rotch thought he was entitled to a little personal benefit. He and his associates took first bite at this particular carrot. In the outcome, the French registered four American-manned ships and only nine Nantucket families moved to Dunkirk, but the door to the duty-free shop was now ajar. Pitt let it be known that Rotch could name his own terms for a Nantucket emigration to Britain. He was told that it was too late.

When Hawkesbury's Act for the Encouragement of the Southern Whale Fishery saw the light of day in Parliament, it still allowed, until 1790, for the American vessels to be licensed as British under Order in Council. The British too could leave doors ajar. The French saw that the Nantuckois, as Thomas Jefferson called the potential emigrants to France, were reluctant to relocate to Dunkirk, and feared that the British might yet entice them. In 1786, therefore, they abated the duty on all imported whale oil, assuming that this would allow more Nantucketers to whale from home. It should have, but the British seized the opportunity to flood the French market with their subsidised oil, which undermined both French and American producers. The French overreacted. In 1788 they closed their ports to all foreign oil. While the British whaling fleet had to contract by one-fifth that year, the Americans again faced near-total ruin. Jefferson, then American Minister in Paris, put a strong case for exemption.

> France cannot expect to raise her fishery, even to the supply of her
> own consumption in one year, or in several years. Is it not better,
> then, by keeping her ports open to the United States, to enable them
> to aid in maintaining the aid against the common adversary [Britain],
> till she shall be in condition to take it herself, and to supply her own
> wants? Otherwise, her supplies must aliment that very force which is
> keeping her under. On our part, we can never be dangerous
> competitors to France. The extent to which we can exercise this
> fishery, is limited to that of the barren island of Nantucket, and a few
> similar barren spots; its duration, to the pleasure of this [French]
> government, as we have no other market.[13]

It was disingenuous but it worked. American oil was readmitted.

When Jefferson claimed that the Americans had no other market he was referring to the common or black oil obtained from right whales, for as yet the British ships in the southern sperm fishery were supplying 'a very small proportion of their own demand'. Rotch and the others could make a profit on sperm oil in London in spite of the duty, although there was increasing competition from the Nantucket colony that had emigrated to Dartmouth, Nova Scotia. The European market was for common oil, and the Americans deployed their ships to meet it. Between 1787 and 1789 they put three vessels into the northern fishery for every one in the southern, and even those that went south, under pressure to make quick voyages for quick profit, were encouraged to take what they could find. In dismissing the oil of the right whale as 'fit only for summer use, as it becomes opaque at 50 degrees of Farenheit's thermometer', Jefferson also noted that 'It is only worth taking, therefore, when it falls in the way of the fisherman, but not worth seeking, except when they have failed of success against the spermaceti whale, in which case, this kind, easily found and taken, serves to moderate their loss'.[14]

The growth of British competition in the southern fishery and European preference for common oil were not the only complications for the spermaceti trade as seen from an American perspective. Spermaceti processing was becoming more efficient. The French had opened a whale oil factory in Rouen, and among its processes was one for extracting spermaceti from sperm oil, no doubt involving the use of white wine as had been reported to the Royal Society in 1666. Hitherto the candle manufacturers had been dependent on head matter for their raw material. Now the additional spermaceti suspended in the oil could be readily retrieved. It made sperm oil more valuable while reducing the number of whales needed to provide any given quantity of spermaceti.

Comprehensively undone by Rotch, the French and their own parsimony in the attempt to relocate Nantucket whalemen directly, the British considered another source. By 1790 the 35

Nantucket families that had emigrated to Nova Scotia in 1785–86 had increased the value of their whale fishery from £22,300 to £31,300. More importantly, protected by duty their 22 ships were exporting more sperm oil to London than the 116 ships of the Massachusetts fleet. This time the proposal to bring them to Britain was in the name of Sir William Hamilton, proprietor of the undeveloped harbour at Milford Haven in Wales, who with his nephew Charles Greville revived a submission they had first put to the government in 1785 in connection with the Rotch discussions. For a net outlay of £2150, they said, 30 families, 19 ships and 271 seamen could be induced to emigrate and create a new whaling port. Compared to Rotch's proposal it was a bargain. The advantages to the Quakers of Dartmouth were less clear. They would be closer to their prime market but far distant, both physically and emotionally, from Nantucket. The decisive factor seems to have been the urging of their leaders, Samuel Starbuck and Timothy Folger. When the community subsequently learnt that both had been granted British annuities of £150 for their persuasiveness, Starbuck was temporarily denied certification as a member of the Society of Friends.

At the end of August 1792 the Dartmouth colony stowed its families, its household goods and its memories into thirteen whalers and sailed for Milford Haven. Religion had driven their ancestors to the New World; worldly considerations were driving them back to the Old. As Jefferson saw it, they were 'postponing country and friends to high premiums' in preference to 'smaller advantages in the neighbourhood of their ancient country and friends'. The British government, encouraged by Greville, again began to think that it might be possible to recruit the remaining Nantucketers from their island home. The Nova Scotian administration disabused them.

> Instead of the circumstances of these people being distressed, it is
> rather the reverse—they are at present Day building many new ships
> and extending their Fishery, so that the Terms which some years ago
> they with joy would have accepted for their removal, I am of the

opinion, although the same should be offered with treble advantage, they would now refuse. Therefore, to make an estimate of the expenses that it would require to remove the whole bulk of the Inhabitants of Nantucket to Great Britain, would be to calculate on a Sum which no nation could afford to give.[15]

So Rotch's Dunkirk initiative had put the Nantucketers beyond any further temptation that could be drawn across their path by either the British or the French. The tug of war to secure the talents of the American whalemen was over. The rope had broken and all three parties were left holding an end. Against all the odds, the Americans had come up with the largest piece, but it was a frayed and fragile thing. Jefferson, now Secretary of State, summed up the state of play so that Congress could see

. . . with what a competition we have to struggle for the continuance of this fishery, not to say its increase. Against prohibitory duties in one country, and bounties to the adventurers in both of those which are contending with each other for the same object, ours have no auxiliaries, but poverty and rigorous economy. The business, unaided, is a wretched one . . .

But less wretched for the South Seamen. The Secretary of State went on to show that it cost $3000 to build, fit out and victual the typical 64-ton vessel that the northern fishery used to get 18 tuns of common oil worth $900. In the southern fishery, a 140-ton vessel ready to sail cost $6500, but would bring back 32 tuns of sperm oil worth $3200. Even allowing for the greater length of the voyage, the return on capital clearly favoured the southern venture. And, with even more ingenuity than the British merchants had given them credit for in 1786, the Yankee whalemen had found yet another way of supplementing their income.

[British oil] is brought here, too, to be reshipped fraudulently, under our [American] flag, into [French] ports where it could not be received under theirs, and ought not to be covered by ours, if we mean to preserve our own admission into them.[16]

It would seem that not all of the oil that was going into Dunkirk on Rotch and other American ships had been caught by them. It was evidence, if any were needed, that the American whalemen that had chosen to tie their fortunes to those of their homeland were among the most resourceful of their kind. The winds of adversity that had blown so many away to Britain, France and Nova Scotia had left only the most determined clinging to Massachusetts shores. Most South Seamen were American, but the best were more American than the rest.

Lay On, Cut In,
Try Out, Stow Down
or From Blubber To Oil

Lay me on, Captain Bunker, I'm hell on a long dart.

American whaling song

The producer/resource interface of sperm whaling, as a modern economist would probably ask us to call it, was six men and a boat in pursuit of tens of tons of live meat. At the outset of a cruise, particularly in the later years of the industry, half or more of those men might never have set foot in any kind of boat before. Unfamiliarity with the equipment and environment was not the greenhand's only difficulty. All of the operations were conducted in trade talk, some of which was foreign even to other seamen. The literature of whaling is replete with bravura passages of chase in which whalemen regale the reader with their patois. None is more immediate or authentic in its apparent artlessness than the description left in the back of his journal by George Gould, a seaman on the *Columbia* in 1844. Its unique interest is that we also have his source material. Gould logged the events of the day in question as follows.

> . . . raised Whales breaching Whales Come up to lee beam lowered and all three boats fastened the waist boat was stove Midships not badly hauled up and Was Stove Again she sank [indecipherable] the gunwales Cut the line Whale went to leeward spouting thick blood

the Mate ran down to us but we did not look for his assistance he ran
off to leeward and picked up the w[aist] boat's Whale after Wafeing
his [whale] so ends[1]

His subsequent elaboration of this manic hour was, literally,
dramatic. A gloss is provided for the greenhands.

23 February

Commenced these 24 hours with a fine brease heading S.S. East for the Marquesas Islands. the watch on deck had Struck four bells, the man at the wheal and mast heads had been relieved but a few moments before the man up forwards Sang out		The three masthead lookouts and the man at the wheel were changed half way through each four hour watch.
Foremast	*there She Breaches*	The whale is throwing itself out of the water.
Captain	*Where away*	
Foremast	*Four points off the larboard bow Sir*	45° off the port (left) bow. Whalers used the older term long after it was superseded in the merchant service.
Captain	*How far off*	
Foremast	*Six miles Sir*	Near maximum distance for seeing spouts.
Captain	*Keep her off three points there, Square in the Main yards and Mizen topsail*	Steer closer to the whale, and trim sail to allow for the wind coming more astern.
Crew	*Aye Aye Sir*	

Captain   *Then belay all that.*   Tie off the yards and sails
haul the topsail brace a   as reset.
Small pull then belay
all, Haul the Weather
fore topsail brace a
Small pull, jump up   The boom is a retractable
there a Couple of you   spar. Its usual function is to
And rig out the fore   carry a light outboard sail
top mast Studing Sail   but it might here have been
Boom. Bear a hand   used to signal whale boats
men if you love Money.   in the chase.

Crew   *Aye Aye Sir*

And a Couple jumped into the   The rigging was always
Weather fore rigen. When the   climbed on the windward
mate from the Main topmast   side so that the seaman
head Sang out   would not be blown off.

Mate   *She blows Close aboard*
Sir

Captain   *What do they look like*

Mate   *Sperm Whales Sir!*   The ridges down the back
there She blows. There   behind the sperm whale's
She ripples regular   hump were an identifying
old Logs   feature.

Captain   *How are they headed*

Mate   *Square to leeward Sir.*   Abeam and directly down
Slow as night.   wind.

Captain	*Bring the Ship to the Wind there. Brace up the fore and mizen topsails. Haul aback the Main yard. Call all hands*	The ship's forward motion will cease. With the front of the mainsail presented to the wind she is hove to.

The Main yard was backed.
And the hoarse and unwelcome
Sounds of all hands ahoy
brought us on deck

Captain	*Do you See Anything of the Whales there*	
Mate	*No Sir. they have gone down*	
Foremast	*There She Blows. one point forward of the lee Beam sir*	
Captain	*Come down there from aloft. Clear away the boats*	Eighteen of the crew will man three boats, leaving only six to work the ship.
2d Mate	*Here Cook Stand by My Boat*	As an 'idler', the cook would not normally take an oar.
Cook	*Aye Aye Sir*	
Mates	*Stand by the boats here*	
Captain	*Hoist and Swing the Cranes all ready there*	Davits hoisted the boats clear of the cranes on which they rested. These were then swung flush against the ship's side.
Mates	*Aye Aye Sir*	

Captain	*Lower away then*	
2d Mate	*Come be lively follow her down bully boat you know, waste boat forever, bend in your line there. down to your oars men, line your oars. Now give her a good stroke. forwards with her. will you beat that boat. you can do it. only Say So. And the whale is ours. What say now a fresh start I will give you all I have but my wife, do men lay back.*	The boats were too fragile to be lowered with the crew aboard. The larboard (stern quarter) boat is the first mate's, the (larboard) waist boat is the second mate's and the (larboard) bow boat is the third's. In the *Columbia* the third mate took the starboard (stern quarter) boat, usually the captain's.

The harpoons are not bent (tied) to the whale line until the boat is afloat.

The mate is racing. Some captains frowned on the added risks of 'victorious whaling'.

Boatsteerer	*They have gone down Sir*	
2d Mate	*Heave up. there peak your oars. take your paddles men*	Paddles made less noise and were less likely to 'gally' the whale.
B.Steerer	*Signal from the ship Sir. Whales are up there She blows Sir one point on Starboard bow*	Every ship had a private combination of sail and flag settings with which its lookout could direct the boats in the chase.

2d Mate	*I see them, take your oars men, What say men give her a good start? only one mile off. Will you pull. a bottle of rum for every man, What say. there they lay as still as night. Waiting for us. there we come up with them hand over hand*	There are five rowing oars, three to starboard and two to larboard. Furthest forward is the harpooner's, to starboard. Looking aft, and alternating from side to side, the order is bow, midships, tub and stroke, or after oar.
B.Steerer	*Whale on lee beam Sir*	Alongside and downwind.
2d Mate	*Take out your oars. Look out for the Sail Warren*	The boat has been chasing under sail and oar but the sail is lowered for the attack.
B.Steerer	*Aye Aye Sir let it Come*	
2d Mate	*Loose the Sail, pass off the Sheat take your paddles men that Whale is ours*	Sheet: rope attached to the foot of the sail.
B.Steerer	*As you go Sir, Steady,,*	
2d Mate	*Lay down your paddles men and Stand by your oars easy men. Stand up Warren*	The oars are needed for rapid manoeuvre in attack. The traditional standby order to the harpooner, who peaks his oar and turns to stand with his left thigh braced in the 'clumsy cleat' cut into the forward thwart.

the whale was but a few feet from us Warren Stood up With the iron in his hand waiting for orders

Iron: harpoon.

2d Mate   *Paddle men one foot More and he is ours. What are you looking over your Shoulder for I will look out for the Whale. do paddle one foot more. ready there Warren?*

Paddling with the oars?

Greenhands had been known to jump out of the boat in terror when close to the whale: 'eyes in the boat' was the rule.

B.Steerer   *Aye Aye Sir*

2d Mate   *Give it to him then*

The traditional order to dart the harpoon.

And the Boat Steerer burried two irons to the Sockets

The whale line had two harpoons attached. They were socketed into wooden poles.

2d Mate   *Stern all, Stern all. I tell you. ever mother Son of you. Stern. Wett line there. trim boat. look out that you do not crab your oars. hold on hard every one of you. hold on. there She fights. haul line Men. Come aft Warren*

'All oars back water', away from the stricken whale. As the whale runs, the tub oarsman pours water on the line to prevent friction setting fire to it.

They begin to pull the boat up to the whale as it slows.

B.Steerer   *Aye Aye Sir*

Lancing into the life (from the Illustrated London News, *1867, National Library of Australia)*

---

the Boatsteerer goes aft And the 2d Mate goes forward		The headsman (usually a mate) is always the most experienced whaleman in the boat and will kill the whale.
2d Mate	*Now haul line men. with a will stand by your oars men. Bowman Stand by to haul the line. haul I tell you haul. pull I tell you there he fights Sixty bbl fellow*	The bow oarsman, whose position is just aft of the harpooner's, takes the line from the bow and runs it to a cleat on the side of the boat nearest the whale. The boat can now be hauled up parallel to the whale.

haul I tell you one good chance and I will Settle his hash for him. (darts his lance) *Stern all. Stern all I tell you Stern if you wish to See Nantucket*

Unlike the harpoon, the lance is unbarbed and can be 'churned' up to 2 metres into the whale seeking the heart and lungs.

the Whale had now gone down and the boat lay in Bloody water. all looking out and waiting for the Whale to rise, he come up the boat happend to be in his way And he Stove her abaft the bow thwart

Between the bow and midship oarsmen.

2d Mate   *Stern you lubbers Stern, Stern I tell you. Stern all to the Devil, off Shirt one of you tear up the Sealing one of you And stuff in your Shirts there. there that's the talk. Now we are off again Haul line bullies Now's your time there he lays like a log. oh do haul will you men. I will pay for your Shirts.* (darts his lance)

Ceiling: the boards lining the bottom of the boat.

The Whale then rounded too
And come for the boat the 2d
Mate Sung out Stern but it was
to late he stove us again and We
Could Not Stuff it up with Shirts,
the 2 Mate And two of the Crew
jumped overboard. the Whale ran
to leeward a Short distance went
into his flurry, headed to the Sun
and turned fin out

The flurry was the last
paroxysm. Whalers believed
that the dying whale always
turned its head to the sun.
The dead whale usually
floated on its side, 'fin out'.

2d Mate   *Jump in Men in to the
boat, the danger is all
gone. rig out your
oars athart ship and
we will weather her
out. Curse old leper I
thought the bloody
buger Would leave me
in Davy Jones locker.
Set the wafes head and
Stern. the old Man
will Soon pick us up.
Keep her headed to
windward there Warren.*

*the bloody thing Cant
Sink Men. Rather wet
here boys. but you will
feel better after you get
dry. we'll Splice the
main brace to pay for
this*

A stove boat that had
settled upright in the water
was kept from capsizing by
lashing the oars across it.

The waif was a flag usually
stuck into a dead whale to
indicate its position.
Old man: Captain
To minimise the risk of
capsize.

Issue a tot of spirits.

Crew *Sail ho! dead a head*
heading us as we
Stern. the old Man
comeing to pick us up
Boys

after backing and filling for a
long time he ran down to us

The set of the wind
requires the captain, being
shorthanded, to back the
ship towards the boat.

Captain *Take in your oars. how*
do you expect to get
along Side

2d Mate *If I take them in She*
will capsize I think Sir

Captain *I don't Care take them*
in I tell you Who
Shiped you to think?

The old rule is. Obey orders if
you break owners. in Comes the
oars And over goes the boat.
Every one for himself And the
Devil for us all.

Captain *There you have done it*
now. oh! you Sap
heads. well jump in.
Come up here Stand by
to take up the waste
boat. all ready to
hoist there

2d Mate *Aye Aye Sir, all ready*

Captain   *Hoist away there fore*
            and aft. lively men up
            with her, there high, put
            her on the Cranes, coil   Falls: hoisting ropes on the
            up the falls.   davits.

Captain George F Joy was not used to having his authority queried. Even solicitude for the owners' property, in this case a boat, was no excuse for disobedience. Gould attempted to continue his dialogue, less convincingly, through the more complicated processes of cutting in the whale and trying out its blubber. For a clearer account we can look to Melville, the prose artist, but he invests them with a kind of glamour that sits ill with such industrial grind. Perhaps, then, we might turn to a struggling poet: Henry Kendall never sullied his muse by versifying about the two miserable years he spent apprenticed on the *Waterwitch*, but necessity was the mother of recollection when it came to scratching a living as a hack writer in Melbourne.

> The cutting in and trying out . . . comprise a large amount of really hard and sometimes nauseous work. In the first place the whale is made fast, fore and aft, to the starboard side of the ship. The head is secured at a site parallel with or a little abaft of the mainmast, the flukes being chained at the bows. There is no need to buoy the animal, a dead [sperm] whale invariably floats; then the cutting in commences. A strong block is affixed immediately under the maintop, and through this a cable-like tackle is carried forward to the windlass; then an auxiliary block and tackle, the latter acted upon by a capstan, is got into working order. To each of the tackles, huge grappling hooks are secured. Then a stage is rigged outside the chains on either side of the gangway—the latter being left clear for the ingress of the blubber. On these stages, the captain and chief officers stand with their cutting in spades . . . The actual cutting in is commenced by an ingenious piece of manipulation on the part of the captain. By careful strokes, he begins the peeling off of the blubber, without losing so much as a scrap. When about a foot is separated from the carcass, the grappling hook of the windlass tackle is lowered and a good swimmer—generally a kanaka—is sent down to affix it to the loose blubber.
>
> Many and many a time, the poor kanaka . . . finds himself in

Welcome Aboard

A muster before the captain on the first morning out was
not uncommon in the merchant service, but it had more
significance on a whaleship given the amount of time the
men were liable to be subject to the rules there laid down.
It was always extempore but with many, like Captain
Alden of the *Bruce*, of Fairhaven, it followed a well-worn
track. J Ross Browne, now a greenhand but formerly a
Congressional shorthand reporter, decided to record for
posterity what he was told on the morning of 18 July 1842.

> I suppose you all know what you came a whaling for? If
> you don't, I'll tell you. You came to make a voyage, and I
> intend you shall make one. You didn't come to play; no,
> you came for oil; you came to work.
> (Here he took a turn on the quarterdeck, and while
> concentrating his ideas for another burst of eloquence,
> amused himself in an undertone, partly addressed to
> himself individually, and partly to the mate, by letting us
> know that it would be 'a greasy voyage, and a monstrous
> greasy one too'.)
> You must do as the officers tell you, and work when
> there's work to be done. We didn't ship you to be idle
> here. No, no, that ain't what we shipped you for, by a
> grand sight. If you think it is, you'll find yourselves
> mistaken. You will that—some, I guess.
> (Here he lost the idea, or, to use a more expressive
> phrase, 'got stumped'.)
> I allow no fighting aboard this ship. Come aft to me
> when you have any quarrels, and I'll settle 'em. I'll do the
> quarrelling for you—I will.
> (Another turn on the quarter deck.)
> If there's any fighting to be done, I want to have a hand
> in it. Any of you that I catch at it, 'll have to FIGHT ME!
> (A frightful doubling up of the fists, and a most
> ferocious gnashing of the teeth.)
> I'll have no swearing, neither. I don't want to hear
> nobody swear. It's a bad practice—an infernal bad one. It

breeds ill will, and don't do no kind o' good. If I catch any
one at it, damme, I'll flog him, that's all.

(A nod of the head, as much as to say he meant to be
as good as his word.)

When it's your watch below, you can stay below or
for'ed, just as you please. When it's your watch on deck,
you must stay on deck, and work, if there's work to be
done. I won't have no skulking. If I see sogers here, I'll
soger 'em with a rope's end. Any of you that I catch below,
except in cases of sickness, or when it's your watch below,
shall stay on deck and work until I think proper to stop
you.

(A stride or two aft, and a glance to windward.)

You shall have good grub to eat, and plenty of it. I'll
give you vittles if you work; if you don't, you may starve.
Don't grumble about your grub neither. You'd better not, I
reckon.

(A mysterious shake of the head, which implied a vast
deal of terrific meaning.)

If you don't get enough, come aft and apply to me. I'm
the man to apply to; I'm the captain.

(Here he surveyed himself with a look of exultation,
which seemed to say that he was not only the captain—the
very man to whom he had special reference, but that it was
a source of infinite satisfaction to him to be the captain.)

Now, the sooner you get a cargo of oil, the sooner you'll
get home. You'll find it to your interest to pay attention to
what I say. Do your duty, and act well your part toward
me, and I'll treat you well; but if you show any obstinacy
or cut up any extras. I'll be damned if it won't be worse for
you! Look out! I ain't a man that's going to be trifled with.
No, I ain't—not myself, I ain't! The officers will all treat
you well, and I intend you shall do as they order you. If
you don't, I'll see about it.

(Three or four strides to and fro on the quarterdeck, and
a portentous silence of five minutes.)

That's all. Go for'ed, where you belong! [*Etchings of a
Whale Cruise*, pp 35–7]

Browne claimed that this was a literal report. What Alden
made of the scribbler by the mainmast is not recorded.

dangerous neighbourhood to the sharks. For it must be noted that the back of a whale affords nothing more than a very slippery footing. However, mishaps, thanks to the vigilant defence of the spadesmen, rarely occur. After the hook is fastened, the man comes on board, and the sailors begin to heave at the windlass. The whale is peeled of its blubber, as one might peel the skin off an orange . . . As the hook of the windlass tackle approaches the block with its burden, which is then called a blanket-piece, the auxiliary hook is made fast to the latter, and drawn taut. Hook number one is then released, and lowered to a level with the scuppers, where it is re-fastened to the blubber. Just above this point the blanket-piece is severed, and its upper portion lowered by the capstan-tackle into the hold, where three or four of the crew are waiting to cut it up into horse-pieces. Meanwhile the spadesmen dig away, and number one hook comes up with a fresh load to be consigned to its auxiliary. This goes on until the whole of the body has been peeled. Then the flukes and head are dealt with. Sometimes the flukes are cast adrift. The brain-pan—known as the case—forms a deep well of spermaceti, which is baled out by buckets. The upper and forward parts of the head (masses of pure blubber) are hoisted on board and cut up on deck; the rest of the huge animal being cast loose to the finned and feathered races.[2]

Other accounts are less restrained. Sharks were known to surf onto the carcass, take a perfectly circular bite out of the blubber and float off, but in the frenzy of feeding they might ignore a seaman who fell in amongst them. They were almost indestructible, in spite of the spadesmen's best efforts, and could suddenly take a limb from the unwary after lying apparently dead on a deck for hours. Practices were not universal: on American ships the captain would seldom stoop to spadework if there were enough officers with expertise.

Removing the head was probably the most difficult part of the operation. The crudest method was to cut a hole in the side nearer the ship and insert the end of a stout baulk of timber, its other end being secured to the ship. The neck vertebrae were then severed with a cutting spade. As the blubber was peeled the body would rotate, eventually twisting free of the fixed head. When the whale was small enough and the tackle heavy enough, the

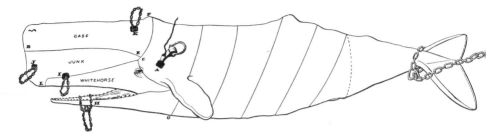

ꝹUTLINE OF A ꟅPERM ꟃHALE, SHOWING THE MANNER OF ꟄUTTING - IN.

*Charles Scammon's diagram for cutting in the sperm whale
(from* Marine Mammals of the North-Western Coast of
North America, *National Library of Australia)*
*A hole is cut at A for the blubber hook attached to the first cutting tackle
and with it the whale is hoisted onto its side. A cut from L–C (and B–E
for a large whale) and another from E–F starts the separation of junk
and case from the upper jaw. A cut from the corner of the mouth to G
precedes the attachment of a chin strap at H, which is hoisted to turn the
whale onto its back. When the tongue has been cut away the jaw can be
wrenched from its socket and hoisted aboard. The blubber hook at A is
now hoisted further, rolling the whale onto its other side, where the earlier
cuts are duplicated. Holes are morticed at I, J and K and the second
cutting tackle is attached to I. Slacking off the fluke chain and the first
tackle while hoisting with the second brings the whale's head to a near
vertical position and the cut L–C is deepened until the weight of the body
tears it away from the upper head. E–F is now completely cut through
and the head is secured astern by J and K. The fluke chain is hauled in
again, returning the whale to the horizontal, and the first tackle unrolls
the blubber from the body as far back as the small, where the spine is
unjointed and the flukes etc. are hoisted aboard. The carcass floats away
and the upper head is brought to the gangway. A tackle is connected to J
and, if the whale is less than forty barrels, the head will be hoisted
aboard entire. If more, junk and case will be separated before hoisting
and, in the case of a very large whale, the case will be hove up to the
plank sheer backwards, with its immense weight still supported by the sea,
and a hole made in its base through which the spermaceti can be bailed
out.*

head would be brought aboard entire to avoid loss of any of the precious head matter. If not, the lower part of the head, the junk, was cut away and hoisted aboard, its 5 or 6 tons calling for the efforts of all hands on the tackles. The case was even heavier and had to be left half suspended in the water, nose down, while the spermaceti was bailed out of its upper end. The cartilage which encased the spermaceti held no oil, nor did the impenetrable 'whitehorse' that separated case from junk. Both were discarded. If the animal appeared unhealthy its intestines would be searched for ambergris, which was even more valuable than spermaceti. When all parts of value had been extracted, the half and more of the animal that remained was just 'kreng', and released from the fluke chain to float away. Then the dirty work began.

> When the spermaceti and blubber are in the hold, the work of trying out the latter commences. Fires are lighted in furnaces under two large copper boilers, set in a frame of brickwork immediately abaft of the forehold. Each boiler has attached to it an immense cauldron of the same metal for cooling the oil. These cauldrons stand at the starboard and larboard sides of the frame, respectively, and are connected to the boilers by copper guttering. As the blanket-pieces are being cut into strips called horse-pieces, the latter are forwarded to the mincing-tub. Here they are dealt with by mincing knives, and then thrown into the boilers. When a pot has been sufficiently tried out, its oil is conveyed, by long-handled ladles, to the cauldron. The cauldrons soon cool their contents, which are emptied into casks lashed on deck. So the work goes on, day and night, till it is finished. Then the deck casks are drained of their oil, by means of hose passed into casks in the hold. Finally, the decks are cleared and scrubbed; and the insatiable spouter starts away after fresh game, with a sort of smug holiday look about her.[3]

Kendall invests the process with the inevitability of an assembly line, which it much resembled. Trying watches were six hours on and six hours off. Continuous processing at a rate of 50 barrels a day could consume even the largest whale in two or three days, but there was much scope for interruption in the incompatibility of fire and wood, oil and water. The fire had to be very

'Jaw Nearly Clear'—cutting in on the Maria Swift
(New Bedford Whaling Museum)

hot, as the boiling point of the oil was far higher than that of
water. Implements were of forged iron because solder would
melt. The tryworks sat in a shallow cistern called the goose pen.
It was kept full of water while the works were in operation.
This was the only safety feature built into the vessel. The oil
in the trypots was difficult to contain unless the sea was dead
calm, and even then a slippery deck or implement might
spill hot oil into the furnace during transfer. The chimneys of
the furnace were located just aft of the foremast, which was
heavy with sails and rigging impregnated with the oil of whales
past. Water was almost as much to be feared, as a sudden
downpour could excite the boiling oil to overflow. And yet,
from this powder trail of circumstance that could be lit at any
point, disaster was almost unknown. The trypots were in the
experienced hands of the boatsteerers, and recorded instances of
oil fires speak of ready containment and quick extinction. What

we lack are accounts of fires from which the ship was just saved, or fires in which the crew took to the boats to watch their ship burn. It leaves the suspicion that if a fire took hold in an oil-soaked, oil-full ship it would spread too quickly and burn too fiercely for control or escape, and of this there are hints in the annals.

In July 1823 the *Lady Adams* was last reported off the coast of Japan with 800 barrels aboard. One night shortly thereafter the captain of a British whaler in the vicinity saw a great light in the distance. He sailed towards it, but by the time he had reached the supposed locality it had disappeared, leaving no clue as to its cause. It was thought that if it were the *Lady Adams* any surviving crew members must have landed in Japan, where they would have been massacred. In March 1846 the French whaler *Asia* was trying out at night off New Zealand when a great fire was seen. The ship's doctor, Felix Maynard, came on deck to view the spectacle.

> There was no doubt about it being a conflagration, and in all probability it was a whaler on fire. I am surprised that these sinister events are not more frequent. At every hour of the day and night, during the fishing, fire threatens . . . [Water in the goose pen] evaporates quickly, and if through forgetfulness it is not renewed, the planks scorch, catch fire, and will no longer support the weight of the furnace, so that both cauldron and fire may suddenly fall into the between-decks. No doubt such a catastrophe had befallen our confrere . . . fifteen miles to windward . . . The fire used for rendering down had become transformed into a gigantic sheaf of flame. The horizon was illuminated, and at the bottom of the flames one perceived, through the telescope, an ignited mass, a colossal coal upon which sudden renderings appeared, which fed the conflagration and gave to the disaster the recurring radiance of an immense intermittent lighthouse . . . Suddenly a more vivid light was diffused over the ocean; then the flames lessened in intensity little by little, and we perceived the colossal coal diminishing in size and becoming extinguished as it sank beneath the sea.[4]

Daylight revealed charred wood and a solitary piece of burnt cotton, which led to speculation that the ship had been American.

There were no survivors to be seen, and Maynard never did learn the identity of the vessel.

The try fires consumed large amounts of fuel, rather more than could conveniently be stored aboard. Wood was used only to start the fires and thereafter, in a irony that appealed to the whaleman's sense of humour, they were sustained with the residue of whaleskin, the 'scraps' or 'crackling' that floated to the surface of the trypots, chip dry, as the blubber dissolved. That was not the end of their usefulness; if the idea of the whale consuming himself was a good heathen joke, there was something redemptive in the last rite of the fire. The ashes of the scraps were raked into a barrel and water poured over them to dissolve the potash. The powerful lye that ran off was the best cleansing agent known for removing sperm oil from decks, gear and clothes.

The pure spermaceti from the case was tryed first, while the pots were clean. It clung tenaciously to its congealed form, leaving in the casks flakes of residue that were known as 'South Seas snow'. In the blubber room, below the main hatch, men cut them into horse-pieces 500 by 15 centimetres with razor-sharp spades and tried to keep their feet and their toes as they stood atop greasy blanket pieces 1 metre wide and 10 metres long. The horse for which they were intended was the mincing horse, on deck hard by the rail, where the pieces were placed skin down. Mincing was a skilled task, for the clumsy two-handed mincing knife, used like a guillotine, had to slice the blubber without severing the skin. The resulting 'bible', skin-spined leaves of blubber, was easy to pike into the pots and quick to melt. No drop of oil was willingly allowed to escape. The scuppers were blocked to save for bailing the leakage from blubber lying on the deck. Again the whale contributed to extracting the last ounce of value from its life; the trailing edges of the flukes were cut into 'lippers' that were used to 'squeegee' the decks free of oil. Even with expert flensing there would occasionally be pieces of blubber with whale flesh adhering and these were set aside to avoid polluting the oil.

Towards the end of the trying out the barrel containing these ends of 'fat lean' was brought up for processing. By now, after a day or two under the tropical sun, the blubber had started to separate from the flesh and could be boiled. There was another change: it was now called 'stink'.

> . . . the meat is green and putrid. Men are now set to work to fish out those pieces not considered of sufficient value to try out, and pitch them overboard. For this purpose one has to lean with his head quite inside the open cask, and inhaling all the noisome stench arising from the decayed mass within, feel around with his hands to grasp the slimy morsels which are not fit for the try kettles. The captain and I worked side by side at one cask for half an hour, at the end of which time I was obliged to say that I could not stand it longer. I was deathly sick. 'That's nothing, Charley', said he, 'just fancy it's dollars you are groping among, and the matter will assume a very different odor'. But I thought that too high a price for dollars.[5]

There was so much of the theatrical in trying out that Kendall is almost alone in his matter-of-factness. Few of the participants who wrote of it could resist the image of hellfire, including E Ross Browne, who sailed on the *Bruce* from Fairhaven in 1842.

> A trying-out scene has something peculiarly wild and savage about it; a kind of indescribable uncouthness, which renders it difficult to describe with any thing like accuracy. There is a murderous appearance about the blood-stained decks, and the huge masses of flesh and blubber lying here and there, and a ferocity in the looks of the men, heightened by the red, fierce glare of the fires, which inspire in the mind of the novice feelings of mingled disgust and awe. But one soon becomes accustomed to such scenes, and regards them with the indifference of a veteran in the field of battle. I know of nothing to which this part of the whaling business can be more appropriately compared than to Dante's pictures of the infernal regions. It requires but little stretch of the imagination to suppose the smoke, the hissing boilers, the savage-looking crew, and the waves of flame that burst now and then from the flues of the furnace, part of the paraphernalia of a scene in the lower regions.[6]

But that, said Charley Nordhoff the stink boy, was the end of romance. It was a filthy process that assaulted most of the senses.

The smell of the burning cracklings is too horribly nauseous for description. It is though all the ill odours of the world were gathered together and being shaken up. Walking on the deck has become an impossibility. The oil washes from one side to the other, as the ship lazily rolls in the seaway, and the safest mode of locomotion is sliding from place to place, on the seat of your pantaloons. Moreover, everything is drenched with oil. Shirts and trowsers are dripping with the loathsome stuff. The pores of the skin seem to be filled with it. Feet, hands and hair are all full. The biscuit you eat glistens with oil, and tastes as though just out of the blubber room. The knife with which you cut your meat leaves upon the morsel, which nearly chokes you as you reluctantly swallow it, plain traces of the abominable blubber . . . From this smell and taste of blubber, raw, boiling and burning, there is no relief or place of refuge. The cabin, the forecastle and even the mastheads, all are filled with it, and were it possible to get for a moment to clean quarters, one would loathe himself—reeking as everybody is, with oil. It is horrible. Yet old whalemen delight in it. The fetid smoke is incense to their nostrils . . . They wallow in blubber, and take a horse-piece for their pillow when lying down . . . [7]

One of the cleaner tasks was extraction of the whale's teeth, useful for trade and a favorite medium for scrimshaw. Dentistry on this scale required implements to match. The lower jaw was severed from the junk, hoisted in and taken forward.

The patient, ie the lower jaw, is bound down to ringbolts in the deck. The dentist, a boatsteerer, with several assistants, first makes a vigorous use of his gum lancet, to wit, a cutting spade wielded in both hands. A start is given to the teeth, while his assistants apply the instrument of extraction to one end of the row, consisting of a powerful purchase of two fold pulleys, and at the tune of 'O! hurrah my hearties O!' the teeth snap from their sockets in quick succession.[8]

Stowage of the oil was the responsibility of the cooper and leakage was his enemy. The casks he set up himself, from shooks carried in the forehold, were untempered and would have to be twice filled with hot oil before shrinkage was complete. The much larger casks of the ground tier were stowed before leaving port and remained in place for the duration. Always stowed fore and aft on their sides, 'bung up and bilge free', they were filled

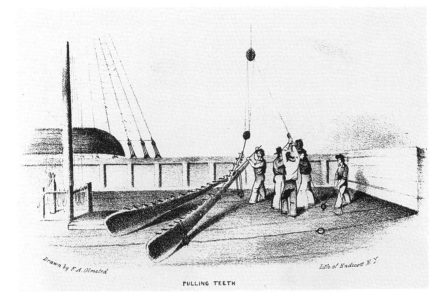

PULLING TEETH

Francis Olmstead's whale dentistry (from Incidents of a
Whaling Voyage*)*

with salted freshwater before sailing to provide ballast and to
preserve the wood. The riding tier that sat atop them could be
'stowed square', one cask immediately over another, or 'bilge and
cuntline', each nestling in the vulva-shaped hollow between the
casks below.[9] The casks in this tier contained drinking water,
provisions, stores and gear, to be broken out and refilled with oil
as consumption and catch dictated. Casks were not left empty. If
there was no oil they would be filled with saltwater to preserve
them.

Once filled from the cooler, a deck cask would be rolled aft to
the quarterdeck and allowed to stand for a day to finish cooling.

> . . . when ready a trap is removed, which is cut through the deck, a
> tub lashed under it between decks, and a hose with a cock attached;
> a cask is now rolled on to this trap, the bung extracted, a vent pipe
> introduced, and soon the whole produce of the fish is in the hold,
> never to be removed, except in case of leakage, during the remainder
> of the voyage.[10]

The immense labour involved in breaking out large casks, particularly from the ground tier, placed a premium on prevention of leakage. In the tropics the practice was to pump water into the hold every other day to inhibit shrinkage. On intervening days the water was pumped out and carefully monitored for admixed oil.

The clean-up that followed a whaler's galvanic burst of activity was in turn followed by a day of rest and cleaning for the men. Duty was confined to manning the wheel and the mastheads. The sequence of activities from raising a whale to looking for another might have taken as little as two days or as much as five, without distraction. If there was the distraction of a second whale, trying out one catch was never an excuse for passing up another, however exhausted a crew might be. That next whale was another whale closer to home. While a ship could be filled in four months, it never was, and the other 44 months were unalloyed boredom. For that reason alone,

> all is cheerfulness and hope at such times, and the prospects of the voyage seem to partake of the brightness of the caboose fires. Wives and children are remembered with new affection at such moments; and each feels nearer to home and friends at each recurring sound of the light-driven bung, and the inspiring cry, 'Away cask!' Truly it is remarked by old whalemen that the most delightful parts of a voyage are 'boiling' and arriving home.[11]

As far as we can tell, neither trying out nor any other aspect of the whaling trade provided inspiration for Henry Kendall. His only solace was the wild and wonderful desolation in which the trade was sometimes practised.

> Down in the South, by the waste without sail on it—
>   Far from the zone of the blossom and tree—
> Lieth, with winter and whirlwind and wail on it,
>   Ghost of a land by the ghost of a sea.[12]

BEYOND THE CAPES

*Fisheries require economy and every indulgence consistent
with Prudence, without which they cannot prosper.*

Samuel Enderby junior

In the post-war revival of whaling the Americans struggled for
markets and the French for expertise, but the British wrestled
mainly among themselves. For all mariners Cape Horn and, to a
lesser extent, the Cape of Good Hope (as the Portuguese had
reassuringly renamed the Cape of Storms) were obstacles to
passage beyond the Atlantic. For British mariners, however, they
presented political and economic barriers as well as natural ones.
Beyond the capes lay the exclusive economic preserves of, to the
east, the Honourable East India Company and, to the west, the
South Seas Company. The latter was moribund and unable to
exercise its prerogatives effectively, but the East India Company
was near the apogee of its wealth and influence, and strongly
resisted any attempt to infringe its chartered rights. Because John
Company did not whale itself, it would consider granting whaling
licences to others, but there could be little profit on such long
voyages without outbound trading cargoes and these the company
reserved to its own ships. The whalemen would not be thwarted.
As early as September 1786 Alexander and Benjamin Champion

had sent the *Triumph*, master Daniel Coffin, far to the south. They only bothered obtaining a South Seas Company licence two months after she sailed. On his return in August 1787, Coffin reported that not only had he taken her as far south as 55° but also east of the Cape of Good Hope, 'where he met very heavy gales of wind and stormy weather which sprung her foremast and occasioned her to leak so constantly that she was obliged to return to England'.[1] Her 50 tuns of sperm oil was one of the largest cargoes taken in the first twenty months of the 1786 Act.

In 1788 Hawkesbury amended the Southern Whale Fishery Act to provide three additional premiums for ships 'which shall double Cape Horn . . . into the South Seas, and carry on the said fishery, during the Space of Four Months', returning after not less than eighteen months' absence. The limits of the fishery for premium purposes were extended and redefined as, to the eastward of the Cape of Good Hope, 51° east and the equator and, to the west of Cape Horn, 180° west and the equator. More importantly, the whalemen had found an outward cargo beyond the control of the East India Company and, like sperm oil, it had come their way courtesy of American independence. Their new freight was British convicts. The new nation was not interested in continuing its colonial role as a dumping ground for felons.

Two of the First Fleet ships that conveyed convicts to the new penal settlement of Botany Bay in 1787–88 were carrying South Seas Company licences 'to fish'. One went off to the sea otter trade of north-west America. The other, James Mather's *Prince of Wales*, discharged the convicts and sailed for the coast of South America, to seas within the bounds of her licence. It is uncertain whether the owner's letter opened by Captain Mason in Sydney on 11 July 1788 directed him to whale, but by the time the ship had crossed the Pacific any sailing instructions were a dead letter. His crew had already been on salt provisions for eighteen months. Scurvy appeared a month out of Sydney, making up to half the crew incapable of duty. On 9 October the captain died 'after a fit of illness of one month and nine days', and the mate steered for

Rio. It seemed to be a less auspicious start to whaling in the Pacific Ocean than the *Triumph* had achieved in the Indian, but while the *Prince of Wales* lay at Rio another whaler came to anchor under the Sugarloaf.[2]

The *Emelia*, an Enderby ship commanded by James Shields, had developed a trifling leak which the captain was anxious to repair before attempting Cape Horn, for there was no uncertainty about his instructions. He was on a mission that the younger Enderby had taken the trouble to explain carefully to the government.

> We have purchased and fitted out a very fine Ship at a great Expense to go round Cape Horn, she is now ready to sail; we are the only Owners intending to send a Ship on that Branch of the Fishery—It appears to be the general Idea of most Persons acquainted with those Seas, that the Sperma Coeti Whales are to the Northward of our Limits—As we appear to be the only Adventurers willing to risk their property at such a great distance for the exploring of a Fishery, we humbly request their Lordships (if there is no impropriety in the request) that in case our Ship should not meet with Sperma Coeti Whales to the Southward of the Line in the South Pacific Ocean, that she, or any other Vessell employ'd in the Fishery, may have Permission to sail as far as 24 Deg. of North Lat. as it is generally allow'd that there are Sperma Coeti Whales on the Spanish Coast, but uncertain whether to the Southward or Northward of the Line. On the Success of our Ship depends the Establishment of the Fishery in the South Pacific Ocean, as many Owners have declar'd they shall wait 'till they hear whether our Ship is likely to succeed there; if she is successfull a large Branch of the Fishery will be carried on in those Seas; if unsuccessfull we shall pay for the Knowledge.[3]

For over a year there was silence, and then the post brought a letter from Deal in Kent. Shields was back. On 20 January 1789 he had doubled Cape Horn, a feat that nine months earlier had been beyond Lieutenant Bligh, commanding HMAV *Bounty*, who had been left with no option other than to turn and run the easting down to Tahiti. Even in midsummer Shields had fallen in with 'a great many Islands of Ice'. Over the ensuing months he had cruised as far north as the island of Lobos, in 7° south,

and up to 900 miles from the coast. On 3 March 1789 Archelus
Hammond of Nantucket, one of the boatsteerers, harpooned the
first sperm whale taken in the Pacific Ocean. It was one of five
taken on that memorable day, of which they saved four. The
weather was very bad all of June, July and August, 'but when the
Wind was moderate, there were always Whales for killing'. In all
the time he had been in the business Shields had never seen so
many large sperm whales. At the island of Massafuero there was
a bonus, for they 'found the Fur Seals lying as thick upon the
Beach as they could lye clear of each other'. Altogether the *Emelia*
had been eight months and two days west of Cape Horn when
she redoubled it on 22 September. Fourteen men were down
with scurvy on that day. Had departure from England been timed
to double the cape in spring, Shields believed, he could have
completed the voyage in ten months. His 278-ton ship had
brought back 147½ tons of sperm oil, of which 41 tons were head
matter, the produce of 27 whales. Of the *Emelia* Shields could
not speak too highly: 'The Ship sails remarkable fast and is one
of the finest Ships in a hard gale of Wind that I ever had my feet
on board of, does not strain one bit of Rigging on board of her,
and one of the compleatest Ships for the Whale Fishery that was
ever built'.[4]

Shields almost embarrassed the Enderbys by having been too
successful too quickly. He was ordered to keep the *Emelia* at Sea
Reach below Gravesend for the few days until 11 March 1790,
when eighteen months would be up and his owners could claim
the premiums, including £800 for bringing back oil from beyond
Cape Horn. Samuel Enderby junior was jubilant, not only for 'a
most uncommon successfull Voyage' but because 'the mines
[whales] of the So: Pacific Ocean are likely to be most profitable'.
Better still, it was the government that had paid for the knowledge. He spared an afterthought for the men who had made it
possible: 'the crew are all return'd in good Health, only one Man
who was killed by a Whale'.[5]

Enderby had not been idle during the *Emelia*'s absence. He

had long since appointed himself unofficial lobbyist for the British industry, and understood that making oneself useful to government was ultimately far more productive than endless petitioning for concessions. In January 1789 he presented statistics he had gathered and proceeded to review the development of the southern fishery, beginning with a flattering acknowledgment of Lord Hawkesbury who, having taken it 'under his protection in 1785', must be pleased to see 'the fishery he patroniz'd succeed so well under his Direction'. Enderby compared the £27,000–28,000 of oil etc brought home by sixteen ships in 1784, for which the government had paid 18 per cent, with the £90,599 earned by 45 ships in 1788. This had cost the government only £6300 in premiums, or less than 7 per cent. Enderby's conclusion?

> In my own opinion nothing is wanted to make this Fishery complete but an unlimited right of Fishing in all the Seas: the British Adventurers would soon explore the most distant parts, and the Settlements of New Holland would often be visited, as there are many whales in those Seas. Our House receiv'd a Letter from America a few Days ago . . . one of their Whaling Captains had been a trading Voyage to China, and had seen more Sperma Coeti Whales about the Streights of Sunda and the Island of Java than he had ever seen before . . . some merchants in Boston have ingage'd him and are going to send him . . . to . . . Sunda. It is hard on us that we cannot send a Ship there: we have 2 Ships upwards of 300 Tons each, which we are beginning to fit for the Southern Whale Fishery, to sail in March, and are undetermined what branch of the Fishery to send them on, we should like to send them to . . . Sunda but dare not without permission.[6]

For the time being Hawkesbury was unable to bully the East India Company into a further relaxation of the whaling limits, but the government took the hint about New South Wales. When the convict transports of the Third Fleet sailed for Sydney in 1791, there were five whalers among their number. Enderby's *Britannia* was commanded by Thomas Melville, who had been sailing Hull and Bristol whalers in the southern fishery since 1786. He saw few whales during the outward passage and was therefore unprepared for the spectacle that unfolded within half a day's sail of Sydney.

> . . . very thick weather and blowing hard till within Fifteen Leagues of the Latitude of Port Jackson. Within three Leagues of the Shore, we saw Sperm Whales in great Plenty: we sailed through different Shoals of them, from twelve o'clock in the day, till after Sunset, all round the Horizon, as far as I could see from the Masthead. In fact I saw a very great prospect in making our Fishery upon this Coast, and establishing a Fishery here. Our People was in the highest spirits at so great a sight, and I was determined as soon as I got in, and got clear of my live Lumber to make all possible dispatch on the Fishery of this Coast.[7]

The wording used by Melville implies that he had not expected to whale off the New South Wales coast, in spite of Enderby's earlier assertions about the whales to be found there, and his subsequent comments confirm it. He found that Governor Phillip wished to have the convicts carried on to Norfolk Island and, worse, to purchase his ship. Melville extricated himself from this delicate situation by confiding 'the secret' of the whales. To Phillip it was a godsend. Here was the opportunity to give his struggling dependency an economic base. Every longboat in the fleet was pressed into unloading the *Britannia*. There was no way the secret could be kept in such a small community, and it became a race among the whalers to get ready for sea. The interest of the Lieutenant-Governor of Norfolk Island, Philip King, a personal friend of the Enderbys, ensured that the *Britannia* was given priority, but even so Melville found that the *William & Ann*, master Eber Bunker, was in close attendance as he sailed out of Port Jackson.

The whales had waited for them. At sunrise the following day the ships were surrounded as far as the eye could see. They had a frustrating wait until two in the afternoon for the weather to abate. Even then the sea was very high.

> I lowered away two boats, and Bunker followed the Example, in less than two hours we had seven whales killed but unfortunately a heavy Gale came on from the SW and took the ship aback, with a Squall,

that the Ship could only fetch two of them, the rest we was obliged to cut from, and make the best of our way on board to save the Boats and Crew. The *William & Ann* saved one, and we took the other, and rode by them all night with a heavy gale of wind. Next morning it moderated. We took her in, she made 12 barrels.[8]

They saw whales every day for a week thereafter but could not lower. All of the whalers straggled back to Sydney with the same story: good whales, bad weather. Melville thought that conditions would improve as summer approached and was prepared to wait a month because 'if a Voyage can be got upon this Coast, it will make it Shorter than going to Peru'. The looked-for improvement failed to occur, and in January 1792 the *Britannia* abandoned the ground. Governor Phillip was bitterly disappointed.

From some information which I have received since that ship sailed, I fear that the fur trade on the north-west coast of America and the trade amongst the islands is too great an object to those who are employed in the fishery ever to admit their giving this coast a fair trial, and apprehend that all the ships have left it.[9]

He was being unfair himself. All five whalers had headed for the more pacific waters off Peru, to the grounds reported by Shields, as it appears the owners had always intended they should. The *Matilda* was wrecked on the way, but the other four reached the South American coast. They found a crowded sea. At least three Dunkirk ships had already come and gone. The *Beaver*, Paul Worth, 240 tons, had become the first American whaler around the Horn at the end of 1791, and was followed by four others. No fewer than eighteen British whalers were reported to be on the coast of Peru in the first half of 1792.

The *Beaver*'s accounts for her seventeen-month voyage survive. Fitted and provisioned for a crew of seventeen, she was valued at $10,212. Her cargo consisted of 400 iron-hooped barrels and about 1400 that were wooden-hooped. There were 40 barrels of salt provisions, 3½ tons of ship's double-baked bread, 30 bushels of beans and peas, 1000 pounds of rice, 40 gallons of molasses and 24 barrels of flour. The only provisions purchased during the voyage were 200 pounds of bread. She brought back 650 barrels of sperm oil, at £30 per tun worth £2437; and 370 barrels of head matter, at £60 per tun worth £2775; and 250 barrels of right whale oil, at £15 per tun worth £468. At the prevailing rate of exchange, even allowing for the British duty, this amounted to a profit of more than the capital ventured.[10] The figures also reveal some-thing of New England whaling practice during these early days in the Pacific, both commercial and prudential. Worth claimed to have taken a barrel of the more valuable head matter for every two barrels of sperm oil, whereas an oil merchant would expect the ratio to be more like one to four: it gives some credence to the jibe made about Yankee captains that their whales' heads extended all the way back to the hump. Worth had also taken less valuable right whales when there appeared to be no shortage of sperm in the Pacific. The reason was Cape Horn: returning captains preferred to double it with a snug but not overloaded ship and fill up in the Atlantic. There they picked up what they could, and more often than not it was right whale.

With returns like these, even the British should have been able to make a profit, but the Champions agitated with Hawkesbury to increase the duty on American oil or to prohibit its importation altogether. Here they parted company with Enderby, who argued that American competition was not a problem. There was so much unmet demand that a quadrupling of supply, which was not within the bounds of possibility, would only lower the price by one-third. Even at that lower price of £40 per tun, the British southern fishery would continue to expand while the Americans 'would be ruined' by the existing duty. It was not as if a prohibition on the Americans would suddenly make the half share of sperm whales taken by them available to British whalers. As many as four in five of those whales were taken off the North American coasts, which the British had given up as unprofitable years earlier. No, further restrictions on the Americans would only drive them elsewhere, especially to Nova Scotia, where they could continue to fit out cheaply and send oil into Britain at the colonial rate of duty, twelve shillings per tun. 'The Nova Scotian Fishery we have always dreaded, and every year convinces us, that it is an improving Fishery; the only check we wish is against that Fishery: the American Fishery is the best Check possible.'[11]

Furthermore, the £11,000–12,000 paid in duty by the Americans reimbursed the government for the premiums with which it encouraged the British industry. Enderby conceded that his view could be criticised as an interested one, given that his firm was also an importer of American oil, but

> Our regular [oil trading] Business we look upon as yielding a certain Profit whether we purchase the oil here or in America; our Whaling Business is the most uncertain possible, in which we are as much interested in making it as profitable as any other Adventurer can be, having a larger Property engag'd in the Fishery than any other Individual at present.[12]

Enderby had his way, and 1791 was the high point of the Champions' involvement in South Sea whaling. Within a decade they had all but withdrawn from the trade. Uncertain or not, the business had expanded remarkably in a short time. Rotch's estimate of 30 British ships was short of the mark; from single figures annually towards the end of the war, sailings had jumped to 39 in the first nine months after the 1786 Act came into effect. By comparison, expansion under the US flag appeared to be slow, but the modest tally of 36 ships on the American register by 1793 was misleading. Thanks to Rotch's Dunkirk strategy, during these years 80 Nantucket captains sailed 55 American-owned whalers out of French ports.[13]

The arrangement was only possible in peacetime, and in 1793 war broke out between Britain and France. Rotch, with his usual foresight, removed most of his whalers from France before hostilities commenced. The fact that war had not yet been declared did not inhibit the British. Two of his ships were seized in the Channel on what Rotch was convinced were the personal orders of Hawkesbury, but the Quaker was a step ahead of him. Their register had already been transferred to London. Other ships went to New Bedford to rebuild the American fleet, and in 1794 Rotch felt safe enough to reopen in Dunkirk under cover of a French associate. His son Benjamin took some of their ships to Milford Haven. The Rotches still believed in spreading their risks.

Some of the British merchants were more interested in risk-making. In previous wars with France, whalers had been armed for self-defence against privateers. Now owners were tempted to seek the letters of marque that would license their own ships as privateers, with the Dunkirk fleet as their chief object. In mid-1793 a British whaler put into Walvis Bay, apparently to join the American and Dunkirk ships fishing there. She then unmasked as a letter of marque mounting twenty guns and seized two Rotch ships. The *Judith* escaped only by cutting her cable. In September a Dutch brig with sixteen guns sprang the same trap at Delagoa Bay on the coast of Mozambique. Two more Dunkirk whalers were taken and a third, after being informed of a war that had already been under way for eight months, managed to slip away under cover of night.

Like Rotch, Enderby anticipated the war. He wanted to warn his whalers about the threat of hostilities and keep them out of harm's way. The Pacific coast of South America was an obvious place, but the Spanish authorities had always been difficult. In 1789 two British sealing vessels had been warned off Patagonia and told that whaling and sealing were prohibited. More serious was the seizure of two British fur-trading ships at Nootka Sound on the North Pacific coast. War had almost ensued in 1790, but a settlement was negotiated in which the right of British whalers to fish outside a 5-league limit was recognised, as was their right temporarily to base themselves ashore in unoccupied territory. Enderby had taken the initiative in exploiting these provisions, and when the French war threatened, with the distinct possibility of Spanish intervention, he and his associates suggested to the Admiralty a joint reconnaissance of the entire western coast of the Americas. Its purpose would be to warn the British whalers there and to find safe anchorages and places for refreshment on the offshore islands, so reducing the need for whalers to call at Spanish ports.

As this was the first of several semi-official, quasi-commercial ventures that the Enderbys undertook with the British government over the next 60 years, the arrangements are of some interest. Enderby needed someone better than the average whaling captain, someone with Pacific sailing experience and an understanding of the politics of Spanish America. James Colnett, then a half-pay naval lieutenant, was an obvious choice. After serving as a midshipman in the *Resolution* on Cook's second voyage, he had pioneered the British fur trade in the North Pacific and in 1789 was captain of one of the vessels seized by the Spanish at Nootka. He was keen to resume naval service and responded positively when the Admiralty suggested that this command would recommend him for promotion and return to the active list. No private vessel was available, so the Admiralty offered one of its own sloops. The *Rattler* was sold out of naval service so that it could be converted for whaling. The Enderbys bought and refitted it and then sold a half share to Colnett. He sailed on 4 January 1793. When later that year the government renewed the charter of the East India Company, it took the opportunity to remove the northern limit on whaling in the Pacific east of 180°. Like the *Triumph*, Colnett's expedition sailed first and was given permission to whale afterwards.

As an early-warning exercise, the expedition was an abject failure. A single British sealer, the *Butterworth*, was encountered. Nor did they take many whales; their success was in the reconnaissance. The *Rattler* visited most of the western offshore islands from the Horn as far north as Cape St Lucas in Baja California. The great whaling discovery was the Galapagos Islands. Sperm whales were found in abundance and there were numerous safe anchorages. As for refreshment, not only did the seas teem with fish but the shores were alive with giant tortoises, which to whalemen's eyes were walking larders. There was no sign of the

Spanish. In August 1794 Colnett redoubled the Horn and
returned to London with his news.

In theory the coasts of Chile and Peru could now be avoided,
if inconveniently, until the shooting stopped. The difficulty was
that, by the time the Spanish got around to entering the war on
the side of France in October 1796, the earlier fears had dissipated. Even Enderby was caught.

> Within these few Days we have receiv'd an Account of the Capture
> of one of our Whalers in the Pacific Ocean, she was loaded with
> Sperm Oil and the Crew being very bad with the Scurvy went into a
> Spanish port (not knowing of the Spanish War) and was there
> detain'd; one of the Crew who escap'd from Prison and cross'd the
> Continent brings the Account, and we are apprehensive it will be the
> case with many others. The Pacific Ocean abounding with Sperma
> Coeti Whales all Adventurers who can afford to venture the risque of
> so large a speculation send their Vessels into those Seas, where we
> consider them safer from the Enemy than in any other part of the
> Ocean where Sperm Whales are found, but it is impossible a Vessel
> can go there and return without going into some Port to refresh . . . [14]

He had a solution, one that would indeed combine the economy
and prudent indulgence that were his watchwords. Would the
government engage the whaler he had ready to sail? He had been
informed by his friend King that there were female convicts
waiting to be transported to New South Wales.

> . . . we will carry them on as low terms as anyone, and we then shall
> have an opportunity of giving the Fishery on the Coast of New South
> Wales a fair trial as we are very sanguine of Success, and if they do
> not succeed they can get sufficiently refresh'd to make a trip to the
> Coast of Peru without going into Port and return to refresh before
> they sail for England.

It was arrangements like this that made the difference between
operating at the margin and making a profit. When Samuel senior
died in 1797, the old cooper had risen so far as to have his passing
noted in the *Gentleman's Magazine*, which linked his large fortune
with the government's wish 'to encourage the trade of the southern hemisphere'.

This circumstance is, we see, exemplified in his arms and crest displayed on a hatchment. His shield is Azure, bearing a ship's topmast in pale proper with a topsail set and dexter pendant flottant between two mullets of six points impaling, Azure a lion rampant Sable, crest a Harpooner also proper in the act of throwing or striking.[15]

The magazine was not so unkind as to suggest that the harpooner's target could as well have been a government subsidy as a whale.

Samuel junior had not been discouraged by Thomas Melville's experience in the *Britannia* in 1791. Indeed, he had sent his captain off to New South Wales again in the *Speedy* in 1794, but Melville, once bitten, had quickly sailed on for the coast of Chile. If the man was not up to it, perhaps his former command was. The *Britannia* was the ship that Enderby had in mind for the female convicts, and his influence was sufficient to gain the contract. When she sailed in 1798, commanded by Robert Turnbull, the ship had the dubious distinction of being the first vessel to make a second convict voyage to Australia. Turnbull found that he had no need to go on to Peru; in fourteen months he filled his ship with 160 tuns of sperm oil. The *Speedy*, now under George Quested, followed him out in 1800 with another cargo of female convicts and a new Governor, who just happened to be Enderby's old friend King. King was as keen as Phillip had been to see a fishery established, and Quested made a point of keeping his employer in London informed through the Governor about prospects on the New South Wales coast.

At my leaving Port Jackson I run to the Northward as far as the Smoaky Cape and between that and Mount Warning I cruiz'd 'till the middle of August and got nothing, although we saw a number of whales, but the Weather was so bad in general that I found enough to do in the Easterly Gales to take care of my Ship . . . in coming from Norfolk [Island] I got 4 Whales . . . and now as the Summer is coming on I have no doubt of getting Oil fast at Norfolk . . . I think that from the 1st Sept to the last of May there is moderate Weather on this Coast with only fresh Blows now and then and during that time I think there is a great deal of Oil to be got, if not a full cargo with persevering, which if that is not used a Man has no Business on

this Coast, or indeed on any other, the other three Months, which is
the breaking up of the Winter and all Coasts in the same Latitudes
the Weather is bad, but on this Coast worse than any other, for there
is such a Sea in these Months and it always keeps up; although you
may have little Wind still the Sea never gets down: from the middle
of June to the middle of August I do not think there were 10 Days
that I could with safety lower a Boat in the Water: in these months
there is little chance of a Ship doing any thing and she had need be
a good Ship to stay out in the Winter. But that there is a Fishery on
this Coast I have no doubt from what I have seen and mean to prove
it if possible by Example.[16]

It took Quested 23 months to prove his point, but 170 tuns of
sperm oil was the result. His optimism confirmed Enderby 'in
the opinion I have long taken up and latterly acted on'. The
weather of the Middle Ground, as the Tasman Sea between
Australia and New Zealand became known, was for the time
being a lesser hazard than French and Spanish privateers in
calmer waters closer to home. Seven London whalers, four of
them belonging to Enderby, were reported to be off the New
South Wales coast at the beginning of 1801, and three of them
had moved on to New Zealand by September 1802. A lesser man
would have been satisfied, but not Enderby. His captains had
told him that there were numerous whales and better weather on
the coast of New Guinea. He immediately began lobbying Sir
Joseph Banks, among others, for another revision of the East India
Company limits to allow whaling around the island.

The whalers continued to enjoy a symbiotic relationship with
the imperial and colonial authorities. When Eber Bunker arrived
in Sydney in 1803 after cruising off New Zealand in the *Albion*,
a whaler belonging to the Champions, he found that the Governor
had a task for him. King intended to found a subordinate settlement in Tasmania, forestalling what were believed to be French
intentions to annex the island. Bunker agreed to take the first
settlers, mainly convict and military, but only if he could whale
while on passage. A compromise was struck. If whales were
encountered Bunker could lower for them, provided that the

convicts were confined below and handcuffed. On the way to the Derwent three sperm whales presented and were promptly taken. As if this were not fortune enough, the Derwent estuary was found to be alive with right whales. Bunker might have taken one or two on speculation, but he quickly sailed on to New Zealand. Who would bother with common oil when there were sperm whales for the asking on the other side of the Tasman? The Tasmanian colonists, that was who. Short on capital but long on initiative, they established a bay whaling industry that replaced sealing as the prime source of Australia's export revenue until it in turn exhausted the resource it exploited.

It might be thought that the difficulties created by France and Britain for the whalers of the other party would have been of considerable benefit to a neutral like the United States, perhaps even an opportunity to regain initiative and dominance in the trade, but it was not so. Their crews were still impressed into the Royal Navy. The French expected them to honour the treaty of 1778, which had created a mutual obligation to come to the assistance of the other in the event that either of them went to war with Britain. In 1796 the United States repudiated the treaty and the French began seizing those of their ships, including whalers, that were trading as neutrals with Britain. The quasi-war that followed between 1798 and 1800 was a squalid end to the partnership that had won independence for the United States. Nantucket was again hard-hit. Six of its whalers were captured, among them the *Active*, master Micajah Gardner, which was intercepted by the French with a record 2380 barrels of oil aboard. To add insult to injury, the prize was taken from the French by a British privateer and sent into Halifax. The loss on this ship alone was $50,000; all in all, the war that never was cost New England over a million dollars. In the end the French had to desist as bigger opponents claimed their attention. The aftermath, the American pursuit of spoliation claims, soured relations between the countries for two generations. Captain Gardner died in 1844 at the age of 85, his claim still unresolved.

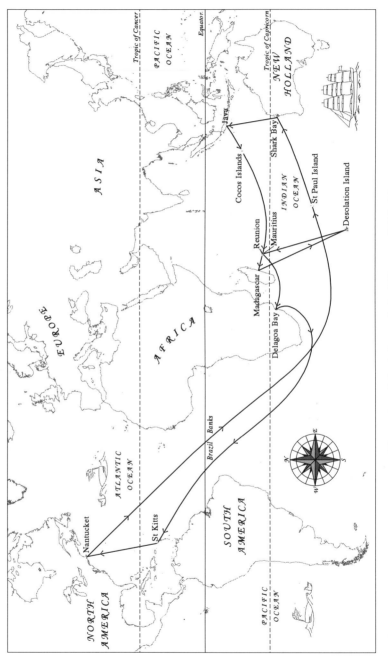

The cruise of the *Asia* and the *Alliance, 1791–94*

If the Americans had found themselves following the British into the Pacific and Indian Oceans, it did not mean that they were any less assiduous in combing the new grounds. As early as October 1791, the *Asia* and *Alliance* of Nantucket had sailed in company on a typically mixed voyage of the day. Their ostensible destination was Delagoa Bay in Mozambique, but they were prepared to take whales of any species they could catch, not to mention sea elephants and seals, wherever they might be found. They first sought seal on St Paul's Island in the southern Indian Ocean, went on to Shark Bay in Western Australia, north to Java (was this the 'Boston merchant' enterprise Enderby had first heard of in 1789?), then Cocos Islands, Mauritius (humpback whales), Madagascar (humpback), Desolation (Kerguelen) Island (sperm and right whales, sea elephants), Mauritius again, Reunion Island and Delagoa Bay (humpback). There both ships narrowly avoided capture by the Dutch privateer mentioned earlier. On the way home they took more sperm off the Brazil Banks, but when the war finally caught up with the *Asia* it inflicted a double wound. She was taken into St Kitts by a British frigate to have some oil confiscated, and then had several men impressed by another frigate at St Eustatia. In the result it was a poor voyage, the more so as the captain of the *Alliance*, Bartlett Coffin, had 'died in great agony' after overstraining himself at Desolation. The ships returned to Nantucket in February 1794.[17]

By the late 1790s sealers and traders of all sorts were criss-crossing the Pacific and discovering islands by the dozen. They found marine resources in abundance, sometimes merely noting the presence of something that was of no use to them but a veritable cornucopia to those in a different line of business. Such was the experience of the sealer Edmund Fanning, in transit from the Marquesas to Canton in June 1798.

> Our route, from about five degrees to the south of the equator to our present situation (9° 35' N, 167° 14' W), must be excellent sperm whale ground, for scarcely a day has passed, but we had sight of those valuable fish, ofttimes in very great shoals, more particularly about the

equator, and in the vicinity of Fanning's Island and the Washington group.[18]

This discovery was of far greater commercial importance than the islands that Fanning was so proud to have found. It would be decades before the whalemen worked their way along his track, but when they did, in the 1820s, 'on the Line' became the most extensive and amongst the most profitable of all sperm whaling grounds.

Fanning had taken his skins at Massafuero off the Chilean coast, and he estimated that there were still between 500,000 and 700,000 seals on the island when he left. In a few years they were gone, and island trawling in higher latitudes increased as the seal populations of the known islands were exhausted. On August 1806 Abraham Bristow was poking around some 300 miles south of New Zealand in the Enderby whaler *Ocean*.

> Moderate and clear; at daylight saw land, bearing West by compass, extending round to the North as far as NE by N, distant from the nearest part about 9 leagues. This island or islands, as being the first discoverer, I shall call Lord Auckland's (my friend through my father), and is situated, according to my observation at noon, in lat 50° 48' S, and 166° 42' E, by a distance I had of the sun and moon at half past ten, a.m. . . . . This place, I should suppose, abounds with seals, and sorry I am that the time and the lumbered state of my ship do not allow me to examine it.[19]

Enderby was even sorrier and immediately sent Bristow back in the *Sarah*. The whaleman took formal possession in 1807, adding this bleak outpost to the British Empire at a time when the imperial authorities were having grave reservations about asserting sovereignty over the far more desirable real estate of New Zealand. More usefully, he left behind some pigs. The Auckland Islands were an acquisition that the Enderbys would come to regret, but Bristow's problems were more immediate. Returning in October 1809, he was captured in the Atlantic by a privateer. Fortunately, the British privateer *Enterprise* was able to retake the hapless explorer a fortnight later.

There were also rediscoveries. On 8 February 1808 Mayhew Folger (Peleg's first cousin, twice removed) was searching for islands that had not been worked by other sealers. Specifically, he was looking for an island not reported by any navigator since its discovery by Carteret in 1767. He found it more by luck than by good navigation because Carteret, in the days before Harrison's chronometer, had miscalculated the longitude and charted the island 3 degrees too far west. To Folger's surprise there was smoke rising from this supposedly unoccupied island. The double canoe that pulled out had a brown-skinned crew, but their words of greeting were English, spoken deliberately, as if unfamiliarly.

Islander Who are you?
Folger I am an American, from Boston.
Islander You are an American? You come from America? Where is America? Is it in Ireland?
Folger Who are you?
Islander We are Englishmen.
Folger Where were you born?
Islander On that island, which you see.
Folger How, then, are you Englishmen if you were born on that island, which the English do not own and never possessed?
Islander We are Englishmen because our father was an Englishman.
Folger Who is your father?
Islander Aleck.
Folger Who is Aleck?
Islander Don't you know Aleck?
Folger How should I know Aleck?
Islander Well then, did you know Captain Bligh of the *Bounty*?[20]

Folger had found, after nineteen years of fruitless searching by the Royal Navy, the hiding place of the *Bounty* mutineers. Fletcher Christian had been right to suppose that Carteret's error would make quick rediscovery of Pitcairn Island unlikely. Alexander Smith, the sole surviving mutineer, gave to Folger the *Bounty*'s chronometer, a Kendall copy of Harrison's revolutionary original which, had it been available to Carteret or unavailable to Christian, might have relocated this little drama in both time and space.

In twenty years of voyages beyond the capes the whalers and sealers had put many islands on the map (or moved them), and had all but commercially exterminated the seals on the known grounds, but as yet there were too few of them to make serious inroads into the pelagic whale populations. Before that could happen, the nations to which they belonged would have to stop preying on each other.

Fast and Loose
or **The Rules of Whaling**

Craft claims the whale.

The First Commandment

On the high seas whalemen were a law unto themselves, and so they made unto themselves some law. They had a body of internationally recognised custom that regulated aspects of whaling in company, but sometimes more elaborate arrangements were thought to be warranted, as in the Articles of Agreement drawn up by seven captains whaling off the Galapagos Islands in 1801.

1st The ship which Discovers a School of Whales will immediately hoist his Ensign to the Miz[en] Topmast head . . .
2nd If in a School of Whales our Lines get foul of each other we will use every endeavour to clear them and Not cut each Other's lines without Mutual Consent.
3rd If a boat is in Danger of losing her line [by having it run out] the Nearest Boat is to give his and without any Exception or Claim whatever.
4th If a Boat Strikes a Whale & parts & then Strikes another, the first whale so Struck becomes the property of Any Boats who shall kill her; but must Return the Craft [harpoon]. Yet, if the first boat is following his whale & hath not been fast to another he claims the whale, even though she is killed by Another Ship's boat.
5th If a ship falls in with Dead whales not having any Craft in them,

a Union Jack will be hoisted for the benefit of those to whom they may belong.

6th If only a Single whale is in sight no Signal will be Made & if more than one Ship's boats are after her tis agreed to render the Fast [secured] boat every assistance, & should any Damage be Sustained in Consequence, it will be Made Good by the Ship who takes the Whale.

7th If Ships be of want of Assistance in the Night, a Tryangular Light will denote it [hung] where best to be seen. Every other Ship who sees it will Render her Every Assistance they Conveniently can.

8th If any Dispute should occur respecting the Claim of a whale or whales, such Disputants shall Chuse two Disinterested Masters, the two so Chosen to Appoint a Third. The Award of Eather Two shall be conclusive.

9th In case of falling in with a Stoven Boat tis agreed to render her all Convenient assistance it being the intent of our present Resolves to promote our Mutual Interest and preserve Amity.

10th It is further Agreed that each Commander will Make Known the Intent of our Present Regulations in order that no Collusion [collision?] may hereafter ensue.

William A Day, *Seringapatam*, London
James Keith, *Favourite*, London
Andrew Myrick, *Aurora*, Milford Haven
Joseph Allen, *Leo*, Nantucket
Ian Frazier, *Euphrates*, London
Thaddeus Folger, *Neutrality*, Nantucket
Micajah Gardner, *Hannah & Eliza*, Milford Haven[1]

There were two ways of identifying the owner of a loose whale. If it had been killed and left it would be marked with a waif, a pole with a distinguishing pennant. If it had escaped with irons in it, these were readily identifiable from the ship's name or initials with which they were marked. When whaling in company, the First Commandment was seldom ignored.

> The *Russell*, South-Seaman, when cruising off the Japan coast, struck a seventy-barrel whale with two harpoons, but at so late a period of the day as to be obliged to cut the line, and let the animal escape without further injury: on the following morning, however, the same whale was found floating dead on the water, and secured by a ship in company; but was subsequently restored to the crew of the *Russell*, upon their establishing their claim.[2]

The Gam

The social round for whalemen at sea consisted of visiting other whalers whenever the opportunity presented. On congested grounds, where a dozen ships might be in sight of each other at any one time, the opportunities were so frequent that some owners tried to forbid socialising as a distraction from whaling. Such bans were a futile attempt to deny the natural impulses of men desperate for fresh company. Viewed sensibly, visiting was healthy relief from the tensions accumulated in the forecastle during long months of uncomfortable proximity to shipmates. The bans were also impossible to enforce and gamming, as visiting was known, was universal.

Gams of a day or two were common, and those of several days were not unknown. They were occasions for exchanging fresh stories, old news and even older newspapers. Stores in short supply would be traded for and letters taken or delivered, depending on how long one had been out or how long before full ship and home. Some writers beat their own letters home, while letters from home could chase addressees around the Pacific for years and end up following them back to New England.

> To whom it may concern . . . If Mr Herman Melville, formerly officer [sic] on board Am[erican] W[hale] S[hip] *Acushnet* is in this part of the world, and will call upon the seaman's chaplain, he may find several letters directed to his address. [*The Friend*, Honolulu, 4 September 1844]

Above all, a gam was company, and a visit to another whaler was governed by an etiquette as strict as any involving morning calls or visiting cards. First, there was the approach, which took the form of a courtship dance. The suitor, usually the ship to windward, would hoist its ensign to indicate a desire to speak, but keep politely off. The party being wooed, should she wish to respond to the invitation, would put helm hard down so as to come up to the wind, backing her yards to bring sails aflutter on the mainmast. At the same time the yards on the foremast would be braced forward to keep those sails full. The sails on the two masts would largely cancel each other, just allowing the ship enough steerage way not to be thought forward. Down towards her the windward ship would sally, as if intending to take her by the waist. Just when unseemly contact seemed inevitable, the suitor would alter course to pass as close astern as possible, losing way by coming up to the wind. The captains were now close enough to converse from their respective quarterdecks without the aid of a speaking trumpet.

> It is quite essential that the speaking ship shall have an experienced man at the wheel during this evolution. Sometimes when it is blowing fresh, and on all ships that steer badly before the wind, two men are put at the wheel with an officer close at hand. Greenhands upon their first experience at the wheel when speaking a ship, have been known to get so badly frightened that they either run away from the wheel or become physically incapable of executing the orders. [Harold Williams, *One Whaling Family*, pp 230–1]

Contact established and intercourse agreed, there was now an exchange of boats. The initiating captain had his whaleboat lowered from the starboard quarter and was rowed across to the second ship. At the same time the first mate made ready to greet his opposite number, who was likewise passing between the ships. One ship now had both captains, the other had both mates, and each had one boat's crew from the other. While the officers enjoyed the hospitality of the main cabin, the boat's crew were guests in the forecastle. These gatherings were part feast, part colloquy and part concert. The practicality of the arrangement lay in the fact that each ship could resume whaling in an instant should a whale present, if necessary without even reclaiming its own boat or officer.

If the boats of more than one ship were involved in a kill while whaling in company, the whale could be divided, head to one ship and remainder to the other. It was usually more convenient, and certainly more acceptable to the crew that had fastened first, for the other crew to have all the labour of cutting in and trying out, with half the fare rafted across to the first ship or stowed down where it was and credited to her account.

It is safe, however, to assume that the fifth article of the Galapagos Agreement was a dead letter. It ran counter to the First Amendment to the First Commandment which, although it understandably lacked formal expression, was to the effect that 'craft claims the whale, *but it will be hard for the owner to sustain the claim if there are no craft in the whale by the time he arrives*'. In the event of a dispute, there was an Appendix to the Amendment which provided that, if the cutting of an unmarked whale had commenced before a legitimate claimant arrived, the finder kept what had already been hoisted above the plank-shear, surrendering only what was still in the water. To such a fine point was this punctilio observed that a blanket piece in the process of being brought aboard would be cut off at the plank-shear. The Appendix also applied to whales in which another ship's irons were discovered only after cutting in had commenced.

The fourth article of the Galapagos Agreement explicitly provided that a loose whale, if being pursued by a boat whose irons were in it, belonged to that boat, whosoever else might kill it. When a large number of boats were engaged against several whales it would often be difficult to know if there were an earlier striker or if he were still in pursuit. This was a prescription for endless disputation, and so when Tasmania came to regulate its whaling industry in 1835 the colony acknowledged joint ownership in certain circumstances, as the Appendix to the Amendment had.

First Where the Harpoon or Instrument shall remain in the Fish so struck and a Line and Boat shall be attached thereto and continue in the power of the Striker or Headsman such Whale shall be deemed a

fast Fish and every Harpoon and Instrument struck by any other
person shall in such case be considered a friendly Harpoon and the
Fish shall be the Property only of the first Striker or Headsman.
Secondly In case the Line affixed to the first Harpoon . . . so struck
shall break or the Line attached thereto shall not be in the power of
the Striker but the Harpoon . . . shall nevertheless remain fast in the
Fish then the Fish if taken or killed by any second or subsequent
Harpoon shall be the joint Property of the first and second or
subsequent Striker.
Thirdly If the first Iron or Harpoon so struck as aforesaid shall break
or shall become disengaged . . . then the Fish shall be considered a
loose Fish and become the Property of the first actual taker thereof.[3]

The difficulty whalemen had with this lawyers' formulation was
the same as that addressed under the second article of the
Galapagos Agreement. Cutting other boats' lines was legitimate
if fouling had created a dangerous situation. Otherwise it had to
be by mutual consent, which was not always easy to obtain.

The boats of two different ships, which were fast to whales, passed
quite near us; and while the officers of each party had no relish for
keeping close company, the two whales exhibited no disposition to
separate; and as the group swiftly approached, we heard loud voices
and saw violent gesticulations. Very soon we heard a burly fellow, who
stood at least six feet in his stockings, bare-headed, with his long
locks steaming behind, shouting to his opponent: 'That won't do! that
won't do! cut your line! I struck my whale first! Cut that line, or
you'll be into us! Cut that line, or I'll put a bomb through you!' But
the officer of the opposing boat very cooly replied: 'Shoot and be
damned, you old lime-juicer! I won't let go this line till we get t'other
side of Jordan!' Then, turning to his crew, he said: 'Haul line, boys!
haul ahead! and I'll give old Rip-sack a dose he can't git to the
'pothecary's! Haul ahead, and I'll tap his claret-bottle!' By this time
the two whales had separated, and the boats were beyond hearing;
but both whales were seen spouting blood, and soon after pyramids of
foam showed that they were in their flurry.[4]

The right to cut a line in an emergency was nonetheless seldom
abused because there was no commercial advantage in it if craft
claimed the whale. There was, however, great advantage if, with
the stroke of a blade, another boat's fast whale could be trans-
formed into a loose fish and half of it subsequently taken by the

line cutter. The Tasmanian Act sought to avoid this with penalties; if a line were cut to prevent the taking of a whale, the offender could be fined between £10 and £100. The sanction appears to have been inadequate and the Act was amended in 1838, but instead of increasing the penalty or reverting to 'craft claims the whale', Tasmania moved further away from the time-honoured custom. If the iron drew or broke, or the line broke or ran out, 'or the fish from any other causes not be in the power or under the management of the striker', it became a loose fish and the property of the taker. The line cutter might now hope to have the profit from a whole whale to pay his fine, and not just half as formerly.

Herman Melville remarked on the absence of international agreements between the whaling nations. The main impediment was the nature of the trade. Nations could regulate relations between their own citizens anywhere (setting aside the difficulty of enforcement beyond their borders), but regulating relations between those citizens and foreign nationals on the open ocean was another matter. Britain, which could do much as it liked on the high seas, largely confined its interference in the business of other significant sea powers to suppression of the slave trade, and even here it proceeded with the agreement of its nominal peers. The Law of the Sea, insofar as it seeks to maintain the rights of the weak against the strong, is a child of our century.

The Tasmanians were not deterred by their weakness. No one would have disputed their right to regulate all whaling activity, their own and other, in the rivers, bays and inlets of the island, but they claimed jurisdiction up to 20 miles from the shore. They acknowledged that this was the high seas. The distance was maximum boat range for their shore-based whalemen but rather more than the maximum cannon range of 3 miles that was generally regarded as the limit of territorial waters. Their law was mainly concerned with regulating shore whaling, but as it made no distinction between shore and pelagic whaling the latter was within its purview. What Tasmania could or would have done in the event of a French or American breach of their law on that 17-mile strip of the high seas remains a moot point. The provisions were repealed in 1842 when shore whaling was no longer viable.

In May 1857 the New Bedford whaler *Pacific* harpooned a whale on the Solander Ground that was found to have been wounded by craft belonging to the Hobart whaler *Sapphire*. Although the whale was not under the *Sapphire*'s control or management, Captain Sherman of the *Pacific* very properly cut his line and consequently lost his irons. The Hobart skipper would have been glad that there was no more local nonsense about loose fish, particularly as he found that the American irons left in the whale were much superior to his own. He took another four whales with those toggle harpoons and, far from returning them, pestered Sherman to let him have a few more.

The question of jurisdiction over foreign ships re-emerged briefly near the end of the century, and again it arose in connection with a whaler. Captain John Carpenter had taken the Sydney whaler *Costa Rica Packet* into Ternate to refresh before a season in the Molucca Sea. He was astonished to find himself arrested, and even more astounded when he was told the charge. In 1888 the *Packet* had come across a derelict proa 32 miles from the nearest land. A few cases of arrack had been found, but Carpenter had ordered that they be jettisoned when his crew began to drink and fight. He reported the whole matter to the Dutch authorities on making port at Batjan, and thought that was an end of it. Without his knowledge, however, one or two of the cases had been hidden by the crew. When this had come to Carpenter's attention he had given permission for the alcohol to be traded for sugar. This was now, nearly four years later, the basis for a charge of piracy.

Once the British consul at Batavia got wind of the affair, the Dutch released Carpenter, but a month had passed and they turned him loose a thousand miles from his ship. It took him another two months to return to the *Packet*, by which time she was in an advanced state of disrepair and the season was lost. There was much agitation in Sydney for compensation for crew and owners as well as for the captain, but the British government seemed reluctant to press the Dutch, denying that the removal of Carpenter need have aborted the cruise. A Select Committee of the New South Wales Legislative Council took a different view. It saw Carpenter's knowledge of when and where whales could be encountered as a trade secret, without which no cruise could be successful. There was also pressure in London.

> The Palmerstonian tradition, that the British flag is a sure and all-sufficient protection against outrage or indignity in any part of the civilized world, has for so long been an accepted rhetorical commonplace, that it comes upon us with quite a shock of indignant surprise, and with all the force of an unpleasantly humiliating revelation, to learn that in the immediate neighbourhood of one of the most important sections of Greater Britain a British captain may be summarily seized by the representatives of a foreign Power . . . [5]

The British decided to put the case to international arbitration. The arbitrator nominated by the Tsar of Russia was Professor de Martens, who found that the incident took place in international waters, beyond Dutch territorial jurisdiction, and that Dutch abandonment of the case was an admission of impropriety on their part. He awarded £8350 compensation, about half of that asked for but more than three times what the British Foreign Office thought would be reasonable for 'personal damage' to Carpenter. More important was the place given to the award in the corpus of international case law. It became a common citation, used to illustrate the proposition that on the high seas a national flag subjects the ship that flies it exclusively to the jurisdiction of that nation. One suspects that Lord Palmerston would simply have sent a gunboat.

One of the reasons that the Australians thought that the officers and crew of the *Costa Rica Packet* were entitled to compensation was that their remuneration was based on the lay, which here

Better times on the Costa Rica Packet, *1891 (photos from the Carpenter Collection, National Library of Australia)*
Above: Boats in pursuit under sail and paddle

Whale alongside, cutting the stage down

Jaw and first blanket piece coming aboard

Small enough to hoist aboard entire—a juvenile sperm whale

Preparing to try out

*Oil stowed, make and mend—Captain Carpenter (upper right)
and crew relax*

computed to no whales, no pay. The lay arrangement allowed too much scope for owners to play fast and loose with the pay of their seamen, but it had a long history in the industry. The notion of working for a share of the proceeds went back at least to the co-operative whaling ventures of the American colonial communities, and perhaps as far as the Dutch Greenland fishery of the seventeenth century. Everyone aboard a whaler was on a lay, from the most experienced captain on his one-eighth to the cabin boy on a two-hundredth or even smaller fraction. Before Herman Melville's day, when New Englanders filled the forecastle and steerage as well as the cabin, a seaman might have hoped for as much as one-sixtieth. This partly reflected the co-operative nature of the early New England ventures and partly the size of their ships, for at any time it was usually the case that the smaller the ship and crew, the shorter the lays. Those on the *Costa Rica Packet* were reasonably typical of officers' and boatsteerers' lays in the latter part of the nineteenth century, but the seamen's lays were shorter on average than in Melville's day because greenhands, prepared to put up with the life for one two-hundredth or less, had become harder to get.

Captain one twelfth	*Fifth Mate* one fifty-fifth
First Mate one eighteenth	*Boatsteerers* one fifty-fifth
Second Mate one twenty-fifth	*Steward* one sixtieth
Third Mate one thirty-fifth	*Cook* one sixtieth
Fourth Mate one forty-fifth	*Seamen* one hundredth to one hundred & fiftieth

In the Hobart of the 1820s and 1830s the crewing of whale ships and shore stations had been a haphazard affair. Articles of agreement, including the terms of employment, were sometimes oral and as such were open to abuse on both sides, but in nothing so much as the seaman's reward for his labour. He signed on for a share, but a share of what? The sale of the oil and bone might take weeks or months to finalise if the owner decided to withhold

them from the market waiting for the price to improve. The
Tasmanian Act of 1835 set out to regulate the lay. It required that
agreements would include the price which the owner would pay
the seaman for his bone and oil, irrespective of the state of the
market at discharge or, if no figure was inscribed, fair market
price. The negotiable figure meant that the seaman could try to
offset a long lay by getting a good price, or only accept a poor
price on a larger share. In reality, the price offered was usually at
a hefty discount to both current and prospective markets. It was
defended by the owners on the grounds that the market might
have fallen by the time the ship returned. To an American, with
no price guarantee, it seemed that the law was of no material
advantage to Tasmanian whalemen. 'The crews receive a large
proportion of the vessels' earnings; but they get only forty pounds
sterling per ton for their oil, no matter what price it brings in the
market; so that, although the lays are shorter, the actual remuneration is about equal to ours.'[6]

The Tasmanian agreements also specified the provisions to be
supplied by the owner. They ameliorated some abuses but
scarcely scratched the surface of the scope for exploitation, much
of which was to be found on the debit side of the whaleman's
account with his ship as opposed to the credit side, where his lay
was usually the sole entry. Fayette Ringgold, the US consul at
Paita in Peru, deplored what he saw as the loss to his country of
thousands of young Americans who each year deserted from
whaleships 'and either from shame or moral corruption never
return'. He was convinced that low earnings were more to blame
than bad treatment, and sent home the following calculation of
average earnings from a four-year cruise.

Ringgold wrote that he had never been able to get a satisfactory
explanation of 'fitting shipping and medicine chest'. No doubt he
knew what it was: he just could not understand why the seaman was
paying for it. It covered the cost of loading the ship, shipping a crew
(the seaman was paying for his own recruitment) and providing the
captain with the means of rendering medical assistance should the

One hundred & eightieth lay of 1200 barrels	$262.25
Less Fitting shipping & medicine chest	$10.00
10% discount on leakage of oil	$26.22
3% insurance for oil	$ 7.86
Outfit	$70.00
Interest on outfit	$16.80
Cash advanced during voyage	$30.00
Interest on advance @ 1% per month	$ 7.20
Slops to make up deficiencies in outfit	$40.00
	$208.08
Amount due	$ 54.14

seaman need it. Ringgold did not mention that there was a similar charge at the end of the voyage, $5 or $6 for discharging the cargo and cleaning the ship. Thus the concept of sharing the profits provided an excuse for dunning the seaman at every turn. Even the insurance he paid to protect his property, the oil, was entirely for the benefit of the owners in whose name the policy was issued. The insurance charge was not levied until the ship returned, at which time it was, by definition, safe. If the cargo were lost, as once happened when a whaler caught fire in Paita Bay, the seamen were unlikely to get anything. On this occasion, as Ringgold tried to salvage something for him, an old whaleman said, 'It's no use, sir, to give me a certificate. The owners play an open and shut game—if the vessel gets home I pay for insurance but if she is lost they pay the insurance and pocket the profits'.[7]

It would not have mattered had the shares themselves been more generous. The rule of thumb was that the returns from a voyage went roughly in thirds, one to cover the cost of the ship's outfit, one to the crew, and one which was the owner's profit. One-third might appear to be generous enough, but take out the lays of the captain, the officers and the petty officers and there could be twenty forecastle hands sharing between one-fifth and one-tenth, before deductions. Ringgold pointed out that if the deductions had not been made and the seaman had received his $262.25, he would have been working for $5.22 per month. After deductions it came to little more than a dollar, which was about as much as the unskilled worker ashore was being paid if room and board were not provided—except that the landsman earned his 90 cents every day, not every month. It was not unknown for a whaleman to finish a voyage owing the owners money. For them, it was not necessarily a bad outcome; a destitute seaman was the more ready to ship again. The sharpest of practice was to have him detained for debt, his release being conditional on signing on for another voyage.

One reason for the difference between the value of the lay and wages ashore was the free room and board allowed the whaleman. Where these were provided for workers ashore, their money wages were usually one-third to one-half lower. Making all due allowance for the difference, it is inescapable that Ringgold's whaleman worked for a small fraction of what he could have earned ashore. The lay system allowed owners to transfer some of the risk of their enterprise to their workforce. It was a unique refinement of sweated labour, and in Ringgold's view it was unnecessary. Appended to his consular report is a table 'showing the amount of profit derived by the owners . . . from which last it will be seen that it would be very easy for them to largely increase the pay of their men and still make an enormous interest on their money'. The table assumed that the crew got their one-third—Ringgold was proposing that deductions be abolished—and put it down as owners' outlay, which would raise their overall investment in whaling to $24,336,226. The $12,040,805 they took in oil and bone would still be giving them an annual return of 46 per cent on their capital.

The lay system nonetheless survived to the very end of the open-boat whaling era, and with deductions.

4

FREE TRADE AND
SAILORS' RIGHTS

*Happily for us, the Mammoth cannot swim, nor the
Leviathan move on dry land.*

Thomas Jefferson

The War of 1812 is the forgotten war of Anglo-American
history, probably because its causes were obscure, its timing
unfortunate and its ostensible objects unrealised. That it occurred
at all says a good deal about American impetuosity and British
insensitivity. The peace of 1783 had not inhibited the Royal Navy
in its accustomed practice of searching American ships for deserters and impressing British nationals. Sometimes they left behind
scarcely enough men to work the ship. Lest this be thought an
excess of zeal it should be noted that in 1807 35 per cent of the
crew of the USS *Constitution* were British subjects. Impressment
intensified when Britain went to war with France again in 1803,
which was understandable in the face of a national emergency,
but there was some prospect of relief after Trafalgar. In the
meantime the New Englanders had been up to their old tricks;
they were breaking the British blockade by transhipping French
colonial goods into European ports under the US flag. These
cargoes were seized as enemy property being transferred between
enemy ports.

Flashpoint was reached on 22 June 1807 with a particularly offensive instance of impressment. The USS *Chesapeake* refused HMS *Leopard* permission to search for a British deserter believed to be aboard the American ship. That piece of impertinence earned the *Chesapeake* three broadsides before her own guns could be brought to action. Thomas Jefferson, then nearing the end of his presidency, was urged to declare war, but instead imposed an embargo on American foreign commerce. If the United States lacked the naval power to enforce either its sailors' rights or its assertion that 'free ships should make free goods', it could at least try to keep its men and ships clear of the death struggle between Mammoth France and Leviathan Britain. It was an expensive policy; Jefferson calculated that the $50 million in exports lost annually was probably three times the cost of a war. New England, the region worst affected, agreed. It began smuggling goods and muttering secession.

The embargo failed to gain any concession from the British and was replaced in 1809 by a Non-Intercourse Act that applied only to Britain and France. An offer was made to both of these parties that, if either would repeal its restrictions on American trade, the United States would apply non-intercourse only to the other, unless it too repealed. Napoleon sensed an opportunity. During the embargo he had 'assisted' Jefferson by confiscating American ships as they arrived in French ports. Now he announced that the relevant decrees were revoked. It was a sham but it took in James Madison, Jefferson's successor. Britain hesitated to repeal its Orders in Council and, when the restrictions on trade with France were lifted, the United States found that it had been manoeuvred out of neutrality. On 18 June 1812 the United States quixotically declared war on Great Britain, but only a week later was offering to negotiate peace if Britain would revoke the Orders in Council and cease impressing American seamen. It was told that the Orders had been revoked on 23 June. This was now a war over the services of a few thousand seamen.

From retirement, Jefferson expressed the hope that America

would devote its efforts to clearing the British from North America, 'leaving the war on the ocean to our privateers . . . [which] will immediately swarm in every sea, and do more injury to British commerce than the regular fleets of all Europe would do'.[1] It was the view of a man who had tried to reduce the United States Navy to little more than a coastal gunboat force and it was well wide of the mark: much of the initial swarming was done by British privateers. Nantucket again feared its full force and again sought relief.

> Experience has taught that the Whale Fishery, for which this place has ever been famed, cannot be prosecuted while it is exposed to the ravages of war; and should it continue, we fear it will in a great degree be lost . . . most of the trading Capital of the Island is now in the Southern Ocean, some of which will not be on its return within one year from the present date; and if the war continues, we fully believe the greater part, if not the whole, will fall an easy Prey to the Enemy . . . requesting . . . Liberty to ask, if in your Wisdom any means can be devised to save our Fleet of Whale Ships now in the Southern Ocean, and if any Method can be adopted, whereby we may prosecute the Cod and Whale Fisheries without the risk of capture by the Enemy.[2]

The Nantucketers' own wisdom suggested exempting the whaling and fishing fleets of both parties from hostilities. This was no more realistic than it had been during the War of Independence, but there was, Jefferson notwithstanding, another option. In the early months of the war the United States Navy had surprised the world. In a series of single-ship actions its few frigates had inflicted embarrassing reverses on the reputedly invincible Royal Navy. Fleet action was out of the question but commerce raiding was not, and in the years following the *Chesapeake* incident some US officers had given the matter much thought. One of them was David Porter, who before the war had suggested to his superiors 'a plan for annoying the enemy's commerce in the Pacific Ocean'. Although it would be far from base, he believed that a US warship would be able to live off her whaleship prizes because they were provisioned for long voyages.

In 1812 he was given command of the USS *Essex*, and in October received orders for a long cruise in the South Atlantic. There he failed to rendezvous with his commodore and, having become a detached unit, determined to round Cape Horn. In his account of the voyage Porter leaves the impression that this was an opportunistic decision. His crew knew better. For some time they had been suspicious that the Pacific was their destination and had been gathering warm clothing. When the decision was made on 11 February 1813, they were dismayed but not surprised. The *Essex* was the first USN vessel into the ocean that its successors would turn into an American lake.

Porter was not the only one who saw the eastern Pacific as a suitable place to annoy the enemy. The British had been busy making manifest the fears of the Nantucketers. Those of their Pacific whalers that carried letters of marque, including three belonging to the Enderbys, headed for the Galapagos Islands, which by then was a rendezvous for whalers from March to July. They began taking American whalers as well as whales. In those months, according to Porter's information, the whales came for the squid 'which are brought into the eddy formed there by the rapid currents that prevail'. The first victim of the British was the *Edward*, of Nantucket. She was taken by the *Seringapatam* of London, fourteen guns, which had the shrewd and experienced William Stavers as master. He had been commanding whalers in the South Seas for twenty years.

The *Essex* sailed north under the British flag and gathered information from the Spanish, but the best source of intelligence was Hathaway's Post Office, a box nailed to a post on Charles Island in the Galapagos. No whaler had been there for nearly a year, and it was 29 April, well into the season, before a relieved Porter took his first three prizes. The prospect of prize money would quieten a grumbling crew, at least for a while.

Sailors and Marines
Fortune has at length smiled on us, because we deserve her smiles, and the first time she has enabled us to display FREE TRADE AND

SAILORS' RIGHTS, assisted by your good conduct, she put in our possession near half a million dollars of the enemy's property. Continue to be zealous, enterprising, and patient, and we will yet render the name of the *Essex* as terrible to the enemy as that of any other vessel before we return to the United States. My plans shall be made known to you at a suitable period.[3]

A month later the *Essex* encountered two more British whalers, both with letters of marque, and captured them by the simple subterfuge of flying British colours. The *Atlantic* and the *Greenwich* were both Enderby ships. The master of the *Atlantic*, Obidiah Weir, was from Nantucket, but he expressed his pleasure at the presence of (as he supposed) a British frigate in those waters and was full of information about where American whalers might be found and taken. Porter led him on, asking how, as an American, he could sail an armed ship under the British flag now that the two countries were at war. Weir replied that although he had been born in America he was an Englishman at heart. Porter at last allowed Weir to be undeceived by the British captains whom he had taken earlier, observing that

> this man appeared the polished gentleman in his manners, but evidently possessed a corrupt heart, and, like all other renegadoes, was desirous of doing his native country all the injury in his power, with the hope of ingratiating himself with his new friends.[4]

Porter had a similarly poor view of John Shuttleworth, master of the *Greenwich*, who was drunk when his ship was taken. He was put in a cabin with Weir, whereupon 'they gave full vent to their anger and indulged in the most abusive language against our government, the ship, and her officers. They lavished on me, in particular, the most scurrilous epithets, giving me appellations that would have suited a buccaneer.'[5]

Soberer and calmer the next day, the two were reminded of their position by Porter and became 'so humbled by a sense of their own conduct that they would have licked the dust from my feet had it been required of them to do so'. More prizes followed, and by the end of June, Porter's fleet numbered nine sail. In July the *Atlantic*, the fastest of the captures, was armed with twenty guns and manned as an auxiliary. Unimaginatively renamed the *Essex Junior*, she was sent to Valparaiso to release prisoners and sell some of the prizes while the *Essex* continued the hunt. Within days another three ships were taken, but this time not without a fight. The *Greenwich*, being used as an armed storeship, exchanged several broadsides with the largest of the three, which struck its colours but attempted to escape although its sails and rigging were much cut about. The *Essex* ran down the cripple as dark fell. To Porter's delight it was the *Seringapatam*, the most formidable British ship in the eastern Pacific. The firm of William Mellish had fitted her out as a whaler but she carried as many guns as a small warship, which indeed had been her original role: she was built at Bombay in 1799 for the navy of Tippoo Sahib. In 1813 the *Seringapatam* was a vessel with a reputation, having taken two Spanish privateers in these same waters in 1807. Her present commander had a reputation for enterprise, and Porter had no doubt that in capturing him he had removed a great threat to the American whalers. It also seems that Porter intended the removal to be permanent.

> On requiring of this man that he should deliver to me his commission, he, with the utmost terror in his countenance, informed me that he had none with him, but was confident that his owners had, before this period, taken one out for him, and he had no doubt would send it to Lima, where he expected to receive it. It was evident he was a pirate . . . I therefore ordered him . . . in irons.[6]

This pirate was among the reasons Porter decided to send one of his early captures, the *Georgiana* (another Enderby ship, with a full cargo of sperm oil), to run the blockade back to the United States. He was getting a little paranoid.

> I was desirous of getting rid of Stavers. He was a man of great cunning and considerable observation, and, however desirous I might be of concealing my intentions, I was apprehensive that some circumstances might lead him to conjecture rightly as to my future views. In order to put it entirely out of his power to obtain and give

such information as was calculated to benefit the enemy or frustrate my plans, I thought it advisable (as I had always intended sending him to America for trial) to dispatch him in the *Georgiana*.[7]

In the meantime the *Seringapatam* was converted from a small warship into a larger, mounting 22 guns. By mid-September Porter believed that he had cleared the eastern Pacific of British whalers, depriving Britain of property to the value of $2.5 million and of the services of 360 seamen, whom he paroled on condition that they not serve against the United States until exchanged. Only one ship, the *Comet*, had escaped his net, and she had fallen into another. She was caught up in the insurrection sweeping the Spanish colonies and detained at Talcahuano for a year. In November the presence of the *Essex* off Galapagos was reported in the British press, and by December there was a rumour afoot that after clearing the islands she would be making for New South Wales.

The rumour flattered Porter and his small command. The *Essex* was now in need of careening and a smoking to kill the rats, which having destroyed much of the food and water had turned their attention to the gun cartridges. When the *Essex Junior* returned, with news that the frigate HMS *Phoebe* and two sloops of war had sailed from Rio in pursuit of the *Essex*, Porter was confirmed in his decision to convoy the most recent prizes to the Marquesas, where his ships were unlikely to be surprised while preparing for the homebound voyage. The day before making landfall at the islands they saw 'immense shoals of spermaceti whales, of all sizes, slowly directing their course to the northward'.

At Nuku Hiva the expedition constructed Fort Madison and on 19 November took possession of the island in the name of the United States. The crew, enjoying the attentions of the wahines, were content as long as they were idle, but when Porter restricted liberty to hasten preparations for sea he found, as Bligh and others had before him, that lotus-eating and discipline do not mix. A report circulated that Robert White, an enlisted man, had declared that the crew would not weigh anchor or, if compelled

Tabua

In October 1997 the Prime Minister of Fiji, Sitiveni Rabuka, met Queen Elizabeth II at Windsor to apologise for the military coup of 1987 that had led to the ostracism of his country by the Commonwealth of Nations. He presented her with *tabua*, a sperm whale's tooth, which in Fijian ceremony betokens, among other things, high **esteem and a** desire for reconciliation.

Tabua (sperm whale tooth) for the Queen, as celebrated on the coin

The first Europeans into the Pacific found that the islanders had an insatiable appetite for iron. Some of the most serviceable metal for the manufacture of edged utensils was hoop iron, which whalers carried in abundance. They soon found, however, that most islanders prized whale teeth above all else and, as the natives did not hunt whales, scarcity ensured demand. As the teeth were otherwise useful to the whalemen only for scrimshaw, they quickly became regular items of trade.

> No jewel, however valuable, is half so much esteemed in Europe or America, as is a whale's tooth here. I have seen them by fits laugh and cry for joy, at the possession of one of these darling treasures. Ivory, however finely wrought

and beautiful in its kind, bears no comparison in their
estimation. Ivory is worn by the lower and poorer classes,
made into the form of whales' teeth, and as ear ornaments,
while the whales' teeth are worn only by persons of rank
and wealth. Some idea may be formed of the value in
which they are held by the natives, when it is known that
a ship of three hundred tons burden, may be loaded with
sandalwood at this island [Nuku Hiva], at the price of ten
whales' teeth of a large size. For these the natives will cut it,
bring it from the distant mountains, and take it on board the
ship. This cargo in China, would be worth near a million of
dollars. [David Porter, *Voyage in the South Seas*, p 83]

The currency became debased as the whalemen
progressively flooded the market. By 1847 one large tooth
would purchase a picul (133.33 pounds) of *bêche-de-mer*.
Twenty would buy 200 gallons of coconut oil, worth about
$113 on the US market. If the captain of a whaler claimed
the teeth for trade and denied the seamen any right to
them, as some did, the financial effect was to reduce
owners' outlays. Strictly, whales' teeth were product of the
voyage and should have been subject to division according
to lay, but they could not be converted into cash and so
the owners had found yet another way to short-change
poor Jack.

to do so, would hoist their own flag within three days of departure.
Porter mustered all hands and promised them that should such
a thing happen he would personally set a match to the magazine.
He then called out White and, seeing a native canoe passing the
ship, 'directed the fellow to get into her and never let me see
his face again'. Leaving some of the prizes behind under marine
Lieutenant Gamble as a refuge should the *Essex* and *Essex Junior*
suffer damage in action, Porter sailed for Valparaiso.

It appears to have been the need for further repairs that led him to put into the Chilean port, but he could hardly have been surprised when four days later the *Phoebe* and the sloop of war *Cherub* came in to anchor nearby, close enough for the British frigate's long guns but beyond the range of the *Essex*'s carronades. Hostilities commenced immediately, but in a neutral port the exchange was of insults rather than shot. The *Essex* was as usual flying 'Free Trade and Sailors' Rights'. Captain Hillyer of the *Phoebe* responded, rather more wordily, with 'God and Country; British Sailors' Best Rights; Traitors Offend Both'. On the following day Porter, with more perseverance than wit, came back with 'God, Our Country, and Liberty—Tyrants Offend Them'. It was all good fun, and when the crew of the *Essex* sang their 'nautical sarcasms' to the tune of 'Yankee Doodle', the men of the British sloop were happy to respond with 'The Sweet Little Cherub That Sits up There'.

It could not last. Porter told Hillyer he was prepared to take his chances against *Phoebe*'s long guns if *Cherub* were sent away. He said he could not issue a challenge because in the event of loss he would be unable to justify risking his ship against a superior opponent, but were Hillyer to challenge he would accept. It was an offer that the British captain could and did refuse; the Admiralty would have been even less understanding than Washington about loss or damage had Hillyer neglected to use all the force at his disposal. The issue was brought to decision on 26 March 1814. A southerly blow made the *Essex* drag her anchors seaward and Porter had no option but to make sail and put out past the blockading British. He had hopes that the speed of the *Essex* and her position to windward would allow an escape to sea, but the frigate was taken aback by a squall and lost her main topmast. No longer able to run, Porter anchored as close to the shore as he could to prevent the British ships from engaging him on both sides and cleared for action. The *Essex* was a sitting target. The British ships positioned themselves off her stern and quarter, where her broadside could not be brought to bear, and proceeded to pound the American into a tangle of splinters and cordage. When Porter struck his colours, two and a half hours later, one in five of his crew was dead and more than half were casualties. 'Free Trade and Sailors' Rights' flew from the fore topmast until the very end.

The *Essex Junior*, out of her league among the men-of-war, had not been engaged, and Hillyer allowed Porter to buy her on behalf of the United States, disarmed, for $25,000 as a means of repatriating his crew under parole. Enderby never saw his money: on arrival in New York the ex-*Atlantic* was seized, condemned and sold for $8100. Mellish was luckier. At Nuku Hiva Robert White had finally succeeded with his mutiny by converting it into a prisoner-of-war escape. In May 1814 the remaining prisoners seized the *Seringapatam*, tied and confined Gamble and his fellow officers, spiked the guns of Fort Madison and the other ships and, after setting the officers adrift in a boat, put to sea. None of the fourteen escapees could navigate; they wandered westward across the Pacific until, half derelict, they fell in with a merchantman en route from China. They were escorted to Sydney. Their story of escape from an American cruiser was initially greeted with some suspicion, but in time their claim for salvage was supported. They sailed for Britain in the *Seringapatam* under the command of Eber Bunker, the same who had helped inaugurate the western Pacific fishery two decades earlier. White made good his own escape by pretending to be a British whaleman rather than an American deserter. At least seven other members of his crew must have been doing the same if Porter is to be believed. He said that he had left twenty seamen but only six prisoners at Nuku Hiva. It is more probable that some of those seamen were Americans from the British whalers whom Porter had persuaded or pressed to enlist in the *Essex*, but there was no hint of it in the petition made to the Vice-Admiralty Court on their behalf: 'your Petitioners occasionally Consulted together on the Means of Effecting their Deliverance from the miserable State of Captivity to which the Chance of War had consigned them, and one and all determined to avail themselves of the first Opportunity that offered to accomplish their purpose'.[8] Anyway, by de-enlisting themselves at this first opportunity they could fairly claim to have lived up to Porter's own motto: were they not exercising a sailor's right to freely trade his services?

Porter's cruise was the war at sea in microcosm. American initiative and spirit were at first rewarded but became ineffectual when the end of Napoleon's war freed the Royal Navy to attend to other annoyances. Most of the prizes sent home by the *Essex* were recaptured as they approached the United States, including, much to William Stavers' relief, the *Georgiana*. Porter had disrupted rather than destroyed British whaling in the eastern Pacific. By attracting the British in strength, he probably did as much damage to the American fishery. The Treaty of Ghent, ratified by President Madison on 17 February 1815, largely confirmed the *status quo ante*. It made no mention of impressment or blockade. The United States declined to recognise Porter's annexation of Nuku Hiva: America was not yet ready for empire in the Pacific.

Nantucket had again been prostrated by war. Thirteen of the 31 whalers that had sailed in 1811 had failed to return, among them the *William Penn*, master George Washington Gardner, which was captured in December 1813 with a full cargo of 1300 barrels and sent into the Cape of Good Hope. Like several others, Gardner lost everything; ship, cargo and personal effects. Undismayed, the islanders started again. They despatched 50 whalers in 1815, twenty of them to the Pacific. New Bedford sent out ten and other ports unrepresented for some years returned to the fray, including Hudson and Sag Harbour. As the full ships began returning from the Pacific in 1817, it was clear that even a brief respite had made the whales on the South American coast approachable again, but within two years the cargoes were smaller and one gloomy captain was predicting that no ship would ever fill again with sperm oil.

Such defeatism was no part of the makeup of George Washington Gardner. On New Year's Day 1818 he brought the *Globe* into Nantucket and landed the first cargo in excess of 2000 barrels. While he had been away, Porter's account of the voyage of the *Essex* had been published, and when he sailed again in March Gardner decided to steer west for the Marquesas. Sure enough, he fell in with Porter's shoals of whales and a new fishery was opened. The Offshore Ground (so called to distinguish it from the Onshore, the coast of Peru) was found to extend due east of the Marquesas between 105° and 120° west and to within 5° of the equator. Within two years 50 ships were whaling there, but by then the *Globe* had already taken home two more 2000-barrel cargoes. Gardner's rediscovery of the Offshore Ground earned him a place in whaling history, but one would never guess it from the modest summary he made of his career.

> I began to follow the sea at 13 years of age, and continued in the service 37 years. I performed three voyages to the coast of Brazil, 12 to the Pacific Ocean, three to Europe, and three to the West Indies. During 37 years I was at home but four years and eight months. There were 23,000 barrels of oil obtained by vessels which I sailed in. During my following the sea, from the best estimate I can make, I have travelled more than one million miles.[9]

The Offshore was the first of the oil rushes that were typical of European exploitation of the Pacific basin in the early years of the century. They were later to be echoed in the gold rushes around the Pacific rim. The next whaling discovery in the Pacific was nearly as far from the Marquesas as it is possible to get. Captain Jonathon Winship, formerly a sealer, was now a trader to China and Hawaii, but he knew that what he had seen near Japan would be of interest to his friends in Nantucket. When the *Maro*, master Joseph Allen, sailed in October 1819, his instructions were to cruise north-west from Hawaii. Only one month earlier Hawaii had received its first visit by American whalers when the crews of the *Equator* and *Balaena*, whaling off Lower California, had been afflicted by scurvy and the captains had decided to recruit (ie refresh) in the islands. Following his instructions, Allen sailed from Hawaii towards the end of May 1820. In early June he discovered a previously uncharted island in 25° 3' north and 167° 40' west, still known as the Gardner Pinnacles. A little further west, 10 degrees further north and there were the whales. By the time he left the ground in September, he was confident that one more season there would fill his ship. He wintered off California and at Hawaii, in what became an established routine for American whalers, and the following year fulfilled his expectations. The *Maro* returned to Nantucket in March 1822 with a full cargo, 2425 barrels. While rounding the Horn, Allen passed the word to Captain Upham of the *George and Susan*, and on the spot Upham aborted his intended voyage to California. The rush was on.

Allen had seen no other ships 'on Japan' and believed that he had been the first whaleman there. He had not reckoned on Samuel Enderby. The Englishman had informants everywhere, including Nantucket, which was the home of Frederick Coffin, master of his ship the *Syren*. Two months before the *Maro* sailed, the *Syren* was on her way from London. By 5 April 1820 she was whaling near Japan. When Coffin brought her back in April 1822, honours were about even; she had taken 346 tons, 14 per cent more than the *Maro*, but the American was a much smaller ship, 315 tons to the *Syren*'s 510. In the following year there were at least nine British and four American ships on Japan. By 1825 the British alone had 24 whalers there. Over the next 30 years it would be the most reliable and prolific of grounds. Allen had found his whales over a huge expanse of ocean, but he encountered none nearer to Japan than 1000 miles from the coast. The area might no less accurately have been described as the Sandwich ground, because its eastern limit was about the same distance from Hawaii.

It might seem that the discovery of new grounds relied more on rumour and good luck than on systematic exploration. As a generalisation this is true enough, but there was an honourable exception. Samuel Enderby seemed prepared to send ships to any untested corner of the ocean on speculation, and the persistence of his efforts over the years was remarkable. A year after the return of the *Syren* he despatched the *Swan*, 150 tons, to the northern Indian Ocean under Captain McLean. Her two-year cruise produced only 40 tuns of oil, less than half a cargo, and has been dismissed as unsuccessful on that score. The criticism is ill-founded. The size of the vessel alone, about half the usual tonnage of an Enderby whaler, is sufficient indication of her mission. Like the *Rattler* 30 years earlier she was on a reconnaissance; where McLean took his oil was more important than the amount he got. Thomas Beale appreciated the significance of the find.

> . . . her want of entire success was not owing to the absence of whales at the places *to which they were sent* [my emphasis], for the crew saw immense numbers, but from a series of misfortunes which befell them, and which rendered them incapable of prosecuting the fishery with all the energy and entire devotion which it requires to bring about a successful termination. The ships which resorted to the Seychelles after the return of the *Swan*, had good reason to be well satisfied with the success which attended their efforts, not only from the number of whales which they found there, but from its being so much nearer home than the Japan fishery, by which much time was saved in the outward and homeward passages.[10]

Enderby was, in his own words, paying for the knowledge. Whether or not it was a good investment for his firm is debatable. As Thomas Melville had found, there were no secrets between sperm whalers, but then they could afford to be more open with each other about new grounds than sealers or right whalers. Sperm whales were nomads of the featureless ocean. In this they were unlike even the right whales, which had a preference for calving in sheltered waters near, with any luck, recognisable landmarks. Enderby seems to have been of the view that in the search for a needle, directions to the haystack would be of limited assistance to his competitors.

A by-product of sealer secrecy was that it was possible to come across them unexpectedly anywhere in high latitudes. On 25 January 1821 Captain Bellingshausen of the Russian exploring expedition was feeling quite pleased with himself. Before this dense fog had blanketed his ships he had made out the group of islands he was looking for. Some months earlier he had been told of the discovery of the South Shetland Islands, and as part of his circumnavigation of the Antarctic ice he had resolved to determine whether it was part of the supposed Southern Continent. Right now he was anxious that his ships should maintain contact, and it was with some relief that he could make out the shape of the *Mirnyi* emerging as the fog lifted. But what was that between her and the *Vostok*? It was the sloop *Hero*, 44 tons, of Stonington, Connecticut. The master, Nathaniel Palmer, came aboard. Yes, he and a fleet of Stonington sealers had been here for four months and, speaking of interesting places, he was just returning from one further south, where he had been sent by his commander Benjamin Pendleton. It was a large landmass with mountains so high that in good weather they would probably be visible from the masthead even now. So at least was the story as handed down in Palmer's family: the Russian's account merely acknowledges the meeting. But it was as Palmer's Land that this first sliver of the Antarctic mainland was placed on the map.[11]

Rope's End
or Discipline and its Dangers

*I am a bloody man! I have a bloody hand and
will be avenged!*

Samuel Comstock

The shipping of malcontents became harder to avoid as the industry expanded after 1815 and captains were less able to pick crews from men they knew. The ship's articles chained master and man together for a sentence of years, from which only death, incapacity or desertion offered escape, and against which the only appeal was to the arbitration of a port's honorary consul, himself often commercially interested. Desertion became one of the industry's most intractable problems, and not only because of the stark contrast between squalor in the forecastle and paradise ashore in the Pacific. Captains were not above making life aboard even more miserable than usual towards the end of a voyage. The whaleman who failed to return to his port of shipping to take his discharge forfeited his lay, and it was in the owner's interest to have him leave the ship (if he did not have to be replaced) with nothing more to show for three or four years work than his outfit and what he had drawn from the slops chest.

It was possible for crews to take collective action against abuse. There was the consul if one's ship visited port, but owners discouraged their captains from visits to some ports for this very reason. Grumbling offered some relief, but no remedy, for it was understood that 'growl you may, but go you must'. Refusal of duty, on the other hand, could certainly be effective if the crew were solid, but it was a risky proceeding. Such action would almost inevitably come before a consul for adjudication sooner or later, and some consuls were not at all averse to calling it mutiny. One such was Charles Wilson, Her Britannic Majesty's Acting Consul at Tahiti, before whom Herman Melville found himself arraigned after joining the Sydney whaler *Lucy Ann* in 1842.

Melville at this stage of his adventures was a deserter from the Fairhaven whaler *Acushnet*, but his new captain, Henry Ventom, was too short-handed to be concerned about such niceties. Ventom sought him out at Nuku Hiva and signed him on for one cruise at the 120th lay. The crew was raddled with venereal disease, the provisions had been obtained at a sale of condemned navy stores, and discipline was largely a matter of the mate laying about him when drunk, which was most of the time.

> He was always for having a fight; but the very men he flogged loved him as a brother, for he had such an irresistibly good-natured way of knocking them down, that no one could find it in his heart to bear him malice . . . Upon an emergency, he flew in among them, showering his kicks and cuffs right and left, and 'creating a sensation' in every direction. A sober, discreet, dignified officer could have done nothing with them; such a set would have thrown him and his dignity overboard.[1]

This robust individual, James German, was on the receiving end on one occasion when he ventured alone into the dark of the forecastle and was ambushed by the carpenter, but in spite of rumblings about a flogging there was no retribution. German had been given as good as he gave, and that was fair enough. The *Lucy Ann* sailed towards Tahiti, but was in too poor a condition to lower even had whales been seen. Ventom was ill as well as incompetent; the crew hoped for discharge or at least a run ashore when the ship reached Papeete, but only the captain landed, intending that the ship should continue cruising under German. The crew, arguing that their agreements were with Ventom,

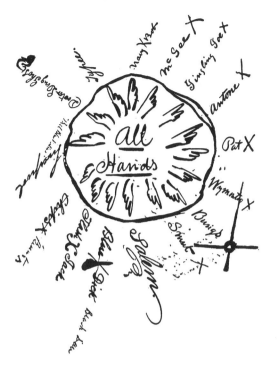

The round robin of Herman Melville, alias Typee
(from Omoo, *National Library of Australia)*

refused duty and presented Consul Wilson with a list of grievances penned by Melville and signed by all in a round robin,

> ... the great object ... being to arrange the signatures in such a way,
> that, although they are all found in a ring, no man can be picked out as
> the leader of it. Few of them had any regular names; many answering to
> some familiar title, expressive of a personal trait; or, oftener still, to the
> name of the place from which they hailed; and in one or two cases were
> known by a handy syllable or two, signifying of nothing in particular but
> the men who bore them. Some, to be sure, had, for the sake of formality,
> shipped under a feigned cognomen, or 'Purser's name'; these, however,
> were almost forgotten by themselves; and so, to give the document an air
> of genuineness, it was decided that every man's name should be put
> down as it went among the crew.[2]

The round robin failed in its object. When Wilson confronted
the men with their claims of 'mistreatment' at the hands of the

mate and insufficient food, a number, among them the most vocal hitherto, not only broke ranks but betrayed the other leaders. Having divided the men, Wilson could afford to give them all the option of returning to duty. To put out any remaining embers, he sought assistance from a French corvette in the harbour that only three weeks earlier had been instrumental in extinguishing Tahitian independence. Ten men who still refused were sent aboard the Frenchman and ironed. Before the corvette sailed the prisoners were removed to the local prison, the Calabooza Beretanee, and there Melville joined them, it becoming apparent that the *Lucy Ann* would soon sail under German's command.

On 5 October depositions against the eleven for 'revolt and refusal of duty' were heard. The men were given a choice; return to duty or be shipped to Sydney for trial when an Australian schooner then in the harbour sailed. All eleven maintained their resolve and were returned to prison. The Calabooza was an open, unfinished building whose only furniture was stocks for the confinement of prisoners' feet. Side by side they lay in this 20-foot bed, leaves for a mattress and a coconut trunk for a pillow. Their Tahitian gaoler left them more and more at liberty as the days passed. Once the *Lucy Ann* had recruited replacements and sailed, it became clear, as all had suspected, that the threat of deportation to Sydney was an idle one. Wilson stopped feeding his prisoners, as a hint for them to depart, but with nowhere else to go the men stayed where they were for the time being, much to the embarrassment of the consul, all of whose stratagems to get them back on the ship were seen to have failed. Melville knew why so much effort had been put into the case.

> Beside an advance of from 15 to 25 dollars demanded by every sailor shipping at Tahiti, an additional sum for each man so shipped has to be paid into the hands of the government, as a charge to the port. Beside this, the men—with here and there an exception—will only ship for one cruise, thus becoming entitled to a discharge before the vessel reaches home; which, in time, creates the necessity of obtaining other men at a similar cost . . . to meet these expenses, a

good part of what little oil there was aboard [the *Lucy Ann*] had to be sold for a song to a merchant of Papeetee.[3]

Melville makes it plain that the complaints of the crew were no more than a device for getting ashore, however abusive German had been. With no real malice involved, it was all in the nature of a rough game, but not all rough games had such a benign outcome.

Samuel Comstock shipped in Edgartown as a boatsteerer on the *Globe*, which in 1822 had just returned from the cruise on which she had opened the Offshore Ground. After a year out her master, Thomas Worth, put into Honolulu to recruit. There were a number of desertions and six men were shipped from the beach as replacements. They were trouble from the first and Captain Worth took a rope's end to Joseph Thomas for insolence on 24 January 1824. The men went forward, vowing to leave the ship at the next island. Comstock had a better idea. Within a week of leaving Honolulu he had been plotting mutiny with the beachcombers. His motives were obscure, but probably had to do with a fantasy about setting himself up as king on a Pacific island. That night he had the watch from 10 p.m., and just before midnight he, Silas Payne, John Oliver and William Humphries descended into the cabin. Joseph Thomas was invited but declined. The captain was their first victim. Comstock found him sleeping in a hammock and took the top of his head off with a single hatchet blow. At the same time Payne attacked the first mate, William Beetle, also asleep, with a boarding knife. The unwieldy, sword-like implement struck bone, and Beetle rose to do battle. He grabbed Comstock by the throat. The mutineer lost his hatchet and was in danger of being choked until Payne returned it to him, and with it he broke Beetle's skull.

The other two mates were in their cabin. 'Don't you open that door', commanded Comstock. John Lombard, the second mate, asked the boatsteerer if he intended to kill him. 'Oh, no. I guess not', was the reply. Comstock then loaded two muskets and fired through the door, hitting third mate Nathaniel Fisher in the mouth. The officers opened the door and Comstock lunged through with musket and bayonet. He missed, was collared by Lombard and lost the musket to Fisher, who put the bayonet to the mutineer's chest. Comstock assured Fisher that his life would be spared if he gave up. The wounded man handed over the weapon which, as soon as it was back in his hands, Comstock used to bayonet Lombard several times. He then told Fisher that he had to die, and alluded to an incident some months earlier.

While the *Globe* had been in company with the whaler *Enterprise*, Comstock had challenged Fisher to a friendly wrestle. Such familiarity between officers and men was rare and, in the eyes of some, subversive, but as a boatsteerer Comstock was rated petty officer and Fisher was the most junior mate so there was no great disparity in rank. In their contest Comstock was no match for Fisher, who handled him easily. Comstock lost his temper and struck out, only to find that Fisher worsted him there as well. The humiliated boatsteerer threatened revenge, but he was not taken seriously. If this seems small enough reason for murder, how much more trivial was the reason Comstock had given Beetle as he struck him: the mate was accused of telling lies about Comstock 'out of the ship', perhaps on the *Enterprise*.

Fisher met his end with dignity. He turned his back as ordered and said, 'I am ready'. Comstock fired into the back of his head. Lombard begged for water and was bayoneted again for his troubles. The other boatsteerer, Gilbert Smith, finding escape impossible, said that he would do whatever the mutineers required. Comstock proceeded to dispose of his night's work. The captain's corpse was disembowelled and thrown overboard, as was Beetle although he was not yet dead. Fisher's body was hauled on deck with a rope around the neck, Lombard's with one around his feet. Amazingly, Lombard was still alive and reminded Comstock of the promise not to kill him. Not only was he pushed from the deck, but when he caught the plank-shear with a hand Comstock called for an axe. Lombard was seen to swim away from the ship and a boat was ordered after him to avoid the possibility that he might be found by another whaler. On a moment's reflection, it seemed just as likely that the boat's crew would also go looking for another whaler and the order was countermanded.

The ship was turned towards the Marshall Islands. Comstock and Payne were in charge of the ship but the mutineers were heavily outnumbered, and became more so when one of their number, Humphries, was found loading pistols. He said he was afraid that Gilbert Smith and another man intended to retake the ship. Comstock's paranoia suggested that the pistols were intended for Payne and him. After a mock trial Humphries was seated on the ship's rail, a noose placed about his neck, and the whole crew told to take the rope's end. 'How long will you give me?', Humphries asked, preparing to meet his Maker. 'Fourteen seconds', said Comstock, turning over the log glass. They swung him from a studding sail boom and then cut the body loose to sink. Comstock promulgated the ship's new laws, which were signed by all but sealed in black only by the mutineers. The others sealed in blue and white.

> If anyone sees a sail and does not report it immediately, he shall be put to death.
> If anyone refuses to fight a ship he shall be put to death; and the manner of their death, this—
> They shall be bound hand and foot and boiled in the try pots, of boiling oil.[4]

On 11 February the *Globe* reached the Mili group in the Marshall Islands. The mutineers anchored beyond the reef of the central lagoon and began rafting stores ashore preparatory to burning the ship. Comstock spent most of his time ingratiating himself with the natives, which aroused the ire of Payne who saw much of their plunder being given away. They fell out, and Comstock destroyed his laws and quitted the ship for a native village. Payne suspected that Comstock was inciting the natives against them and, when Comstock approached the ship's camp on 17 February, sword in hand, he was shot. Payne took an axe to him to make sure that he was dead. Now in sole charge, Payne told off Gilbert Smith and five of the others to look after the ship, having taken the precaution of removing the binnacle compasses. Smith found another, substituted it for a binnacle compass, cut the cable that night and set sail for Valparaiso.

With only six men to work the ship, it took nearly four months to cross the Pacific. It would have been easier had Joseph Thomas pulled his weight, but he remained as insolent as when Worth had flogged him. He was subsequently tried for mutiny but acquitted in the absence of evidence of direct involvement. A year later the USS *Dolphin* was sent to apprehend the remaining mutineers and release the other crewmen. On 19 November 1825 the schooner reached the islands, but for ten days found no sign. Then they came across the deserted remains of the mutineers' camp and a buried skeleton. Lieutenant-Commandant Percival decided to send his launch into the lagoon. For a month it combed the islets until one day it happened upon a large group of natives, one of whom, dressed in a mat and as dark as any of them, warned the crew in English that they were in danger of attack. It was William Lay, and he was able to direct them to where Cyrus Hussey was being held. These were the only survivors of the *Globe*, but they were able to tell what had become of the others.

After the escape of the *Globe*, Payne had begun decking one of the whaleboats for flight. He also went exploring and returned with some native women. The one he kept for his own pleasure ran back to her people. Payne retook her by force, flogged her and ironed her. From this point relations with the natives deteriorated rapidly. Theft increased and Payne decided to make an issue of it. He armed four men, but loaded their muskets with bird shot rather than ball, fearing that the weapons might be used against him. At the village Hussey and the others recovered the missing property but were surrounded by a large throng which began stoning them. The crowd's rage and confidence grew when the bird shot was ineffectually fired into them, and in the chaotic retreat to the camp Roland Jones was overwhelmed and stoned to death. Thoroughly rattled, and having dissipated the natives' fear of firearms, Payne tried to negotiate. Lay and Hussey were quietly taken aside and held by natives they had befriended. Payne offered to surrender all the ship's goods and seemed to be making some headway with the chiefs until a huge shout went up and the white men were attacked. They tried to run but six were pursued and killed, including Payne and Oliver. Lay and Hussey were taken into the families of their protectors and lived among them for 22 months.

Payne and Oliver were pieces of windblown refuse from a Pacific beach, but Comstock was to all the world a typical upright Nantucketer. Quaker-educated, at sea at thirteen and a boat-steerer at twenty, he would certainly have become an officer and probably a captain. But it was Payne and Oliver, the murderer's assistants, who had the nightmares, while Comstock revelled in his deeds.

> After the death of the officers, Comstock made us all live in the cabin with him, where the mutineers used to sing, and carouse, and tell over the story of the murder, and what they had dreamed. Payne and Oliver who could hardly ever sleep, spoke with horror of their dreams, and of the ghosts which appeared to them at night, but Comstock always made a light of it, and appeared to exult in what he had done. He said once that the captain came to him with his wounded and bloody head, and showed him what he had done, when he told the captain to depart and never come again, or he would kill him a second time.[5]

At his own death Comstock appeared disoriented, calling on the other mutineers not to shoot him even though he held a naked sword in his hand. It was of a kind with his other irrational and disproportionate behaviour. Whether he was clinically insane is something that can only be guessed at, but it may be significant that none of his contemporaries described him as mad. It seems more likely that small festering grievances, too long harboured and too seldom banished during the interminable idleness of

Owners' Instructions

The mutiny on the *Globe* reverberated through the offices of the Nantucket owners. The only device available to them for controlling a voyage was the owner's instructions to the captain. These sometimes presumed to tell the captain how to go about catching whales, or where, but were more often concerned with management of assets and control of the men. After the *Globe*, some paid particular attention to boatsteerers' watches.

> To Captain Elisha H Fisher
> Sir
>   Having appointed you to the command of the ship *Maria*, we wish you to proceed to sea with all convenient dispatch, and as the ship is furnished with everything necessary for you to proceed to the Pacific ocean, we do not think it necessary for you to touch at any port this side of Cape Horn, unless you should be so fortunate as to get oil on your passage before passing the Western [Azores] or Cape Verde Islands, in which case you can touch at the most convenient port of the islands and ship it home.
>   On your arrival in the Pacific Ocean, you will consider yourself at liberty to cruise wherever you may think the prospect best for a cargo of sperm oil.
>   You are at liberty to go into port as often as it becomes necessary to recruit & refit the ship, but you must not prolong your stay for social purposes; and while cruising at sea you will suffer no visiting to interfere with the interests of the voyage. We have had much cause heretofore to complain of visiting & carousing, and expect it will be avoided by you. When in port do not suffer your men to sell their clothes to buy fruit & liquor, but rather give them fruit at the ship's expense, where it is plenty, and at no rate suffer liquor to be brought on board, except in a very small quantity, & that for medical purposes only.
>   Serious losses have occurred by suffering the officers to neglect a part of their duty, which you must not allow; we mean the practice of leaving the deck in care of boatsteerers, who are not paid for that service. And that you

may not misunderstand us in this respect, we repeat that it is our desire that you require the mates to take their regular watch in the night time while at sea, through the whole voyage; it will be no justification for them to omit this part of their duty because it is not practised on some other ship.

We wish you to bear in mind that perfect order is to be maintained on board the ship by you, & that no quarreling is to be allowed among the officers, nor between them and the crew, as the success of the voyage depends very much on harmony and united exertion.

Christopher Mitchell & Co, Nantucket
October 1836

whale searching, developed into an obsession. It would have been something that his shipmates understood. According to E A Stackpole, the *Globe* mutiny had two consequences. US naval vessels became more active in suppressing mutiny in whaling ships—and the navy flogged far harder than whaling masters— and owners forbade boatsteerers to stand watch at night, thus effectively demoting them from under-officers to senior seamen.[6]

Twenty years later, when J Ross Browne served as a greenhand on the *Bruce*, of Fairhaven, it appeared to him that, if anything, workplace relations had deteriorated further. The book he subsequently wrote was an exposé of working conditions in the whaling trade, much as Richard Dana's *Two Years Before The Mast* had been for the merchant service. In his consideration of which was chicken and which was egg when it came to the relationship between discipline and mutiny, Browne was firmly of the view that mutiny was usually provoked, and that respectable young men like himself could not be expected to be attracted to whaling while masters had an unfettered right to punish and consuls were

J Ross Browne condemns flogging (from Etchings of a Whale Cruise,
National Library of Australia)

unwilling, even when they were able, to provide redress. He
believed that corporal punishment was more frequently resorted
to than formerly.

> To such perfection has [the] system of flogging been carried of
> late years that, whether a man be innocent or guilty, if it is
> supposed it can in any way add to the dignity of the quarter-deck, he
> is seized up and flogged. This power was designed for useful
> purposes; but its abuse prevails to a far greater extent than could
> have been apprehended. It is the primary cause of mutiny and
> bloodshed on the high seas . . . Its abuses far exceed, in their
> demoralizing tendency, the good done by its appropriate and judicious
> exercise . . . Would it be safe to abolish flogging? I answer, not only
> would it be safe to do so, but it would be the strongest bulwark
> against insubordination and mutiny. Let flogging in every form, and
> under all circumstances, be abolished, and there will no longer exist
> any occasion for (mutiny).[7]

Browne had a hard time on the *Bruce*. Had he been less engaged, he might have given more weight to another factor.

> ... I freely confess a large proportion of the Americans who continue to seek refuge in [the whale fishery] are not of the most reputable character. It is the existence of the very evils complained of that furnishes the excuse for oppression. Remove them, and the alleged necessity for this severity will be removed.[8]

He offered no suggestion as to how the riffraff were to be excluded when they and the islanders made up rather more than half of most crews, but the course he and others urged was adopted in 1850. Flogging was outlawed in both the navy and the merchant marine.

The *Globe* might have been the worst of whaling mutinies, but it had an eerie echo in another that took place 34 years later. On Christmas Day 1857 the *Junior*, of New Bedford, was crossing the Tasman Sea headed for New Zealand. For one of the boatsteerers, Cyrus Plummer, these were familiar waters. A few years earlier he had made a hero of himself by getting a line ashore from the steamer *Monumental City* when she was wrecked off the Victorian coast. Now he was aggrieved. Some time earlier he had complained too loudly about the food and conditions, and Captain Mellen had ordered first mate Nelson Provost to trice him up to the shrouds and give him twenty strokes with a rope's end. So much for legal prohibition, but had boatsteerers so far slipped in status since the *Globe* mutiny that they could be subjected to illegal punishment with apparent impunity, as if they were common seamen? Something else was unchanged; as with the *Globe*, and in spite of owners' strictures, when the officers retired for the night with a skinful of Christmas cheer—which the hands had shared—Plummer and the other boatsteerers were left to stand boat watches. At 1 a.m. on 26 December Plummer and four accomplices entered the cabin and took post beside the berths of the officers. At Plummer's signal all were attacked simultaneously.

The whaling gun with which Plummer shot Mellen put three

balls right through him and into the side of the ship, but still he
grappled with his assailant until struck with a hatchet. Provost
was hit by six balls from a single shot and the flash ignited his
bedding. Third mate Hall was run through several times with a
boarding knife, but a similar attempt on Lord, the second mate,
failed when he deflected the blade. He was shot instead. The
mutineers went forward to prevent other crewmen from coming
to assist the officers. The petty officers, including boatsteerer
Alonzo Sampson, were then able to get into the cabin from the
steerage.

> The room was dark and full of smoke, and we could not see what the
> trouble was. We asked 'what's the matter?' The mate replied that he
> had been shot. On examination we found that both he and the
> second mate had been shot in the shoulder, one in the right and the
> other in the left. We went into the captain's state room, and found
> him kneeling down at his chest, apparently trying to open it. We
> spoke to him but he made no reply. The mate then took hold of him
> and so ascertained that he was quite dead. He had been struck in the
> shoulder with some heavy weapon, an axe apparently, and split right
> down into the body. He had other cuts upon him, and 'all cut to
> pieces' is the only phrase that fully describes his condition. The third
> mate not making his appearance, we went to his berth. He had got
> out of his bunk and was seated on his chest with a boarding knife
> . . . in his hand. Like the captain, he was entirely lifeless.[9]

Provost was able to half-load the captain's revolver. Finding him
armed, the mutineers were afraid to re-enter the cabin but the
spreading fire forced the mate into the hold. The mutineers
extinguished the fire and then, as was done on the *Globe*, they
dragged the corpses on deck with ropes to throw them overboard,
as if it were unlucky to handle them. From his hiding place
Provost thought he heard Plummer order the second mate's death
and decided that he would prefer to die of his wound rather than
surrender to be shot. And die he nearly did. After two days he
found a water cask with an upright bung. Careful not to make
the slightest sound, he drew water by pushing a piece of his collar
through the bung hole. He enlarged the bung hole of a bread

cask by rubbing at it with his revolver's sight. For five days he hid, but when he was found and told that he would not be shot if he came up he was at the end of his endurance.

> While I was in the hold I was as strong as a lion but when I came on deck I could scarcely stand. When I was in the hold I could hear a kind of suction in my shoulder and I knew then that I was badly hurt. It smelled very bad. My shirt being bloody, cold and stiff I shifted it round and put the soft side on the lame shoulder . . . The foremast hands said that if there had been any other person with me they could not have told who it was, I was so much altered.[10]

He found that the second mate had not been killed after all, but Plummer needed Provost alive because Lord could not navigate and nor could anyone else. To reach Australia it was a simple matter of steering west, but Plummer had a particular landfall in mind. He wanted to be landed at Cape Howe, only a few miles north of the wreck of the *Monumental City*. If Provost would take him there he could have the ship. On 4 January 1858, off Cape Howe, Plummer and his accomplices took to two of the boats after stripping the ship of its weapons and whaling blades. Before they left they wrote an entry in the logbook that exonerated the remainder of the crew but gave no reason for the mutiny. Provost noted that Plummer had said that he would not shoot him because 'you never misused me'. While this seems a likely explanation for the killing of the captain, it sits uneasily with Plummer's boast that he had taken two or three ships previously, and had nearly done the same with the *Daniel Wood* while he was returning to America in 1856. The mutineer also told Provost that he had shipped in the *Junior* with the intention of seizing the vessel, and to that purpose had brought aboard pistols and ammunition.

Whether Plummer was trying to recover valuables secreted near the wreck of the *Monumental City*, or simply wanting to be landed on a deserted but familiar shore, he quickly abandoned whatever plans he had and rowed north to Twofold Bay. He dallied long enough at the port of Eden for Provost to sail the *Junior* to Sydney and raise the alarm, and the local police took the mutineers into custody without a fight. They were shipped back to America on the *Junior*, in deck cells made of sheet iron, and put on trial. Plummer was convicted of piracy and first-degree murder. He was condemned to hang but escaped the rope after political agitation on his behalf had the sentence commuted to life imprisonment. The illegality of his mistreatment aboard the ship was probably the mitigating factor. His accomplices were sentenced to five years and ten months each for second-degree murder.

James German's man-management on the *Lucy Ann* had been rough and ready, but it did not involve degradation and humiliation. Even those commentators who supported flogging because they could see no alternative agreed that it made a good man bad and a bad man worse. It might have been less serious in its consequences, even when legal, had better avenues for appeal against grievance been available. As it was, pressure was suffered to build up until crews exploded, and who could tell when that time might come, or over what trifle. Even had Worth and Mellen been given time to ponder the cause of their deaths, they might still have died puzzled men.

HONOUR WITHOUT
PROFIT

*Australians, yet unborn, must go down to the sea in
ships, and do business in the great waters; or they will
do but little business.*

South Asian Register, 1828

The *Pax Britannica* should have encouraged the British adventurers in the sperm whale fishery as never before. There were more imperial ports and more British consuls. The White Ensign dominated the high seas, and the American whaling fleet had again suffered severe losses during the war. Yet it was the American fleet that grew and grew, while most of the British firms struggled. Some of the pioneers, like the Champions, unable to convince the government to provide more protection, had already withdrawn from the trade. There were several factors at work, one of which was the inability of the British, like the French and before them the Dutch, to sustain the industry without protection and/or financial encouragement. So single-minded were the British whalemen in pursuit of government money that even national pride was no obstacle. When the French again attempted to revive their war-devastated industry in 1816, the Enderbys found that by employing a few Frenchmen—one-third of each crew—they qualified for a bounty of 50 francs (£2) per man for the entire crew. From 1829, if the ship's crew was two-thirds French the owner could get a bounty of 40 francs per register ton, doubled if the vessel passed Cape Horn. Payment was not conditional on taking whales; it was enough that you had been there. It was a small price for British owners to pay for the support of the French taxpayer.

The British taxpayer was less sympathetic. With Britain unchallenged at sea, there was no force in the 'nursery for seamen' rationale. There was also no shortage of opportunities for the employment of capital in industries that would generate revenue for the exchequer rather than drain it. In 1824 the premiums were withdrawn but, on the other side of the ledger, between 1823 and 1825 the duty on oil was reduced from more than eight shillings to just one shilling per tun. As compensation it was illusory because colonial oil was no longer discriminated against, attracting the same nominal duty. The British merchants were aggrieved by the exposure to colonial competition, but equally so by the threat of substitutes in their markets. In the case of sperm oil, one substitute was coal gas; it was coming into widespread use at a time when the postwar revival of whaling was pushing up oil production. Between 1820 and 1822 sperm oil imports more than doubled and the price fell from £85 per tun to £53. Municipal authorities had been quickly persuaded of the merits of gas lighting for their thoroughfares, but the whalemen fought a dogged rearguard action against its use for private purposes, petitioning the government in 1817 for protection on the grounds that

> . . . they deny its being a public benefit to light shops, houses and other building internally. They contend it is a private benefit to individuals which ought not to be allowed to interfere with the existence of important national fisheries, and therefore the Shipowners say they hope they [the gas companies] will not be allowed to light houses, shops, etc, with gas—There being no consumption for spermaceti oil except in shops, houses and public places, it is not used in our manufactories, and for that reason the fishery must be lost if the light from gas is allowed to be used indoors.[1]

It was an argument unlikely to prevail at a time when Adam Smith's case for the merits of free trade had insinuated itself into the thinking of most political economists. As a Parliamentary Select Committee put it in 1820, with perhaps a hint of regret, 'the time when monopolies could be successfully supported, or would be patiently endured . . . seems to have passed away'. Even the biggest owners like Daniel Bennett were discouraged, and the number of whalers fitted out for the South Seas fell from 68 in 1820 to 44 in 1822 and 31 in 1824. After 1824 those that remained increasingly concentrated on taking sperm oil, leaving the less profitable black oil of the right whale to the colonials. Samuel Enderby junior died in 1829. He had done his best to keep the faith, but even this most committed of firms had reduced its fleet from thirteen ships in 1821 to ten by 1827. The firm passed into the hands of his sons Charles, Henry and George.

Part of the motivation for reducing colonial duty was to stimulate colonial whaling and sealing, particularly in Australia and at the Cape of Good Hope. It was an opportunity for which the Australians had long been agitating. Robert Campbell, Sydney's first merchant, had taken colonial sea-elephant oil to England in a Bengal-registered ship as early as 1805 to test the East India Company monopoly. On this occasion Enderby had been one of the most vocal upholders of the company's rights, rights he had for years argued should be curtailed in his own interests. He did not prevail, but there was more than one way to keep the colonials in check: in 1809 the duty on their oil was increased to the point where profit and interest disappeared, although in the interim Campbell had inaugurated Australian sperm whaling by purchasing the London-registered *Elizabeth* and having Eber Bunker take her to the New Zealand grounds. William Charles Wentworth knew who was to blame.

> The act which authorizes these duties, is one of those smuggled acts by which, to the disgrace of our [British] legislature, the welfare and happiness of helpless unprotected thousands have been so frequently sacrificed on the shrine of individual avarice or ambition. It originated

in a certain great mercantile house extensively concerned in the
South Sea fisheries, and could never have been passed, had there
been a single person in either house of parliament, at all interested in
the prosperity of this colony. This act, indeed, is such a terrible
deviation, such a monstrous exception to the usual policy of this
country with respect to the fisheries, that it carries with itself the
strongest internal evidence of its polluted origin.[2]

Wentworth, already famous at the age of 29 as an Australian
explorer, patriot and angry young man, had a point. The domestic
rate of duty on sperm oil was 8s 3¾d per tun. Oil from any British
colony attracted a discriminatory duty, but for Newfoundland oil
it was £1/4/11¼ and for British North America £4/19/9. For the
rest (read Australia and the Cape, Enderby's competitors) it was
a prohibitory £24/18/9. Where might such manifest injustices, of
which this was but one instance, lead if not redressed?

> Let [Britain] from the midst of the glory with which she is environed
> compare her situation, brilliant and imposing as it is, with what might
> have been; let her look at the consequences of her former injustice. Is
> not the most formidible on the list of her enemies, a nation [the
> United States], which might have this day been the most attached
> and faithful of her friends? A nation which, instead of watching every
> occasion to circumscribe her power, would, if its rights had been
> respected, have been still embodied with her empire and confirmatory
> of her strength. Will this terrible lesson have no influence on the
> regulation of her future conduct?[3]

Wentworth was acutely conscious that a penal settlement of
20,000 people counted for little in the imperial scheme of things
and that secession on the American model was not an option, but
America itself was a possible factor in the equation. He conjured
up the spectre of Porter.

> Let [Britain] ask herself, what would have been the consequence if,
> during the late war with America, the ports of this colony had been
> open to the vessels of that nation? How many hundreds of the
> valuable captures, which the Americans made in the Indian seas and
> on the coast of Peru, might have safely awaited there [in Australia]
> the termination of the war, which were recaptured by [British] cruisers
> in view of the ports of their country? How many hundreds of
> [American] vessels, that shared the same fate, would have still

belonged to their merchants? And is there no probability, that a
perseverance in the present system of injustice and oppression, may
on some future occasion, urge the colonists to shake off this
intolerable yoke, and throw themselves into the arms of so powerful a
protector? May they not by these means acquire independence long
before the epoch when they would have obtained it by their own
force and maturity?[4]

It was not as if Wentworth was a lone voice. In March 1819
Governor Macquarie forwarded to London a petition that pro-
tested against, among other things, high duties on whale products
'which do not produce one shilling of Revenue and merely
operate as a prohibition'. The petition was signed by 1261 'Merchants, Settlers etc.' a large part of the free population. Even
Commissioner Bigge, who had been sent out by the home government to inquire into Macquarie's administration, could see that
the duties had reduced employment for young colonials and
deprived British ships of return freights. He conceded that more
colonial whaling ships meant more opportunities for convicts to
escape, but reminded his masters in Whitehall that in proportion
to the availability of return cargoes for British ships 'will the rate
of freight be diminished to the government for the transport of
the convicts'.[5] The subsequent decision by the British government to remove the discriminatory duty reflected a new maturity
in imperial policy, an acknowledgement that colonies settled from
the motherland could not forever be treated like children; they
might grow up to be America.

In 1820 Richard Jones, a 34-year-old Sydney merchant, revived
the sperm whaling trade by taking up the *Prince Regent* after she
had unloaded her convicts. It took just sixteen months for her to
take 1400 barrels and land it back in London. By using a British
ship, British-manned, to catch his whales, Jones could avoid
paying the colonial rate of duty. For some time the artificiality of
these arrangements inhibited expansion, but in the year that the
duty was equalised Jones and his partner William Walker sent
five whalers to sea.

One was the *Mercury*. Jones had sent the 156-ton brig to whale in New Zealand waters and in March 1825 Captain Edwards put into Whangaroa on the North Island for refreshment. Maoris swarmed aboard, as was their wont, but they were intent on pilfering rather than trade or prostitution and Edwards was unable to eject them. After a local missionary had persuaded some to go ashore, Edwards put out his boats to tow and attempted to weigh anchor. Directing from the bows, he detected a sudden movement behind him and ducked. The hatchet buried itself in the windlass. Edwards jumped from his ship and swam for the boats, leaving the mate, cook and steward in Maori hands. The natives proceeded to strip the brig. The missionary, William White, again interceded and at considerable personal risk slipped the cable and attempted, with the aid of the remaining crew, to get the derelict under way. She was uncontrollable and had to be abandoned 15 miles out to sea. In the meantime Edwards had reached the Bay of Islands and assembled a force of six well-armed whaleboats to retake his ship. The *Mercury* was already gone by the time he returned to Whangaroa and was not found for twelve days. She had drifted aground and had been burnt by the Maoris for her iron. The mission was abandoned and some of its members returned to Sydney with Edwards and his men in another Jones whaler, the *Pocklington*. The *Sydney Gazette* was glad to report that no one was hurt and that Jones was insured, but it was not disposed to turn the other cheek.

> . . . some example should be made, which no doubt would have the effect of affording them a lesson that might be remembered for years to come . . . We must confess that we never had any predilection in favour of a mission to the New Zealanders, being the most savage, barbarous, and warlike race of cannibals on the face of the globe, and in all likelihood they will be about the last of the Creation that will bow to the mild and convincing dictates of the Christian Religion.[6]

Jones had hardly had time to absorb this blow when, a fortnight later, his ship *Alfred*, 248 tons, was reported to be entering Sydney 'in distress'. It was something of an understatement. Commanded by the ubiquitous Eber Bunker, now 63, the *Alfred* had cruised to the Solomon Islands and in April had been whaling off Santa Cruz. There she had been caught by one of the season's tropical cyclones. The onslaught knocked her down and carried away the rudder and all three topmasts, which was probably a blessing as she might not otherwise have righted. For the next month Bunker patiently nursed his jury-rigged vessel across the 2000 miles that separated them from safety. By the time they reached Sydney Heads there was 9 feet of water in the hold. The *Alfred* could probably sink no further, buoyed up by the 1000 barrels of oil trapped below the deck beams. Bunker had had enough. The 'father of Australian whaling', as he became known, retired to his farm near Sydney, 39 years after he had first commanded a South Seas whaler.

Two years and two cruises later, the *Alfred* almost went the way of the *Mercury*, but this time the cost was measured in lives. The ship was whaling off Malaita in the Solomons. The natives had come alongside in numbers to trade, but there had been no unfriendliness and Captain Phillips had no misgivings about lowering all his boats when whales presented. Without provocation or warning, he found his own boat cut off and he, the second mate and three crewmen disappeared in a hail of missiles. The other boats raced to regain the ship and the first mate, Banks, got the *Alfred* under way. Several natives were killed as the ship fought her way through the canoes towards open water. A witness to these events described the tactics employed by the natives in an attack made on his own ship a few weeks later. There is a remarkable similarity to the conventional image of a wagon train under Indian attack.

> . . . the natives had formed their canoes into a large ring, which completely encompassed the ship; they kept constantly paddling around us in this position, leaving several small canoes out of the ring each time they went round, thus making the ring smaller and smaller and drawing nearer to the ship. After having paddled round the ship several times, their ring which was now composed of large war canoes,

being sufficiently near for their arrows to reach us, they commenced
shooting arrows and slinging stones, which fell in and against the ship
by showers; at the same time they made tremendous and terrific yells,
which struck the ear with horror and dismay.[7]

And that was as far as the demonstration was allowed to go.
Grapeshot and musket fire from the ship killed an estimated 200
natives, with as many wounded.

Banks was not disposed to abandon the cruise just because he
had lost his captain and one-sixth of the crew. He stayed out for
another half-year and returned with 96 tuns of oil. With such
commitment on the part of his men, Jones prospered in spite of
the setbacks. It was estimated that he and Walker had made a
net profit of £35,000 from sperm whaling by 1829. The local press
urged emulation.

All other ships of all other Nations have a voyage of 12,000 miles to
perform, to take up their fishing ground. We are here on the spot, in
the very heart of the preserve. The London or Boston owner has
from two to three years to wait for the return of his capital. Our ships
would be filled in one-third of the time. Merchants of Australia, open
your eyes,—use your reason! If you would but fairly set to work, what
Nation in the world could compete with you. The example is before
you. One Mercantile house has had the wit to avail itself of the
advantages of its situation. Is that House the least wealthy in Sydney?[8]

The Merchants of Australia responded with enthusiasm and in
the course of the next few years the colonial fleet grew rapidly
while the British fleet struggled to regain its pre-1824 strength.
By 1832 the 106 British south whalers at sea were competing with
55 ships, mainly colonial-registered, operating out of Sydney and
Hobart. Supply and demand for sperm oil reached a new equi-
librium in the late 1820s and price recovery, to £79 per tun in
1827, added impetus to colonial expansion. Their share of the
British market rose from 4 per cent in 1824 to 43 per cent in
1833. Proximity to the best whaling grounds was one of their
advantages. Another was the size of ship employed.

It was an iron law of whaling commerce that the longer the
voyage, the larger the ship had to be. Whaling ships sailed

outfitted for the voyage, and if the voyage was to the Pacific for three or four years that meant large amounts of consumables, edible and otherwise, and especially water. A whaler might go months with no better opportunity to refill casks than that offered by a passing shower. Average tonnage did not stop rising until every corner of the ocean could be reached from London or Nantucket and the ship could stay thereabouts until she filled. A ship or barque of about 350 tons met this requirement. The colonials, out into the western Pacific for a year or less, could make do with about 250 tons.

The difference that ship size and distance made to potential profit could be dramatic. When in 1828 the *Australian Quarterly Journal* was attempting to persuade its readers of the merits of sperm whaling, it printed a notional budget that can be compared with the skeletal but actual British costs provided by Charles Enderby to a Parliamentary Committee five years later.

	Australian	*British*
Length of voyage	1 year	3–4 years
Cost of ship	£5500	£9000
	(250–270 tons)	(say 350 tons)
Outfit		£7000
20 whale lines	£80	
5 boats	£150	
blocks, tackle, harpoons, lances	£200	
beef & pork	£600	
	(for 30 men)	
bread	£200 (ditto)	
cabin stores & spirits	£200	
220 tons of casks	£550	
Total outlay	£7480	£16,000

Sale of cargo	£10,000 (200	[£14,000]
	tuns @ £50)	(say 280 tuns)
less captain's lay	£1000	[£1400]
mates' lays	£400	[£560]
6 petty officer lays	£1500	[£2100]
20 crew lays	£2000	[£2800]
wear & tear	£500	[£2100]
		(3 years)
Profit	£4600	[£5040]
Return on capital	61.5%	31.5%

When the three-year return on British capital is annualised it falls to 10.5 per cent and a bad comparison becomes worse. As the figures assume a full ship and do not include insurance, the British owner was facing small and uncertain profit at high risk. Even allowing that the Australians had to add freight of about £6 a tun to get their oil to the London market, they enjoyed a clear competitive edge.[9] The Australian career of the *Alfred* illustrates the profitability as well as the risks of colonial sperm whaling in the 1820s. On five cruises between 1824 and 1829, averaging 8½ months, the *Alfred* took an average of 145 tuns of oil, 83 per cent of her potential carrying capacity. If it had not been for cyclone and massacre, the figure could have been close to 100 per cent. Compare this with the record of the Enderby ship *Indian*, 385 tons, which completed two cruises averaging 28 months between 1823 and 1828. On the best of these she returned a full ship, with about 270 tuns of oil, but it had been taken at a rate of 11 tuns a month. The *Alfred* took hers at 17 tuns a month, cruise after cruise. The difference was not in ships and men but in the amount of empty ocean a British ship had to traverse going to and from the grounds.

In time the Sydney and Hobart whalers had to venture further afield for their whales, as all whalers eventually did, and contact with the island peoples of the Pacific increased. There was frequently trouble, but nowhere worse than in New Zealand, where long familiarity and mutual exploitation had bred suspicion and fear in the whalers and contempt and fear in the Maori. In 1834 the whaler *Harriet* was wrecked at Cape Egmont while attempting to land a shore whaling party under John Guard. Most of the crew were killed and eaten or enslaved by the Maoris. Guard, his wife and their two children were held until he persuaded his captors to release him so that he could arrange for their ransom. This was a man who was of the opinion that 'a musket ball for every New Zealander was the best mode of civilizing the country', and who was moreover suspected of giving effect to this view whenever he could, but the Maoris took him at his word.

On arrival in Sydney, where the news had preceded him, Guard found the colony in a mood for reprisals like those called for by the *Sydney Gazette* nine years earlier. He asked for military assistance and was sent back to New Zealand in a visiting frigate, HMS *Alligator*, with 60 redcoats. Faced with this show of force the Maoris surrendered the crew members, but Mrs Guard and the children had been taken elsewhere. Ransom was again promised but Mrs Guard and her daughter were surrendered without payment. Finally, an old chief who had protected and adopted Guard's son appeared with the boy on his shoulders and asked for the ransom. On being refused, he turned to run and was shot. Indiscriminate firing then broke out and many Maoris were killed before the officers could regain control. The captain of the *Alligator* gave other tribes notice that this was how the King of England punished cruelty to his subjects. The House of Commons committee that subsequently inquired into the incident thought it poor policy.

> The impression left with that tribe of savages must have been one of extreme dread of our power, accompanied with one of deep indignation. The Committee cannot refrain from expressing their regret at the transaction, because it may be fatal to many innocent

persons [by Maori reprisal]; and because it seems calculated to
obstruct those measures of benevolence which the legislature designs
to native and barbarous tribes.[10]

The committee felt that these evils could have been avoided by
further efforts to negotiate. Certainly the expense could have
been avoided; the Maoris would have been happy to settle for a
pound of tobacco and a blanket for each of the crew members.
At the heart of the issue was the reality summed up in the
whalemen's phrase 'no law in New Zealand'. The solution recommended by the Governor of New South Wales was to have a
warship permanently stationed in the southern seas. In the
absence of the King's Justice it could at least attempt to enforce
the King's Peace, protecting commerce and repressing the out-
rages of Europeans and natives alike.

In 1823 Samuel Enderby had advocated annexation of New
Zealand to protect British whalers and inhibit the Americans and,
although Charles would be associated with a similar petition in
1837, the son was more interested in continuing his father's other
campaign, that of inhibiting the colonial whalers. He had become
chief spokesman for the family firm and was particularly critical
of what he saw as colonial advantages in outfitting, advantages
like those that 40 years earlier had made his father fearful of the
Nova Scotian whalers. He complained to the Commons Select
Committee on Manufactures, Commerce and Shipping that it cost
him £179 in duty when he bought Baltic staves for his oil casks,
whereas colonial whalers could get theirs second-hand and duty-
free when convict transports disposed of water casks in Sydney.
He estimated that it would require a duty of £8/10/- per tun on
colonial oil to overcome their advantages. Six months earlier,
overproduction had driven the price down to £51: Enderby said
he could just about break even at the current price of £63 per
tun. It was 'a most irregular trade' but he did not wish to give
up if the government would support it. He was asked if he had
thought of refitting at Sydney and shipping his oil home in a
merchant ship, as his colonial competitors did? 'That I might do',

he said, and went home to think about it, but his mind was really on other things.

While his father lived, exploration had been a means of expanding the horizons of the business and ingratiating the firm with governments. For Charles, it was an enthusiasm he could now indulge without having to justify it to anyone. Shortly before complaining to the Parliamentary Committee about how difficult it was to make whaling pay, he had reported with great pride to the Royal Geographical Society, of which he was a councillor, on the discoveries of his vessels *Tula* and *Lively*. In 1830 he had sent them sealing under the command of John Biscoe, a former acting Master in the Royal Navy, with explicit instructions to explore in high southern latitudes.

Sailing via the Falklands, Biscoe pressed south and east to cross Cook's 1773 track on 19 February 1831, skirting the ice. There was the appearance of land on the 25th but two days later, in 65° 57' south and 47° 20' east, there was no mistaking a coastline of considerable extent bound by field ice. He named its eminence Cape Ann, believing it to be 'the head land of a continent.'[11] It became known as Enderby Land. Aurora australis provided fireworks to celebrate their discovery,

> . . . at times rolling, as it were, over our heads in the form of beautiful columns, then as suddenly changing like the fringe of a curtain, and again shooting across the hemisphere like a serpent; frequently appearing not many yards above our heads, and decidedly within our atmosphere. It was by much the most magnificent phenomenon of that kind that I ever witnessed; and although the vessel was in considerable danger, running with a smart breeze and much beset [with ice], the people could scarcely be kept from looking at the heavens instead of attending to the course.[12]

In autumn Biscoe was forced into Hobart to refresh, arriving with only three men and a boy fit to work his brig. He resumed the voyage in October and, after sealing in New Zealand waters with little success, continued eastwards until he fell in with the Antarctic Peninsula. Biscoe believed that the land he could see

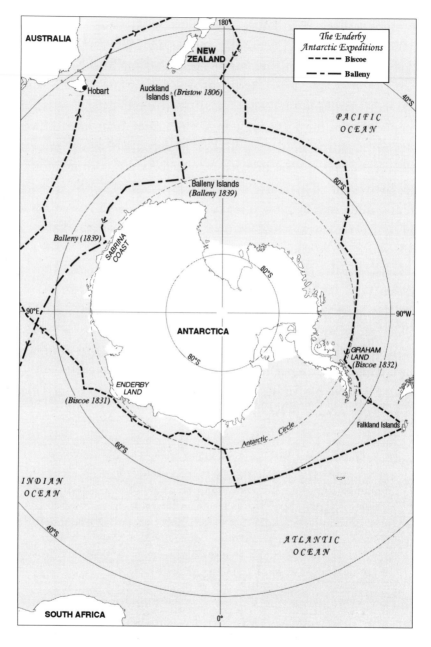

The Enderby Antarctic expeditions

extending south from 66° to 69° adjoined Palmer's Land but was a new discovery, the farthest known land to the south (he was unaware of Bellingshausen's discovery of Alexander Island even further south). He took possession on 14 February 1832 and British charts subsequently showed it as Graham Land. Having completed a circumnavigation but not gained a cargo, Biscoe prepared the *Tula* for sperm whaling. The whales were spared when the brig grounded in the South Shetlands and was so badly damaged that there was no option but to turn for home. In 2½ years the expedition had taken only 30 seals. The Royal Geographical Society awarded Biscoe its gold medal, noting that

> Two distinct discoveries have been made, at a great distance the one
> from the other; and each in the highest southern latitude, with very
> few exceptions, which has yet been attained, or in which land has yet
> been discovered. The probability seems thus to be revived of the
> existence of a great Southern Land, yet to be brought upon our
> charts, and possibly made subservient to the prosperity of our
> fisheries; so strongly, indeed, are Messrs Enderby impressed with this
> probability, that, undeterred by the heavy loss which they have
> incurred in the late voyage, they propose again sending out Captain
> Biscoe this season, on the same research.[13]

With the encouragement of a £3000 grant from the Treasury and without his father to caution him about throwing good money after bad, Charles sent out the cutter *Rose* and the schooner *Hopefull*. Wishful would have been closer to the mark. Before the expedition even sailed, Biscoe had been superseded by Henry Rea, a surveying officer provided by the Admiralty. The *Rose* was crushed in the ice south of the Falklands early in 1834, and the expedition was abandoned. This time the return was two cases of sealskins. Nothing daunted, in 1838 Charles tried again; it says much for his powers of persuasion that, unable to fund the whole expense from his firm's emptying coffers, he could recruit as associates a number of owners still active in whaling and sealing, including Young, Buckle and Sturge. The schooner *Eliza Scott*, 154 tons, and the cutter *Sabrina*, 54 tons, were put under the command of John Balleny and departed in July with instructions to sail as far south as possible looking for land. From New Zealand the expedition dropped down to Campbell Island. Here they found a four-person sealing gang left on the island four years earlier by the *New Zealander*. Balleny recruited them to his ships and engaged to buy their miserable stock of 165 skins. In Perseverance Harbour he also came across the colonial brig *Emma* and found that her captain had also been searching for land to the south. It was John Biscoe, long parted from the Enderbys but employed by a consortium of Sydney merchants on 'a secret expedition towards the South Pole'.[14] Subsequently a report circulated that he had been as far south as 75°.

For another fortnight Balleny sailed south-east until his ships were embayed in field ice in 69° south. Working north-west to clear the ice, on the morning of 9 February 1839 they saw land to the south-west and by sunset could make it out to be three unwelcoming islands.

> There is no landing or beach on this land; in fact, but for the bare rocks where the icebergs had broken from, we should scarce have known it for land at first, but, as we stood in for it, we plainly perceived smoke arising from the mountain tops. It is evidently volcanic, as the specimens of stone, or cinders will prove. The cliffs are perpendicular, and what in all probability would have been valleys and beaches are occupied by solid blocks of ice. I could not see a beach or harbour, or anything like one.[15]

The expedition continued west along the ice edge until a clear sea on 18 February again tempted them southwards. Fourteen days later, in 64° 58' south and 121° 8' east, they saw land to the south, but were surrounded by immense icebergs and were forced northward. Duty done, the ships were held to the course until the ice was gone. Then came the wind. The westerly gale grew for three days until at midnight on 25 March those aboard the schooner saw a blue distress light burning on the tiny *Sabrina*. She was only a mile distant, but the sea was so high that the schooner could not close. There was no sign of the cutter in the morning and by then the *Eliza Scott* was struggling for her own survival. A sea cleared the decks and laid the schooner on her beam ends. For ten minutes they feared that the vessel was settling, but eventually she righted without making too much water. The *Sabrina* was not seen again.

If Balleny and his crew took any sealskins other than those gathered by the Campbell Island gang there appears to be no record of it, but there was plenty of glory. The islands they had seen were named after Balleny. Sabrina Coast honoured the lost cutter. The Geographical Society was fulsome about 'the spirited exertions of Mr Charles Enderby, and other British merchants, so honourable to the commercial enterprise of our country'. Enderby himself was lauded as 'this disinterested and praiseworthy owner'. Indeed, in the light of subsequent confirmation the discoveries he made possible are even more impressive than they seemed to contemporaries, who were used to 'discoveries' that could not be found again. Before Biscoe, all that was known of Antarctica was that there was an archipelago or peninsula south of Tierra del Fuego that might or might not be the outlier of a larger landmass. By the time Balleny had finished his work, Enderby ships had seen land on the Antarctic Circle in 47° east, 121° east, 163° east and 63° west—almost a discovery in each quadrant. Were it not so disrespectful of the subsequent achievements of Ross, D'Urville, Wilkes and others on the Antarctic coast, it could be said that after Balleny the task was to join up the dots.

By the mid-1830s one-third and more of the sperm oil imported into Britain was of Australian origin. In the five years to 1833 colonial production had risen tenfold, peaking at 3048 tuns. There was something of the enthusiasm that had made William Rotch catch his breath in London nearly half a century earlier: 'Wool is very well, and so are horses and horned cattle, and skins, and hides, and timber, but for lucrative investment of capital, and Colonial advancement, choose we the SPERM WHALE FISHERY!'[16]

As a long-term investment, it was the wrong choice. Wool production had only doubled between 1828 and 1833 but in the next five years it trebled, while sperm oil production fell by one-third. In 1834 the value of the export wool clip exceeded that of sperm oil for the first time since the oil rush had started, and it never looked back. The Australians had found their staple. They would do their greatest business on the great plains.

Not that they abandoned whaling. It remained profitable and appealed to something in the emerging Australian character.

> The pursuit is, after all, to be considered rather as a species of gambling adventure than as partaking of the nature of a regular branch of commercial enterprise. As in many other games skill has, indeed, a certain part to play; but still the issue depends mainly upon chance. The same captain, in the same vessel, and exerting himself with the same ability and energy, may bring home a valuable cargo one year and a clean ship the next. It is what has repeatedly happened.[17]

Jones and the other Australian firms continued to take their chances, with fair success, throughout the 1830s: in 1840 production was well past its peak, but value, thanks to rising prices, reached an all-time high. Their nemesis was not bad luck with the whales but another change in British tariff policy. For all their efforts the British and colonial whalers had been unable to satisfy British demand, which continued to grow in spite of the emergence of substitutes. Enderby had tried to widen the market by singing the praises of sperm oil as a lubricant which, he said, would get 500 revolutions per minute more out of a cotton spinner than the 4000 obtainable with common oil. Mill-owners preferred rapeseed oil, the duty on which had been lowered from £10 to 10s. per tun in 1834, but the price of sperm oil held up anyway because of the large duty levied on American oil. It was a constraint on industry that the government was not prepared to maintain, the more so as American oil was still able to force its way on to the market. In 1842 the duty was reduced from £26/12/- to £15 per tun.

Fiercer American competition undermined the business of British and colonial whalemen alike, but in Australia it accelerated a downturn already setting in because of drought. Capital and water were both in short supply. As the depression approached its nadir in the early 1840s, Jones and many like him lacked the reserves to ride it out. In their generally futile efforts to save land-based businesses and property they found that whaleships were assets that could still be readily converted to cash. The buyers did not necessarily wish to employ them as whalers. Jones was declared insolvent in 1843 but the collapse of colonial whaling was not complete. Joseph Somes, one of the latecomers to the British trade, was premature when he said, in 1844, that 'it did not pay . . . The colonies gave up whaling after the alteration of the [tariff] law.' Sydney was not yet finished and Hobart became one of the great whaling ports of the world, with 29 of its own ships employed in 1848 and 26 foreign-owned whalers using it for refit or replenishment.

Somes was better informed about the present state and prospects of the British South Seas trade. For seven years, he said, it had been 'a losing concern', but since the admission of American oil five out of every six ships returning were being withdrawn from the trade. He attributed American superiority to better and cheaper ships, better and cheaper seamen, and weight of numbers.

> There are so many Americans upon the fishing ground that it makes our voyages longer; they are now four years, and formerly they were not more than three and a half or three years; and I account for that by the great increase of American ships for the fisheries in all directions.[18]

Somes gave up, as did most of the British firms. G F Young, another of the new owners of the 1820s, did not believe that a revival was possible and was convinced that nothing the Parliament could do to reduce costs would enable British whalemen to meet the American competition. As to tariffs, he wryly noted that the Americans justified their £10 duty on seed oil, and the higher consumer prices that followed, as the price they paid for the advantages of a large whaling fleet. But he recognised that in Britain this was a lost cause.

> That is one of those questions in political economy on which I am quite aware that theoretical and practical men have entertained differences, and may reasonably entertain them . . . but . . . if you will follow out the policy which has for its object solely the benefit of the consumer, as far as that is connected with subjects of maritime commerce, you will destroy British navigation.[19]

In 1842 there were 64 South Sea whalers on Lloyd's register; by 1848 the number had shrunk to fifteen. Enderby clung on, just. By 1843 the only survivor of his fleet was the *Samuel Enderby*, itself testimony to the firm's improvident pride in their trade. Purpose-built at West Cowes in 1834, in appearance she was more like the yachts that came from the Isle of Wight yards than a whaler. Imposing as well as beautiful at 422 tons, in her the firm had a floating advertisement as insubstantial as a painted hoarding. Her later voyages were mortgaged and shares in her were sold, until by 1846 the Enderbys were little more than the name on the transom and the registry. True to the family's coat of arms, the firm kept up appearances for the honour of South Sea whaling, and did so long after there was any profit in it.

Melting Pots
or Race, Rations and Other Accommodations

*The forecastle was black and slimy with filth, very
small, and as hot as an oven.*

J Ross Browne

Put 30 or more men on a ship 100 feet long, push it out to sea for four years, and it would be reasonable to expect a measure of familiarity to develop, even allowing for the formal divide between officers and men. Such was not the usual experience of whalemen, and when they encountered it, as William Whitecar did aboard the New Zealand schooner *Eliza* in 1857, they marvelled.

> . . . her captain and mate are of the [Maori/white] half-caste . . . The
> half-caste consider themselves a peg above the native, and take good
> care to let strangers know the distinction . . . All lived alike, fore and
> aft. Little discipline prevailed; the captain was called Tom, and the
> mate Bill . . . From us these people obtained tobacco, and captain,
> mate and crew engaged at a game of all fours for it . . . I asked the
> captain how he managed to preserve subordination where he allowed
> so much familiarity. He was a powerful, brawny figure, and a smile
> passed over his features at my question; extending his bared arm,
> corrugated with sinews, he said, 'I play this fellow right and left
> amongst them, whenever they make too much noise.' The English
> part of the vessel's crew professed a great contempt for these savages,

as they called them; but a good understanding appeared to exist
between the parties.[1]

Race created obvious lines of demarcation, but the white man's
claim to superiority over all 'lesser breeds without the law' was
not the only one. Language was at least as divisive, particularly
in the forecastle, where at any one time a dozen voices and half
as many languages might be competing for air time in a space
with the area of a bedroom and the headroom of a chicken coop.

> In that repulsive hole called the forecastle, of scarce twelve feet
> square capacity, not high enough to allow a tall man to stand upright,
> with little or no light or ventilation but what comes down the narrow
> hatchway (and even this must be closed in rough weather), here some
> twenty or five-and-twenty men are to eat, and sleep, and live, if such
> a state can be called living; here, in sickness and in health, by day
> and by night, without fire in the rigours of the polar regions, or by
> cooling appliances under the equator, these men, with their chests
> and hammocks, or bunks, are to find stowage. After again and again
> examining this feature of their arrangements, and comparing it with
> the cells prepared for and enjoyed by the felons in all our principal
> prisons in more than half the states of our Union which I have
> visited, the latter would be pronounced princely, enviable even in all
> the requisites of roominess, light, ventilation, and facility for seclusion![2]

Even so, it was large enough for segregation. Whitecar remarked
of some Hobart whalers that the forecastle was partitioned, one
side for blacks, the other for whites. This was unusually blatant,
but he had no need to look to foreign vessels for intolerance. Two
Portuguese boys were recruited to his ship at Flores and he was
glad that there were not more.

> If there be only one or two of this race aboard, and they are
> separated in different parts of the ship, and not allowed too
> frequently to converse with each other, they soon acquire English and
> become useful; but if there are half a dozen together in the forecastle,
> they jabber and chatter in their unmusical jargon from morning until
> night . . .[3]

Be it noted that Whitecar's complaint was about language, not
colour. Two Portuguese might be assimilated, but six would form

Australian whaling in the South Pacific (from the Graphic,
Australian National Maritime Museum)

a ghetto. J Ross Browne was equally scathing about them, and
not only for their behaviour in the forecastle.

> In this loathsome den, the Portuguese were in their element, revelling
> in filth, beating harsh discord on an old viola, jabbering in their native
> language, smoking, cursing, and blackguarding. Their chief recreation,
> however, was quarreling, at which they were incessantly engaged. Nor
> was it confined to week-days, for not the slightest regard was paid to
> the Sabbath. The most horrible profanity was indulged in, and to an
> excess that was truly revolting . . . A more ignorant, heartless,
> treacherous, beastly set of men, I think, never existed; and, with two
> exceptions, I would rather live among the most degraded of the
> savage tribes.[4]

This prejudice is as much linguistic, religious and social as racial,
for in the whaleman's world the Portuguese were a conundrum.
Those from the Azores were sometimes white; those from the
Cape Verde Islands usually black or mulatto. Among themselves,
language was a bulwark against Anglo-Saxon pretension. Between

them colour was a barrier, although not as high as that between black and white English-speakers.

The captain and mates promoted the assimilation favoured by Whitecar for entirely practical reasons. The working unit on a whaler was the boat, and when the mates took turns picking their crewmen it was a broad back and a previous cruise that recommended the individual, not a white skin or good English. Boats' crews were selected on merit and thereby were multi-racial. As each watch was made up of two boats' crews, they too were multi-racial. The difficulty came when those watches went below. In a merchant ship the starboard watch, technically the captain's watch but in fact kept by the second mate, occupied the starboard side of the forecastle. The mate's watch occupied the larboard side. Watches usually also messed together. In a whaler, the Portuguese, the Negroes, the Kanakas and the native Americans automatically took themselves to the larboard side of the forecastle, irrespective of boat, watch, or mess. It reduced friction and, incidentally, improved opportunities for avoiding duty: it was said of 'sogers' (soldiers, i.e. slackers) that they were in everyone's mess but no-one's watch.

For all Browne's loathing of life at close quarters with the Portuguese, when he left the *Bruce* at Zanzibar he found that his attitude had been changed by the months spent with them: 'We had endured the same hardships, faced the same dangers, suffered together, and stood night-watches together; and, although I did not regret that the tie of our fellowship was broken, I sincerely wished them well'.[5]

Standard fare in the forecastle of a whaler, breakfast and supper, was salt junk and hard tack—salted meat and double-baked ship's bread, also known as sea biscuit. Alonzo Sampson found that these unpromising ingredients could be conjured into many varieties of scouse, which was 'prepared by soaking hard bread in water, and then baking with pork etc.'.[6] On American ships molasses was the universal sweetener in beverages and on the bread taken from the forecastle's bottomless kid, or bucket.

Coffee and tea were merely descriptions of convenience, as burnt peas were sometimes substituted for the former and the massive stalks found in the latter gave rise to the term 'studding sail boom tea'.

> The difference between the tea and the coffee is less discernable by the taste, than by the different texture of the grounds. I always thought that the tea most resembled a weak vegetable-soup, floating grease being somewhat more apparent on it than on the coffee. But both decoctions are dished boiling hot, and this is their chief recommendation, inasmuch as the heat is pretty sure to dislodge any of the white bread-worms, say an inch long, which may lurk in the soaking biscuit.[7]

And anything was better than the water. 'He must slake his thirst with water of so high a temperature as to answer very well as an emetic, and of so powerful an odor frequently, when just pumped into the skuttle butt, as to make him hold his breath for a long interval after drinking it.'[8]

Unlike the British and French whalers, where alcohol was often part of the ration, most American ships were at least nominally dry if not formally Temperance. For refreshment the men manufactured switchel, a concoction of molasses, vinegar and water, with ginger for flavouring. If the captain would allow something a little stronger, there was swankey.

> . . . we built a big tank down in the hold, just abaft the mainmast. It was round and would hold forty or more barrels. Then we cut a number of bushels of potatoes, put them in the tank with a barrel or two of molasses, and filled it up with water . . . It would take nearly a year for it to ferment and then be about as strong as wine.[9]

Sunday was duff day, and we are indebted to Francis Olmstead for the 'receipt' (recipe) he coaxed from 'Mr Freeman', otherwise the *North America*'s 'doctor' (as black cooks were usually called).

> To a quantity of flour, more or less, (more would be preferable in Mr F's opinion), wet up with equal parts of salt and fresh water and well stirred, add a quantity of 'slush' or lard, and yeast; the mixture to be boiled in a bag, until it can be dropped from the top-gallant cross-trees upon deck, without breaking, when it is cooked.[10]

Slush was the fat skimmed from the boiler after salt meat had been cooked. Persuading the cook to part with some of it to spread on biscuit, or even to slush down the rigging, could be difficult; selling it at the conclusion of the voyage was one of his perquisites. Real variety in the diet was found only on the dinner menu, and even there it could be as regular as the calendar.

> *Monday* corn, beans and pork
> *Tuesday* codfish and potatoes
> *Wednesday* mush and beef
> *Thursday* corn, beans and pork
> *Friday* rice and beef
> *Saturday* codfish and potatoes
> *Sunday* beef and duff[11]

There were few chores associated with meals. The men sat around the communal kid on their sea-chests or the deck and extracted morsels with their sheath knives. A tin plate and mug completed the mess kit. There was no need to wash them afterwards; the cockroaches would attend to the scraps before the next meal. For clothes that became too stiff with dirt to wear there was the urine barrel to soften them and, after a trying out, the miraculous lye that could restore the greasiest fabric to its original condition.

> This whale lye completely emulsifies the oil and greasy substances, so that a jersey which would stand upright owing to the amount of contained fat, becomes, after being rubbed for a few minutes, as supple and clean as though it had never been dipped into any thing save fresh water.[12]

Fresh provisions were known to be essential if scurvy was to be avoided, and the keeping qualities of potatoes recommended them. Port visits to refresh were avoided, even when the potatoes were gone, because they presented opportunities to desert. Some captains kept at sea until crewmen were so incapacitated that they had to be lowered by rope into their boats to whale. The main symptoms were softening of the gums, painful inflammation of the joints and failure of open wounds to heal. Inability to chew

Receipts

Whale Balls
Ingredients Sperm whale brains, flour.
Preparation Break open the skull of a small sperm whale with an axe. Mince the brains (each lobe about the size of a pudding) and mix with the flour. Form into balls and fry.
Serve As a substitute for calf's head.
Variant Use minced porpoise meat instead of brains.

Lobscouse
Ingredients 3 buckets of hard bread, 7 pounds of salt pork and beef, ¼ pound of pepper.
Preparation Cut the meat into small pieces and break the bread into fragments. Add water and bring to the boil, stirring to mix. Reduce the heat, add the pepper and simmer until the meat is cooked.
Serve Smoking hot in a wooden kid. This quantity will serve all hands.
Variant For potato-scouse, substitute potatoes for some of the bread.

Whale's Lip
Ingredients Gelatinous outer edge of the right whale's lip.
Preparation Place in the hot oil of the cooler for about 6 hours, or until it becomes the consistency of jelly.
Serve With salt, pepper and vinegar. Closely resembles pig's feet.
Variant Often accompanied by the tubular shellfish from the nib of the whale's nose, similarly prepared.

Dandyfunk
Ingredients 4 buckets of hard bread, 2 pounds of salt pork fat, molasses to taste.
Preparation Chop the pork fat and break the bread into fragments. Add a little water and mix, then heat the mixture until lukewarm. Add molasses until the mixture is sweet. Increase heat and stir until boiling.
Serve Hot. Enough for all hands.

Variant For dundee-pudding, pound the bread and add sufficient flour with the water to make the mixture adhere.

Whale Steak à la Melville
Ingredients Steaks cut from the small of the sperm whale's back.
Preparation Hold the steak in one hand and 'show a live coal to it with the other'.
Serve Washed down with a pint of whale oil.
Variant For a rare steak, omit the coal.

hard rations further debilitated the sufferers, but the main challenge was to save teeth.

> The malady made frightful progress each day, and the least crippled among us had loosened teeth and decomposing gums. Several times I saw canines on the point of falling out, so much had they become exposed. One of our men plucked out two of his and showed them to me in the hollow of his hand. I immediately made him open his mouth, and I replaced them in their sockets, inserting them even more firmly than they had been previously, and advised him not to let them come out again, but, on the contrary, to press them home from time to time with his finger . . . Thanks to these instructions, which were followed to the letter, I obtained a complete success which our friends the dentists will probably scarcely credit. So much was this so that, after the disappearance of all effects of the scurvy, the teeth remained as firmly fixed as if they had never formed the idea of taking a voyage to foreign parts in their owner's hand.[13]

The whalemen's remedy for this scourge, now known to be caused by vitamin C deficiency, arouses scarcely less disbelief than reseating lost teeth, yet time and again their accounts insist that when invalids were taken ashore and buried up to their necks in earth for a day or so, improvement invariably followed. Even a land breeze was said to afford relief, although the land might be out of sight.

It would be wrong to think that in the absence of a port visit the only provisions aboard were those shipped at home. In the Pacific Islands, away from the ports, desertion was easier to control; the natives could usually be relied upon to return runaways to the ship for tobacco or trade goods. Fruit and coconuts were readily available, and in New Zealand and elsewhere potatoes and other vegetables were grown for the purpose of trading with whalemen as well as for domestic consumption. The most welcome addition to the whaleman's diet, however, was not fruit from a hothouse island but meat from a desert. The giant Galapagos tortoise was a self-maintained storehouse.

> I have known them to live several months without food; but they always in that case grow lighter and their fat diminishes . . . notwithstanding some writers have asserted to the contrary . . . Their flesh, without exception, is of as sweet and pleasant a flavour as any that I ever eat. It was common to take out of one of them ten or twelve pounds of fat, when they were opened, besides what was necessary to cook them with. This was as yellow as our best butter, and of a sweeter flavour than hog's lard.[14]

If stored in the dark of the hold they became dormant and lasted longer, up to eighteen months if the taller tales are to be believed. A reservoir at the base of the neck contained about two gallons of potable water, sweeter than any other stored at sea. Roasting in rock from their native islands was the preferred method of cooking.

> Place two pieces of . . . lava, with spoon-like cavities to catch the gravy, before the blazing fire, until they become frying hot. Then place the meat upon the stone with the largest cavity; lay a piece of sweet fat on top, sprinkle a little salt over it, and cover all with the second lump of lava. In a short time you will have a dish that none but good whalemen or honest landsmen deserve to eat.[15]

Sea as well as land provided the whalemen with bounty for the table, some of which was unfamiliar even to other seamen.

There was whalemeat in quantities beyond the most gargantuan appetite but, possibly because of this very excess, or because it was tough and fibrous, whale steak was not particularly favoured.

> The flesh of the whale is of a deep red colour, darker than beef, and appears full of blood; its flavour very much resembling that of black puddings. We had it frequently on table—sometimes stewed, sometimes in steaks, sometimes chopped up with onions and pepper, like sausage meat—and it is not a bad relish in any way, although I preferred it in the sausage manner.[16]

An alternative was whale's brains mixed with flour and fried as fritters. The greatest treat was doughnuts, made in industrial quantities during trying out watches. Cakes of dough were fried in the boiling oil or, if the cook were ungenerous, the men could make do with biscuit.

> The oil while cooking smelled so sweet and clean (like lard) that I got my share of the ship's bread served out to us, great square crackers so hard you need a hammer to break them, and held them in the boiling oil. They immediately became as tender as pie crust, and I gorged myself with them. But O! didn't I pay for my feast! It brought out boils all over me. I had twenty-six on me at once and thought of Job.[17]

It was perhaps to postpone the effects of such over-indulgence that on some ships the frying of doughnuts was prohibited until a thousand barrels had been taken.

One indulgence that no captain would have dared to regulate was the solace of nicotine. Whalemen smoked, chewed and inhaled tobacco in immense quantities, but that was the least of it. Aboard it served as currency, being good for wagers and ship's rewards like those for whale sighting. Smuggled ashore (and the Azorean authorities in particular took a dim view of this), it could be traded for anything the whaleman's heart desired. When it could be landed duty-free it was one of the captain's preferred trade goods, not to mention one of his main sources of profit from the slops chest. In 1844 it was estimated that each of the 242 American whalers fitted out for the sperm fishery that year had sailed with an average of 2500 pounds of tobacco, more than a ton per ship, as part of its outfit. In addition, many of the seamen on those ships would have taken as much as 50–70 pounds for personal use.

If the forecastle was the ship's hell hole, steerage was its purgatory. Here, just forward of the mizzenmast and adjacent to the main cabin, the boatsteerers and the 'idlers' (cooper, carpenter and steward) were almost as crowded as the men. The space where they enjoyed the separation that went with rank was named not for the boatsteerers but because it had housed the helmsman and the tiller in the days before ships were steered by wheel. All of those in the steerage had earned their places through merit and/or skill. Melville indicates that discrimination had no place there by making all of the *Pequod*'s boatsteerers exotic; Queequeg is a South Sea Islander, Daggoo a black African, Tashtego a Gay Head Indian, and Fedallah an 'oriental'. From steerage the boatsteerer could aspire to the heaven of the cabin, with its dining table and two-berth staterooms for the mates. Many non-whites made the transition. If particularly ambitious, a boatsteerer might fancy himself eventually in the holy of holies, the captain's stateroom. This, the most salubrious accommodation aboard, was a box perhaps 8 feet by 6 into which had to be crammed all the impedimenta needed for a four-year absence from home. Luxury took the form of a personal privy. Achieving this final dignity was far harder for a non-Yankee in American service than it was, for example, for a part-Maori on a New Zealand ship, but some succeeded. The Azorean Portuguese in particular worked hard at assimilation, and the colony they established in the New Bedford precinct known as Fayal produced some distinguished captains in the declining years of the industry.

The boatsteerer had a glimpse of the kingdom of heaven three times a day, for he and the other petty officers dined there as a 'second table' after the officers had finished. It was the only privilege of rank that meant anything in terms of personal well-being, and that mainly because of one item—flour. It was part of the standard weekly ration on Australian ships—7

pounds of biscuit, 3½ of flour, 10½ of meat, 1½ of sugar and 3½
ounces of tea—but discretionary on American vessels. There the
cook baked soft bread and such breakfast delicacies as slapjacks
(flapjacks), or flippers, but only for the cabin. Butter too figured
rather more prominently on the cabin table than in the forecastle
kid, but it was a mixed blessing. After three or four crossings of
the equator it was said to be indifferent as butter, but a passable
cheese. The cabin's duff included raisins (at 5 cents a pound),
while the forecastle had to be content with dried apples (at a
more economical 4 cents a pound). Otherwise the cabin ate what
the forecastle ate. Food was never far from the whaleman's
thoughts, probably because it was often so far from his stomach.

> Heave him up! O he yo!
>   Butter and cheese for breakfast.
> Raise the dead! O he yo!
>   The steward he's a makin' swankey.
> Heave away! O he yo!
>   Duff for dinner! Duff for dinner!
> Now I see it! O he yo!
>   Hurrah for the Cape Cod gals!
> Now I don't. O he yo!
>   Round the corner, Sally!
> Up she comes! O he yo!
>   Slap-jacks for supper!
> Re-re-ra-ra-oo-we ye yo ho!
>   Them's 'um![18]

An invisible line ran across the ship at the mainmast. Aft of it
was the quarterdeck, the captain's domain, although a landsman
would have been hard-pressed to show you where it began and
ended on a flush-decked ship. Foremast hands mustered there
only by direction, as when called to witness punishment or to be
addressed by the captain. Duty at the wheel took individual
seamen aft, but then only by the lee side, leaving the captain or
the officer of the watch in splendid isolation to windward. If for
some reason a foremast hand was summoned to the cabin, he
would leave his hat on the deck by the companionway.

Medical arrangements were primitive. British and French whalers by law carried doctors, but Americans were made of sterner stuff. One of the deductions from the seaman's lay was a contribution to the medical chest, which was usually of good quality, but if he was in need of something from it he was at the mercy of the captain's skill as a pharmacist. The ingredients in the chest were labelled with numbers and there were instructions about what to combine with which to treat that. One is reluctant to dismiss as altogether apocryphal the story of the captain who, having run out of number 9, dispensed a mixture of 4 and 5. Dentistry was taught in the same school.

> During the night I had had the toothache. It was still causing me a great deal of pain, so I went to the Mate and asked him to pull it out . . . he came out of the cabin with a pair of those old-fashioned tooth pullers in his hand . . . he looked into my mouth and found the right tooth, shoved the instrument of torture over it, and bringing a sudden jerk on it, brought it out of my mouth with the tooth in its claw . . . I remarked as soon as possible, that if he had no more use for my jaw to please put it back where he had taken it from. 'Pooh', he said, 'you will not miss the piece I have. It is not more than half an inch long.' He was right, I did not miss it, or some three or four more pieces that afterwards came out . . . 'Such times as these, people must not be too exacting', he said. I thanked him.[19]

If American whalers had carried medical officers, they would undoubtedly have tried to persuade the captains that morale was as important as diet and cleanliness in maintaining health, and that two of the keys to morale are recreation and exercise. They would have found that trial and error had led whalemen to the same conclusion, and that the leading agent in providing recreation and exercise aboard was none other than the 'doctor'. The cook was expected to be far more than a boiler of salt junk. After he had dispensed supper it would be 6 p.m. Then, during the last dogwatch, when all hands were expected to be on deck but the only duty was the wheel, he would take his fiddle to the windlass and invite 'the gentlemen to digest themselves into readiness to make a few molestations on the floor'. With more enthusiasm than skill, the seamen would then 'trip the light fantastic toe' until eight bells, when 'skylarking' ceased and regular watch-keeping resumed. Cook was also expected to do duty as the chantyman when there was windlass work.

His other function was as a safety valve. Olmstead could liken him to nothing so much as a court jester. On the *North America* he was Mr Freeman, Doctor, Spot, Jumbo, Kidneyfoot and Skillet—if Olmstead knew his real name, he kept it to himself.

> . . . although the captain and officers would consider it impairing their dignity to descend to any familiarity with the men, yet Spot is regarded as the privileged character on board, and the discipline is not relaxed by any amusement at his expense, which the captain and officers choose to indulge in. He receives a serio-comic punishment from the captain and officers every day, when his grimaces and exclamations are so ludicrous that I am sometimes almost faint with laughing. We call him down into the cabin now and then, and give him presents, to amuse ourselves with his elegant bows and expressive exclamations of satisfaction. He possesses all the negro accomplishments in full perfection, embellishing his conversation by the use of language in all the variations of which it is susceptible.[20]

Cook was less the butt of humour in the forecastle and more its instigator. He was able to make fun of the embarassments and humiliations of the men with a licence that taken by any other would have led to fighting. A thick coating of humour was laid on to make insolence palatable, and much was tolerated from a black man playing buffoon that would have been mortal offence from a white. Besides, in the galley cooks had opportunities to take terrible revenge if crossed. They are whaling's unsung heroes, their identities and dignity sacrificed in the cause of peace and harmony aboard. History has stripped most of them of individuality as well as identity, but occasionally a personality shines through the clutter of a white author's stereotyping to display qualities that, in a more equal world, would have taken their possessor far.

Britannia, the first Enderby whaler in Australian waters (Thomas Whitcombe, Departure of the Whaler Britannia from Sydney Cove, 1798; Nan Kivell Collection, National Library of Australia)

i Whales in Sight, A Shore Whaling Party
Coming Out of Twofold Bay, 1844 (*Mitchell
Library, State Library of New South Wales*)

ii Amateur Whaling, or a Tale of the Pacific,
1847 (*Australian National Maritime Museum*)

iii The Death Flurry *(National Library of Australia)*

iv South Sea Whalers Boiling Blubber, Boats Preparing to get Whale Alongside *(Dixson Galleries, State Library of New South Wales)*

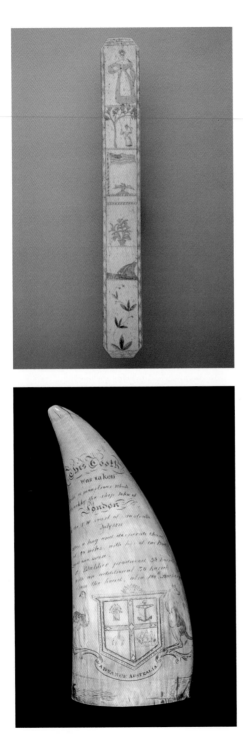

For the loved one at home—a scrimshaw busk (Australian National Maritime Museum)

A trophy of the chase—scrimshaw whale tooth recording a big catch by the John of London (Australian National Maritime Museum)

Coloured engraving by Edward Duncan, after WJ Huggins South Sea Whale Fishery:
A Representation of Boats Attacking a Sperm Whale, from Descriptions given by Experienced
Masters and Officers in the South Sea Fishery *(Australian National Maritime Museum)*

i 'Glad tidings to the whalemen—"There she blows!"
"There she blows!"'

ii 'The "flurry". He came rapidly onward towards the
captain's boat, throwing huge sheets of water on the
crew at every sweep of his gigantic tail, and filling it to
the very brim.'

iii 'The whale attacks the boat, seizes it in his huge jaws—perilous position of the crew.'

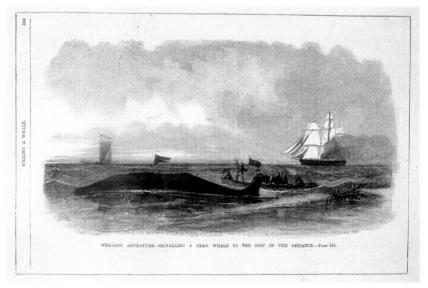

iv 'Signalling a dead whale to the ship in the distance.'

A record of the chase: Surgeon William Lewis Roderick of the London whaler Adventure scrimshawed this scene on a plaque taken from the lower jaw of a sperm whale (Whaling off the Islands of Flores & Pulo Comba in the Flores Sea, Indian Ocean, July 30 1853 (A Good Cut); *Nan Kivell Collection, National Library of Australia*)

OF CURRENTS AND BACKWATERS

We trust to establish satisfactorily that the course of the
great currents of the ocean, sweeping with them the
proper food of the great cetaceous animals, determines
not only the places to which they are in the habit of
resorting, but the seasons at which they are to be found
frequenting them.

Charles Wilkes, USN

The expansion of the American whaling fleet in the years after the War of 1812 was a matter of astonishment to contemporary observers and it hardly seems less so even today. In 1816, 61 whalers sailed from American ports, of which 38 were Nantucket-registered. Thirty years later, at its peak in 1846, the American whaling fleet numbered 722 vessels, about half of them sperm whalers, when the rest of the world could muster perhaps 230. If the Nantucketers had been able to maintain their dominance, more than 400 of those American vessels would have been theirs; in truth, their fleet had peaked in 1843 with 88 ships and over the following three years the number fell to 74. The bulk of the expansion was coming from elsewhere; to be precise, from New Bedford. In 1823 the village that had been burnt to the ground in the War of Independence sent more whalers to sea than

Nantucket. When the New Bedford fleet was at its largest—329 ships in 1857—it comprised nearly half of the world's whalers.

In this contest for world whaling supremacy between small towns only 80 kilometres apart, Nantucket had an insidious handicap. The island sand, so poor for crops that it had been responsible for driving the Nantucketers to sea in the first place, was also an obstacle when they tried to return. There had always been a bar across the entrance to the island's only port, but it was of no consequence to the small, light-draughted vessels with which Nantucket had started in the whale fishery. By the time the ships had grown to be 350 tons, however, the fathom and a half over the bar at high water was insufficient to float them across. If the chain cables were piled on one side of the deck to offset the keel, an empty ship might bluff her way through, bumping and rubbing, but loading and unloading had to be done outside the bar, which meant double handling—twice. The stevedores had no complaints, but the additional cost, estimated at $1000 per voyage, was anathema to the owners and there were many proposals for remedy. In 1828 a channel was dredged, but no breakwaters were constructed to create scouring currents and it quickly refilled. In 1842, with matters becoming critical, Peter Ewer was authorised to construct 'camels' on the Dutch pattern. These were a species of shallow draughted floating dock. Two 40-metre buoyant caissons, each concave on the inside to fit the side of a ship, and joined by fifteen heavy chains underneath, were flooded until their intended burden could be slid onto the chains. These were then tightened by windlass to make the ship snug and a steam engine pumped out the caissons. The whaler rose with them until the whole could be floated over the bar. It was ingenious and it worked, but it still involved additional cost.

Nantucket's other disability was human rather than hydrological. One of the consequences of the embargo and the War of 1812, a consequence that Jefferson had foreseen and feared as a threat to his ideal, the agrarian republic of self-sufficient freemen, had been the growth of manufacturing. So insistent was domestic demand that capital had turned to import-substitution. Where traditional avenues for capital investment were closed off, as the sea was to New England, the impetus was particularly strong, and places like New Bedford set aside the harpoon for the loom, at least for the time being. By the end of the war jenny was spinning at a such a rate that the British market for sperm oil, so long the arbiter of American whalemen's fortunes, had become an irrelevance. What did it matter that London was still the destination of 85 per cent of American sperm oil exports when 90 per cent of production was being consumed at home? The British found that their tariff barrier against American oil, while it might preserve their own fishery, was no longer an impediment to the American industry. By the late 1830s the Americans were producing four barrels to Britain's one.

The industrialisation of New England passed Nantucket by. The favoured child of the sea had found that its parent was a gaoler. During the war its means of setting up factories, importing raw materials and exporting finished product had all been at the mercy of the Royal Navy, which showed little. Obed Macy listed 77 long-term residents who emigrated to the mainland, many with their families. As far back as the 1790s it had no longer been possible to find Nattick Indians for whalemen and the last of them died in 1822. Gay Head Indians from Martha's Vineyard and American blacks from the mainland had taken their place. Macy thought the latter a mixed blessing because 'their inebriety and want of economy generally kept them poor, although they made great voyages'.[1] The census of 1820 counted 7000 whites and 274 'coloured persons' so the island was not depopulating, but as the whaling fleet alone required 2000 seamen it must have been difficult to man the ships, especially with a continuing outflow from the old families. As many as 600 individuals left in the 1820s. The position worsened in the 1830s and Nantucket, like New Bedford, was forced to accept what it could get, with singular ill-grace.

Too many ungovernable lads, runaways from parental authority, or candidate for corrective treatment, too many vagabonds just from the clutches of the police of European and American cities—too many convicts—. . . are suffered to enlist in this service . . . From materials thus gathered, it is not surprising that revolts, mutinies, and murders, conflagrations and immense destruction of property so frequently arise . . . The whale-fishery shall not be converted into a mere engine for the repair of cracked reputations and the chastisement of those against the reception of whom even the jail doors revolt.[2]

Scarce twelve months after this outburst, in 1837, the undesirables brought home the largest fare in the history of the American sperm fishery—5,329,138 gallons. The quantity drove the average price down from 89 to 82½ cents per gallon, but the gross return was still a record. The owners were pleased but not overjoyed. They were looking at the other side of the ledger. Productivity was declining. In each year of hunting throughout the decade 1816–25 the New Bedford barques took an average of 2.12 barrels of sperm oil per vessel ton; in 1826–35 the figure was 1.81; even though this was temporarily offset by increased averages for ship-rigged and smaller vessels, these too declined in the following decade. In 1836–45 the averages for the three classes of vessel fell to 1.06, 1.11 and 1.42 respectively.[3] There was an even more precipitous decline in the proportion of sperm oil taken. In 1827, 72½ per cent of all whale oil imported into the United States was sperm. By 1837 the figure was down to 45½ per cent and ten years later it was only 28 per cent.[4] The year 1845 was the last one in which importation exceeded 4 million gallons, but it was easier to blame the help than to admit that there might be too many ships or that sperm whales were scarcer and/or harder to find.

Other sources of labour, increasingly important as the years went on, were Portuguese-speakers from the Azores and the Cape Verde Islands, picked up on the outward passage, and the native peoples of the Pacific. There were Kanakas from Hawaii and the Marquesas, Maoris from New Zealand, Pitcairners resettled on Norfolk Island and Spanish speakers from Guam. They were universally valued for their keen sight and bravery in the hunt, but equally condemned as poor seamen, 'lazy and shiftless'. The industry's pool of casual labour was made up of white and native 'seasoners' who could be recruited in Pacific ports for a few months' cruise, and beachcombers who were usually deserters from other ships. The latter were regarded as much less reliable than natives, being apt to desert again as soon as they had drawn clothing from the slop chest and been fed at the ship's expense for a few days or weeks. It was a far cry from the tight-knit community of the previous century, in which Peleg Folger had been related to everyone else.

The economy and efficiency that continued to characterise Yankee whaling, even as productivity declined, carried with it scorn for the dependence of foreign whalemen on government financial support (although Americans were grateful for their own government's efforts to exclude seed oil imports). Where they wanted to see their taxes at work was in the protection of their assets at sea. Of the 750 vessels in the New Bedford fleet from 1816 to 1905, 231 failed to return from their last voyages. Insurance rates, usually around 2½ per cent, were not exorbitant but owners could nonetheless be relied on to support any government initiative that might lower them. The United States Navy might not be much use against Acts of God but it could certainly raise the hand of wrath against natives, renegades, mutineers and the other maritime low-life that threatened the property of the whaling merchants in the South Seas. Enter Jeremiah Reynolds.

Reynolds was an Ohio lawyer who had been seduced by books of travel and discovery long before he ever saw the ocean. He became a one-man lobby for an exploring expedition to the Pacific Ocean but, conscious of the need for allies, built into his case the need to protect American commerce. In 1828 he petitioned the House of Representatives, producing letters of support from senior state politicians the length of the Atlantic seaboard. He furnished the Committee on Naval Affairs with a report on, principally, 'the nature and extent of the whale-fishery, and of its importance to the welfare of our country', and received timely support from his friends in Nantucket, whence came most of his information.

> The increased extent of the voyages now pursued by the trading and whaling ships into seas but little explored, and in parts of the world before unknown, has increased the cares, the dangers and the losses of our merchants and mariners. Within a few years, their cruises have extended from the coasts of Peru and Chili to the Northwest coast, New Zealand and the isles of Japan. This increase of risk has been attended by an increase of loss. Several vessels have been wrecked on islands and reefs not laid down on any chart: and the matter acquires a painful interest from the fact, that many ships have gone into those seas, and no soul has survived to tell their fate. Your petitioners consider it a matter of earnest importance that those seas should be explored; that they should be surveyed in an accurate and authentic manner, and the position of new islands, and reefs, and shoals, definitely ascertained. The advancement of science, and not their private interest only, but the general interests of the nation, seem, to them, imperiously to demand it.[5]

There was general political support, but when it came to the point the Navy did not have a suitable vessel and Congress procrastinated about finding the money. Andrew Jackson's veto, exercised on his accession to the presidency in January 1829, scuttled the project as an official expedition, but matters had been sufficiently far advanced for Reynolds to arrange with Edmund Fanning for the charter of two brigs. Fanning, himself a thwarted Antarctic explorer whose ambitions had been frustrated by political developments (in his case by the War of 1812), adopted the Enderby approach. With New Bedford confederate Benjamin Rodman he engaged his old associates Benjamin Pendleton and Nathaniel Palmer to command the *Seraph* and *Annawan*. They allowed Reynolds to go along with Palmer as half of a two-man 'scientific corps'. The expedition's first mission was to search for land west of Palmer's Land and south-west of Cape Horn. They found nothing, not even the seals that would have paid their way, for the crew members were mainly on a lay in lieu of wages. When scurvy threatened, Pendleton bore away for Chile. There most of the crew deserted. With barely enough men left to work the brigs, Pendleton was forced to abandon the expedition. The only commercial information obtained was that south-west of Chiloe Island on the Chilean coast there was a feeding ground for sperm whales between September and December, and that right whales could be found inshore there until March. Pendleton gloomily reported to Fanning.

> . . . I am now convinced from experience in this enterprise, that an exploring expedition, under private means, never can produce any great of important national benefits, the same must be under authority from the government, and the officers and men under regular pay and discipline, as in the navy. Had our companies been thus situated, I have no hesitation in saying, your instructions would have been carried fully into effect, the result of which would have been highly beneficial to the commerce, navigation, whale and seal fishery, &c, of our nation.[6]

Reynolds stayed in Chile and spent the next four years on and off the Pacific coast of South America. At Valparaiso he was offered the post of private secretary by the captain of the USS *Potomac*. This was no other than John Downes, Porter's second-in-command and erstwhile commander of the *Essex Junior*. After returning to the United States, Reynolds volunteered to write an account of the *Potomac*'s cruise and took the opportunity to agitate once more for protection of the whaling interest. The main threat, as he perceived it, was carried into the Pacific by the whaling masters themselves. He quoted the complaint of the US consul at Honolulu.

> I have never before seen so much the importance of having a vessel of war stationed at these islands, for the protection of the whale-fishery; there has hardly been one vessel in the harbour that has not had more or less difficulties. I have at one time had sixty Americans confined in irons at the fort; and hardly a day has passed that I have not been compelled to visit one or more ships to quell a mutiny, or compel by force whole crews to their duty, who had united to work no longer. I should say, too, that there were over one hundred deserters now on shore from the American ships this season, regular outlaws, ready to embark in any adventure.[7]

The whaling masters blamed 'a class of worthless keepers of grog-shops, who entice away and conceal their men, to the great hazard, and even ruin of their voyages'. One bright spot was the newly founded Colombian colony on the Galapagos Islands, whose governor had turned it into something of a reformatory for his subjects. There was no alcohol. The first execution was for an attack on an American whaleman. Minor offences were punished by shipping the offender off on a short-handed whaler for a cruise of six, eight or ten months. Masters availing themselves of this service were bound to return the recruit before leaving for the United States. Reynolds thought that this was an admirable arrangement: 'the whaler is benefited, the offender punished, and also improved by a knowledge of a new business, and by earning something for himself'.

Back in New York in 1834, Reynolds renewed his campaign for an exploring expedition. The growth of the whaling fleet was his principal argument and, like all successful publicists, he was acutely aware that one dramatic instance of the need for protection was worth a thousand generalisations. There was no shortage of examples, and when in 1836 he was allowed to make his case in the hall of the House of Representatives, he chose to remind his audience of the loss of the *Mentor*.

On 21 May 1832 the New Bedford whaler *Mentor*, master Edward Barnard, was caught in a gale and wrecked near midnight on an uncharted reef off the Palau Islands, east of the Philippines. Eleven of the 22 crewmen were lost attempting to get ashore. On the following morning another boat was launched and made for the nearest land, about 2 miles distant. The first natives they encountered stole from them but were no threat, unlike the 30 canoes that descended on them shortly thereafter. These newcomers were more interested in the wreck than the boat, but one canoe remained with it, offering to tow them to shore. The folly of accepting quickly became apparent and plunder was only avoided by cutting the tow rope. The Americans made their escape seawards under a hail of missiles that badly injured one of them. A day later they reached another island, whose inhabitants seemed more kindly disposed; although they were stripped, they were given refreshment while the island's prophetess was asked what should be done with them. Into this scene came a chief who, to the astonishment of the Americans, addressed them in English. Charles Washington had deserted from HMS *Lion* 29 years earlier and through his good offices the Americans got their clothes back, were given a house to live in and were well fed without being called on to do any work in return.

The only cloud on the horizon of this seaman's paradise was the prospect of having to endure it forever, and they tried to construct a boat. When that failed they induced the natives, by promise of 200 muskets, to build them a canoe. Five months after landing they again took to the sea, steering south-west for the Moluccas. Three of their number remained on the island as hostages for the reward. The canoe proved unseaworthy and soon all were crowded into their old ship's boat. After six weeks' passage and at the end of their provisions they came in sight of Lord North's Island, or Tobi. They received the by-now familiar rough reception from the local canoe fleet, but this time matters did not subsequently improve. They were distributed as possessions among the local dignitaries and put to work. The islanders themselves lived close to starvation and the Americans fared worse. Two months later a ship was seen off the island. Captain Barnard and Bartlett Rollins contrived to escape but could do nothing for their compatriots, who found themselves blamed for the escape and treated even worse than formerly. As their condition deteriorated and they began to fail, one by one they were turned out to fend for themselves, as was the islanders' custom with their own people. Peter Andrews was beaten to death for some obscure offence. After nineteen months only two of the men, Horace Holden and Benjamin Nute, remained alive. As it seemed that they might live after all, the natives decided that they should be tattooed.

We expostulated against it—we entreated—we begged to be spared this additional affliction: but our entreaties were of no use. Those savages were not to be moved . . . We were in the first place securely bound down to the ground, and there held by our tormentors. They then proceeded to draw with a sharp stick the figures designed to be imprinted on the skin. This done, the skin was thickly punctured with a little instrument made of sharpened fish bones, and somewhat resembling a carpenter's adze in miniature, but having teeth, instead of a smooth, sharp edge. This instrument was held within an inch or two of the flesh, and struck into it rapidly with a piece of wood, applied to it in such a manner as to cause it to rebound at every stroke. In this way our breasts and arms were prepared; and subsequently the ink, which was made of a vegetable found on the island . . . was applied. The operation caused such an inflammation of our bodies, that only a portion could be done at one time; and as soon as the inflammation abated another portion was done, as fast as we could bear it, till our bodies were covered. It was effectually done; for to this day the figures remain as distinct as they were when first imprinted, and the marks will be carried by us to the grave.[8]

They drew a line of their own when the natives wanted to start on their faces. They would rather die, they said, and were left alone. They were nonetheless obliged to pluck all of their body hair and, every ten days, their beards, an operation that became increasingly painful as the chin hair grew harder and stiffer with each repetition. By September 1834 Holden and Nute were at the end of their endurance; near death, they persuaded their captors that they would be more use alive than dead if put aboard a ship for a reward. The natives agreed and ceased both working and feeding them. For two months they 'crawled from place to place, subsisting on leaves, and now and then begging of the natives a morsel of cocoa-nut' until they were surrendered to the British barque *Britannia*, en route to Canton. Short, her commander, gave the natives what he could and brought the men on board. He was sure that another two or three days would have seen the death of Nute. The whalemen returned to the United States in May 1835 after an absence of four years, two of which had been spent in captivity.

Reynolds made much of this story, which he had from Holden

personally, because it combined the hazards of uncharted reefs with the abuse of unprotected American citizens. He was able to make another point by reference to proceedings on Palau after Barnard and the others had left. The three hostages were held in different parts of the islands and two were subsequently released, presumably ransomed by a passing ship. Young Carl Alden was not so lucky and remained for over a year with his captors, who treated him well. One day they put out to a passing whaler to trade and the captain took a shine to one of their canoes. The chief who owned it was not disposed to trade for the few old muskets offered but, after being kept on board the ship for four days while she rode out a gale, said he would agree if the captain would return him to his own settlement, now some distance away. Instead the captain forced the chief to swim ashore to a part of the coast controlled by his enemies and then sailed off with the canoe, the muskets and Alden. The chief survived and, according to his own testimony, would recognise the captain and officers should he meet them again, in which case his spear would 'drink their heart's blood'. Reynolds did not blame him, particularly as his intended revenge would not be indiscriminate, which was all too often the case.

> Although personal experience, during an intercourse of years with our South Sea whaling captains, enables us to bear testimony to their intelligence, great enterprise, and humanity, as a body; yet there are necessarily exceptions to this general character. Among a class so daring and adventurous, it is not surprising that we occasionally meet with unprincipled men—and what profession or pursuit in life in which they may not be found?—who require to be held in subjection by the arm of coercive power, and the dread of legal penalties. To persons of this stamp, the South Sea trade and fishery open a wide field for the indulgence of their vicious propensities. Placed beyond the reach of penal influence, governed by no other law than their own will, it is not wonderful such men should be guilty of oppression and violence in their dealings with the natives. The savage does not pause to discriminate between individuals, and the flagitious act of one man may consign hundreds of his fellows to captivity or massacre.[9]

Reynolds got his exploring expedition but, alas, not the post of its 'historiographer', which he had long coveted and to which, if devotion to the cause had been any criterion, he was more than entitled. It is much to his credit that he persevered with his agitation in favour of the expedition even after it was obvious that the Secretary of the Navy considered him an annoyingly influential crank. The address in the House of Representatives was his swan song.

> We feel that we have discharged our duty, and that the subject is now committed to other hands, to be disposed of by those whose decision will have no connexion with our individual feelings or wishes, nor do we wish that it should . . . The time was, when we felt differently—far differently—but that time has gone by. For us there is no disappointment in store. We sought adventure, and have had it without the aid of patronage and government.[10]

Two years went by before the government could find the ships or a commander. In the end a long-serving but relatively junior officer, Lieutenant Charles Wilkes, was given USS *Vincennes*, USS *Peacock*, USS *Porpoise*, some smaller tenders, and an immense task. He was to explore and survey the great Southern Ocean, 'having in view the important interests of our commerce embarked in the whale-fisheries and other adventures', to determine doubtful islands and shoals, and discover those along the frequented tracks that had escaped Cook and his successors. Among other things, he was to look for harbours of refreshment and refuge for the whalers. He was forbidden to interfere with the natives or to use force against them except in self-defence, or if there were a need to defend lives and property 'placed within reach of your protection'. Instead, he was to appeal to the goodwill of the natives 'until it shall become apparent that they can only be restrained from violence by fear or force'.

Between 1838 and 1842 Wilkes' little squadron found, fixed and surveyed scores of islands, reefs and shoals. South of Australia he charted a longer stretch of the Antarctic coastline than had hitherto been seen. It must all have seemed relatively straightforward compared with the task of conducting relations with the natives. Wherever the expedition touched among the islands, there seemed to be aggrieved islanders or whalers—or both—appealing to him for redress. The main problem, as he was only too acutely aware, was that his power to mediate or protect extended no further inland than the range of his guns—not even that far where shoal and reef kept his larger vessels in the offing—and then only so long as they were in sight. Wilkes knew that as he could not permanently overawe he must treat. In Samoa he successfully negotiated rules and regulations for the reception of foreign vessels. They embraced protection for consuls, ships and shipwrecks, apprehension of murderers and deserters, and the prohibition of alcohol. In return, the chiefs were to have port charges and pilotage. It was a significant advance, and Wilkes immediately tested the arrangements by asking the chiefs to give up Opotuno, a notorious murderer of American whalemen.

One of Opotuno's more recent atrocities had been to intercept two boats from the Falmouth whaler *William Penn*, killing the first mate and two boatsteerers. The third mate had been left on the beach for dead, but was found and nursed back to health by native women. He did not rejoin his ship, perhaps because the sense of social responsibility that he had found on the beach was so clearly superior to that in the whale fleet: Captain Lewis Tobey of the *Swift*, short of a boat or two, had purchased the stolen craft from Opotuno knowing their bloody history. No questions had been asked. Wilkes had first tried to capture Opotuno by stratagem. Under a pretence of surveying, Captain Hudson of USS *Peacock* was sent to Savaii and with just two men walked into Opotuno's village. They were a mile from the security of the boats. Far from fleeing, the chief contemplated shooting Hudson but was persuaded by his followers that the act would bring great retribution. Instead he simply faded into the mountains, as he had some years earlier when the USS *Vincennes* had been sent to Samoa expressly to apprehend him.

Much as the other chiefs disliked Opotuno for offences against them they would not agree to retrospective operation of the regulations, but neither would they stand in the way of American efforts to take him. Honour was satisfied all around when the chiefs agreed to publish a 'wanted—dead or alive' poster offering a large reward. It was nailed to a pillar of the council house but, to no-one's surprise, elicited no response. Fifteen months later Hudson returned to Samoa to conclude unfinished business and attempted to take a number of chiefs hostage for the surrender of Opotuno. They were as skilful as he at disappearing when necessary, and the episode would have undermined whatever faith the Samoan chiefs had in American notions of justice.

Agreements regulating relations with American whalers were also drawn up with the chiefs of Fiji and the Sultan of Sulu. The success of the former can be judged by the fact that the expedition here lost two officers, one of them Wilkes' nephew, when the natives of Malolo attacked his surveying boats. The difficulty was that the islands were in a state of perpetual upheaval in which the goodwill of one chief, or even a group of them, was no guarantee for the behaviour of others. At Malolo reprisal seemed the only option and 57 Fijians died. In another incident a chief named Vendovi, who had been responsible for the killing and eating of a number of American seamen, was surrendered, but again only after hostages had been seized. He readily confessed and showed no contrition for what he clearly regarded as normal behaviour. His followers were even aggrieved that the seamen, especially a Negro, had tasted of tobacco. Vendovi was taken back to the United States in irons and died in hospital soon after arrival. It was a futile demonstration of commitment to order in the midst of chaos, but Wilkes was convinced that he had improved matters.

> The character of the navigation in a sea abounding with reefs and shoals, of which no chart possessing any claim to confidence has hitherto been published, has not been the cause of less danger than the treachery, covetousness, and cannibal propensities of the inhabitants. Eight vessels, of which five were American, are known to have been lost within the Feejee Group between the years 1828 and

1840. In one of these instances every soul on board perished . . .
Considering how small a number of vessels have as yet visited these
islands, these instances of total or partial loss bear an enormous
proportion to those of escape without injury. I confidently trust that
the labours of our squadron will have so far diminished the risks
which have previously attended communication with this group, as to
render a visit to them much less perilous.[11]

Wherever the squadron went, Wilkes took a keen interest in
the doings of the whalers. Much of what he saw of his own
countrymen offended him, not least as a seaman. Early in the
voyage he encountered the *America*, of Hudson, homebound and
leaky 35 days out from New Zealand. The master, Topham, was
nonetheless in high spirits, as well he might be with 3800 barrels
stowed after only eighteen months out. Wilkes was happy for the
opportunity to send letters home, but

I have seldom seen at sea a more uncombed and dirty set than his
crew. How they preserve any tolerable state of health I know not, and
it is not at all surprising that the ravages of scurvy should be felt on
board of some vessels belonging to the whaling fleet, if this is the
state in which they are kept.[12]

He subsequently learnt that appearances counted for very little
and that American whalemen were still enjoying their traditional
superiority. He was in Sydney at the height of its whaling boom
and noted that the colonists had the advantage of short voyages
to the grounds, but concluded that they were not as skilful,
economical or enterprising as the Americans.

I heard many complaints that our whalers were in the habit of taking
whales and obtained much of their oil in the bays of the western
coast of New Holland; and the remark was made, that if the colonists
were not brought into collision with the Yankees, they would succeed
well enough. This, I suppose, may be considered as complimentary to
the energy and skill of this enterprising portion of our citizens.[13]

Not that the colonists deferred to these superior beings. Wilkes felt
that few places surpassed Australia and New Zealand for 'the
commission of all kinds of vice', and rivalry among whalers frequently led to conflict and bloodshed which the British authorities

seemed disposed to ignore. At the Bay of Islands the American
consul was petitioned by the master and crew of the New Bedford
whaler *Adeline* for action against pirates at Kapiti. One of their
boats had been towing a raft of water casks out to the ship when
it was intercepted by a whaleboat in the charge of James Harrison,
of Raymond and Young's station. Harrison, whose men were
armed,

> forcibly took possession of the boat and cut off the raft, threatening
> instant death to any one who should make resistance. Having thus
> captured the boat, they at once made sail, and ran for their
> establishment, on the shore, about six miles distant. The captain, on
> perceiving the piratical act, at once followed with two boats, but did
> not succeed in overtaking them until they reached the shore and had
> hauled the captured boat up on the beach. While on his way he was
> pursued by another boat, which kept firing at him. The captured boat
> was surrounded on the beach by from thirty to forty desperate-looking
> wretches, more or less armed. Of these, Harrison became the
> spokesman, declaring that they had taken the boat and meant to keep
> it, at the risk of his and all the party's lives, to which speech they all
> signified their assent. Captain Brown repeatedly cautioned them
> against such acts of piracy; but his caution was received with curses
> and all kinds of abuse, and finally a pistol was presented, with the
> declaration that he, Harrison, would blow out the brains of Captain
> Brown if he attempted to rescue the boat.[14]

Wilkes decided that he could not afford to be diverted from
the program laid out in his instructions every time his intervention
was sought: there were 100 American vessels whaling off the coast
of New Zealand alone in the spring of 1840. Besides, he believed
that in the long run his work as a navigator and oceanographer
would be far more beneficial to the whaling interest than anything
he could do as an itinerant US marshal. And so it was that the
last chapter of his five-volume narrative was not narrative at all,
but sailing directions for whalemen based on the expedition's
work on ocean currents.

Wilkes' current log was only able to measure surface currents
and therefore told only a partial tale. He was also aware that the
expedition was seldom in the one place for long enough to

observe seasonal variation in the ocean currents. Given these limitations, the model he constructed was impressive, and is easiest understood by reference to its operation in the Pacific, where it was least distorted by the influence of landmasses. He drew attention to what he called 'eddies', about 300 miles wide and lying along the 30° parallel in both hemispheres, 'in which the polar and equatorial flow of waters neutralize each other, and where therefore, all the floating matter that is brought by both must accumulate'. Among this floating matter was the 'gelatinous medusa' on which the sperm whales fed. Spawned in high latitudes in summer, the squid would be carried towards the equator by submarine polar currents in the winter months; they seemed to be most prolific in the eddies or nearer the equator where islands like the Galapagos interrupted the submarine current and brought the cold water favoured by the squid closer to the surface. 'The sperm whale, it must be expected, will leave the higher latitudes and follow the currents which transport his food.'

Although the theory explained sperm whale migration, Wilkes conceded that too little was then known of the natural history of the squid and of the submarine polar currents to predict whale movements. But the whaling captains knew. They had to anticipate the migrating whales on the cruising grounds if they were to have first cut of the year's harvest. Wilkes valued their information, even though it was sometimes contradictory, because they succeeded or failed by it.

> By a large majority of persons, it is believed that the whale-fishery is a mere lottery, in which success is more owing to good luck than to good management. Those, however, who entertain such an opinion, are in error. There is, perhaps, no employment on the ocean wherein a sound judgement is more necessary, and no business where success depends more upon the experience, enterprise, and industry, of the commander, than in that of whaling.[15]

He absorbed the experience of the most successful commanders he encountered and digested it into a system of ocean belts.

The Kraken

For centuries seamen frightened landlubbers with tales of a sea monster as big as a ship, with arms long enough to wrap around a vessel and strong enough to drag it down. It acquired literary form when Erik Pontoppidan mentioned this 'kraken' in his *Natural History of Norway* (1752–53) being responsible for whirlpools when it submerged. In the 1830s Frederick Bennett, who had seen the 'solid masses of enormous size and weight' of squid vomited up by dying sperm whales, speculated about 'an animal with which naturalists are but little acquainted; but which has been known to attain such huge dimensions, that, when spread out beneath the surface of the sea, it has alarmed navigators by its resemblance to a reef, or shoal'. Sperm whales were sometimes seen to bear circular marks the size of a dinner plate about their heads. Naturalists compared these with the tiny suction cups of the common octopus and squid and could only speculate about the size of a creature capable of leaving such an impression.

Off Sumatra in the 1870s, Frank Bullen's ship took a sperm whale which, as they often did, gave up its last meal. Some of the pieces ejected were estimated to be the size of the hatch house, i.e. 8 feet by 6 feet by 6 feet. That night, while on watch, he saw in the moonlight a commotion in the water some distance from the ship.

> Getting the night-glasses out of the cabin scuttle, where they were always hung in readiness, I focussed them on the troubled spot . . . A very large sperm whale was locked in deadly conflict with a cuttle-fish, or squid, almost as large as himself, whose interminable tentacles seemed to enlace the whole of his great body. The head of the whale especially seemed a perfect network of writhing arms—naturally, I suppose, for it appeared as if the whale had the tail part of the mollusc in his jaws, and, in a business-like, methodical way, was sawing through it. By the side of the black columnar head of the whale appeared the head of the great squid, as awful an object as one

could well imagine even in a fevered dream. Judging as carefully as possible, I estimated it to be at least as large as one of our pipes [casks], which contained 350 gallons; but it may have been, and probably was a good deal larger. The eyes were very remarkable from their size and blackness, which, contrasted with the livid whiteness of the head, made their appearance all the more striking. They were, at least, a foot in diameter, and, seen under such conditions, looked decidedly eerie and hobgoblin-like . . . So the titanic struggle went on, in perfect silence as far as we were concerned, because, even had there been any noise, our distance from the scene of conflict would not have permitted us to hear it. [*Cruise of the Cachalot*, pp. 143–4]

Such tales were regarded as wonderful even in Bullen's day, although, as he pointed out, some specimens were by then available for study. His observations, supposing them to be genuine, are well within the bounds of possibility. At 60 feet, a large sperm whale is only slightly longer than the largest known specimen of *Architeuthis princeps*, the colossus of molluscs, which with tentacles extended is 59 feet. Sightings off the coast of Norway are not unknown.

- *Equator to the Tropic of Cancer*: south of Hawaii and west to the Mulgrave Islands at most times; west of Galapagos in the 'season'.
- *Tropic of Cancer to 50° north*: coast of Japan to north-west coast of America and California from May to November; Bonin Islands to the coast of Japan in July; north of Hawaii between 28°–35° north and 145°–165° west from June to October; north-west coast of America in August and September; coast of California in November and January.
- *Equator to the Tropic of Capricorn*: coast of South America to the

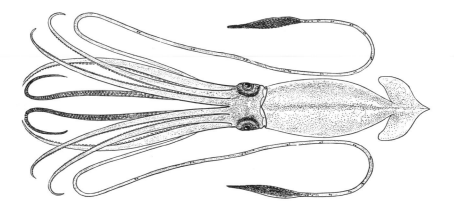

The kraken, one-sixtieth scale (from G B Goode's The Fisheries and Fishery Industries of the United States, *National Library of Australia)*

Kingsmill Islands, including the Marquesas, Tahiti, Tonga, Samoa and Fiji, in July and August; Offshore Ground between Galapagos and Marquesas in July and August; stragglers at all seasons.

• *Tropic of Capricorn to 50° south*: east of New Zealand from March to May; from May, between 22° and 28° south from the coast of New Holland to the coast of South America.

Comparing their experience with his eddies and 'spaces of no current', Wilkes found the coincidence striking, and he was so bold as to predict that with more oceanographic information 'theory may serve in some degree to shorten the apprenticeship which is now necessary in order to acquire the requisite knowledge of the places and seasons wherein to meet the game in this adventurous employment'. Although his data was ambiguous in some respects, he was prepared to assert that the reason sperm whales were to be found around certain islands between the beginning and the end of summer was that they had been moving with the currents until they found concentrations of squid, and there they stayed until the food was exhausted.

In the map he published to illustrate the whaling grounds Wilkes combined his two tropical belts, and the three belts so arrived at have largely been confirmed by twentieth-century research. In the Pacific there are several discrete stocks of sperm whales, but the great divide between them is the equator. In both hemispheres the whales are found in the middle latitudes in summer and move closer to the equator in winter. Those seemingly present along the equator at all times of year are not permanent residents but tourists. Escaping in their turn from the northern and southern winters respectively, they keep the tropical resorts full all the year round.

If the whales had itineraries it stood to reason that whalers needed them too, and like a good travel agent Wilkes offered alternative tours of all the best spots tailored to one's preferred date of departure. An autumn sailing from New England taking the Cape of Good Hope route would get you to the New Zealand ground in good time to recuperate before the start of the season in March: as winter approached it would be best to move east between 22° and 28° south, arriving off the coast of Chile in September and ready to go north for the Offshore season in November. Late arrivals could start at Tonga in June, head north and west with the season to Samoa and Fiji, continue eddying south to the Middle Ground and then join up with next year's crowd in New Zealand the following March. If you preferred to sail at the beginning of summer, the better route was around Cape Horn, which would get you to the Offshore Ground for November after recruiting in Peru or Chile: after one to three months you should move west and north, via the Marquesas and the Mulgrave Islands, to the coast of Japan, thence to the northwest coast of America and California, finally reaching Hawaii to recruit in October or November. Alternatively, as the whaling was good around Hawaii from February to April, it could be visited

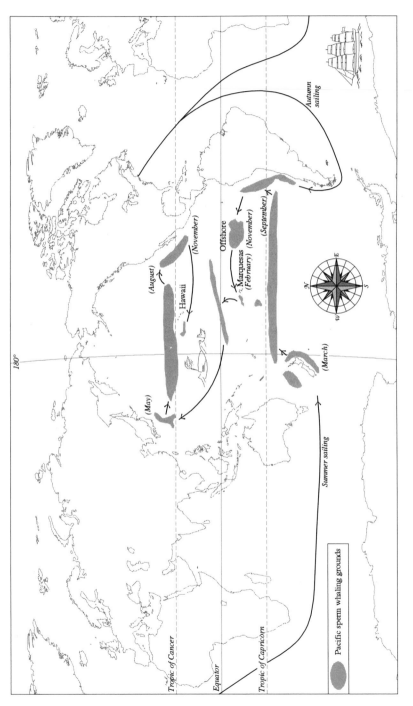

Charles Wilkes' Pacific itineraries for sperm whalers

immediately after the Offshore Ground, this to be followed in turn by a cruise westward along 30° north until October, when the party could join up again in Hawaii. Wouldn't it be crowded? Not at all, said Wilkes; 'there is ample room for a vast fleet to operate in these numerous and extensive spaces, without the vessels interfering with each other, and many more might be advantageously employed'.

Although the picture was more complicated in the Atlantic and Indian Oceans, Wilkes held that here too the most successful grounds were associated with the obstruction or termination of submarine currents, and that the seasons for exploiting them coincided with the movement of squid towards the equator. The Atlantic offered the prospect of cut-rate cruises using smaller vessels. The 'plum pud'n'ers' sailed east to the Azores for the summer, thence south to the Cape Verde Islands, across to South America, north to the Caribbean for January and February, were at Yucatan and Cuba in April, and sailed via the Gulf of Mexico to the Bahamas and Cape Hatteras in May, finishing on the eastern side of the Grand Banks of Newfoundland. The longer sweep, south of the equator, took the larger Atlantic vessels along the same track as far as the coast of Brazil but then turned south to take in the River Plate in January and February, the Carroll ground to the south-east of St Helena in March, April and May, and took them home via the South American coast, the Windward Islands and the Bahamas.

Not surprisingly, Wilkes' information was sketchiest for the Indian Ocean, which the expedition visited only in transit: here he recommended southern Madagascar in March and April, the Mozambique Channel in May, June and July, and then north along the African coast to the Comoros Islands. During the north-east monsoon, from October to April, some ships cruised the Arabian coast. The Chagos Archipelago south of India was doubtful and little frequented. The best profit was to be had was on the west and north-west coasts of Australia, as far north as Java and Timor and as far west as the Cocos Islands. The English were reported to have had some success in the Sulu Sea, but to American whalemen it was an unknown.

And what did Wilkes conclude about the issue that was agitating sperm whalemen like no other?

> An opinion had indeed gained ground within a few years that the whales are diminishing in numbers; but this surmise, as far as I have learned from the numerous inquiries, does not appear to be well founded. They have indeed become wilder, or as some of the whalers express it, 'more scary', and, in consequence, not so easy to capture; but if we consider the numbers that continue to be yearly taken, there will, I think, be no reason to suppose that any great decrease has occurred. On an average, it requires fifty whales to fill a ship, and it would therefore take about five thousand whales annually, to supply the quantity of oil that is imported . . . Of late years there has been much fluctuation in the price of oil, which has caused those to make losing voyages who returned at the time of its depression; but at the steady prices of eighty-five cents per gallon for sperm oil . . . voyages would generally yield a handsome return.[16]

He believed that better attention to the well-being of whaling crews was the key to improving both efficiency and standards of behaviour in the industry, hence his emphasis on rest and re-creation, not least as a ward against scurvy. Better accommodation and rations would also help, as would an end to the price-gouging that went with regarding the slops chest as a perquisite of the master rather than a source of reasonably priced necessities and comforts for the crew. Warships stationed on the grounds during the season could support the consuls in their adjudications between masters and men, saving owners much time and expense, and might reduce the numbers of beachcombers created by unscrupulous masters who turned men out of their ships for the least cause near the end of a voyage to cheat them of their pay. Some of the resources currently devoted to missionary activity would still indirectly serve that cause if they were directed to improving the condition and morals of seamen.

> Our ships might, by proper exertions at home, be soon made to carry on every breeze, to the ports and islands of the Pacific, such an

example as would promote the great cause of morality, religion and temperance . . . and instead of our 'tars' being considered, as they now frequently are, worthless reprobates, opposed to everything that is sacred, they will be found a band of industrious advocates in the cause of civilization.[17]

It was, in fact, a precondition for successful missionary activity among the natives. The bad example of the whalers was everywhere. Ironically, on his return to Washington Wilkes found that some of his own actions were unacceptable. There was criticism of his reprisal at Malolo and he was court-martialled and reprimanded for illegal punishment of some of his crew.

The expedition returned to the United States at the time Nantucket was beginning its experiment with the camels. Within a few years they were rusting on the beach. The final blow to the island's whaling industry came with the California gold rush. At the outset Nantucket whalers were numbered amongst the vast abandoned fleet that choked the port of San Francisco, but so were whalers from many of the other New England ports. More ominous was the use of fourteen Nantucket whalers, one of them commanded by George F Joy, who featured in George Gould's little drama, to transport the young men of the island to the diggings in 1849. They were followed by another four in 1850. Altogether, more than 400 men left and many never returned. Only seven of the ships came back and only two, the *Edward* and the *Citizen*, ever resumed whaling from Nantucket. By the late 1850s the fleet could be counted on the fingers of one hand. The *Oak*, Nantucket's last, was sold at Panama in 1872. The island that had taught the world how to catch the cachalot, and had endured through revolution and war, finally succumbed to natural disadvantage and the lure of other American adventures. Wilkes' currents and eddies held the promise of good whaling still to come but they could not keep open the Nantucket bar: the island had become a backwater.

Trouble in Paradise

For most of the nineteenth century the independent
Kingdom of Hawaii was ground between the upper and
nether millstones of evangelical American missionaries and
godless American whalemen. Contemporary opinion was in
two minds about which of them did most damage to the
social fabric of the islands. Alcohol brought out the worst
in the whalemen when ashore, but attempts to control it
by licensing its distribution pleased the Temperance lobby
little better than it did the sailors.

To His Excellency John Young, Governor of Maui
Sir
    We regret most sincerely the affray that took place on
Saturday last, resulting in the serious, if not fatal injury, to
not only one of your own countrymen, but also to a
number of seamen, many, if not all of whom were injured,
being peaceable men, not being concerned in the riot . . .
    It is absolutely necessary, for the preservation of the
health of our crews, that they should have liberty on shore
as much as possible—being, as often the case, seven or
eight months at sea, and it is our wish that liberty should
not be abused; but we PROTEST against being held
responsible for the conduct of our men, when the sale of
ardent spirits, the prime, nay, SOLE CAUSE of their ill
conduct, is legally authorized by the authorities of these
islands . . .
    It is hard that peaceable men cannot walk through the
streets without having their lives endangered by stones
thrown, or clubs wielded, by the authority of the police, to
quell a disturbance originating with a few drunken men,
made so at your LICENSED GROG-SHOPS; and we think it
would more redound to the credit of this government, to
punish the unprincipled men who sell rum to drunken
sailors, than to drag from those miserable men a large part
of their hard earnings, as fines for breaking one law, when
by another you compel the grog-shop keeper to sell as
much as possible, so that he may be able to pay for his
license.

If therefore, you still, after all the representations made to you, and the memorials sent into you by so large a number of the respectable part of your community, persevere in your intention of legalizing the sale of ardent spirits, we assure you that we shall no longer consider ourselves responsible for the conduct of our crews . . .

Respectfully, your ob't serv'ts
Signed by the masters of 24 American whalers at Lahaina, Maui,
18 March 1844
[*The Friend*, Honolulu, 3 April 1844]

Honolulu's Port Regulations also seemed to be at least as concerned with raising revenue as with maintaining peace and social order.

All boats and seamen are required to return to their ships at nine o'clock PM, when the first gun is fired from the fort.

The undermentioned fines are enforced: . . .

Hanging, as a murderer, for knowingly and maliciously violating those laws, whereby a contagious disease is communicated on shore . . .
$10 for coming on shore with a knife sword-cane, or any other dangerous weapon.
$2 for every seaman on shore, after the firing of the second gun . . . at half past nine . . .
$10 on every person who aids, secretes or entertains a seaman on shore, after that hour; and the same on every person who, by force, opposes the police, in their search
$1 to 5 for hallooing or making a noise in the streets, at night.
$6 for striking another in a quarrel.
$5 for racing or swift riding in the streets or frequented roads.
$1 for desecrating the Sabbath for the first time.
$2 for . . . the second time, and then the fine is doubled for every repetition . . .
$6 for drunkenness.
$5 for fornication.
$30 for adultery.

$50 for rape.

$10 for lewd, seductive and lascivious conduct.

[*The Friend*, Honolulu, 1 May 1844]

When things boiled over, a not infrequent occurrence, the ensuing fracas was sometimes more like an insurrection than a civil disturbance, and never more so than in 1851.

> In a common way we entertained no particular ill will against [the native police], but there was an auxiliary force of English, from Australia, known as the 'Sidney Rangers', whom we hated cordially. Besides the overbearing manner natural to their nation, they usually displayed peculiar brutality, acquired during a lawless life among the islands of the Pacific, and collisions between them and the seamen were marked with considerable animosity . . .
>
> On one occasion half the crew of the *Eagle*, of Sag Harbour, were out on an excursion . . . , and upon their return, being boisterous with animal and other spirits, one of their number announced his intention to ride into town at full speed, which he did . . . The native police immediately gathered around to arrest him, and he was hurried before the authorities. There he refused to pay his fine and was ordered to be taken to the fort for confinement . . . When there, and helpless, he continued to resist in the only practicable way, that is, with his tongue; abusing his captors, yelling and roaring, to the great annoyance of the Sidney men, one of whom at length struck the unlucky whaleman on the head with his club and killed him.

The news soon got round, and roused the seamen. A deputation proceeded to find the American consul and demanded that the murderer should be given up. As nothing was done, they threatened violence. The captains and ships' officers discreetly retired to their ships.

> Then we 'went in'. We were about 500 in number, and although mostly unarmed, there were probably no 5000 men on the islands that could have withstood our charge. In a few minutes the streets were cleared, and in an hour

the entire population was flying pell mell, in a confused and frightened mass, for the mountains. The custom house was fired and the assailants pushed on to the fort, which was given up without a struggle by the horror stricken native soldiers, who retired and took up a position on . . . Punch Bowl Hill. The king and the consuls did their utmost to restrain the rage of the rioters and succeeded in extinguishing most of the fires that had been kindled, but further than that their efforts were in vain. We followed the soldiers and chased them from Punch Bowl Hill, dispersing them utterly.

We now returned to plunder the city. Stores, grog shops, dwellings, all were thrown open and ransacked. The king dispatched a messenger to Lahaina, where there were ships of war, for assistance, but in the meantime, having held the town for three days without molestation, and having gratified our vengeance and enjoyed our spree, we retired quietly, as the humour took us, on board our several vessels, leaving the city a solitude. For our satisfaction it was told us that the Ranger, whose crime had been the cause of so much trouble and loss, had been banished to the island of Lanai for life; whether it was true or not I cannot say. And so ended the 'Great Sailors Riot', in which, singular to relate, not a single life was lost. [Alonzo Sampson, *Three Times Around the World*, pp 57–8]

The whalemen left but the missionaries stayed, and in 1893 their sons overthrew the native monarchy and established a republic. Five years later the islands were annexed by the United States.

Clouds
or How a Whaleman Vanished and a Whale Appeared

Hamlet: *Do you see yonder cloud that's almost in the*
                 shape of a camel?
Polonius: *By the mass, and 'tis like a camel, indeed.*
Hamlet: *Methinks it is like a weasel.*
Polonius: *It is backed like a weasel.*
Hamlet: *Or like a whale?*
Polonius: *Very like a whale.*

W e do not know if Nathaniel Worth kept the promise he made in 1751 to put in a good word for Peleg Folger, but we do know that Peleg did not marry Anna Pitts, nor anyone else. He left whaling to teach Nantucket's young and became a local character, which is a polite way of saying that he was regarded as eccentric. He was nonetheless a respected Elder among the Friends and in 1789 he died as he had lived, dispensing advice to the friends and neighbours who visited in his last days. To the rest of the world he would have been no more than a reference in Obed Macy's *History of Nantucket*; no more, that is, until Joseph Hart decided to write a novel based on information he had gathered during a stay on the island. Published in 1834, his *Miriam Coffin* strongly supported Reynolds' agitation for a Pacific expedition, but looked back rather than forward. The action takes place in the revolutionary era, and while there is something of

whaling there is much more of Nantucket society. The significance of Hart's book was that it was the first 'whaling' novel.
And it treated Peleg Folger rather poorly, describing him as 'one
of those prying, good for nothing, meddlesome bodies that vex
every community, and yet he was not vicious, nor would he
designedly do an ill turn to his neighbour for the world'.[1] Hart
represented Folger as an asthmatic, choleric old oil merchant and
teamed him up with another whom he called Jethro Coffin,
Miriam's husband. In their vaudeville Peleg was cast as the
buffoon, and self-revelation allegedly from his own pen was used
to sketch him in.

> Peleg Folger lived to an advanced age and, in his latter years, took to
> writing the history of his times. He embodied, in an antique dress,
> many curious incidents and stirring events of the day. In turning over
> his notes, to which we have had access, we came across one sentence
> that struck us as particularly faithful. It was that 'the females of
> Nantucket are good-looking, and some of them even beautiful!' Well
> done, Peleg! We have heard that after labouring hard at this gallant
> sentence, for half a day, Peleg got upon his legs, and, snapping his
> fingers, shouted 'Minnows and mack'rel! What will posterity and the
> brethren say to that!'[2]

Posthumous indignity could not have gone much further, but
Peleg was destined for another metamorphosis. *Miriam Coffin*
became one of Melville's source books for *Moby Dick*, and sure
enough Peleg turns up again, this time as a former whaling
captain and co-owner of the *Pequod*. His straight man now is
Captain Bildad, and they turn on a good captain/bad captain
routine to flim-flam Ishmael into signing on for a very long lay.
Only glimpses of the real Peleg survive this second reincarnation.
He is still short and excitable, but he has lost his learning
and acquired the shrewdness and aura of a whaling captain. He
and Bildad, and Ahab with them, are different aspects of the one
type.

> Now, Bildad, like Peleg, and indeed many other Nantucketers, was a
> Quaker, the island having originally been settled by that sect; and to
> this day its inhabitants in general retain in an uncommon measure the

God and Mammal

Yankee thrift and Quaker piety usually rubbed along well enough together but there was one major point of friction—Sunday whaling. Whaling captains became practised in their excuses for Sabbath-breaking. John Stetson, deputy US consul at Lahaina, had heard them all.

> Without stopping to notice the many quaint sayings among Seamen, such as 'There is no Sabbath in five fathoms water'; and that 'When we bid adieu to our native shores, we bid adieu to all the Sabbath privileges and enjoyments', we pass on to take a view of what may more properly be called their reasons for violating a plain command of God . . . One is, that if they do not take whales on the Sabbath, they may not have an opportunity again during the week, or even the month. Again, . . . we at least lose one seventh of the time, and our voyage will be proportionably lengthened. Again, . . . the crews would become dissatisfied and mutinous—would curse and swear, and we should indirectly be the cause of more sin, than we should directly, by whaling on that day. Again, . . . we should not be acting honestly with our employers; they expect us to do so, and improve every opportunity that offers to advance the interests of the voyage; besides, we are absent from our families, and we deem it our duty to return to them as soon as possible. If we should attempt to prosecute this business without whaling on the Sabbath, we should be thrown out of employment; as but few if any of the owners of whale ships would be willing to furnish ships on such conditions. Our dependent families would be brought to want, and we be deprived of the means of relieving their wants . . . [*The Friend*, Honolulu, 3 April, 1844]

Providence was clearly at fault in presenting temptation. The Reverend Henry Cheever had a ready response.

> God has revealed no indulgence in favour of Sabbath whaling, any more than Sabbath-breaking railroad companies . . . It is an unfounded presumption, that a steady and well-grounded refusal to have nothing to do

with Sabbath whaling will produce discontent among the men. Experience has proved that they like the rest of the Sabbath as well as any other men.

He then undermined his own point by admitting that the men 'would like now and then to improve any rare chance offered on that day as well as on any other'. The solution was to avoid temptation: if no lookout were kept whales would not often be seen. Captain Lafayette Ludlow of the *Commodore Preble* had converted to the practice, Cheever said, and whaled with a new heart. Unfortunately, Providence had not yet seen fit to reward his conversion.

> He took one season afterward on the North-west, but, for reasons which it were easy to mention, not the least of which was not being well officered or manned for North-west whaling, the ship did not succeed so well as many others. Several boats were stove early in the season, some of the men got upset and frightened, tow-lines parted, and many things went ill: but, so far from repenting of his purpose to keep the Sabbath, he is more strong in it than ever, well persuaded and well content that, if God do not pay him in oil here, durable riches and righteousness are his in heaven.

It was uphill fight enough, even without discouraging examples like Ludlow's. Cheever was told by many captains that their owners, many of them members of evangelical churches in the New England whaling ports, positively insisted on Sunday whaling as a condition of employment. On the other hand, 'some owners say nothing to their captains on the subject; but if their ships do but return full, no inquiries are made how or on what days the oil was obtained'. A captain was unlikely to be wide of the mark if he assumed that his pious owners believed that 'oil got on the Sabbath burns as well, sells as well, and . . . spends as well as oil got lawfully on week days' (*The Whaleman's Adventures in the Southern Ocean*, pp 226–39).

peculiarities of the Quaker, only variously and anomalously modified by things altogether alien and heterogeneous. For some of these same Quakers are the most sanguinary of all sailors and whale-hunters. They are fighting Quakers; they are Quakers with a vengeance.[3]

Hart and Melville took what they wanted of Peleg, as novelists are wont to do, and discarded the rest. They turned a real whaleman, or a whaleman as real as could be when all that remained of him was caricature and some private papers, into a stereotype. Peleg Folger is entitled to speak for himself, and how more fittingly than in the poem that brought together his literary ambition, his brushes with death while whaling, and the faith that so buoyed him up that, at the end, 'the sting of death was entirely removed'.

Thou didst, O Lord, create the mighty whale,
    That wondrous monster of a mighty length;
Vast is his head and body, vast his tail,
    Beyond conception his unmeasured strength.

When he the surface of the sea hath broke,
    Arising from the abyss below,
His breath appears a lofty stream of smoke.
    The circling waves like glitt'ring banks of snow.

But, everlasting God, thou dost ordain
    That we, poor feeble mortals should engage
(Ourselves, our wives and children to maintain,)
    This dreadful monster with a martial rage.

And though he furiously doth us assail,
    Thou dost preserve us from all dangers free;
He cuts our boat in pieces with his tail,
    And spills us all at once into the sea.

I twice into the dark abyss was cast,
    Straining and struggling to retain my breath;
Thy waves and billows over me were past;
    Thou didst, O Lord, deliver me from death.

Expecting every moment still to die,
    Methought I nevermore should see the light;
Well nigh the gates of vast eternity
    Environed me with everlasting night.

Thou savedst me from the dangers of the sea,
That I might praise thy name for ever more.
Thy love and power the same will ever be;
Thy mercy is an inexhaustible store.[4]

Another of Melville's inspirations, but of greater consequence, was the Great White Whale. As Joel Polack had noted in New Zealand, sperm whales can vary widely in colour. Old sperm bulls not uncommonly carry grey or white markings, particularly about the head. Sometime around 1810 one or more of the greybeards that were being encountered by the whalemen off the Chilean island of Mocha began to acquire a reputation for boat chewing. In time he or they became notorious for destructiveness and indestructibility. Re-enter Jeremiah Reynolds. In 1839 Reynolds published *Mocha Dick or The White Whale of the Pacific (a leaf from a manuscript Journal)*. He related that while on the *Annawan* in 1829 he and Captain Palmer had gammed with an unnamed whaler off the coast of Chile, whose mate, a Nantucketer, was introduced to them as the Man Who Slew Mocha Dick. Reynolds proceeded to tell the mate's story which, as it varied little from a hundred other accounts of killing fighting whales—other than the terror inspired in his crew by the thought of dealing with this legendary beast—there is no reason to doubt. The conclusion of the mate's narrative, with its emphasis on outcome, is another earnest of its authenticity.

> Mocha-Dick was the longest whale I ever looked upon: he measured more than 70 feet from his noddle to the tip of his flukes, and yielded one hundred barrels of clear oil, with a proportionate quantity of head matter. It may emphatically be said that 'the scars of his old wounds were near his new', for not less than twenty harpoons did we draw from his back, the rusted momentoes of many a desperate encounter.[5]

From this story Melville derived the name of his whale and one of its distinguishing characteristics, for it was 'white as the surf'. But Mocha Dick was merely a boat-eater like many other aggressive whales that were associated with various grounds, as Timor

Jack and New Zealand Tom (which in 1804 had destroyed nine boats 'before breakfast'); in Melville's hands Moby Dick became the Whale That Sank a Ship. Such a whale also sank Jethro Coffin's *Grampus* in *Miriam Coffin*, and for that story both Hart and Melville were indebted to the most famous whaling tale of all, the sinking of the *Essex*.

The *Essex*, under the command of George Pollard, sailed from Nantucket in August 1819. For fifteen months it cruised the Pacific and the morning of 20 November 1820 found it just south of the equator in 119° west. Whales were sighted and three boats lowered. That of the first mate, Owen Chase, was soon stove and returned to the ship, jackets plugging the hole. While heading the ship towards the chasing boats and making repairs to his own with a view to rejoining the fray, Chase noticed that a large sperm whale had broken water about 100 yards away. It settled but immediately resurfaced a ship's length ahead and came directly at the ship at normal cruising speed. Chase ordered helm up, but before the ship could answer the whale suddenly accelerated and struck the *Essex* just forward of the mainmast.

> . . . he gave us such an appalling and tremendous jar, as nearly threw us all on our faces. The ship brought up as suddenly and violently as if she had struck a rock, and trembled for a few seconds like a leaf. We looked at each other with perfect amazement, deprived almost of the power of speech.[6]

The whale scraped along the keel and surfaced to leeward as if stunned. Chase considered lancing it, but its tail was under the stern and he feared that the rudder might be unshipped. Although the whale then moved off and began thrashing the sea about 100 yards distant from the ship, those aboard were too busy rigging the pumps to pay it much attention, for the ship was settling quickly by the head. Chase had signalled the away boats to return and was preparing to launch the spare when a crewman shouted 'Here he is—he is making for us again'. A quarter of a mile ahead, at twice its previous speed, the whale was coming on in a fury. Again Chase put the helm up but again failed to avert the

collision, which this time was at a combined speed of about
7 knots. The impact stove in the bows below the cathead. The
whale again passed under the ship to leeward and disappeared
from sight. There was just enough time to load some navigation
tables and instruments into the only serviceable boat before the
Essex fell over to windward and settled. No more than ten minutes
had elapsed since the first attack. Far out in the chasing boats,
the captain's boatsteerer looked back over Pollard's shoulder:
'Look! Look! What ails the ship, she is upsetting.'

Pollard could not comprehend what he found. 'My God, Mr
Chase, what is the matter?' was all he could say. For three days
the boats hovered around the wreck. By cutting away the masts
and breaking through the deck, the men were able to get to about
600 pounds of hard bread, 195 gallons of water, two small hogs
and half a dozen tortoises. It was little enough for twenty men
adrift more than 1000 miles from the nearest land. Pollard took
a sight. The Marquesas were closest, then Tahiti; both were
believed to be populated by savages who were, Pollard feared,
cannibals. He seemed unaware that missionaries had been there
for many years. Towards Hawaii it was the hurricane season. The
best course seemed to be to sail south to about 25° latitude in
search of a westerly that could take them to Peru or Chile. Chase's
boat was in the poorest condition, it having been stove several
times, but he was unconcerned.

> At best, a whale-boat is an extremely frail thing; the most so of any
> other kind of boat; they are what is called clinker built [with
> overlapping planks], and constructed of the lightest materials, for the
> purpose of being rowed with the greatest possible celerity according
> to the necessities of the business for which they are intended. Of
> all species of vessels, they are the weakest, and most fragile, and
> possess but one advantage over any other—that of lightness and
> buoyancy, that enables them to keep above the dash of the sea with
> more facility than heavier ones. This qualification is, however,
> preferable to that of any other, and, situated as we were, I would not
> have exchanged her, old and crazy as she was, for even a ship's
> launch.[7]

But they raised the gunwales 6 inches to be on the safe side and rigged two masts in place of the usual one. The daily ration was fixed at a cake of ship's bread (3 ounces) and a pint of water per man. On 24 November they left the wreck, and four weeks later reached what they thought was Ducie Island in 24° 40' south. They had in fact come upon Henderson Island, 200 miles to the west-north-west of Ducie. The boats had been weakened by the voyage and the men had been unable to collect water because the spray-coated sails turned rain water to salt. Some of them had resorted to urine. In mid-December the bread ration had been halved while they were becalmed and three of the men now declared that they would rather take their chances on the desert isle than continue. They were left and the boats proceeded eastwards towards Easter Island. There had been a discussion about sailing independently so that any mishap to one would not lead to overloading of the others, but the comfort of companion-ship overrode the prudence of selfishness. Within a week Pollard found that they had come too far south and decided to make for Juan Fernandez, off Chile and over 2000 miles distant. The first man to die was the second mate, Matthew Joy, on 10 January 1821. His body was slipped overside.

Two days later a storm separated Chase's boat from the other two. Richard Peterson, a black man, died and was cast overboard on 20 January. When offered the ration on his last day he refused, saying 'Keep it, it may be of service to someone but can be of none to me'. A week later there was only fourteen days of half ration left and they agreed that to maintain their strength for the boat work it would be better to increase consumption even if all the food would then be gone in five days. By early February Chase was confiding to his journal that the end for them all could not be far off, as they were too weak even to steer. When Isaac Cole became demented and died in a convulsive fit, the mate raised with the remaining men, Benjamin Lawrence and Thomas Nickerson, the question of use of the body. There were three

days' provisions left. Once those were gone, the only course
would be to cast lots. Better to eat Cole. It was agreed.

> We separated his limbs from his body, and cut all the flesh from the
> bones; after which, we opened the body, took out the heart, and then
> closed it up again—sewed it up decently as we could and committed
> it to the sea. We now first commenced to satisfy the immediate
> cravings of nature from the heart, which we eagerly devoured, and
> then eat sparingly of a few pieces of the flesh; after which we hung
> up the remainder, cut in thin strips about the boat, to dry in the sun;
> we made a fire and roasted some of it, to serve us during the next
> day. In this manner we dispose of our fellow-sufferer; the painful
> recollection of which, brings to mind at this moment, some of the
> most disagreeable and revolting ideas that it is capable of conceiving.
> . . . Humanity must shudder at the dreadful recital.[8]

Cole sustained them until 15 February. Chase thought that they
were now near Masafuera, the westernmost of the Juan Fernandez
Islands, but before daylight on the eighteenth Nickerson bailed
the boat, lay down, covered himself with a canvas, and announced
that he wished to die. Chase upbraided him with the wickedness
of losing faith in Providence, but the teenager was resolute in his
despair.

> A fixed look of settled and forsaken despondency came over his face.
> He lay for some time silent, sullen and sorrowful. I felt at once
> certain that the coldness of death was fast gathering upon him. There
> was a sudden and unaccountable earnestness in his manner that
> alarmed me and made me fear that I myself might unexpectedly be
> overtaken by a like weakness or dizziness of nature, which would
> bereave me at once of both reason and life.[9]

At seven that morning Chase was woken by a loud cry from
Lawrence, who was steering: 'There's a sail!' Nickerson's despon-
dency fell from him and they hastened to overhaul their salvation.
They were taken aboard the brig *Indian* and a few hours later
Masafuera was in sight, 53 days after they had left Henderson
Island. It was a remarkable feat of navigation without a chart.

    After separating from Chase, Pollard's boat and the other, now
under the command of third mate Obed Hendricks, continued to

head for Juan Fernandez. Of the eleven men aboard, five were black Americans. One by one the blacks died and were eaten until on the night of 28–29 January the boats became separated in the darkness. Hendricks' boat, with Joseph West and the last black, William Bond, was not seen again. Pollard's crew was reduced to Charles Ramsdell, Barzillai Ray and the captain's nephew, Owen Coffin. On 1 February Ramsdell proposed that they draw lots. Pollard resisted, but said that if he were first to die the others were welcome to his remains. Coffin supported Ramsdell and paper slips were placed in a hat. It fell to young Coffin to be the victim. Pollard was distraught.

> I started forward instantly, and cried out, 'My lad, my lad, if you don't like your lot, I'll shoot the first man that touches you!' The poor emaciated boy hesitated a moment or two; then, quietly laying his head down on the gunnel [gunwale] of the boat, he said, 'I like it as well as any other.' He was soon dispatched, and nothing of him left . . . But I can tell you no more—my head is on fire at the recollection; I hardly know what I say.[10]

Pollard's words, as reported second-hand, do not name Coffin's executioner. Chase's account, for long the only other version, says it was Ramsdell. Not until 1981 did a third account come to light. Like Chase, Thomas Nickerson was not in the captain's boat, but his version explains Pollard's reticence and anguish.

> . . . they were compelled again to cast lots that who should draw the fatal trigger. As if the fate would have it, the awful die turned upon Captain Pollard [who] for a long time declared he could never do it, but finally had to submit. Coffin then called to them to come near whilst he breathed a parting message to his dear mother and family, then, craving a few moments in silence, he told them that he knew the lots had been fairly drawn. Peace to his memory.[11]

Ray died two days later, and the two corpses kept Pollard and Ramsdell alive until they were picked up within sight of Santa Maria Island, near Talcahuano, by the whaler *Dauphin* on 23 February, 60 days after leaving Henderson Island. It was arranged that the *Surry*, an English trader in Valparaiso en route to Australia, would pick up the castaways on Henderson Island. Their rescuer was Thomas Raine, who later inaugurated shore whaling at Twofold Bay in New South Wales.

It was hardly to be expected that men could revert to normality after such experiences. Pollard had to tell his sister what had become of her son. She could never afterwards endure his presence. He was given command of the *Two Brothers* and again sailed for the Pacific. Seventeen months after the wreck of the *Essex*, his new command struck a reef near Hawaii. His thoughts can only be imagined as he again took to the boats, but this time he was picked up by the whaler *Martha* after a few days. He knew that after two such blows he would never get another ship and so retired from the sea, to all the world a Jonah, in his thirties. For many years he was a nightwatchman on the Nantucket docks, and it was there that Herman Melville was taken to meet him in 1851, after the publication of *Moby Dick*. The author found him 'unassuming, even humble', but withal the most impressive man he had ever met.

> . . . Never he smiled;
> Call him and he would come; not sour
> In spirit, but meek and reconciled;
> Patient he was, he none withstood;
> Oft on some secret thing would brood.[12]

Owen Chase became a celebrated captain and lived to a ripe old age, but in his last years he would hurry to the attic after a visit to the grocery store, there to hide biscuit and other provisions. Ramsdell would not talk about his experience, even to his son, except in the most cursory way. Nickerson committed his recollections to a hundred pages of manuscript but kept them to himself until they were found in a Connecticut attic 88 years after his death. And for three generations it was impolite to mention the *Essex* in Nantucket.

Melville first heard the story when the whaler on which he was serving, the *Acushnet*, gammed with the *Lima* of Nantucket in the Pacific near the equator in 1841. One of the *Lima*'s foremast hands was a son of Owen Chase, and the boy showed Melville a copy of his father's narrative. 'The reading of this wondrous story upon the landless sea, and close to the very latitude of the shipwreck had a surprising effect on me.' Ten years later he published his own 'whaling' novel.

Peleg Folger had been passed from pen to pen until he became as insubstantial as a cloud. Conversely, tales of fighting whales were conflated by Melville to make manifest all the nimbus of the soul. A week before the publication of *Moby Dick* a letter arrived from a friend telling of the wreck of the whaler *Ann Alexander*. On 20 August 1850 Captain Deblois and his crew had been attacked by a rogue whale on the Offshore Ground. It had stove and sunk the ship after destroying several boats. Five months later the *Rebecca Simms* took a large bull without much trouble. It was badly damaged about the head, in which pieces of wood were embedded. In its blubber were two of the *Ann Alexander*'s irons. Melville's return letter was worthy of Edgar Allen Poe.

> It is really and truly a surprising coincidence—to say the least. I make no doubt it is Moby Dick himself, for there is no account of his capture after the sad fate of the *Pequod* about fourteen years ago.—Ye Gods! what a Commentator is this *Ann Alexander* whale. What he has to say is short and pithy and very much to the point. I wonder if my evil art has raised this monster.[13]

Mocha Dick, having inspired Moby Dick, might be thought thereby to have exhausted his literary potential, but writers are not known for letting the dead rest. In 1892 the *Detroit Free Press* published a confection entitled 'The Career of Mocha Dick'. It had him ranging the oceans of the world, from Chile and the Falklands to Japan, and held him responsible for the destruction of fourteen boats and over 30 men. Identifiable by an 8-foot white scar across his head, he was said to have sunk a French merchant-man and an Australian trader, and stove in three whalers over a period of nineteen years. When age had enfeebled him he was taken off the Brazil Banks in August 1859 by a Swedish whaler

TUE WHALE OF CAPTAIN DEBLOIS.

The publication of Moby Dick *conjures him up from the depths*
(from Harper's New Monthly Magazine, *1856)*

that found nineteen irons in him. 'He measured 110 feet long; his girth was 57 feet; his jaw was 25 feet 6 inches long. Eight of his teeth were broken off and all others badly worn down. His big head was a mass of scars, and he had apparently lost the sight of his right eye.'[14]

All that was missing from this deluge of detail was an eye patch, a parrot and a black flag.

THE PRINCES
OF WHALES

*. . . two estoiles in fesse or, representing the Arctic and
Antarctic polar stars.*

Enderby blazon, 1778

By the early 1840s London was as much a whaling backwater
as Nantucket, but it still had its entrepreneurs and dreamers
who believed that there was profit to be made. By accident and
design they turned to the approach that had long since suggested
itself to thoughtful observers in the colonies. If the ships were
based where the whales were, and not 12,000 thousand miles
away, they could be employed on their proper business almost
continuously, with the oil going to market in Britain as ordinary
freight. The busiest British port near the best grounds was
Sydney, and into its bustling harbour on 18 July 1842 sailed the
handsomest craft its inhabitants had ever beheld.

The *Wanderer* was a rakish topsail schooner, sharp enough for
slaver or smuggler, but flying the White Ensign of the Royal
Navy. Her owner and master, Benjamin Boyd, was exercising his
privilege as a member of the Royal Yacht Squadron. The juxta-
position of flag and ship suggested influential connections and
dubious enterprise, a suitably ambiguous signal to herald the
advent of such a mercurial character. Boyd came to Australia

ostensibly to found a bank, but he brought with him two sailing ships that subsequently became whalers and a number of steamers with which to establish a shipping business. His capital had been subscribed by shareholders in the Royal Bank of Australia, but it seemed to Boyd that there were much better uses for their money than banking. The whole country was for sale at clearance prices. Drought and depression had so reduced the value of squatting runs that if one bought sheep, licence to the land on which they grazed was thrown in for nothing. Like a child in a sweet shop, Boyd laid his hands on whatever he could, including *Fame* and *Juno*, the remains of Richard Jones' whaling fleet. Nothing if not a man of vision, he built his own settlement, Boydtown, 400 kilometres south of Sydney on Twofold Bay, to function as a way station for his coastal steamers, a shipping point for his wool and a refreshment port for his pelagic whalers. It was near enough to a feudal fief, with its own currency and Boyd employees as magistrates. He also had shore-based boats in the bay that competed with those of other stations for passing right whales.

If he could retain these assets for long enough, especially the land, economic upturn would eventually restore their value and produce great profits for himself and the bank. Unfortunately his co-shareholders would not wait so long, the more so as it became clear that Boyd's flair for acquiring assets was much better than his ability to generate income from them, and that some of his projects were little more than expensive self-promotion. The lighthouse he built at Twofold Bay was a case in point. An elegant tower of beautifully dressed stone shipped from Sydney, its ramparts still display to the four quarters the name of the Ozymandias who had it built. Because he had neglected to obtain official permission, it was never lit. The assets safest from Boyd's dreams and self-indulgence appeared to be his whalers. *Terror* and *Velocity* he had brought from England. Another ten were purchased in the colony, including such well-known ships as *Margaret* and *Lucy Ann*. At sea his captains were beyond his

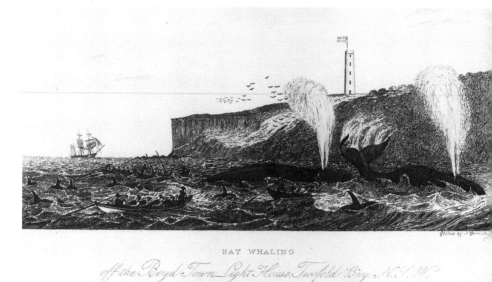

BAY WHALING
of the Boyd Town Light House Twofold Bay. N.S.W.

*Ben Boyd's Folly—the light at Twofold Bay (by J Carmichael in Wells'
Geographical Dictionary of the Australian Colonies,
National Library of Australia)*

interference and their voyages were profitable. Less promising
was the appointment of one of his gentlemen companions from
the *Wanderer*, Oswald Brierly, as manager of the Twofold Bay
whaling station. Brierly was an artist with no experience of shipping or whaling. It was typical of Boyd that his friend was given
the job to rest his eyes. The Medici would have done no less.
Brierly saw himself as a Phidias to Boyd's Pericles and was alive
to the possibilities for his art, going so far as to take an oar for
the experience.

> . . . there was a call from the Lookout under which we lay, after
> about three quarters of an hour hard pulling we . . . first caught sight
> of the whale—a large Black one—There! it has struck one of the
> headsmen and knocked him out of the Boat in an instant he was
> hauled in again and sends a Lance deep into his side—the sight gave
> us redoubled energy—'Spring' was the word . . . and the gig darted
> forward with increased velocity, and in a few minutes we were within

a Boats length of the animal (Huge mass)—it spurts Blood mingled
with water which was now in its last agonies. Blood pouring from
gashes in its sides and Back and discolouring the water around—what
a scene the shouts and men the splash of the Whale the more
Languid motions where the Fish comes up to Blow becomes
exhausted . . . sometimes a sudden rush to rid itself of pursuers the
Boat flying along with terrific rapidity. Oars peaked Water boiling on
each side—the hollow Burst when compelled to return to the surface
to Blow then all the Boats tailing away after him to fasten if he
should get Loose.[1]

Labour troubles led Boyd to reconsider the practice of sending
oil to England in the ship that had taken it. In March 1846 the
Margaret returned to Sydney with 185 tuns of sperm oil from the
season's cruise. The crew were all articled to take her on to
London but the cook deserted. Although his lay was technically
forfeit, he sued for non-payment of wages to the tune of £100.
The ship was arrested by the Vice Admiralty Court pending
hearing of the case. To avoid the costs of delay the captain paid
off the cook and other grumblers in order to get the ship released.
Boyd drew two conclusions: Sydney men were troublesome and
expensive; and smaller, cheaper ships could be used for whaling
if they did not have to make the voyage to and from England.

If I had twenty small Brigs varying from 150 to 200 Tons . . . which
. . . ought to be got for £2500 each I would almost engage with cheap
provisions supplied from Twofold bay & one half manned by South
Sea Islanders, to send home after paying all expenses including
freight of Oil, £50,000 a year.[2]

Boyd and his associates saw islanders as the solution to most
of their labour problems, whether on land or sea, and the *Velocity*
resorted to practices little short of kidnapping to recruit them.
Allegations of slavery were made, to be fended off with the
specious argument that as slavery was prohibited in the British
Empire, and as Australia was part thereof, whatever these inden-
tured labour practices might be they could not be slavery. The
attraction of the islanders as whalemen was that they put the
British on a more even footing with the Americans, who recruited

them in large numbers on small lays. The annexation of New Zealand, with its attendant enrolment of the Maoris as British subjects, made it easier to sign on islanders while keeping within the limits imposed by the Navigation Act on the employment of foreigners. But by 1847 a scheme like Boyd's 'small brigs' was pie in the sky, at least for him. The capital was spent, the shareholders were restless and, as Boyd was to discover, whaling returns could not be relied upon.

Boyd predicted for 1848 and 1849, on the basis of earlier returns, that his then current fleet of seven whalers would average 40 barrels per month each. At £70 per tun, the expected 336 tuns of sperm oil would realise £23,520, one-half and one-third respectively of the two years' income from all of the bank's investments. For a while it looked as though they might do even better; oil to the value of £42,000 was sent home in 1848. But by now solvency was hostage to the return of every whaler and in July 1849 the *Fame*, after thirteen months out, came in unsuccessful. The lay system ensured that Boyd was not alone in his disappointment. The ship's captain, Kean, took himself to his bedroom, tidily placed a basin and mirror on the floor before him, and cut his throat. He was found with his head in the basin.

Three months later the *Wanderer* exercised her right as an honorary British warship to leave Sydney without customs clearance and Boyd slipped off in search of Californian gold. That too proved illusory, and he was killed on Guadalcanal in 1851 while pursuing another dream, that of creating his own private empire as Brooke had done in Sarawak and Raffles in Singapore. He appears to have been killed for breaking a tabu, but had the natives associated him with the recruitment practices of his former enterprises they might have felt they had double cause. The *Fame* also sailed to California, with diggers for passengers. Like her erstwhile owner, and the Nantucket fleet, she never returned. It is somehow appropriate that Boyd's lasting contribution to whaling was artistic rather than commercial; Brierly's watercolours of his Twofold Bay experiences, mostly painted many years later but replete with detail, are rendered with an energy and freedom untypical of nineteenth-century marine painting. They glow with the remembrance of youth.

If in the 1840s Boyd was a meteor that blazed briefly across southern skies, Charles Enderby was more like a dull comet making a periodic return. The man was a Bourbon by nature, forgetting nothing and learning nothing, and the idea of colonial whaling operations that had been tossed to him by the House of Commons Committee on Manufactures had simply been waiting its turn. With New Zealand annexed and the report of Captain James Ross' Antarctic expedition to hand it must have seemed to Charles that a heavenly conjunction had occurred, one that would restore the fortunes of his house and gain for it the dignity and recognition which he believed was its due. In 1839 he had given his friend Ross news of John Balleny's discoveries. In 1840 Ross visited another Enderby discovery, the Auckland Islands, to make magnetic observations before proceeding south. He reported that many right whales and some sperm whales had entered Laurie Harbour while his ships were there. The place was uninhabited and well suited for a whaling station. Enderby began to make plans to claim his patrimony. After all, as Ross wrote, 'from the circumstance of their having been discovered by the commander of one of his ships, he may with some justice claim to be entitled to greater privileges than others'.[3]

In 1843 Charles asked the government to lease the Auckland Islands to the Enderby brothers for 30 years. The government was reluctant and suggested that if whaling was the object it would be more practicable to operate from the existing infrastructure of the Australasian colonies. Perhaps so, but Charles intended a financial coup in which the islands would be his leverage, and the government gave way on condition that a settlement would not involve it in any expense. His next step was to excite public interest, for the enterprise was beyond Enderby resources and would need to attract investors. One Thomas Preston was prompted to write to Charles Enderby in July 1846, purportedly on behalf of 'certain parties connected with the British Shipping Interest', asking him to unfold his plans for the revival of the British southern whale fishery.

> They are of opinion, that the system generally upon which the fishery has been of late years carried on from the ports of Great Britain, has not sufficiently adapted itself to the changes which time has brought, to bear up with advantage against foreign and colonial competition, and the diminution of profits induced as well by this cause, as by legislative enactments, more especially the reduction of duties upon oils and oil seeds imported.[4]

British prestige demanded its 'speedy resuscitation' by concentration of the national effort in the hands of a public body under the direction of those with the necessary qualifications. The letter could have been written by Enderby himself, and probably was. The nub of his lengthy response was to propose the formation of a Southern Whale Fishery Company, to be incorporated by Royal Charter (like the East India Company). In place of the uncertainty inherent in individual enterprise, where one poor voyage might be enough to ruin a firm, a large company would be able to average the bad with the good over an extended period. It should be based in the Auckland Islands, wherein he and his brothers would assign their rights 'upon equitable conditions'. If this arrangement were acceptable, the brothers would also invest heavily in the company. The proposal was self-serving in the extreme, especially as the terms on which the brothers admitted the company to joint proprietorship of the islands—equal shares in profits from the sale of land to colonists—were probably expected to generate the funds they said they would invest. One of the 'advantages' claimed for the islands was that in sailing thence to the California right whale grounds a whaler would twice traverse the sperm grounds on the equator, taking 15 tuns of oil each way. There could be few franker admissions of the failure of the British sperm fishery.

In developing his case, Enderby attempted to explain how the Americans were making whaling pay when the British manifestly were not. It was not a matter of skill, he said; if anything, both had to defer to the colonials on that point, at least in the most recent year for which he had figures. In 1845 the Australian sperm whalers, smaller ships with smaller crews, had averaged 71 barrels per month against 50 for the Americans (which included 11 barrels of right whale oil) and 40 for the British, which figures included allowance for passage time. American success was attributable, he believed, to a strong domestic market protected by a duty of 25 cents per gallon on foreign oil but in which competition between domestic producers kept the price down. By contrast, lower duty on vegetable oil substitutes in Britain had so depressed the supply of sperm oil—even though demand for oil generally had more than doubled since 1821—that the little there was commanded a high price. Unfortunately for Enderby, he undermined his own argument with figures that showed imports of sperm oil had also risen over the period, albeit much more slowly. The point he chose to ignore was that in 1821 the imported oil had all been of British origin, whereas in 1845 only a quarter of it was. In 1845 the colonials were supplying as much as British whalers; the other half was foreign, for which read American. The Americans did profitable business at home at only two-thirds of the average London price of £82 per tun, and the extra £4 in freight to Britain (for American whaleships could not land their oil direct) was no impediment. Enderby had to be wilfully blind not to see that the British whalers had been displaced in their own premium market by more efficient producers.

One point on which Enderby was adamant was the availability of whales, 'since the Americans, at least, capture them in abundance'. It was simply a matter of finding them.

> . . . if whales disappear for a time from one part where they had previously abounded, they are to be found in another; nor is there any greater popular error than that which inculcates a contrary belief; or, in other words, that the effect of the fishery is to exterminate the tribe of cetacea. All experience proves that whales do not entirely disappear, but merely migrate in consequence of their favourite

haunts being too continuously invaded; while everyone familiar with their habits is equally aware that they do not permanently abandon those haunts, but resort to them again in the course of time. The apparent failure of the Spermaceti Whale Fishery is attributable to the natural shyness and wildness of the fish being increased, in consequence of the unremitting pursuit to which they are subjected wherever encountered, rather than to any actual decrease of numbers.[5]

His own figures showed that the search had become less and less rewarding. From 1800 to 1845 the average duration of sperm voyages had steadily increased while the average produce from them had unsteadily declined, 'these fluctuations . . . chiefly owing to the opening of new fisheries, and to the decline of old ones, from the whales becoming more wild and shy'.

	Voyage in months	Produce in tuns	Tuns per month
1800–10	25	129	5.16
1810–15	24	165	6.87
1815–20	30	181	6.03
1820–25	na	na	na
1825–30	33	190	5.76
1830–35	37	186	5.03
1835–40	40	172	4.30
1840–42	42	168	4.00
1843	43	158	3.67
1844	42	142	3.39
1845	45	143	3.18

Enderby then factored the price of oil into the equation so as to calculate seamen's wages, taking their average lay as 1/160th of net proceeds. He found that from £3/-/6 per month in the last years of the Napoleonic wars, wages had fallen by more than half, to £1/7/-, by 1845. A seaman on a trader would expect to get between £2/5/- and £3/10/-. It was hardly surprising that it was difficult to recruit and retain whalemen of any quality, but British owners could consider themselves well off by comparison with the Americans, who might ship 80 men in the course of a voyage just to keep a 30-man crew up to strength, such was the rate of desertion. Part of the answer would be more money, but Enderby also had another proposal. If the Auckland Islands were colonised by the families of the whalemen,

> first, a character of permanence and stability would be imparted to the whaling establishment itself; secondly, the whaling crews would have their home, their families, and their connexions close at hand. Upon the importance of the last consideration, I need not dilate. It will be sufficient to remark, that the cause of morality would be largely promoted by the arrangement; since it is only too much a matter of notoriety, that, owing to the want of domestic associations, the greatest immorality has hitherto marked the intercourse of the crews of whaling ships with the natives of the islands in the Pacific, whither they are in the habit of resorting to refit.[6]

As to the economics of operating from the islands, that could be calculated by reference to colonial experience. Enderby showed the advantage that colony-based sperm whalers had enjoyed over vessels sailing from Britain and America by using figures much like those that had excited the *Australian Quarterly* in 1828. They begged the question why British interest was stirring so late in the day, but Enderby did not want to offend his potential fellow investors. He denied that the British owner could be accused of lack of enterprise 'because he has not expatriated himself to carry on from a distant colony, an under-taking which he had been accustomed to conduct from home'. The figures told another story, one of twenty years' wasted opportunity.

As the table on the next page shows, the colonial vessel returned £12/18/10 per ton per annum against £7/14/11 for the British and American vessels.

The calculations appeared sound enough, but a cautious investor might have looked askance at the remoteness of the islands, the costs of establishing a whaling port, and the way in which most of the potential for profit seemed based on the price of sperm oil whereas most of the projected catch was of right

	Britain/America	Pacific Colonies
Expenses		
Ship and outfit	£9100 (350 tons, for 4 years)	£5000 (250 tons, for 1 year)
Extra outfits	–	£1650 (for 3 years)
Four years' interest @ 5% (foregone on oil in ship)	£1820	£610 (net of 2 years interest saved on remitted oil)
Total	£10,920	£7260
Returns		
Sperm oil @ £80 per tun	£12,000 (150 tuns)	£16,000 (50 tuns for 4 years)
Less		
freight @ £6 per tun	–	£1200
crew's share	£3500	£4000
Plus		
Residual value of ship	£3000	£2125
Total	£11,500	£12,925
Profit	£580	£5665

whales. Not Enderby's investors. Shamed into it or keeping an eye on the opposition, a number of prominent merchants who should have known better associated themselves with the enterprise. Among the directors were Charles Enderby and Robert Brooks, a merchant in the Australia trade, and shipowners W S Lindsay and Frederic Somes, Joseph's nephew. The shareholders included shipowner Money Wigram and William Greener, maker of harpoon-guns. The Earl of Hardwicke brought prestige to the governorship of the company and Thomas Preston, Enderby's stalking horse, became its secretary. The prospectus spoke of 30 ships initially, to yield a gross return of £61,440 per annum on a capital of £100,000. It also announced that Enderby

DEPARTURE OF THE WHALING-SHIP, "SAMUEL ENDERBY," FOR THE AUCKLAND ISLANDS.

Charles Enderby sails for the Auckland Islands in the Samuel Enderby,
the last remnant of the family fleet (from the
Illustrated London News, *1849)*

would be proceeding to the islands to organise the fishery 'and to remain there a sufficient time to place it on a sure foundation'.[7]

The prospect of colonists brought into play the government's condition that the company should bear the expense of any public services, including the provision of a chief magistrate. As Chief Commissioner of the company in the islands—salary £500 per annum and £250 'table money'—Enderby was available to take on the second function. New Zealand was now a fully-fledged colony and had a governor: Charles Enderby would be Lieutenant-Governor of the Auckland Islands. On 18 April 1849 he was given a public dinner at the London Tavern, Bishopsgate, where he heard his praises sung by distinguished men of Westminster and the City. A Lord of the Admiralty was in the chair and the President of the Board of Trade wished Enderby success on behalf of the government. It was the high point of his life. He sailed on the *Samuel Enderby* in August. Two months later *The Times* announced that the family firm was unable to meet its commitments which, although small, would fall heavily on the family members. 'It is hardly necessary to add that the difficulties of the firm have not in any way been caused by their connexion with the Southern Whale-fishery Company, and which, in fact, was not of a nature to lead to anything else than their advantage.'[8]

So Charles Enderby would have hoped, but the reality was otherwise. The company did not have 30 ships: it had eight, of which only five, purpose-built in 1850, were around the desired 250-ton mark. The islands were not uninhabited; in the years since Ross' visit Maoris had taken up residence. An accommodation was reached with them, which was just as well, for few colonists came and only the New Zealanders could get anything to grow. The colonists complained that Enderby broke his own regulations when it suited him, but petty administration was the least of his difficulties. Where were the whales? In February 1850 Enderby despatched the *Brisk*, Captain Tapsell, south to the Balleny Islands in search of the whales reported by Ross. Sailing west from the islands as far as 143° east, over seas reported by the Wilkes expedition as land, they encountered many whales but the weather was always too rough to lower. In April and May the right whales failed to appear off the islands and the pelagic catch was poor. In September the right whales did come on their return migration but shore whaling was unsuccessful; the ships, short-handed because the Maoris were planting their potatoes, fared little better. The company's Australian agent, Robert Towns, reported that the California gold rush had stripped Sydney of possible replacements.

Enderby made matters worse by deploying his little fleet as if he had the 30 ships he dreamed of. To cover as much ocean as possible in search of the new haunts of his displaced whales, he denied his captains the discretion to seek whales where their experience suggested. Where Wilkes had recommended concentration, Enderby favoured dispersal. His few ships ranged from East Africa to California, from the Bering Strait to Antarctica. In some cases they took what little oil they found in places that were closer to London than to the Auckland Islands, making a mockery of the depot-and-ship strategy that was supposed to revive British South Sea whaling. Enderby preferred to blame his captains' failure on lack of zeal or neglect of his instructions.

The first year's whaling brought in £3000, less than one-twentieth of the forecast return and about one-fifth of what would have been expected of eight ships. The directors became anxious. In August 1851 they sent two Special Commissioners, George Dundas MP and Thomas Preston, with powers to relocate the establishment if necessary. Their arrival in December was the end of Enderby's dream. It was clear that there was no prospect of recovering most of the £30,000 sunk into the settlement at Port Ross, money that could have been spent on ships if they had been based in Australia or New Zealand. Enderby had been playing the vice-regal role to the hilt, even approaching the Bishop of New Zealand to appoint a clergyman for his colony. The bishop had made plans to visit 'the principality of Enderby, the Antarctic Prince of Whales',[9] but when the Special Commissioners recommended abandoning the settlement Enderby resigned both as Chief Commissioner and Lieutenant-Governor. Only the government could accept the latter; Enderby awaited their pleasure at the islands, his relations with Dundas and Preston deteriorating as they ignored his gratuitous advice.

Matters came to a head on 21 February 1852 when a seaman died of scurvy and neglect in the makeshift hospital, an unlined work shed with a few rough bunks. Enderby had been in the habit of visiting the hospital every day. The Special Commissioners left it to the doctor, a drunkard who in turn delegated the irksome task to an invalid seaman. Three days before the death the patients had been left without food, water or medical attention for seventeen hours. Enderby tried to refuse burial until cause of death was properly certified. His authority was defied. He was turned out of his house, ordered off the islands and, under threat of being placed in irons if he would not comply, constrained to accompany the Special Commissioners to Wellington. There Enderby had Dundas and Preston arrested for forcing him to leave the islands and for arrears of salary. They were released on bail and two days later all three made an appearance at the Governor's Queen's birthday levee, Enderby resplendent 'in full dress, Windsor uniform'. The Governor, Sir George Grey, declined to return Enderby to the Auckland Islands and he lingered in Wellington for a year, unwilling to face the humiliation of returning to London.

In the meantime Port Ross had been abandoned. The Acting Commissioner, Mackworth, had asked for a warship to remain at the islands during the breakup of the settlement, fearing that news of the Australian gold rush would move his already restless seamen to violence. The final cruise of the last ship to return, the *Earl of Hardwicke*, exemplified much of what had gone wrong. Out four months, of which three weeks had been spent trying to beat up to the anchorage, she brought in only 40 barrels. The provisions were exhausted and all of the crew were down with scurvy. One man had died and four were in irons. Towns wrote to his associate Brooks, one of the directors, opining that 'English whalers are not the men for our colonial ships, they are accustomed to too much extravagance and their own way'. The Southern Whale Fishery Company was wound up in 1855.

On his eventual return to London, Enderby cut a sad figure. The family firm was no more. The last tenuous connection with the *Samuel Enderby* was severed at its sale in 1855. For years Charles pursued the company and the Special Commissioners. They in turn blamed him for the failure but both were at fault, Enderby for princely ambition and the directors for blindness about the prince's lack of clothes. Although he was alleging usurpation of the authority of the Crown and manslaughter, Enderby was unable to excite much interest in the Colonial Office or the general public. When the second batch of Commissioners' replies to Enderby's accusations was published as a Parliamentary Paper in 1855 *The Times* did not try very hard to explain why the Colonial Office had declined to act, confining itself to 'the most salient points of a very prolix and uninteresting correspondence'.[10]

In his old age, Enderby lived at the back of his daughter's house in Kensington. It was understood in the family that he was not to be trusted with money.[11] In 1874 he tried to write a brief account of the family's involvement in South Sea whaling for his nieces and nephews. It was a rambling valediction for the trade, and typically wrong-headed in explaining the cause of its demise.

> . . . the Southern Whale Fishery although ostensibly only catching fish in the Ocean kept up communication and gradually opened up trade with all of the minuter parts of the world ending in a flourishing trade to every inhabited portion of the world and having thus performed its function it died away so entirely that for the last ten years not a single ship has been fitted from England . . . [12]

With the death of Charles in 1876, the House of Enderby passed into history. Its fame endures, not in dusty narratives of Antarctic exploration or commercial hazard and failure, but in the encomium of an American whaleman who in the early months of 1841 encountered the *Samuel Enderby* off the coast of Chile.

> Ere the English ship fades from sight, be it set down here, that she hailed from London, and was named after the late Samuel Enderby, merchant of that city, the original of the famous house of Enderby & Sons; a house which in my poor whaleman's opinion, comes not far behind the united royal houses of the Tudors and Bourbons, in point of real historical interest. How long, prior to the year of our Lord 1775, this great whaling house was in existence, my numerous fish-documents do not make plain; but in that year it fitted out the first English ships that ever regularly hunted the Sperm Whale . . . In 1788, a fine ship, the *Amelia*, fitted out for the express purpose, and at the sole charge of the vigorous Enderbys, boldly rounded Cape Horn, and was the first among the nations to lower a whale-boat of any sort in the great South Sea . . . All honour to the Enderbies, therefore, whose house, I think exists to the present day; though doubtless the original Samuel must long ago have slipped his cable for the great South Sea of the other world.[13]

As Charles had written, the British trade did not long outlive Enderby involvement. In 1859 Her Majesty's Customs recorded the last British cargoes of sperm oil to be landed in London. The *Cowlitz* and the *Caroline* brought in 196 barrels between them.

Cowlitz had been out 39 months: the oil she took would not have kept the crew in beef and biscuit. Robert Towns, who had continued in the trade with Brooks as a partner, tried to keep Sydney whaling going in the 1850s, but the labour shortages of the gold rushes and a shortage of accessible whales defeated him and the handful of others who persevered.

> I little expected the change that has taken place in our whaling property—I am at a final stand what to do. Carpenters wages continue fifteen shillings per day and neither masters nor officers to be found for whalers—I did hope we should have a change for the better but the news from Port Phillip today puts an end to all such hopes—it appears gold is now being found in greater and more wonderful abundance than ever . . . what is all this to end in—our sailors will be more unsettled than ever.[14]

In 1861 Henry Kendall's old school of hard knocks, the *Waterwitch*, reported from 34° south and 159° east that she had not seen a whale, much less caught one, in five months. Nine months' cruising had yielded only 300 barrels. If it were true that the whales were not lost, but merely displaced, then finding them appeared to be beyond both the British and their Australasian colonists.

Boat and Barque
or The Mother Ship and Her Offspring

*I never saw anything so ready and so smart as the way
that whaler, rolling desperately all the time, lowered one
of her boats . . . the microscopic white speck of the boat
seemed to come into the game instantly, as if shot out
from a catapult on the enormous and lonely stage.*

Joseph Conrad

It was the boats that set the whaleship apart from her sea-
going sisters. Viewed from afar she was an anxious old mother,
with four offspring under her wings and another two on her back.
She might be worn out and dowdy, her best years behind her,
but her children were all youth and dash, and she tended them
with nervous pride. The design criteria for these small charges
were speed under oars, carrying capacity, seaworthiness and
manoeuvrability. Strength was desirable, but that meant weight
and weight was the enemy of speed. Ease of repair was the
trade-off but, even so, few boats made more than one cruise. They
were expendable and therefore had to be cheap.

In an emergency Charles Beetle, master boatbuilder of New
Bedford, could make you one in 28 hours. In the 1840s it would
have cost you $50. There never was a standard whaleboat, but
many features had become conventional long before the great

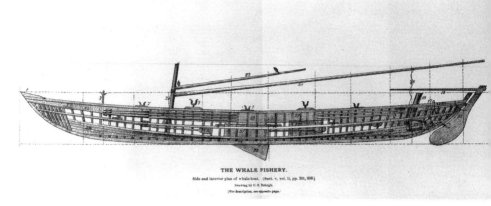

THE WHALE FISHERY.
Side and interior plan of whale-boat. (Sect. v, vol. ii, pp. 241, 256.)
Drawing by C. S. Raleigh.
[For description, see opposite page.

SIDE AND INTERIOR PLAN OF WHALE-BOAT,

Length, 30 feet.

1, Bow, chock, and roller. 2, Clumsy cleat, and hoisting eyebolt. 3, Crotch for bow harpoon irons. 4, Harpooner thwart. 5, Paddles. 6, Harpoon irons, lances on opposite side. 7, Rowlocks for oars. 8, Bow thwart. 9, Midship thwart. 10, Tub thwart. 11. After thwart. 12, Boat spades and waifs (i. e., small flags to locate dead whale). 13, Lantern keg. 14, Piggin (for bailing boat, &c.). 15. Rudder. 16, Rowlock for steering, oar. 17. Hoisting eyebolt. 18, Tiller. 19, Loggerhead. 20, Boom for sail 21, Center case (small tub for 75 fathom-line other side). 22, Large tub for whale line, 225 fathoms. 23, Gaff for sail. 24, Mast for sail. 25, Keel and floor timbers 26, Main sheet. 27, Gunwale streak plank, 9 inches in widest part, generally colored blue in new boats. Timber of boat of this size, about 6 inches apart (generally). 28, Center-board partly down. 29, Boat's ceiling.

NOTE.—*Oars* omitted on this draft, full length being given on front and interior plan.

Whaleboat elevation and interior plan (from G B Goode's The Fisheries and Fishery Industries of the United States, *National Library of Australia)*

American artisans of the mid-nineteenth century gave them final form. The double-ended, single-banked, oar-steered, lapstake-built boat constructed around 1700 would have been almost as familiar to the whaleman of 1900 as his own. The later classics built by Beetle, Leonard, Edwards and others were long for their breadth and shallow, with a pronounced sheer and raked ends. Amidships they were slightly flared. Using the half-inch cedar planking that had characterised Nantucket boats since Christopher Hussey's time, they could build a 28–30 foot whaleboat with a 6-foot beam that weighed no more than 1000 pounds. In no

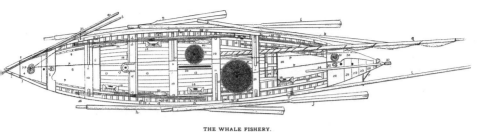

THE WHALE FISHERY.

Deck view of whale-boat ready for the chase; scale, ⅜ inch to foot. (Sect. v, vol. ii, pp. 241, 258.)

Drawing by C. S. Raleigh.

[For description, see opposite page.]

DECK VIEW OF WHALE BOAT READY FOR THE CHASE.

[Scale ⅜ inch to foot. Parts of boats designated by figures and, utensils by letters.]

1, Bow-chocks through which tow-line runs when fast to a whale. 2, Lance straightener; a slot in gunwale or straightening bent irons. 3, 3, Top or false chocks, nailed on gunwhales. 4, Box of boat. 5, Clumsy-cleat or high thwart used by boat-steerer to steady himself during the capture. 6, Shackle or iron strap, for hoisting and lowering the boat to and from the ship. 7, 7, 7, Timbers of boat. 8, Platform (forward) upon which boat-steerer and officer stand when striking and working a whale. 9, 9, Risings, or top board of ceiling, on which the thwarts are placed and nailed. 10, Harpooner thwart. 11, 11, 11, 11, Knees on all thwarts. 12, 12, 12, 12, Dunnage for all thwarts; the main thwart (16) is dunnage all the way across. 13, 13, 13, Boat ceiling (inside planking); the bottom of boat. 14, 14, 14, 14, Peak cleats; wooden cleats for the reception of the handles of the oars when apeak; used when fast to a whale, when the oarsmen are resting, &c. 15, Peak cleat for tub-oar. 16, Bow-thwart; a seat for the bow oarsman. 17, Mast-hinge and strap, showing mast-hinge block. 18, 18, 18, Sail-cleats. 19, Mid-ship thwart or mid-ship oarsman. 20, Center-board, box and well. 21, Gunwales. 22, Tub-thwart for tub oarsman. 23, After thwart. 24, Well for bailing boat. 25, Plug for letting water out of boat when on the cranes. 26, Platform (aft) on which officer and boat-steerer stand when steering boat. 27, Standing cleats upon which officer stands when going on to a whale in order to get a *longer view*. 28, Cuddy-board. 29, 29, 29, 29, 29, Cuddy-boards; cedar boards filling up the stern of boat from the cuddy-b· ard aft to stern-post. 30, Logger head strip, or *lion's tongue*. 31, Logger-head; an upright post with enlarged head, around the neck of which runs the tow-line when fast to a whale and by which the line is managed. 32, Boat-iron, or shackle, same as 6. 33, Rudder. 34, Tiller. 35, 35, 35, High and low rowlocks (wooden), wi h holes for the reception of shanks of rowlocks. 36, 36, Bow-cleats; nailed to gunwales, and used in *bowing on a whale*, and also as safeguard in case the tow-line should jump from bow-chocks and preventing it from sweeping the boat aft.

A, First iron, shank resting in bow-chocks and handle in boat-crotch. *B*, Second iron, placed in same position as first iron; the handle of first iron, which is the first instrument used, is placed in the top crotch; the handle of second iron is placed in the lower crotch; the extreme end of tow-line is bent in the eye of the first iron strap; these two irons are known as the live irons or live harpoons. *C, C*, Spare irons on port side of boat above thwarts (the two other spare irons, one on either side of boat under thwarts cannot be shown in this plan). *D, D, D*, Three lances (thrust by hand) on starboard side of boat, used in killing the whale. *E*, Boat spade on starboard side aft. *G*, Harpooner oar. *H*, Bow-oar. *I*, Mid-ship oar. *J*, Tub oar. *K*, Stroke-oar. *L*, Steering-oar, manipulated by officer of boat when going on to a whale. *M, M, M, M, M*, Paddles. *N*, Small tub with tow-line coiled down, containing 75 fathoms of line. *O*, Large tub with tow line coiled down, containing 225 fathoms of line. *P, P, P*, Tow-line extending aft from large tub around loggerhead and forward across the thwarts to box of boat (4), where it is coiled and known as box-warp (*PP*); thence extending to and bent in eye-splice of first iron strap. *Q, Q*, Mast and sail. *R*, Steering-oar brace. *S*, Lashing or strap for handle of steering-oar when not in use or fast to a whale.

Whaleboat deck plan (from G B Goode's The Fisheries and Fishery Industries of the United States, *National Library of Australia)* other type of working boat did form and function find such an elegant synthesis. But then they put in the gear.

Mast, sail, oars, paddles, line tubs, harpoons, lances, boat spade, waifs, drogues, bucket, bailing piggin, lantern keg—these were only the large items, and all up the load was some 900 pounds before the crew got in. To make sense of the arrangement of this mass of men and matériel we should follow what was in effect the boat's right of way, the path taken by the whale line. The line had absolute priority in the boat, as befitted the boatsteerer's pampered pet. In the ropewalks of New England, three strands of Manilla or tar-vapoured hemp, thirteen or fifteen yarns to the strand, had been drawn together to make a line 2 inches in circumference with a breaking strain of about 6000 pounds. To ensure that it was kink-free, all 75 fathoms had been run astern or to the masthead. Three lengths were carefully spliced to make a 225-fathom line that was then Flemish-coiled in a wooden tub, with both ends free. Stored on the ship's deck under cover, the tub was loaded into the boat before lowering, and sat to larboard beside the feet of the tub oarsman. Its uncentred weight of 230 pounds was partially offset by that of its little brother, which with 75 fathoms inside was placed just forward on the starboard side of the centreboard trunk next to the midship oarsman. There was a more substantial weight offset in the form of the mast which, when not erect, had its heel jammed under the after thwart and its length draped inelegantly over the starboard quarter.

With their loose ends no more than a foot apart, it was the work of an instant to bend the second tub line to the eye of the first if the whale demanded more. If all that went too and there were no other boats present to add their lines, the whale would take it all, because it was anathema to secure the line to the boat. To do so would risk losing boat and crew as well as the line. Resuming our tour, we find that the line is drawing aft rather than forward. This excursion is so that it can pass around the loggerhead, a short, stout wooden post that protrudes from the starboard side of the afterdeck. Here it cannot impede use of the steering oar that trails to larboard. A few turns around the loggerhead will retard the rate at which the whale takes the line, but the friction can be fierce enough to set fire to the wood and one of the tub oarsman's duties is to ensure that the line is wet as it leaves the tub.

The view forward as we turn around the loggerhead reveals the line undulating over the oars towards the bow. There are five rowing oars, three to starboard and two to larboard. Each oarsman sits on the side opposite his rowlock to extract maximum leverage for his oar. The two/three arrangement is convenient for the headsman because he can shorten his orders, as in 'pull three, stern two', which will turn the boat around in its own length, but its rationale is to balance the pulling power once the harpooner has peaked his oar to 'stand up'. The length of the oars is calculated to maintain the balance of power in the absence of the harpooner. If his oar is 14 feet long, the others on his side of the boat, midship and aft, will be 18 and 14 feet respectively. The bow and tub oars on the other side will both be 16 feet long. Lines painted across the blades permit easy identification. The power-to-weight ratio with all oars in play is so high that from full speed the boat can be stopped within a length. Any imbalance when the harpooner is at his oar can be redressed by the headsman, whose 23-foot steering oar has great sculling power in the hands of a man powerful enough to manage it. With all other oars apeak, the steering oar alone can propel the boat and spin it like a top. Unlike a racing shell, of which the stroke oarsman is the powerhouse, the whaleboat has the lightest man at the after oar because the headsman has a hand free to back up.

Beyond the harpooner, at the leading edge of the clumsy cleat, the line passes under a kicking strap and crosses the bow box to leave the boat through lead-lined bow chocks. The chock pin that holds the line in the channel is made weak enough to break if fouled. Outside of the boat the line doubles back and comes in over the starboard gunwale, where a few fathoms are coiled as the box warp. The harpooner may hold the warp in his left hand to keep it clear while the harpoon is in his right. We have come to the end of the line: the serpent is about to acquire teeth. The two harpoons to be used have lines of their own, lashings that hold the iron to its hickory pole and run the length of the pole to end in a loop at its base. The first of the live irons is bent directly onto the end of the whale line. The second is loosely attached to the line by a short warp with a running bowline. Both are placed ready for use in a crotch at the starboard bow.

A smartly drilled crew will have plug and line tubs in, gripes and gig tackle off, cranes swung in, boat lowered, davit tackles cast off and oars manned in one minute flat. In a calm sea under oars alone, the men will be able to make 5 knots for the first hour and 4 knots in the second. The oars will flex as they make the 'white ash breeze', but as the men can row only marginally faster than the cruising speed of the whale the race is an even contest. Towards the middle of the century, as the whales became increasingly difficult to approach, sailing on to them became common, and whaling captains became as keen as their naval counterparts to manoeuvre for the advantage of the weather gauge, positioning their ships to windward. It is possible that the whales came to understand that their pursuers were unable to sail directly into the wind; humpbacks in particular were notorious for fleeing dead to windward when gallied.

While sailing on might have saved the oarsmen's arms, lowering the mast and sail added considerably to movement and instability in the boat once the whale had been struck. The boatsteerer cast off the halyards to lower the sail, which was furled and tied by the other men who remained in their seats. The bow oarsman cast off the shrouds and wrapped them around the mast, which was then lifted by the boatsteerer and caught by the headsman and aft oarsmen as it fell back. Only then could the boatsteerer and headsman change places. Whalemen were inordinately proud of their boats. To the speed and grace of these flyers can be attributed much of the spirit of competition that attended a whale chase, and of the ability of crews to pull 20 miles in a day, fight a whale, and if necessary do it all again the next.

> It is the fruit of a century's experience, and the sharpened sense and ingenuity of an inventive people, urged by the peril of the chase and the value of the prize. For lightness and form; for carrying capacity as compared with its weight and sea-going qualities; for speed and facility of movement at the word of command; for the placing of the men at the best advantage in the exercise of their power; by the nicest adaptation of the varying length of the oar to its position in the boat; and, lastly, for a simplicity of construction which renders repairs practicable on board the ship, the whale-boat is simply as perfect as the skill of the million men [sic] who have risked life and limb in service could make it.[1]

Until the boatsteerer struck, the whale line was a benignly inanimate object that hardly seemed to warrant the fuss made of it. All that changed on the instant. The boatsteerer aimed for an area behind the fin, from about 4 or 5 fathoms distance if he had a good eye and arm, or point blank, 'wood on blackskin', if the headsman lacked confidence in him. His most urgent task then was to get rid of the second iron which, with the line running, would very soon be wild in the boat. His preference was to put it into the whale, even though it would only take the weight if the first iron drew. Otherwise he would jettison it, to be retrieved with the line.

The whale could settle, making a disconcertingly effortless disappearance, but more often than not it would run or sound after making its displeasure clear with an angry sweep of the flukes. Sounding was the more dangerous. The sperm whale might choose to descend almost vertically, which could mean the line going straight down from the bow and running out at as much as $7\frac{1}{2}$ fathoms per second. At such a rate the line would be exhausted in 40 seconds. Any attempt to brake it with the loggerhead would simply take the boat down, and a foul line could produce the same result. At this point the line is in full tantrum, its voice a discord of scream and thunder. The flakes spring from the tub at a speed the eye can scarcely follow.

Inadvertently to touch the banshee in its wild career is as to be struck by a club. Bare skin it does not burn, but tears like a serrated knife. If the flakes give the slightest appearance of coming out unevenly, or an obstruction threatens to divert the line from its ramrod course, the order will be to cut, accompanied by a silent prayer that the hatchet or knife will be in time and not itself deflected. Usually the descent stopped before the line was out, which was fortunate for the whalemen because the whale could dive much deeper than their line could reach.

If the whale ran, the boat was off on a Nantucket sleigh ride. With a sprint speed of around 20 knots, trumpo could tow a boat into a head sea with enough force to start the planks as cedar slammed through one crest after another, the keel not even finding the troughs between. All hands huddled in the stern sheets to keep the bow up, which made balancing the boat that much more difficult. 'Trim boat', was the order, 'Don't shift your tobacco!' When the pace slackened sufficiently, all the line that had run out with such abandon had to be hauled in, hand over hand, and coiled in the sternsheets by the aft oarsman in case the whale ran again. As the boat came up to the whale, the bow oarsman took the line from the bow chocks and brought it to a cleat on the side, which drew the boat alongside and parallel to the whale. The headsman now began to ply the lance, either by hand or by throwing and retrieving it with a short warp. A more hazardous proceeding, employed only if the whale appeared likely to run again, was to use the boat spade (a narrow-bladed cutting spade) to sever the tendons in the small of the back, immobilising the flukes.

There was always a danger that a sperm whale would fight rather than struggle to escape. A well-directed fluke stroke was invariably the end of the boat but, as the whale relied on touch to find the target and then swept its tail away before striking with the recoil, it could often be avoided. The jaw, on the other hand, was less powerful but more precise. In attack, the whale would roll almost onto its back and come up under the boat, lower jaw open and poised, but so poorly placed were its eyes for viewing ahead at close quarters that a boat might escape even from this extremity.

> Being thus ingulfed in the whale's mouth and threatened with immediate destruction by the shutting of his jaws, which stood erect eight feet above water exhibiting two tremendous rows of teeth the sight of which were sufficient to dismay and terrify our hearts, there was but one alternative for us if we would save ourselves and that was to take a hold of his jaw which was one foot from my shoulder, and keep the boat from touching his teeth. This was the most important thing to be done as he was only waiting for something to touch his teeth in order to crush it in a moment; and as I was the nearest to it, it came to my lot to perform this most dangerous duty, and seeing our immediate, and imminent danger I did not hesitate, but instantly rose and stood upon the gun-wale of the boat, placing each of my hands and fingers between each row of teeth and kept the boat off, and at the same time pushed the boat ahead and she cleared the whale.[2]

More often than not a boat that found itself in that position would be hopelessly stove, with perhaps a man or two missing. Once capsized, the boats were difficult to right and impossible to bail. If, however, attempts to right a boat failed, the overlapping planks of lapstrake, or clinker construction, allowed the crew a handhold. When carvel construction came into vogue in the middle of the nineteenth century, because its batten-seamed flush planking was quieter in the water and less likely to alarm the whales, some boatbuilders did not forget the old safety feature. The plank second from the keel still overlapped the garboard.

The boats were singular and expendable: their mother ships were motley and enduring. Purpose-built whaleships were a comparatively late development. Until the second quarter of the nineteenth century it would be no exaggeration to say that almost any vessel of the desired size would do provided that it had two decks, or a second could be built above the hold. Merchant sailers were built to be maids of all work, and the whaleman's only special requirements were for space between decks for a blubber room and steerage accommodation, and a clear area on the main

The Joust

The boat moves smoothly through the water, rowlocks thrummed to make as little noise as possible. The bull comes on. He has only just commenced spouting out after a dive and can be relied on to spout once for each foot of his length before sounding again. At three respirations a minute, this one should be up for twenty minutes. Enough time to close, bless his huge hide. Given the option, the mate prefers head-on attack. Coming from astern is more oar work for the men and it is difficult to avoid the oily 'glip' that marks the whale's passage and which all whalemen swear will alert him if crossed. And then the boat would have to cross the flukes to get within sure darting range.

The massive forehead grows with each passing minute but the whale shows no sign of seeing the boat, and cannot unless the mate strays a few degrees to right or left. The forehead, wide as a locomotive, presents a tempting but deceitful target; it is so dense that the sharpest harpoon will not penetrate far enough to hold. Whale and boat are closing at a combined speed of about 8 knots. Wind is not a factor and so the mate decides to pass the whale to larboard, which will give his right-handed boatsteerer the easiest dart. At perhaps 50 fathoms from the whale comes the order to arm: 'Stand up'.

The boatsteerer peaks his oar and takes the covers from the heads of the live irons in their crotch. Unhooded, the razor edges blink in the sunlight. With box warp in his left hand and first iron in the right, the boatsteerer braces his left thigh in the clumsy cleat. For once, he has not been drained by an exhausting pull after the whale. This will be a strong dart. Then a rank oily mist envelops the boat and the whale is with them.

Just short of collision, the mate sweeps the long steering oar to larboard and boat and whale are passing in parallel. Instantly he makes another, wider sweep, this time to starboard, to bring the side of the whale bow on. 'Give it

to him!', and from a distance of no more than 4 fathoms
the harpoon darts, flat and hard. The boatsteerer's window
of opportunity is a matter of seconds if he is to strike the
whale between fin and small. By the time he can get the
second iron into his hand, the whale has felt the prick of
the first and begun to settle. So quickly can this effortless
disappearing trick be accomplished that the second iron
may find nothing but water. It would probably have failed
to bite even had it made contact, for another of the
whale's defences is to bow his body, compacting his side
blubber to the impenetrability of his forehead.

The mate's control over events ends with the order
'Stern all!' (traditionally and realistically accompanied by
the incentive 'for your lives'). All now depends on the
whale. He can sound until the 300 fathoms of line are
gone, against which the only option is to tie off the line,
abandon ship and 'give him the boat', thus converting it
into an expensive drogue. He can go 'head out' at
20 knots or more and although the speed cannot be
sustained for long it might be long enough, if crashing
through a head sea, to start the boat's planking. He can
maintain escape speed of 11 knots or so for some hours
which, if interspersed with judicious sounding when the
boat has been hauled up to him, will exhaust the crew and
leave the mate with no option but to cut the line at
nightfall.

These are the mate's nightmares, but he can also dream.
He would have the whale, after settling or sounding,
quickly return to the surface to try conclusions between
jaw and lance. Because the whale's teeth are located only
in its lower jaw, its instinct is to bite at objects on the
surface from below. To do this it must roll on its side, into
what whalemen call the 'first biting position'. While the
boat is now at its most vulnerable so is the whale, for in
turning it has exposed its 'life', the small area immediately
abaft the fin through which the lance can reach heart and
lungs. It is then merely a question of who can strike first.

The mate is a confident man, as all must be who have such dangerous dreams. In the short interval between his sharp challenge and the whale's acceptance, he and the boatsteerer must somehow manage to change places. To stand is hazardous in a small boat on the open sea. To move is worse; if it must be done, it should be done one person at a time along the centreline. For two men to do it simultaneously in opposite directions, clambering over four oars while avoiding the centreline, where the whaleline is in full cry, is an act of consummate boatmanship. The mate has the honour of the lance, and puts the boat at risk to claim it, not because he is the senior man, but because he is the most experienced. The esquire makes way for the knight.

The lance can be thrown and retrieved by the short warp attached to it, but it is much more effective held and churned in the whale. If the boatsteerer can hold the boat parallel to the whale while the mate delves, neither jaw nor flukes will be able to engage. The whale signals his defeat with the 'red flag', spouting a pink mist punctuated with barrel-sized gouts of blood. 'Fire in the chimney!' announces the triumph, and the boat draws off to avoid the uncontrolled power of the 'flurry' as the whale drowns in his own blood. With 'fin out' a whale may be presumed dead, but whalemen who have had a nasty surprise while cutting a tow-hole in the head will take the precaution of pricking the eye with a lance before taking liberties.

An eruption in the water ahead spoils the daydream. This whale is up but running. It may be several exhausting hours before they can close to lancing range, and there will be flukes as well as jaw to contend with. 'Haul line!'

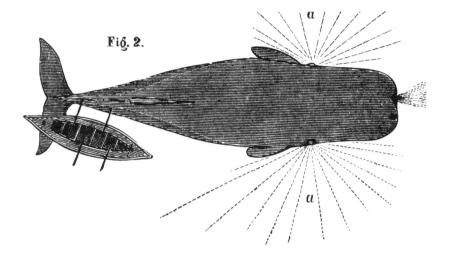

The difficulty of avoiding eyes and flukes at the same time in a stern approach (from William Davis's Nimrod of the Sea*)*

deck abaft the foremast large enough for tryworks. Just as time was no object to a whaler, so age was no impediment. The *Maria*, the ship that carried William Rotch to London in 1785, whaled almost continuously until 1863, when she was condemned at Talcahuano. After three years as a coaler, local interests returned her to whaling. At 202 tons she was amongst the largest of whalers when she entered the trade; when she left it she was one of the smaller three-masters.

Some of these veterans inspired fierce loyalty in their crews, and an affection that was almost perverse. It had nothing to do with speed or appearance, the points of honour that seamen most often found themselves defending in bar-room brawls. Perhaps it grew out of the length of time spent in the ship, the sentimental attachment to a home, whatever it might be. Melville spent only two months on the *Lucy Ann*, which he called the *Julia*, but fell under her spell. She had been built in New Brunswick after the War of 1812, and only sent a-whaling in the 1830s after government service in Australia. To Melville she seemed very old, with unsound lower masts, worn rigging and rotten bulwarks, and only 'tolerably tight'.

> But all this had nothing to do with her sailing; at that, brave little
> Jule, plump little Jule, was a witch. Blow high, or blow low, she was
> always ready for the breeze; and when she dashed the waves from her
> prow, and pranced, and pawed the sea, you never thought of her
> patched sails and blistered hull. How the fleet creature would fly
> before the wind! rolling, now and then, to be sure, but in very
> playfulness. Sailing to windward, no gale could bow her over: with
> spars erect, she looked right up into the wind's eye, and so she went.
> But after all, Little Jule was not to be confided in. Lively enough,
> and playful she was, but on that very account the more to be
> distrusted. Who knew, but that like some vivacious old mortal all at
> once sinking into a decline, she might, some dark night, spring a leak
> and carry us all to the bottom? However, she played us no such ugly
> trick, and therefore I wrong Little Jule in supposing it.[3]

South Sea whaling had a lifetime beyond the span of any of the men or ships or firms that pursued the trade, but there are threads that connect them through the years like the fibrous network that runs through the flesh of the sperm whale. The man who succeeded Henry Ventom as master of the *Lucy Ann* was William Lee, who in turn parted from the ship shortly before she was bought by Ben Boyd in 1845. Lee subsequently commanded the *Waterwitch* on the 1855–57 cruise during which Henry Kendall served his apprenticeship. But Kendall left no fond literary memoir of 'the slave ship', so it would be unwise to assume that too many whaleman were as prepared as Melville to find virtue in their 'home on the rolling sea'.

But we digress. In the course of her 80-year whaling career, the *Maria* underwent only one significant change. In 1840 she was converted from ship-rig, with square sails on all three masts, to barque-rig, with only fore and aft sails on the mizzen. The change was a common one at the time, driven by an opinion among owners that any loss of speed (which was irrelevant as well as debatable) was more than offset by greater ease of handling. Of all the whalemen's odd practices, the one that gave other seamen the most nightmares was the virtual abandonment of the ship when all of the boats were launched at once. A 350-ton vessel would often be left in the keeping of the cooper, the cook and the cabin boy. With the main topsail left aback, they drifted. Their duty was to man the masthead and helm and signal the whale's movements to the boats, but a shift in the wind or the need to assist exhausted boat crews might require them to work the ship, and this was much easier to do using fore and aft sails. Presumably the owners then felt able to dispense with the cabin boy. The practice was not quite as risky as it appeared. Unless the ship were actively being sailed away from the boats, they could easily overtake her—provided that she was in sight.

The 1820s and 1830s also saw the advent of the purpose-built whaler. The explosive growth of American whaling made it harder for owners to pick up second-hand merchantmen cheaply. At the same time the industry was so prosperous and its long-term prospects so good that owners were prepared to build. One such was Charles Waln Morgan, grandson-in-law to William Rotch. The old man had died in New Bedford in 1828, but by then Charles had not only served for several years in the Rotch counting house but, with brother-in-law Samuel Rodman, had aquired his own interests in whaleships. Now, in 1841, after a number of his ships had returned with good cargoes, he commissioned the Hillman brothers to build him another. The keel was laid in early February and the unnamed ship was launched on 21 July. Building time would have been under five months had not seventeen days been lost to a strike when the carpenters were refused the ten-hour day. They had to settle for ten and a half hours, worked six days a week. Altogether, the carpenters, caulkers and joiners were paid less than $8000 from a total outlay of $31,000.

In August, Charles returned from a business trip to find that the ship now bore his name, a decision taken by his nephew and one with which he did not altogether agree, perhaps wondering about the reaction of his partners. For although Charles was the largest shareholder, in his own right he owned but one-quarter of the ship. The Nantucket tradition of active partnership, capital's equivalent of the lay, was still strong. Samuel Rodman and Charles' firm of Pope and Morgan both held one-eighth shares, as did the ship's captain, Thomas Norton. The remainder was held as sixteenths, one by the Hillmans and one by David Brayton, the yard foreman. The certificate of admeasurement lodged at the New Bedford Customs House described the *Charles W Morgan* as carvel-built, two decks, three masts, 106 feet and 6 inches in length, 27 feet and 2½ inches in breadth, 13 feet and 7¼ inches in depth, and of 351 and 31/94ths tons burthen. True depth was 17.6 feet; the certificated figure was a register measurement calculated as half of the breadth. Just another merchantman—except for the deck fittings.

The tryworks are unavoidable, a brick wall blocking the way as you emerge from the forecastle scuttle. Looking aft from the windlass (the good old-fashioned barrel and handspike, none of your new-fangled patented pump-types here) greenhands might remark on the large section of bulwark missing at the starboard gangway and the scaffolding over the gap. This is not work in progress but the cutting stage, which when lowered outboard parallel to the deck will provide the platform from which the mates will perform surgery on the whale. The deck underfoot is double-planked; its top layer, which will be much cut about by the end of the cruise, will follow the tryworks bricks overboard as the ship approaches home. Further aft, over the booby hatch which gives entry to the steerage, there are two gallows-like structures. Across them lie two inverted boats, which seems a bit excessive when there are already four sitting outboard on cranes, three down the larboard side and one on the starboard quarter. Right aft along the flush deck is the wheel, a standard fitting one might think, but this device is just one remove from a tiller, on which it in fact sits. The wheel travels to starboard or larboard with the tiller when it is turned, and the tyros will soon discover why it is called toejammer and shincracker. Altogether, when the greenhands contemplate these things and the bluff bows that are so unlike those of a Baltimore clipper, they may conclude that the Hillman brothers have not built a new ship, but an old one.

In 1867 the *Morgan*, like the *Maria* before her, was cut down from ship to barque. At some time in her 80-year career an afterhouse was built over the cabin skylight and wheel. It housed the galley, the bosun's locker, the paint locker and the cabin stairs. The stern windows were timbered over to exclude following seas. The windlass was moved forward of the foremast to make more space for the tryworks. As to whaling arrangements, the only change of note in all that time was the addition of a fifth boat, carried at the starboard bow. In the course of 37 voyages she brought home cargoes worth a total of $1.4 million for her successive owners. On the first voyage the officers and crew were mainly New Englanders; on the last, Portuguese almost to a man.

After the industry began its long decline in the 1850s, there should have been no need to build new whaleships. Demand was down and for the time being there was no shortage of superannuated wooden vessels as the long-term advantages of building in iron began to outweigh the costs. Yet such was the havoc wreaked by the Civil War and the Arctic disasters of the 1870s that when the whalebone market boomed it again became worthwhile to build wooden whalers, the more so as the builders in this outdated material were desperate for business. The enthusiasm was brief, but it called forth a generation of wooden whalers, the last, that was quite different from its predecessors. They were different because they were pretty, even dainty. Shipbuilders were still building what they knew, and by now what they knew was the smart moderate-clipper type that had replaced the extreme clippers of the 1840s and 1850s. The barque *Alice Knowles*, 302 tons, built in 1879, was representative of her kind.

In place of the square bows and upright masts characteristic of the *Charles W Morgan* and her predecessors ('built by the mile and cut off by the length'), the *Alice Knowles* had a cutaway bow and raked masts. The foremast was also stepped further aft, which

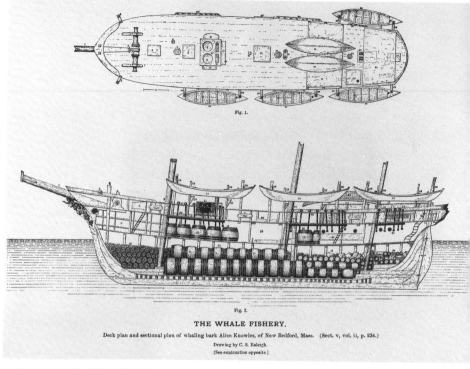

Fig. 1.

Fig. 2.

THE WHALE FISHERY.

Deck plan and sectional plan of whaling bark Alice Knowles, of New Bedford, Mass. (Sect. v, vol. ii, p. 234.)

Drawing by C. S. Raleigh.

[See explanation opposite.]

DECK PLAN AND SIDE AND INTERIOR PLAN OF WHALING BARK ALICE KNOWLES OF NEW BED FORD, MASS.

302.78 TONS.

FIG. 1. DECK PLAN.—1, Heel of bowsprit. 2, Paul-bitt. 3, Cat-heads. 4, Windlass and bitts. 5, Forecastl companions. 6, Fluke-chain bitt. 7, Foremast. 8, Fore hatch. 9, Try-pots. 10, Try-works. 11, Cooler. 12, Scra hopper. 13, Work-bench. 14, Chimney and flue. 15, Main hatch. 16, Mainmast. 17, Pumps. 18, Deck-house 19, Spare boats. 20, Galley. 21, Mizzen-mast. 22, Cabin skylight. 23, After deck house. 24, Wheel and screw box 25, Fore channels. 26, Main channels. 27, Cutting-in gangway. 28, 28, 28, 28, Whale boats on cranes for activ service. 29, Boat-davits. 30, Mizzen-chains. 31, Bit (for the belly-chain of the whale).

FIG. 2. SIDE AND INTERIOR PLAN.—(Scale one-sixteenth inch to foot.) 1, Bowsprit. 2, Paul-bitt. 3, Cat-head 4, Windlass and bitts. 5, Figure-head. 6, Forecastle companion. 7, Hawse-chocks. 8, Foremast. 9, Forecastl 10, Fore hold shooks, gear, &c. 11, Casks for oil (riders). 12, Casks for oil (between decks). 13, Fore 'tween deck 14, Blubber room. 15, Try-works. 16, Steerage. 17, Chain locker and pumps. 18, After hold (stores, gear, &c.). 1 After peak (captain's stores, &c.). 20, Captain's cabin. 21, Galley. 22, Skids for spare boats. 23, Mainmast. 2 Mizzen-mast. 25, After house. 26, Boat davits. 27, Whale boats. 28, Boat bearers. 29, Main hatch. 30, For hatch. 31, Booby hatch. 32, Cabin skylight. 33, Wheel and screw box. 34, Cranes for boats. 35, Lower mai hold. 36, After 'tween deck. 37, Fore channels. 38, Main channels. 39, Mizzen channels.

Deck plan and elevation of the whaling barque Alice Knowles *(from* G B Goode's The Fisheries and Fishery Industries of the United States, *National Library of Australia)* left space for a larger forecastle and forehold. No doubt the crew were grateful, and there was more space for storing shooks, but the trade-off was a smaller main hold. Fewer large casks could be carried and oil-carrying capacity was thereby reduced. To a whaler speed was of no consequence, and crew comfort was neither here nor there to owners, but oil was her life's blood. The last whalers exposed a paradox: the *Maria* generation had no pedigree but had a form appropriate to function, so appropriate that the builders of the 1840s eschewed innovation and sought only to build to the desired size. The builders of the 1870s failed to adapt their standard product, and functionality was sacrificed to form.

The whaleboats retained their design integrity to the very end. Mother fell victim to fashion.

8

SEAS AFLAME

*New England enterprise: It grapples with the monsters
of the Pacific to illuminate our dwellings, and with the
problems of science to enlighten our minds.*

Toast at the New England Society's dinner, 1848

The 1850s were the uncertain decade for the American whaling industry. Engrossing the world had been exciting; business as usual was not. It was not that the public was necessarily bored with its former darling, but it had other things on its mind: things like North versus South, and Out West. Besides, the whaling struggle was over and the Yankees had won. The British had been forced from the field and their colonials had seen better days. The French were still active in the South Seas but their interest was in right whales. The few Bremen and Hamburg ships were no competition. The sperm fishery was reverting to the American monopoly it had been before the War of Independence, which was just as well because the catch was in serious decline. The 2,694,000 gallons imported between 1851 and 1855 were 601,000 fewer than those imported during the previous five years. The next five years saw a further fall of 137,000 gallons. Captain Francis Post of New Bedford looked back.

When, half a century ago, our ships first ventured into the Pacific in quest of sperm whales, the coasts of Chili and Peru abounded in them; and our hardy pioneers in this daring occupation, were there enabled to fill their ships, without the necessity of penetrating further. But the whaling fleet increased extensively; the persecuted whales were in a measure killed and driven from their haunts; so that later voyages, to insure success, have been compelled to push their adventures into still farther and comparatively unknown seas. One unexplored track after another has been traversed, until it may now be said that, from Chili to New Holland, from California to the Japan Isles, and China Sea, with the whole intermediate space—in a word, over a square expanse comprehending above eighty degrees of latitude, and more than one hundred of longitude, there is scarce a spot of any extent but what has been furrowed by the keels of a whaler, and been a place of privation to her enduring crew.[1]

In New Bedford the conviction remained strong that the sperm whales were still out there. It was just a matter of finding them and the key to that seemed to be the kind of oceanographic research on which Charles Wilkes had made a tentative start. In the meantime, less profitable though it might be, there was the right whale of the Arctic. As early as 1835 the Nantucket whaler *Ganges*, master Barzillai T Folger, had taken a right whale off the north-west coast of America and so opened the Kodiak ground. It was a measure of Nantucket's decline that he stooped to take such inferior stuff. Peleg would have lamented the extremity to which his kin had been reduced. Eight years later, off the coast of Kamchatka, two New Bedford whalers took baleen whales with much bigger bone and twice the blubber expected in a right whale. They had found the bowhead, the western Arctic stock of the Greenland *mysticetus* that had been exploited for centuries by the Dutch and British whalers of the far North Atlantic. In 1848, pursuing these easy prey into their summer haunts, the Sag Harbour barque *Superior*, Captain Thomas Roys, passed through Bering Strait and inaugurated the Western Arctic fishery. By the following year there were 154 vessels in the Okhotsk, Anadir and Bering seas and the bowhead quickly became the stockfish of the American industry.

Wilkes' expedition had gathered its data first-hand, on the water. Even so, Wilkes had depended on the whalemen for much of his information. The man who continued the work was Lieutenant Matthew Maury of the Naval Observatory. Like Wilkes, he drew on the whalemen's knowledge but, following Reynolds' example, he did it by consulting their logbooks. He persuaded whaling and other captains to record wind, current, temperature, whales and more in a standard format three times a day. In Washington the information from these abstract logs was meticulously entered, year in and year out, against 5-degree squares of ocean. For the naval officers who compiled the 'fives and tallies' that, month by month, recorded the total ship days devoted to searching and the number of sperm and right whales seen, the whale charts were cell walls on which they scratched off the tedious days until release to sea duty. Their vast mosaic covered the whole world ocean between 60° north and 60° south. At first the tiles appeared random but, as the years went on and the data accumulated, Maury could see a pattern emerging.

> As observation after observation in such an immense field was recorded day by day, with the most untiring industry, and as the oft-repeated process finally began to express a meaning, I was surprised to find the lines for entering the right whales were blanks, through certain districts of the ocean, from one side of the Chart to the other. Finally, it was discovered that the torrid zone is to this animal forbidden ground, and that it is as physically impossible for him to cross the equator as it would be to cross a sea of flame.[2]

As the bowhead was found in both the Atlantic and Pacific Arctic, and could not cross the equator, was this not evidence for the existence of the fabled North-West Passage between the two oceans? Using the same technique, Maury charted the northern and southern limits of the sperm whale and modified Wilkes' findings. There were sperm whales in higher latitudes; in the South Atlantic they had been encountered between 30° and 35°, in the South Pacific between 35° and 60°, and in the North Pacific as far as 40° north. Maury inferred that the presence of the whales so far north and south meant warm water: 'These investigations . . . have taught me to regard sperm whales as much out of place in cold water, as the whalers themselves would regard out of place a wilderness of howling monkeys of the Amazon among the Green Mountains of Vermont'.[3]

Right whales in cold water, sperm whales in warm; it was neat but simplistic. Whereas Wilkes used what he knew of the movements of current-carried squid to predict sperm whale movements, Maury took the whales as his predictor of warm-water currents. If there were areas where sperm whales and cold currents coincided, as off the coast of Chile, or areas of ocean in which the ranges of right and sperm overlapped, as in the North Pacific, these were anomalies that could be ignored. So convinced was he that there was a submarine current from the South Atlantic to the Pacific that neither absence of evidence in logbooks nor lack of scientific observation would be sufficient evidence to the contrary. Only the thermometer would tell.

> . . . if . . . it should so turn out, . . . that the sea climate is not an extra-tropical one, as its latitude indicates, that it is the inter-tropical temperature of its waters which tempts the sperm whales to gambol there in such multitudes—then the discovery of the fact that the sea-water here is a little warmer, and that, therefore, there is a current running hither from the equator, should be regarded as one which is due to the information which the study of the habits of this animal has given us.[4]

What study? Maury systematically recorded time and place, but that was all. Otherwise he relied on whalemen's anecdotes. If one were to take Maury at face value, sperm whales are just carefree hedonists looking for another warm bath to frolic in. And frivolous too, for they disappointed him; the waters of Cape Horn, surface and submarine, are as cold as one would expect them to be that far south. There were also flaws in his collection of data. If squares were left unvisited by whalemen, whales were unlikely to be reported there. Such omissions were usually prejudice based on experience but there could be other factors, like the closed

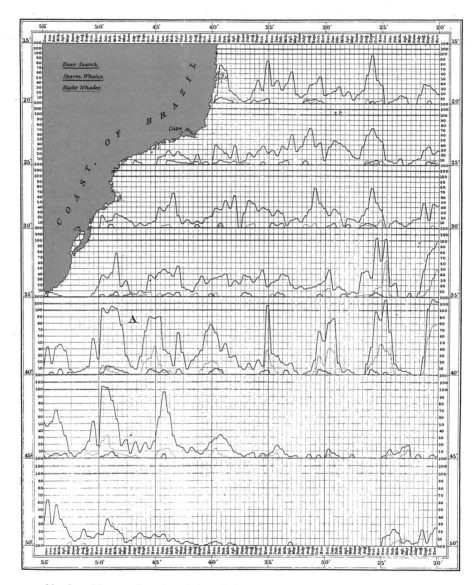

Matthew Maury plots the whales off the coast of Brazil in five degree squares (from the Whale Chart (series F) in his Explanations and Sailing Directions to Accompany the Wind and Current Charts, *National Library of Australia)*

door of Tokugawa Japan which kept whalemen out until Commodore Perry shouldered his way through in 1853. 'Coast of Japan' then became among the most prolific of the later grounds. Despite its limitations, Maury's Whale Chart was a powerful tool in the hands of the industry. It brought science to the task of whale search. An intelligent captain could look for those areas that reported little search but numerous sightings, and plan his cruise accordingly. He might avoid areas reported to be rich in whales if they also reported long periods between sightings. Off Brazil in February, for example, he would prefer Cape Frio, where only sperm whales were taken and one was seen for every 2.8 days' cruising, to square 40–45° south and 45–50° west where there were 2.3 times as many fish but most of them were right whales and there was only one sighting every 3.7 days.

The extent of their co-operation is the best indication of the seriousness with which the whalemen viewed Maury's work. Hundreds filled in his logs. Many corresponded with him on the haunts and habits of the whale. Thomas Roys was happy to find 'one man in our Government who will condescend to take notice of a business the annual income from which is millions, and at the present time has broken down all competition of other nations'. He had acquired the charts, and found them useful. Captain Crocker of New Bedford, having only heard of Maury's work after returning from a long cruise, was anxious to 'furnish his mite' in return for benefits he was sure he would receive in a new age of scientific whaling. He had taken sperm whales in the Sulu Sea: 'I was considered very lucky in finding them; perhaps I was, but I had read Wilkes on Currents and Whaling and paid attention to the temperature and currents.'[5]

In dollar terms, 1854 was the apogee of the American industry. Ship numbers and tonnage had fallen away since 1846 but in 1854 they brought home oil and bone to the value of $10,766,521. Thereafter the clouds gathered quickly. In 1857 an economic downturn depressed the domestic demand for sperm oil and accelerated the push into the British market. The domestic price came off its historic high (averaging a real price of $1.44 per gallon between 1851 and 1855) and began a long, slow decline from which it never recovered. One of the culprits was petroleum. The distillation of kerosene, or paraffin, from coal oil and oil shale began in the 1850s. It came into its own when commercial exploitation of the Pennsylvania oilfields began in 1859. Here was a cheap and plentiful source of light. It rapidly displaced whale oil for domestic illumination and particularly undermined the market for sperm oil, which had few other uses. Another product of the oil refinery added to the injury; paraffin wax was cheaper than spermaceti, but in the public mind the spermaceti candle remained the standard of excellence. One manufacturer solved the dilemma by patenting a blend of the two to produce a candle that was said to be of 'superior quality'.

Captain Post's half-century of expansion had been a by-product of *Pax Britannica*, which had allowed American whalemen to sail where they would without fear of naval molestation, even from the British themselves, who had quietly abandoned the practice of impressment. The outbreak of the American Civil War was a rude reminder of how vulnerable whaling fleets were. Suddenly, Americans who whaled had an enemy again, and it was themselves. The Confederate states did not whale or do much else on the export front except grow cotton, but in that they believed they held a trump card. Cotton would generate the income the South needed to purchase the tools of war in Europe. Northern interference with the cotton trade, on which the Lancashire spinning mills were almost totally dependent for their raw material, might well bring Britain into the conflict on the side of the Confederacy. Many southern officers in the United States Navy, including Maury, offered their services, but nearly all of the ships remained in Union hands. The Confederate naval effort was perforce one of defending ports, running blockades and raiding commerce. In the commerce of the North there were few targets larger or easier than the Yankee whaling fleet.

The steamer *Calhoun* opened hostilities near Belize in May

1861. Three Provincetown whalers were rounded up in the space of two hours and taken as prizes to New Orleans. The Union blockade of southern ports soon precluded prize-taking and the Confederates resorted to burning their captures. The whalemen alleged that they combined the practice with a particularly nasty method of ambush. In 1862 the British-built and largely British-manned raider CSS *Alabama* descended on the Azores whalers. Her commander, Raphael Semmes, declared that his intention was to follow Porter's example of 50 years earlier.

> Unlike the ships of commerce, the whalers are obliged to congregate within small well-known spaces of ocean, and remain there for weeks at a time, whilst the whaling season lasts. It was the most obvious thing in the world, that these vessels, thus clustered together, should attract the attention of the Confederate cruisers, and be struck at.[6]

On 8 September, off Fayal, Semmes captured the *Ocean Rover* of Mattapoisett as she was returning from a three-year cruise. The whalemen's charge against him was that he waited until nightfall and then set her afire to attract other whalers in the vicinity. While he did run down the *Weather Gauge* that evening, it is unlikely that the schooner had seen any flames from the *Ocean Rover* and the two other victims Semmes had burnt that day. The last of them had been lit at 4 p.m. and if seen the smoke would have been taken for trying out. In his memoirs Semmes asserted that he deliberately avoided burning at night for fear of 'flushing the remainder of the game'. In the course of a fortnight he destroyed nine whalers, uncovering the birds 'no faster than I could bag them'. In vain did Washington protest that the British had violated their neutrality by allowing the *Alabama* to be constructed at Birkenhead. The Confederate strategy was to cause such havoc amongst northern commercial shipping that the federal government would be under domestic pressure to provide protection. As the Union could only do this by taking warships away from an already leaky blockade, the pressure had to be resisted. Conscious, however, of the need to be seen to be doing something, Washington came up with a plan that would in theory improve the blockade and also keep the whalemen quiet. The Navy Department would buy up whalers and use them as blockships.

The Stone Fleets, as they were known, are usually said to have been made up of 'old whalers', the implication being that the ships were past usefulness and their owners were being paid for an otherwise worthless asset. The fact is that two-thirds of them had returned from their most recent cruises only a few months before enlistment for naval service and in the absence of hostilities would almost certainly have gone a-whaling again. Most whalers were old: the average age of the New Bedford fleet in the decade 1856–65 was 22 years. In November 1861 the first of two fleets was sent south. Twenty-four whalers and a solitary merchantman, mainly under whaling captains, sailed with secret orders. Only when these were opened, after the pilot had been dropped, did they know where to deliver their cargoes of solid New England granite.

> You will proceed from this port . . . and when clear of the land make a direct passage to the port of Savannah, and there deliver your ship to the commanding officer of the blockading fleet off said port . . . On the voyage down it would be well, as far as practicable, to keep in company of your consorts, to exhibit lights by night and sound horns or bells in case of fog near the coast. You will also examine daily the pipe in the quarter of your ship under water, to see that it remains safe. The only service required of you is the safe delivery of your vessel; and as she is old and heavily laden, you will use special care that she sustains no damage from unskillful seamanship or want of prudence and care . . . In case of disaster to preclude going on, you can call at Fortress Monroe, Hampton Roads, to repair damages . . .[7]

The 'pipe' was of lead, 125 millimetres in diameter and fitted with a valve. It passed through the hull of the ship and when opened would sink it in 15–20 minutes. Some of the captains might have sailed just for the money but Henry Chase of the *America* was doing his bit for the Union cause. He called his voyage 'a rat hole cruise' to stop up the rebel port. He was unsentimental about the fate of his ship but permitted himself a small joke: 'I should think there has been a great manny whales here by the looks of the whalers here tonight for Charleston Bay'. After being tugged up the river, some of the lightest ships were sunk together 'like a nest of eels'.[8] The *America* and the other large ships were more strategically placed. They were anchored broadside in rows across the main channel. The plan was to interrupt the flow of water on the crests of the bar, thus artificially creating eddies, whirlpools and counter-currents that would make an already difficult channel positively hazardous. The 7500 tons of stone the ships were carrying held them in place, but they were of limited effectiveness as obstacles. Charleston and Savannah had many sea entrances: blockage of their main channels, while it might restrict larger ships, could do little to inhibit blockade running. One of the sacrificial blockships was the *Herald*, nearly 100 years old and a survivor from the whaling revival of 1815. She had finished her last cruise, 1339 barrels to the good, only five months earlier.

The *Alabama* was at large for nearly two years; by the time she was sunk off Cherbourg by the USS *Kearsage* on 19 June 1864, she had cruised as far as Singapore and her tally was 63 victims, of which thirteen were whalers. By then, two-thirds of the freight that had been carried by American ships pre-war was being carried under neutral flags. So slim had the pickings become that of 100 ships intercepted in late 1863 by the CSS *Tuscaloosa* in the South Atlantic, only one was flying the Stars and Stripes. The raiders had been a great success as a deterrent except, apparently, to the Yankee whaleship owners. They put 98 ships to sea in 1864, trusting that the Pacific grounds would remain beyond the range of southern warships. The Confederate Navy rose to the challenge. Another British steamer was surreptitiously purchased, spirited out of Liverpool before the British authorities could respond to Union protests, and commissioned at sea on 19 October 1864 as the CSS *Shenandoah*. Her Lieutenant Commanding, James Waddell, was ordered 'to do the enemy's property the greatest injury in the shortest time'.

His instructions directed Waddell to cruise as far as the Sea of

Okhotsk and then position himself north of Oahu in September 1865 to intercept the whalers returning from their Arctic summer cruise. On the way he was to destroy what he could, and his first whaler was the *Edward*, of New Bedford, which was taken unawares while cutting in off Tristan da Cunha. Waddell has left us his recipe for disposal.

> To prepare a vessel for destruction by fire, first remove all living animals, take out all useful equipment which may be wanted, discover what combustibles are in her hold . . . and see to the removal of gunpowder. All of these things should be thrown into the sea. Combustibles are then scattered throughout the vessel, bulkheads torn down and piled up in her cabins and forecastle. All hatches are opened and all halyards let go that the sails may hang loosely and the yards counter braced. Fire is then taken from the galley or cooking stove and deposited in various parts of her hold and about her deck. If she is very old she burns like tinder. This painful duty which sometimes became necessary would have been avoided had we been allowed to take our prizes into port for ajudication.[9]

And the whalers that he found were old, some of them very old.

> The strength of these vessels, many of which were built fifty years ago, prove the high estimate which American shipwrights then placed upon the power necessary to enable vessels to contend successfully against the storms of the ocean. The timber then used was double that now employed, and while greater strength was secured by the introduction of such large timbers, space for cargo was diminished. The improvements which the last thirty years have introduced in naval architecture have so revolutionized former theories that those old hulks have been turned over to whaling, and it was found to be a profitable trade until the *Shenandoah* got among them.[10]

After Tristan da Cunha, trouble with the propeller ostensibly forced the raider to head for Melbourne for repairs. On arrival most of the crew, largely drawn from captured ships, deserted. Waddell was left with 27 men against a complement of 120. As usual, the Confederates pushed British neutrality to its limits and, although the local populace feted the officers, the authorities were anxious for the *Shenandoah* to be gone. Britain's Foreign Enlistment Act forbade Waddell any Australian recruits but, fortuitously,

45 'stowaways' were discovered aboard after sailing. In a similarly fortunate occurrence a collier from England, bearing a name associated with the Confederacy's financial agents in Britain, just happened to be in port and was able to provide Waddell with 250 tons of good Cardiff steaming coal. The US consul was beside himself.

The 26 days spent in Melbourne had been sufficient warning of the raider's presence to ensure that no whaler was in evidence when Waddell crossed the Middle Ground in February 1865. New Zealand, Fiji, Rotuma and the Ellice Islands were likewise barren ground, but the alert had spent itself by the time the *Shenandoah* reached the Caroline Islands. There, conveniently bottled up in the little harbour of Ponape, were three American whalers and one flying the Hawaiian flag. Waddell found that the Hawaiian, *Harvester*, had an American register, American captain, American mates and no bill of sale to anyone else. He burned her with the *Pearl*, *Edward Casey* and *Hector*. One item of plunder was particularly welcome: the whalers' charts, thanks to Maury, showed their tracks and their successes.

> With such charts in my possession, I not only held a key to the navigation of all the Pacific Islands, the Okhotsk and Bering Seas, and the Arctic ocean, but the most probable localities for finding the great Arctic whaling fleet of New England, without a tiresome search.[11]

On 21 May the *Shenandoah* entered the Sea of Ohkotsk but found only one whaler, the *Abigail* of New Bedford, which was approached under Russian colours. Captain Ebenezer Nye could not believe his bad luck. Three years earlier his previous ship had been taken by the *Alabama*. One of his mates could see the funny side: 'you are more fortunate in picking up Confederate cruisers than whales. I will never again go with you, for if there is a cruiser out, you will find her.'[12] In June Waddell passed into the Bering Sea, making for Cape Thaddeus on the Siberian shore. There were no whalers present, but on midsummer's eve blubber was seen drifting up from the south-west on the current. In less than an hour the greasy trail led them to the *William Thompson* and *Euphrates* of New Bedford, which were seized, and the *Robert Towns* of Sydney, which was not. The Australian demanded to know to whom he was speaking. '*Petropauluski*', was the reply. The disguise was invariably effective because there was a widespread expectation in the whaling fleet that a Russian telegraph vessel would be operating in the northern seas that summer.

On the following day five more whalers were encountered. Captain Hawes of the *Milo* had disturbing news. He had left San Francisco in April, when the news had been of Lee's surrender, but he had no documentary evidence. Waddell declined to believe that the Confederacy had been defeated. A shot through the main topsail brought the *Sophia Thornton* to, but the *Jeriah Swift*, trusting to her reputation for near-clipper speed, raced through the ice floes for the neutral waters of the Siberian coast. Three years earlier her fleetness had enabled her to avoid the *Alabama* off the Azores. Even under steam it took the *Shenandoah* three hours to run her down, but once it was demonstrated to Captain Thomas Williams that he was within range of a Whitworth 32-pounder he was not prepared to continue risking the lives of his men. Within twenty minutes his ship was ablaze. The numerous prisoners were placed aboard the *Milo*, which agreed to be sent to San Francisco under ransom bond. Before she headed south with 182 aboard, Captain Nye, late of the *Abigail*, manned two whaleboats with volunteers and struck north to warn the fleet. Hawes accommodated the remainder on the *Milo* with extreme difficulty.

> The first thing to do was to get them a place to sleep. This we did by heaving overboard cask, 500 barrels, 30 barrels of blubber, wood, etc, and everything that was in the way for that purpose. We used our lumber, nails, spikes and canvas, and some sails; one suit of sails to make berths for the men, and then they could not sleep all at one time. We made our way to San Francisco as best we could, and arrived there in 28 days, without much sickness.[13]

On 23 June Waddell captured a trading brig that was carrying Californian newspapers. Lee had indeed surrendered, Richmond had been evacuated and the Confederate government was in Danville, where Jefferson Davis had issued a proclamation calling for renewed efforts. That was good enough for Waddell. He continued to find whalers to the north of St Lawrence Island and he continued to burn them. Six were destroyed between 24 and 26 June, and a seventh was ransomed to take their crews south. It was plain that the whalers' own telegraph had yet to register the presence of the raider, although many captains knew her to have been reported in Australia. And so it was that on 27 June, when five sail were seen to windward, Waddell had hopes of taking them all.

For a whole day, fires banked and funnel retracted, the *Shenandoah* loitered up wind, a wolf in sheep's clothing. Patience was rewarded with a flat calm on the following morning and at 10 a.m. the *Waverly* was taken. The raider then steamed into East Cape Bay at the entrance to Bering Strait to find not five but ten whalers becalmed. The American flag was displayed and all ten victims returned the compliment, disclosing that there were no neutrals among them. The reason for their gathering then became plain. The *Brunswick* had been stove by ice, was lying on her side, and was only being kept afloat by her oil. The others had come to her assistance or, less charitably, to buy her oil at impromptu auction. Could the steamer help?, asked the officer who came across from the stricken vessel. He was assured that the *Brunswick*'s troubles were over. The Confederate flag was unfurled and nine Yankee skippers immediately struck theirs. The exception was Captain Thomas Young of the *Favorite*.

When a boarding crew from the raider pulled alongside, Captain Young and his crew were standing to arms and made it clear that that they would not surrender. Nonplussed, Lieutenant Bulloch asked Waddell if he should attempt to board against resistance. Instead, the whalemen were told that they had five minutes before their ship would be sunk under them. The crew took the prompt and came off in boats, but Young was obdurate. Unwilling to use force in such an unequal contest, the more so as Young was suspected to be three sheets to the wind, Waddell sent a second boat across under the diplomatic Lieutenant Whittle. When diplomacy failed, Whittle boarded. He is perhaps the only person who ever had a loaded whaling bomb gun snapped at him in earnest and lived to tell the tale; the crew had removed the percussion caps from the weapons before leaving the ship. Southern gallantry did not extend to forgiving the attempt though; Young was placed in irons and souvenired of everything he had, including his shirt studs.

Among Waddell's captures was the *James Maury*, complete with the captain's widow, her two children, and her late spouse's remains preserved in a keg of whisky for burial in New England. Mrs Gray was taking him home, but not until their ship was full. Waddell had heard of the indomitable widow while in Ponape and released her ship under ransom. Three hundred whalemen were crowded into the *James Maury* and the *Nile*. The other ships were burnt in the midnight twilight. It was by now familiar work for master's mate Cornelius Hunt, but he had seen nothing on this scale before.

> We hauled off to a little distance and anchored . . . to watch the mighty conflagration our hand had lighted. It was a scene never to be forgotten by anyone who beheld it, the red glare from the eight burning vessels shone far and wide over the drifting ice of those savage seas; the crackling of the fire as it made its devouring way through each doomed ship fell on the still air like upbraiding voices. The sea was filled with boats driving hither and thither, with no hand to guide them, and with yards, sails, and cordage, remnants of the stupendous ruin there progressing. In the distance, but where the light fell strong and red upon them, bringing out in bold relief each spar and line, were the two ransomed vessels, the Noah's arks that were to bear away the human life which in a few hours would be all that was left of the gallant whaling fleet. Imagination assisted us no doubt, but we fancied we could see the varied expressions of anger, disappointment, fear, or wonder, that marked the faces of the multitude on those decks, as their eyes rested on this last great holocaust . . .[14]

A whaleman who had joined the raider from the *Abigail* assured Waddell that there were whalers further north, but Ebenezer Nye had achieved his end. His men had rowed 180 miles to the ice edge and raised the alarm. The *Shenandoah* searched in vain. At 66° 40' north Waddell was sufficiently nervous of the ice to abort the chase. Still intent on his mission, he toyed with the idea of a raid on San Francisco, but took the precaution of intercepting an outbound merchantman on 2 August to ascertain the lie of the land. The English barque *Barracouta* informed him that the war was long over, and had been ever since he was at Ponape. The *Shenandoah*'s guns were sent below and the ship was disarmed. After some debate, in which the crew almost to a man declared a preference for discharge in Sydney, the *Shenandoah* made an unmolested return to Liverpool. In the last act of the American Civil War she had taken 24 whalers after the surrender of the Confederacy and burnt twenty of them. It could have been construed as piracy, and desultory efforts were made to pursue Waddell and others, but of far greater import were the claims made by the US government against Britain for the damage done by the raiders. Britain, they said, had at the very least allowed the raiders to go to sea instead of detaining them as neutrality required.

Britain resisted these '*Alabama* claims' for years but in 1871 allowed them to go to international arbitration. The tribunal decided that Britain was indeed liable for the damage directly caused by the *Alabama* and the *Florida*, and by the *Shenandoah* after her recruiting drive in Melbourne. The *Shenandoah*'s bonfires of 28 June 1865 alone were worth $400,000. The British were not unhappy to have the matter settled for $15.5 million in gold; it ducked the question of indirect damage, such as the disruption of trade, for which claims of many times that amount were being made.

The raiders and the Stone Fleets between them accounted for the loss of nearly 100 whalers during the war. Before that, the financial crisis of the late 1850s had removed well over another

100. In the last year of peace, 1860, the number of vessels fell below 600 for the first time in a decade. Between 1860 and 1865 what had been a downturn became a precipice, with numbers down from 561 to 271. The American industry was in deep trouble and it could not all be blamed on the rebellion.

Spun Yarn,
Being An Attempt to Find the
Truth in Art, and Vice Versa

Captain William Scoresby, jr (of the Greenland Fishery):
*Can you furnish any anecdotes as to the dangers
attendant on the southern fishery?*
Captain William Day (South Seaman):
*Many, but they would appear rather of a marvellous
description. They might be misunderstood, or
considered as exaggerated, if communicated.*

Among the routine tasks aboard a whaler was the recycling of
old rope. It was unpicked and respun into lengths of yarn
suitable for the innumerable uses of a sailing ship. There was an
element of make-work in this, but it was seldom grumbled at by
the crew because it was easy labour and its mechanical nature
left minds and voices free to roam. Yarn spinning became synony-
mous with story-telling; the longer and more fanciful, the better
to beguile the hour—not for nothing has 'a whale of a tale'
acquired proverbial status.

Whalemen's stories, whether of whales or men, were large in
subject and large in treatment. Whales were always villains, albeit
sometimes admired: a man could be hero or villain, and made famous
or infamous far beyond the confines of his ship. Some captains were
both—admired for their whaling skills but avoided by foremast hands
for brutality or stinginess. The lay system ensured, however, that the

reverse was never true; a captain who could not catch whales could no more command the respect of his men than he could keep the confidence of his owners, no matter how much butter there was in the forecastle. Ahab was a tyrant, as much to the *Pequod*'s officers as to the men, but there was the smell of oil about him and an ivory leg was entirely fitting for one who seemed part whale himself. Men would put up with much for the prospect of success, and a charismatic personality might recruit even a sceptic like Ishmael to the service of his obsession. But Ahab is an invention, much as some scholars would have you believe that he was modelled on Captain Valentine Pease of Melville's first whaler, the *Acushnet*. To find the men behind the stories, and to understand how their attributes could grow with the telling, it is necessary to find evidence independent of the yarn-spinners.

One of the very best yarn-spinners was William Davis. He made only one whaling cruise, as a greenhand on the *Chelsea* of New London in 1834–38, but went on to become a highly respected captain in the merchant service. When, 40 years on, he turned his hand to writing, his book was on whaling. *Nimrod of the Sea* told his own story but he was not its hero. That role was filled by a procession of whaling captains personally known to Davis, but particularly by James Huntting of Southampton, Long Island. He is the 'mighty hunter' of the title and the references to him, sometimes poorly cloaked in anonymity, are unabashed hero-worship.

> I call him an old man, as his snowy hair and beard indicate the snows of many winters; yet he has only filled forty-six years of life. Gigantic in form and power, with a head to attract the sculptor's attention, and a countenance to arrest the eye of a woman . . . As I regarded him, with the battle-fire lighting up his pleasant, beautiful eye, and as I measured his brawny figure, it seemed to me that he was just the man to jump into a struggle with the leviathan . . . still hale and hearty, erect and powerful, with the rosy complexion of youth. There is not much damage, considering the terrible wear and tear on as splendid a physique as ever trod deck on whaleboat.[1]

The battle-fire had been kindled by a reference to fighting whales, of which Huntting had rather more experience than he

A NIMROD OF THE SEA.

Captain James Huntting of Sag Harbour, Davis's Nimrod of the Sea

would have wished. He recalled an incident off the River Plate in which a sperm whale, when struck, cut the boat in two with its jaw and then thrashed the wreck to splinters. The crew were rescued and two other boats went on. They fastened, but were also crushed by the jaw. Those who could swam for their lives, but two terror-stricken non-swimmers climbed on to the whale's back and seated themselves forward of the hump. The whale, although trailing six harpoons and 900 fathoms of line, showed no disposition to retire from the fray, so the men in the water were rescued and the spare boats rigged. Huntting pulled on and managed to avoid the jaw. Rather than fasten, he fired a bomb-lance, which exploded in the whale behind its fin. It did not even distract the whale, which 'tore right through my boat, like a hurricane, scattering all hands right and left'. That night, as they fitted other boats, they could hear the whale as it continued to rampage amongst the wreckage. Rough weather at daybreak caused them to lose track, much to the crew's relief. At Buenos Aires most of them deserted.

Unusually, Huntting had also had a very personal encounter with a right whale that chose to fight. His boat had been stove and overturned by the flukes. From the water, he told the second mate's boat not to rescue them but to pursue the whale. Davis quotes him at length.

Just then the whale came up on the full breach, and striking the boat, she went right through it, knocking men and wreck high in the air. Next the great bulk fell over sideways, like a small avalanche, right in our midst; and spitefully cut the corners of her flukes right and left. In the surge and confusion, two poor fellows went down: we saw no sign of them afterward, and the water was so dark, stained with blood, that we could not see into it. As the whale came feeling around with her nose, she passed close by me. I was afraid of the flukes, and got hold of the warp, or iron pole, or her small, or something, and towed a little way till she slacked speed a little. Then I dove under, so as to clear the flukes, and came up astern of them. I was in good time; for having felt the boat, she turned over and threshed the spot with a number of blows in quick succession, pounding the wreck into splinters. She must have caught sight of me, for she came up on a half breach, and dropped her head on me, and drove me, half stunned, deep under water. Again I came up near the small, and again dove under the flukes. From this time she seemed to keep me in sight. Again and again—the mate told me afterward—she would run her head in the air and fall on my back, bruising and half drowning me as I was driven down in the water.

Sometimes I caught hold of the line, or something attached to the mad brute, and would hold until a sweep of the flukes would take my long legs and break my hold. The second mate's boat had cut long ago, and watched her chance to pick up the surviving crew, but had not been able to reach me; for when the whale's eye caught the boat, she would dash for it so wickedly that the whole crew became demoralized.

. . . To husband my strength, I gave over swimming, and, treading water, I faced the danger, and several times by sinking avoided the blow from her head. As a desperate resource, I strove with my pointed sheath-knife to prick her nose: I did all a strong man was in duty bound to do to save his life. The cooper, who was ship-keeper, ran down with the ship, intending to cut between the whale and myself; but we were at too close quarters. He was afraid to run me down, lest he might tear me with the ragged copper [sheathing on the ship's bottom]. Thus for three-quarters of an hour that whale and

I were fighting: the act of breathing became laboured and painful; my head and shoulders were sore from bruises, and my legs had been pounded by her flukes; but it was not until I found myself swimming with my arms alone, and that my legs were hanging paralysed, that I felt actually scared. Then it looked as if I couldn't hold out much longer; I had seen the ship close beside me, and the second mate's boat trying to get in to me, and throwing me lines, or something to float on. But I failed to reach them. Now these things seemed very far off; that was the last I remembered, until I came to on board the ship.[2]

His rescuer had been the first mate's boat. It had dashed in, the mate had seized Huntting's collar, and with the crew pulling for their lives they had towed him to safety. It was several weeks before Huntting could head a boat again.

A Paul Bunyan of the South Seas, he was built to the scale of his exploits; 6 feet 6 inches and 250 pounds, with not enough fat on him to grease a skillet. A newspaper in 1881 breathlessly reported that on one occasion a line had fouled his ankle and he had been taken down by a sounding whale at 20 miles per hour. It was said that he had 'the presence of mind, resolution and bodily strength' to double over and cut the line below his foot. Huntting demurred. It was true that in the Sea of Japan in July 1846, when acting mate on the *Portland*, he had been taken out by a foul line and towed underwater for some distance, 'but the whale rose to the surface and stopped his headway, and I was then able to cut myself clear. Had the whale continued to sound, I could not have done it.' The only damage had been a broken ankle and besides, he had witnessed a much more remarkable case.

I will give you an instance of a man who was caught in a foul line by the upsetting of a boat, and carried almost instantly fifty rods [137.5 fathoms] under water. He was picked up with his foot and hand gone, torn off by the line. I amputated the limb above the ankle, and took out the crushed bones of the hand, and the man lived at least ten years after, and may be alive at this day . . . This occurred in April, 1853, on the coast of Chili, when I was master of the ship *Jefferson*, of Sag Harbour. How this man could have lived under water so long is a most unaccountable thing. I could not have believed it had I not seen it with my own eyes.[3]

Thus the modest and laconic hero, disinclined to tolerate exaggeration. Compare his account with Davis' embellishment.

> After being drawn with frightful speed some 125 fathoms from the boat, he was released by his limbs giving way to the strain. Thus freed, and almost unconscious, he rose to the surface and was picked up and carried on board the ship. On examination, it was found that a portion of the hand, including four fingers, had been torn away, and the foot sawed through at the ankle, leaving only the great tendon and the heel suspended to the lacerated stump. From the knee downward the muscular flesh had been rasped away by the line, leaving the protruding bone enveloped in a tangled mat of tendons and bleeding arteries. Saved from drowning, the man seemed likely to meet a more cruel death, unless some one had the nerve to perform the necessary amputation . . . Captain Jim was not the man to allow any one to perish on slight provocation. He had his carving knife, carpenter's saw, and a fish hook. The injury was so frightful, and the poor fellow's groans and cries so touching, that several of the crew fainted in their endeavours to aid the captain in the operation, and others sickened and turned away from the sight. Unaided, the captain then lashed his screaming patient on the carpenter's bench, amputated the leg, and dressed the hand as best he could.[4]

It seems clear-cut. The basic facts are agreed; the art is in the presentation. It would be churlish to point out that on the dates mentioned both the *Portland* and the *Jefferson*, according to Alexander Starbuck's *History*, were snug in Sag Harbour between cruises. Let us rather put the error down to lapse of memory after 30-odd years, and reflect that a disadvantage of detail is that it invites checking. Whaling lent itself so well to exaggeration, with the endless hours available for yarning and the temptation to embroider for the sake of novelty, that unvarnished accounts, whether first- or second-hand, are not easy to come by. Logbooks are one such source because they were written within 24 hours of the incidents they record, and even when they have vindication in the eyes of owners, officialdom or posterity in mind it is usually transparent.

Spinning

The rope was unpicked by hand but respun by a machine called the spun yarn wench [sic]. In keeping with size of the stories told around it, it was an exaggerated version of the cottage spinning wheel.

When there is nothing else to do, they pick to pieces old ropes, and splice together the separate yarns, which are then twisted together and form spun yarn. The apparatus made use of consists of a heavy wheel of about eighteen inches in diameter, giving momentum to an axle about three feet in length upon the end of which furthest from the wheel, is the spindle, to which motion is communicated by means of a rope wound around the axle two or three times, drawn tight, and relaxed alternately, until the required velocity is produced.

The machine is set upon one of the windlass-bitts, and the yarns lead along the deck as far back as the mizzen mast. As the spindle revolves, the man who makes the spun yarn, commencing close to the spindle, moves backwards from it, rubbing the yarns vigorously with a piece of cloth dipped in oil, so as to render the spun yarn fine and smooth.

In this way, thousands of yards of spun yarn are made every voyage, an indispensable article aboard ship. Three yarns are also often spun together by means of three spindles to which motion is communicated by large tooth wheels acting upon three smaller ones.

All the shrouds and stays of a ship are carefully protected from the friction of the running rigging, by being 'served' or wound around with spun yarn. Some of them are covered with mats of spun yarn woven very neatly together. [Francis Olmstead's *Incidents of a Whaling Voyage*, p 87]

Among other functions, a log could justify, obscure or condemn, but surely the most unusual use to which it could be put was found by Captain Clothier Pierce, for whom the log of the *Minnesota* was prayer wheel, scourge and confessional. The stories circulated by whalemen earned him the nickname Crazy Pierce. To disagree would be to argue with the melancholy evidence from the man's own pen. In 1868 the litany started just six days out of New York.

Remarks on Board the Unfortunate *Minnesota*

1 July No signs of LIFE here Nothing for us June has passed & we get Now-wheir No chanc for us this season I fear three seasons in the North Atlantic to get One Whale in this Unfortunate Vessel

2 July Will the Lord ever favour us to get One Whale I fear not very soon Fresh Breeze from East wheir it will continue for all future time

4 July will the Wind ever change . . . No Whales in the Ocean that we can find . . . No Chanc to do anything or to ever get One Whale The LORDS Hand appears to be against the Poor Old *Minnesota* and all concerned in her Will the Lord in his infinite Mercy ever suffer us to get One Whale

13 July No Whale this season for the Poor Old *Minnesota*: The LORD will not suffer us to get One (I am so wicked) . . . Stearing East over the desert Nothing to be seen: Oh if the LORD would but favour us to get something all in vain I fear Nothing for us

14 July the Ocean is Barren wheir we go Not a Whale can this Poor vessel get The last Whale has been Caught here; Non now Live here—the *Commadore Morris* or som Lucky Ship Has Bioled the Last One: Never did I feel more cast down this a dark Period in my Live: why did I come Whaling but for my own distruction: I think my damnation is fixed now

16 July If I am or can be blessed to get One Whale this season: I will try to become a better Man & strive to be a Cristian for the future

18 July I, Pray that Heavenly favours & May attend this Poor and Unfortunate vessel with favour

19 July Heavenly Father if we are but favoured I will try to be A humble and devoted Cristian

20 July No Chance for this Unfortunate Vessel to get One Whale this Year & I allmost fear she never will: The time passes swiftly and we get Nothing The Lords Power is against this Poor Bark . . . 9 AM Saw Sperm Whales going to Windward . . . Lowered the boats and chased . . . could not get up to them: Such is this Unfortunate Vessels: Hard Luck

22 July I Believe the Hand of Providence is against me for beeing so Uncharitable to my Brother [Lorenzo, the ship's agent] in his Day of misfortune and trial

26 July Lorenzo Pierce is certainly a ruined Man! my damnation is certain this voyage I have previously been favoured but now ruined: The Hand of devine Providence is against this Unfortunate vessel it is impossible to get One Whale We have seen Whales twice and got Nothing. I do not expect to get a Whale it seems utterly impossible for us to get One

1 August No signs of Life here: I am ruined No Oil in the Ocean for the Poor Old *Minnesota* Lorenzo Pierce is undone and must fail in consequence of our hard Luck; My ruin is fixed . . . This brings us to the close of another Week Spent in vain our Ruin is fixed My destiny is sealed to destruction. I am a Ruined Man in consequence of ingratitude to my Brother and Parents . . . I know that I have reached the greatest highth of my prosperity and means: I am now in the decline of my Life my limited means in regard to Money is now leaving me: I shall yet be without Money or Friends in consequence of this Unfortunate voyage: I shall yet be reduced to want and beggary I know the very Hand of Providence is against us on this Voyage in consequence of my Sins and ingratitude to my Parents and Brother the Lord will Not suffer me to prosper any more—His Mercy is clean gorn forever: all blessings are withheald from this Poor Unfortunate vessel

And so it went, on and on, for 1449 days and 1448 nights. When the One Whale was taken, in March 1869, did it lift the pall? Not a bit.

24 March The Elements is bound to distroy our Whale and ruin all concerned: No prospect of [the weather] Moderating: Halled the Whale alongside this Morning to Hook on Could Not impossible: to save the Body

25 March Still Blowing a Severe Gale from SW wheir it will Continue until I am a ruined Man . . . Not the least Chance to save a particle of the Whale

26 March Whale rotting in the Sea . . . No Human Power Can save the Whale No Vessel so unfortunate as this: Except the *Addison* when she was here . . . Such is my Hard Fortune

27 March Remarks on Board the Most Unfortunate Vessel in the Whaleing Buisness. Cut off some of what was once good Blubber; but Now Spoiled . . . Such is: Lorenzo Pierces Unfortunate Vessels Fate: A Terable Gale to ruin their Voyages It is no use to try in his Ship to

make a Voyage Impossible: The Hand of Providence is against him
. . . commenced to Boil a Littile[5]

How did the crew deal with this—to be charitable—eccentric-
ity? At the Bay of Islands Pierce had to call on the US consul to
quell a mutiny. After several brawls with the first mate, Pierce
discharged him. The replacement was no improvement: he was
sent below for refusing to flog a seaman who had struck Pierce.
The third mate died. Another officer attacked Pierce over some
gratuitous advice about how to kill a pig. In Hobart the captain
was arrested over a dispute with a one-legged outfitter. Not a
pleasant voyage perhaps, but not the family's ruin either. The
Minnesota sent or took home a total of 1176 barrels of sperm and
130 barrels of whale oil. It was not a large fare, but the best of
the four-year voyages by the other ships that sailed in 1868, that
of the *James Maury*, realised only 1420 barrels. Even depression
is relative.

Pierce's personal problems adversely affected his ability to
control his crew but, according to his own account at least, he
had no difficulty controlling himself. A captain who succumbed
to the corruption of unbridled power afloat was a terror to his
crew and ultimately a danger to himself if he could not modify
his behaviour when ashore. Court records occasionally give us a
glimpse of such tyranny at sea, but only rarely do they reveal the
difficulty of making the transition to shore. One such case was
that of Noah Pease Folger (Peleg's second cousin, thrice removed,
and Valentine's kinsman).

On 18 February 1833 William Mellish, an extremely wealthy
wholesale butcher and long-time whaleship owner who we have
previously encountered as the owner of the *Seringapatam*, was
walking through Spread-eagle Court in London. Folger came up
behind him, presented a pistol to the back of the old man's head,
and shot him. Mellish fell and onlookers rushed up to apprehend
Folger, who did not resist. 'I shot him—he injured me of my living;
I know the laws of my country, and I shall be hung for it', he was

reported to have said, and added that he had been looking for this opportunity for three months. To his apprehenders he appeared to be in his senses, and sober. He was remanded in custody by the Lord Mayor of London who, with a fine disregard for the golden thread said to run through British justice, called him an assassin and examined him as though he were a witness rather than a prisoner. At the Old Bailey two months later, the plea was insanity.

Mellish, who was not badly hurt, testified that he had given Folger command of the whaler *Partridge* in 1826. On the ship's return in 1830 they had argued over deductions from Folger's lay for damage to Mellish's property. Folger sought arbitration and nominated a fellow American, a Mr Rotch. Mellish knew him, and agreed: it was probably Benjamin, founder of the Nantucket colony at Milford Haven. Rotch awarded Folger £848 against his claim for more than £1200. Mellish paid, but he did not employ Folger again. The American needed a reference to obtain another command but would not ask Mellish directly. For three years he vainly sought employment, increasingly drunk and distraught, persuaded that Mellish was to blame. Relatively normal at other times, except when drunk, he would become deranged at the mention of Mellish's name and threaten horsewhipping or worse. Witnesses testified that in his youth (he was now 36) he had been a fine officer but that since employment with Mellish his mind had become disordered. Andrew Hitter, fourth mate on the *Partridge*, was called to the witness box in an attempt to find a cause for the change. He had no psychological insights to offer, but his evidence made it clear that if Folger had not actually taken his problems aboard with him he had started displaying symptoms quite early in the voyage. Had Hitter been yarning, rather than giving evidence under oath, his story could not have been more bizarre.

> We made to Cape de Verd in the course of our voyage . . . the chief of our crew went on shore there by the captain's orders; . . . he ordered them to work on Sunday, and they would not, so he sent about twelve men on shore—he got others in their stead—part of them were slaves; they were decidedly unfit men to work the ship

> . . . I remember one Sunday his nearly shooting the third mate . . .
> he called the third mate down into the cabin to have conversation
> with him; the pistols were in a case—he took one up, and fired it—it
> just grazed the mate's ear . . . the prisoner laughed, and spoke of it as
> a joke to every ship we passed—the pistol had a ball in it, for it
> lodged in the rudder-case; I saw it there; the ball was in the ship
> when we came home—he kept it there to show.

At Galapagos Folger had sent Hitter and five men 20 miles in
a boat without water or provisions. When they returned a day and
a half later and told the captain that some of the men had been
reduced to drinking salt water, he laughed.

> He was very proud of his office as commander; he was always
> boasting of his big ship, saying he was master and commander of the
> fine ship the *Partridge*, and placed in the shoes of Mr Mellish himself,
> and would show his authority—I considered that indicated deficiency
> of mind and weakness—we all spoke of it as such . . . nothing
> particular had happened to have affected his mind then, he might
> have drank a little, but we had not the opportunity of knowing that.

At the Marquesas the ship was nearly wrecked by a local pilot,
'a cannibal almost', who was employed by the captain although
Hitter knew the waters well. The mate, Thompson, had to take
action to save the ship when Folger only laughed at his officers'
warnings of danger.

> He would have one of the Welch sailors on the sofa, saying the
> Lord's prayer in Welch, and he would drink with him too . . . talking
> all manner of foolishness . . . and asking him about whales, and that
> repeatedly . . . we went down after a large whale, and he hove two
> irons at her, which missed, and then he jumped overboard upon
> her—I did not expect to see him come up again, but he swam back
> to the boat . . . I have often seen him strip himself; he would dance
> about in his own cabin, or in the common cabin . . . and sometimes
> he would break about a dozen panes of glass with his fists at a time,
> and cut his hands; sometimes he would fall with his head against the
> window of the berth, and cut his head—sometimes he would break
> half a dozen tumblers, and dance on them with his bare feet; he did
> this frequently for months—he would have the doctor take the glass
> out of his feet, forehead and hands, and go at it again just the same;
> he said that it was through family fits, that the family were troubled
> with them. He would often tell the boy, after dinner or supper, to

heave the plates and knives and forks out of the cabin window, or else he would flog him.

At Hawaii Folger gave away the cabin sofa and had the cooper make him a cradle to sleep in. More often he slept with his head on the cabin table, a loaded horse pistol with a 10-inch barrel by his ear. He reacted badly when the danger was pointed out to him.

> He was very impatient of controul; he was a passionate man, and very jealous of his power and station in the ship . . . I have seen the prisoner jump on the top of [the mate] when he has been in bed and asleep, with a pistol in each hand . . . he would sometimes come and throw a jug of cold water into my face when I have been asleep; I always remonstrated with him—he said it was to show his authority as master and commander; he sometimes put the bottles on the cabin table, and took his steel or knife and fenced with them, and sent them away to the other side of the cabin, liquor and all; he would often jump out of his bed in the night, and say the devil was in the cabin—he often said we were going to rob him, and he would lock every thing up—these symptoms increased more and more.

The cook died, and for weeks afterwards Folger would not sleep below for fear of his ghost. He was under medical treatment for six weeks in Hawaii. The officers appealed to the British consul but got short shrift. He threatened to have them taken out of the ship and flogged because, as Hitter saw it, they were questioning the captain's 'authority, madness and stupidness'. At Guam the governor sold Folger some iron, there was a dispute over payment, and Folger threatened to shoot him: the sum in question was a dollar or so.

> I thought his mind in the worst state when we got nearer home. Some of us locked him in his berth, for he had got mad altogether; (we had been out 45 months; he was going to blow the ship up in the chops of the Channel)—we locked him up by common consent, for the safety of the ship: he continued always so till we got into the Downs . . . he was worse then, and the pilot had to put him below—the prisoner said he would shoot him if he could get a pistol.[6]

Hitter's account did not go unchallenged by the defence. Under cross-examination, he could not say that Folger had jumped right on to the whale's back, but 'he jumped after her, and into the vortex of the water where it had gone down'. Asked if there was anything unusual about sailors being afraid of ghosts, Hitter assured the court that he knew of many who were not. The jury returned a verdict of not guilty, the accused being found of unsound mind. Folger was committed to Hanwell lunatic asylum, to be detained there at His Majesty's pleasure. A year later Mellish died of old age. The Home Office, reasoning that the obsession would die with its object, released the whaleman in 1836. He was never heard of again. The story of this landlocked Ahab with a horse pistol, pursuing his White Whale for months through the streets of London, is a salutary reminder that, although Melville and his fellow whalemen had a weakness for embellishing stories until they were unrecognisable, it would be folly to dismiss them as altogether untrue.

Consider the last of many surreal passages in *Moby Dick*. Ishmael uses the coffin made for Queequeg, slung from the *Pequod*'s stern, as a lifebuoy. Thirty years earlier Captain William Scoresby had asked Captain Day for South Seamen's anecdotes and, as we know, had been warned and refused. In the following year, 1821, Scoresby was in command of the northern whaler *Baffin* when she spoke the *Vigilant*. It was recorded that 'in the boat hanging over her stern was a coffin containing the remains of one of her boat-steerers who had been killed by a whale'.

But no sound mind will give any weight to the fact that the man who passed on Scoresby's initial request to Captain Day was William Mellish.

FROZEN FLEETS

Hereafter, doubtless, many ships will go there [to the Arctic], and I think there ought to be some provision made to save the lives of those who go there should they be cast away.

Captain Thomas Roys

The concentration of whalers that fell victim to the *Shenandoah* in the Arctic demonstrated how much the Pacific whaleman's itinerary had changed since Wilkes' day. The yearly average catch in the late 1830s had landed three barrels of sperm to every four of common oil: by the early 1860s the ratio was two to four. Both catches had declined in volume but the price differential in favour of sperm had also eroded, having fallen over the same period from 2.66 times the price of common oil to 1.79 times. The only port capable of making sperm whaling pay appeared to be Provincetown, whose 70–140-ton plum pud'n'ers were finding enough in the Atlantic to fill small ships on short and cheap cruises. The size of these vessels meant that a short-lived revival of fleet numbers at the end of the war was illusory. The British had been forced to use substitutes for whale products during the Civil War, had found them satisfactory, and did not come back into the market to the former extent. They were also still being supplied in a modest way by their colonies, 7200 barrels in 1869 as against 25,500 from the United States. For the New Bedford ships in the Pacific bowhead hunting was easier, at least in the chase. There was much more oil per whale (an average of 200 barrels from the large 'browns' against the sperm whaler's standard 'five and forty' barrel bull) and a bonus in the form of whalebone, the plates of baleen through which the whale filtered its food. Light, strong and flexible, whalebone found a place in women's hands (as brooms) and close to their hearts (as corset stays). Their husbands were familiar with it as material for buggy whips, fishing rods and umbrella ribs. Its real price had risen fivefold since the late 1830s.

It is therefore hardly surprising that the bowhead season, the northern summer, dictated the deployment of the fleet in the North Pacific. An autumn departure from New England would put a whaler round Cape Horn in good time to recruit in Hawaii before sailing for the Arctic in March. During April some bowheads might be intercepted on their northern migration through the Bering Sea, but sometimes it would be July before the ice had retreated far enough to allow whalers through Bering Strait in pursuit. There were walruses to hunt along the ice edge while waiting. Thereafter the ships would make as far to the north-east along the Alaskan coast as conditions permitted, again intercepting the whales on their return journey and following them as they made their way from the Beaufort Sea to the autumn feeding grounds of the Chukchi Sea. In early October the returning ice would force the whalers south to Hawaii or San Francisco. There they could outfit for a winter sperm cruise towards Japan or off California before heading north again in spring.

The South Pacific fleet was not distracted to the same extent and three out of every four American whalers were still primarily in the sperm business. The reasonable sperm hunting to be had around New Zealand and other islands kept them in southern waters. They filled in the off season by intercepting the winter migration of humpbacks, taking the whales as they calved among the islands of New Zealand and Tonga and along the east coast of Australia and the west coast of South America. These were a second-best whale, dangerously fast, prone to sink, and with short bone, but the 22,000 barrels they yielded in 1872 equalled the Arctic catch. Frank Bullen, who sailed on the *Splendid* out of Otago, wondered if the game was worth the candle.

> In spite of their well-known speed, we were several times so close in their wake that the harpooners loosed the tacks of the jibs to get a clear shot; but as they did so the nimble monsters shot ahead a length or two, leaving us just out of reach. It was a fine chase while it lasted, though annoying . . . At last, after nearly two hours of the fun, they seemed to have had enough of it, and with one accord headed seaward at a greatly accelerated pace, as who should say, 'Well, s'long boys; company's very pleasant and all that, but we've got important business over at Fiji, and can't stay fooling around here any longer.' In a quarter of an hour they were out of sight, leaving us disgusted and outclassed pursuers sneaking back again to shelter, feeling very small.[1]

The completion of the first American transcontinental railroad in 1869 stimulated the development of San Francisco as a home port for whalers. Whalebone could be freighted across the continent for two cents a pound. Oil still went east on a returning whaler or was transhipped across the Isthmus of Panama at six cents per gallon: in either case Hawaii was just as convenient as San Francisco and had other advantages, of which the chief, according to a roving reporter for the *Sacramento Union*, was the absence of land sharks: 'The lawyer who took charge of a sailor's complaint against his captain might as well emigrate—he could practice no more in Honolulu'. Another advantage had more to do with ego.

> A whaleman don't amount to much in San Francisco, but here he is the biggest frog in the pond. Up there the agent lets him dance attendance until more important business is attended to, and then goes out with him and assists him in just such of his concerns as absolutely require assistance, and then leaves him to paddle his own canoe with the remainder . . . If I were going to advise San Franciscans as to the best strategy to employ in order to secure the

whaling trade, I would say, cripple your facilities for 'pulling' sea
captains on every pretence that sailors can trump up, and show the
whaler a little more consideration when he is in port. All other
objections will die of themselves. A nucleus is already formed up
there. Swift and Allen have opened a branch of their New Bedford
house in San Francisco, and their ships (they have eight at sea now)
will rendezvous there hereafter.[2]

The migratory habits of the bowheads were their undoing.
More predictable in their movements than the sperm whales, year
by year they were eliminated from the more accessible areas of
their range. In the 1850s significant numbers were caught south
of 60° north in the western Arctic, and few whalers went north
of 69° north. By the late 1860s whales south of 60° were rare and
there was significant whaling effort between 69° and 72° north.
New London, which had been among the first ports to exploit
the right whales of the north-west coast, soon found prey closer
to home; in 1847 the *McLellan* resumed the long-neglected Davis
Straits fishery. The bowhead population was now under attack
from both sides of the continent. In a reversal of the circumstances under which Nantucket had taught the British sperm
whaling, some of the *McLellan*'s officers and men were English,
from the Greenland fishery. The South Sea whalers now ranged
wherever sperm, right or bowhead could be found.

In the pursuit of bowheads, that meant pushing further into
the ice every year. What was always risky in 1871 became disastrous. The fleet was south of Cape Thaddeus on the Siberian
shore in March, at the edge of dense pack-ice and with a contrary
wind. Not until June did the ice loosen enough to allow a push
through to Cape Navarine, where a few whales were taken but
many more were heard spouting with impunity deeper in the
pack. At the end of June the fleet was able to pass through Bering
Strait and in the second half of July they found open water along
the Alaskan coast south of Cape Lisburne. The ice continued to
peel back from the land as the season advanced and the ships
coasted to the north-east until stopped by ice lying on Blossom

Shoals beyond Icy Cape. That ice started on 6 August and by the following day the advance guard had reached Wainwright Inlet, where plentiful whales promised a good season. The whalers anchored or made fast to the dense ice and some of their number went on to Point Franklin. Only one or two made it around Point Barrow, the most northerly point of Alaska but usually passable at this time of year.

On 11 August a sudden wind shift began driving the ice on shore. The ships worked inshore, leaving their lowered boats to be dragged back to them over the broken ice. Two days later the ice grounded, leaving only a narrow strip of water between Point Belcher and Wainwright Inlet. The whalemen looked for a north-east wind to release them but got a westerly instead. It closed up the ice to within half a mile of the shore until on 25 August the tardy north-easter reopened the water as far as 4–8 miles offshore and whaling resumed in earnest. The Inuit warned them that this reprieve was temporary and that the ice would soon return to set in for the winter, but the whalemen thought they knew better. Four days later the ice came back, so quickly that some of the ships were trapped in the pack and the remainder were saved only when the ice grounded on the beach shoals. Most of the fleet was trapped along the 20 miles of coast between Point Belcher and Wainwright Inlet, iced in from east and west. On 2 September a cracking and groaning announced the death of the first ship. The *Comet* was held in a giant hand that pushed her aloft. For three or four days she hung, stern forced out, until the ice, tiring of the broken toy, released her to sink. And still the whalemen were more worried about the loss of the season than the threat to their ships. By 8 September the *Roman* and the *Awashonks* had also been crushed and discussion finally turned to means of escape.

One of the smaller vessels, the brig *Kohola*, was emptied with a view to floating her over the bar at Wainwright Inlet. Her draught was reduced to 9 feet but there was only 5 or 6 feet over the bar. Three boats were sent down the coast under the command of Captain Frazer of the *Florida* to discover how far the ice extended, the chances of getting through it, and whether there were whalers beyond that could provide relief. He returned with mixed tidings. The ice extended beyond Blossom Shoals, 80 miles south. There was no prospect of getting a ship through. He had found scarcely enough water for boats and that might not last another 24 hours, given that young ice had cut up his own boats severely. There were two whalers beyond the ice and another five that might be able to work their way out of its edge. 'Will you wait?', he had asked Captain James Dowden of the *Progress*: 'as long as I have an anchor left or a spar to carry a sail' was the reply. The captains quickly took a collective decision to abandon their ships, looking to the safety of numbers against the expected displeasure of their owners. On 12 September they drew up a statement protesting the necessity of their action.

> Know all men by these presents, that we, the undersigned, masters of whale-ships now lying at Port Belcher, after holding a meeting concerning our dreadful situation, have come to the conclusion that our ships cannot be got out this year, and there being no harbour that we can get our vessels into, and not having provisions enough to feed our crews to exceed three months, and being in a barren country, where there is neither food nor fuel to be obtained, we feel ourselves under the painful necessity of abandoning our vessels, and trying to work our way south with our boats, and, if possible, get on board of ships that are south of the ice. We think it would not be prudent to leave a single soul to look after our vessels, as the first westerly gale will crowd the ice ashore, and either crush the ships or drive them high upon the beach. Three of the fleet have already been crushed, and two are now lying hove out, which have been crushed by the ice, and are leaking badly. We have now five wrecked crews distributed among us. We have barely room to swing at anchor, between the pack of ice and the beach, and we are lying in three fathoms of water. Should we be cast on the beach it would be at least eleven months before we could look for assistance, and in all probability nine out of ten would die of starvation or scurvy before the opening of spring . . .[3]

Thirty-two captains signed the document and at noon on 14 September the prearranged signal—ensign at the masthead, union down—passed along the line. A total of 1219 persons, including wives and children who had accompanied some of the captains, took to the boats. For Eliza Williams and her family it was becoming an annual routine; a year earlier the *Hibernia* had sunk from under them after striking a submerged floe off Cape Barrow. In the current emergency gunwales had been built up and bows and keels sheathed to improve the chances of the frail craft, but they were little reassurance. Another passenger was David Wilkinson of the Melbourne whaler *Japan*, also shipwrecked the previous year. Only weeks earlier he and the other survivors had been rescued from the north shore of Siberia by the *Henry Taber*. Their harrowing tales of a winter spent with the Chukchi, half-starved on decomposing walrus blubber, had reinforced the resolve of the captains to avoid similar misery. Now Wilkinson had the loss of a second ship to record, and a second escape.

> The boats were hauled over the ice toward the open water close in shore. It was fortunate that the narrow strip of water kept open so long, as it allowed the boats to pass south, comparatively without much trouble, though in some few cases it was miserable work for the crews to drag their boats over the rough ice, for miles at a stretch.[4]

On the first night of the voyage the boats were pulled ashore across the sandhills, overturned and covered with sails to provide shelter for the women and children. William Fish Williams, the son of Eliza and her husband Thomas, the man who had tried to save the *Jeriah Swift* from the *Shenandoah*, was twelve at the time. With his mother, his sister, clothing, bedding, provisions and himself in addition to the six oarsmen, their boat was grossly overloaded. The ships were lying 5 miles offshore on the other side of a huge tongue of ice that projected 10 miles out from Icy Cape. The whaleboats were safe enough in its lee but rounding the point would expose them to a south-west gale and a sea big enough to be testing the ground tackle of the waiting ships.

> We still had several miles to go to reach the ships, and as it was in the open ocean outside the ice, there were some fears as to our ability to make it with our boats loaded so deep . . . Our boat made the trip under sail and although we put in several reefs, it was a

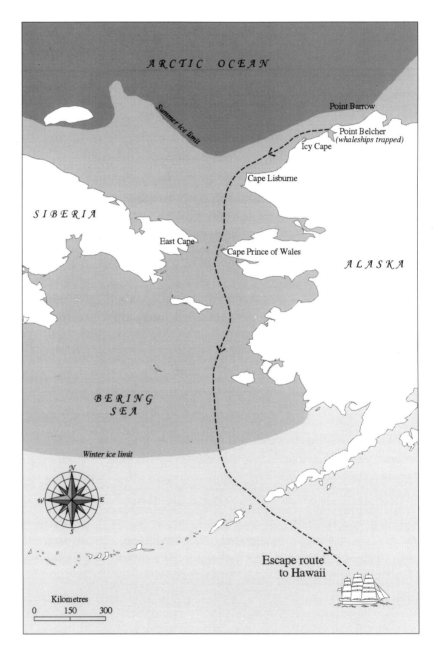

Escape from the Arctic, 1871

hair-raising experience. My father had decided to go aboard the
Progress. She was still at anchor and pitching into the heavy seas, that
were then running in a way that would have made you wonder how
we would ever get the men aboard, let alone a woman and two
children; but it was all accomplished without accident, or even the
wetting of a foot. As fast as the boats were unloaded they were cast
adrift, to be destroyed against the ice pack a short distance under our
lee where the waves were breaking masthead high.[5]

It is testimony to the boat skills of the whaleman that 120 or more
overloaded boats made the passage safely. Thirty-two ships worth
$1,477,000 were lost, but not a single life. The rescuers divided the
boat people between them. The five American vessels took 909,
the Hawaiian ship *Arctic* took 250 and 60 went in the *Chance*, of
Sydney. By the end of October all were safely in Honolulu. The
sperm market panicked and the price rose from $1.30 to $1.60 per
gallon until buyers realised that it was whale oil that was going to
be in short supply that year. Shortage of ships was the least of the
sperm whalemen's worries. Indeed, there were 30 of their ships for
sale at the time of the disaster and by early 1871 four former sperm
whalers were among the ships sent on their way from New Bedford
to replace the Arctic losses. Three others already on the sperm
whaling grounds were directed to the Arctic. It was only part of a
longer-term reorientation; five former sperm whalers had been
among the ships that had sailed for the Arctic before news of the
disaster even reached New Bedford. But still there were surplus
whalers. Owners were looking elsewhere.

> The continued purpose to sell whalers after so great a depletion in
> little more than a year shows the judgement of those who have long
> and successfully been engaged in the business, viz, that it has
> become too hazardous, and its results too uncertain to continue it,
> when capital is promised a safer employment and surer rewards in
> enterprises on the land, and in our own city [New Bedford], where
> the products of two large cotton mills equal very nearly the aggregate
> value of the fishery yearly.[6]

It was hoped to salvage something from the Arctic wrecks. The
Inuit had been taking whalebone even as the ships had been

abandoned and it was thought that up to half might be recovered from them by trading. Little hope was held for any of the ships, but in the summer Captain William Kelley took the *James Allen* in search of his command of the previous year, the *Gay Head*.

> The *Minerva* lay at the entrance to Wainwright Inlet, as good in hull as when abandoned. The *Thomas Dickason* lay on her beam ends on the bank, bilged and full of water. The *Seneca* was dragged by the ice up the coast some distance; her bowsprit was gone, bulwarks stove, and rudder carried away, and she was frozen in solid. The *Reindeer* sank, and the *Florida* was ashore on Sea Horse Islands, burned to the water's edge. The rest of the fleet were either carried away by the ice, crushed to pieces, or burned by the natives. The *Gay Head* and *Concordia* were burned where they lay.[7]

It was recalled that the *Massachusetts* had rounded Point Barrow; and when the point was reached by the 1872 fleet the crews were amazed to see an emaciated figure coming towards them across the ice. One of the men had stayed to save the bone. The Inuit had taken it from him and would have killed him but for the intervention of their women. He had survived in the care of an old chief. He told the whalemen that four days after the ships had been abandoned the water had frozen and the natives had walked across. A fortnight later the north-east gale had belatedly arrived and cleared the surface ice away. Whether this would have allowed the ships to escape had they still been manned was problematical; the ground ice remained locked solid. A further gale then drove the ships into each other. The captains had taken the precaution of destroying the alcohol stores, but to little avail; 'what the ice spared the natives soon destroyed, after pillaging them of everything they pleased'. Some of the Inuit died from sampling the contents of medicine chests.

Thomas Williams had decided to see what could be retrieved and fitted out the *Florence* in San Francisco for a salvage voyage. He made the *Minerva* seaworthy and sent her home loaded with recovered oil, but she never whaled again. His own ship, the

Monticello, had sunk where she had been left and was only recognisable by the portion of her bows that still protruded from the water, unique in the fleet for their iron sheathing. Of the 12,000 barrels of oil and 100,000 pounds of whalebone abandoned, only 250 barrels of sperm, 1200 of whale and 50,000 pounds of bone were recovered by Williams and others. The main marine insurance companies in the east, the Commercial Mutual and the Union Mutual, had to issue stock notes to the value of $410,000 to meet the claims against them. The additional premium for Arctic insurance rose to 3 per cent, further discouraging owners: although 60 whalers sailed in 1872, only six fewer than the previous year, in 1873 the number was down to 37. San Francisco underwriters, having had to pay on every Arctic whaler that had sailed from the port up to that time, flatly refused to insure and, apart from the *Florence*, it was 1875 before the west coast whalers returned to the Arctic.

It was bad timing. In 1876 twenty vessels, including two San Franciscans, passed through Bering Strait in August. In what was almost a repeat of the events of 1871, the ice set in early, there was no north-easter to release the ships, and the masters of twelve decided to abandon them near Point Barrow. William Kelley, who had been making the seasonal voyage in the *James Allen* since he lost the *Gay Head*, was among them. On the basis of his earlier experience he had reason to be confident that all would be well, but the weather was execrable. Several men died making their way from wrecked ships to those yet intact. Many died on the trek to the refuge ships and 53 decided that it was safer to stay with the wrecks than make the attempt. Three hundred made their escape. The twelve ships were valued at $442,000 and their cargoes at $375,000. Among them was the *Arctic*, a survivor of 1871, and the *Clara Bell* of San Francisco, keeping up her city's lamentable record of losses. The captain of the latter, the perennial Thomas Williams, at least had had the foresight this time to leave his family at home.

Whaling Wives

For a South Seaman, a whaling wife came in one of two
forms. From the earliest times of whaling in the Pacific,
island visits had been the occasion for unbridled sexual
licence between whalemen and native women wherever
local custom permitted it. For captains these casual liaisons
could grow into more durable relationships, particularly if
there was a need to cement alliances with local notables
during a protracted stay. A 'season wife' supplemented
more conventional conjugal arrangements that a whaling
captain had left at home. As the Pacific became 'civilised'
more and more of these New England wives began
accompanying their husbands on whaling voyages, in some
cases for reasons not unconnected with the competition for
their husbands' favours. More often, though, it was born of
a refusal to accept that married life was otherwise rationed
to three-month interludes between four-year voyages.
Some immersed themselves in their husbands' work,
learning how to navigate and even doing duty as
shipkeeper. Others were content with domestic duties, and
their sewing and embroidery rivalled scrimshaw in the
elaboration born of boredom.

Eliza Azelia Griswold of Wethersfield, Connecticut, was
24 when she married Captain Thomas Williams in 1851.
She was tiny, and could stand erect under her husband's
arm. A reticent, retiring woman, she hated the
responsibility for managing her husband's interests that
devolved on her during his absences and in 1858, although
five months pregnant, resolved to go with him. Their third
son, William, was born in January 1859 in the Tasman Sea.
Daughter Mary was born in Banderas Bay, Mexico, in
1861, and her sister Flora five years later in the Sea of
Japan. Eliza was wrecked in the Arctic twice. Her longest
voyage was 38 months but she sailed on every voyage with
her husband, other than during the Civil War, until 1874,
after which the children's schooling kept her at home. No
skills were wasted on a whaleship; when a man's face was

torn apart in a bomb gun accident, Eliza finished stitching him back together after crewmen could not bear to hold his head steady for the captain to sew. In Eliza's journals, only the encounters with other 'Lady Ships' give some hint of the isolation and the longing for female company.

> *5 August* This afternoon I have been with my Husband and Baby on board the *Eliza F Mason* and have had a nice gam with the Ladies. This is their second season out from home. They are going to Honolulu after they leave here. Mrs Smith likes the Sea much. She has been going on the water now 10 years and has been at home a little over one year out of that, in all . . . They have a very fine Boy Baby about 15 months old. It seemed very pleasant to me to see a Lady. They were quite sociable and seemed quite pleased to see me. We stopped there until evening and then came home. We would have stopped all the evening, had it not breezed up so strong that it was getting quite rugged. Mrs Smith tried to coax my Husband to let me stop all night, but he wanted to get under way in the morning. [Harold Williams, *One Whaling Family*, p 82]

While most captains seemed able to keep their domestic arrangements at home and abroad separate, the consequences weighed heavy on the consciences of some. In 1846 Captain Ichabod Handy of the *Belle*, 24 years married to Mary Warren of New Bedford, took a beautiful Maori woman as a season wife at the Bay of Islands. At the end of the season he sailed away without her, as was the custom. Eleven years later he was again at the Bay of Islands and sought out his sometime wife. She was not to be found but her sister was, and in her charge was a niece, a ten-year-old of mixed extraction. Handy recognised the girl as his daughter and named her Alice Henrietta. It would have been impolitic, to say the least, to take her home to New Bedford, and so her upbringing was entrusted to Handy's sisters in Boston, where she had a proper Bostonian education and married a proper Bostonian

carpenter. She bore him two children but died of
consumption at the age of 28.

Alexander Starbuck was putting his monumental compilation,
History of the American Whale Fishery, to press when the news
reached the east and he quickly added a footnote on the overwintering whalemen.

> These men are still there, and there seems no feasible way to
> communicate with them until the summer of 1877. Judging by the
> experience of Arctic navigators and by the condition of several of the
> former abandoned fleet when found in the ensuing season, their
> chance for a comfortable survival seems good, unless attacked by the
> avaricious natives. Provisions and fuel are reported amply sufficient for
> them, and with the first clear water of 1877 ready hands and willing
> hearts will hasten to their assistance.[8]

When the 1877 fleet was able to push through to Point Barrow,
they found that the whalemen had been treated kindly by the
Inuit. The only inconvenience had been the need to flee from
one dwelling to another when the natives were on a drunken
spree; this time no precautions had been taken with the ships'
alcohol. Only two ships were to be seen. The *Acors Barns* had
been burnt but, miracle of miracles, Captain Barnes of the *Sea
Breeze* saw the *Clara Bell* exactly where she had been left.

> She was found lying at her anchor, wholly clear from ice, and with no
> further damage than was done by the natives, who took whatever was
> any use to them, and cut and hacked until they had made a bad
> looking vessel of her. The first few vessels helped themselves to
> whatever was left of value . . . The *Clara Bell* lay there at her anchor
> till about the 20th of September, when she broke adrift and came up
> with the current and went out of sight in the ice to the northeast . . .
> I cannot learn that anything certain is known concerning the other

abandoned ships . . . It seems probable to me that in the strong northeast gales of the fall the abandoned ships were driven to the southwest, and were drifting around with the ice in the winter, and if not sooner broken to pieces, were carried away in the spring among the ice moving north.[9]

And so Thomas Williams lost a third ship to the Arctic ice. The losses of 1871 and 1876 were exceptional only for their number. Hardly a year went by without at least one whaler being lost: three in 1877, one in 1878 (the *Florence*), three in 1879, one in 1881. Steam began to be accepted in spite of its expense and the lack of bunkering facilities. In the Arctic, its dependability promised safety as well as efficiency. On his last voyage, in 1879, Williams carried a steam launch on the barque *Francis Palmer*. In 1880 the first auxiliary steam whaler was added to the Arctic fleet and by 1884 there were eight, two from New Bedford and the remainder from San Francisco. A transitional phase in the rise of San Francisco as a whaling port, years after Mark Twain had reported on its potential, began with the introduction of railway tank cars that could transport whale oil to eastern markets. The first experimental shipment was made in 1880 and the following year proved the viability of the route. Demand was so strong along the right of way that much of the modest shipment failed to reach the eastern states. More significant was the opening of processing facilities for sperm and whale oil in 1883, including a spermaceti candle factory. In that year the whole of the Arctic catch was sold and processed in San Francisco.

By 1886 San Francisco could put 44 whalers to sea, ten of them steamers and all directed to the Arctic or 'Japan and Okhotsk'. Provincetown had fourteen vessels working the Atlantic, all but one of them schooners and none larger than 117 tons. New Bedford strove to maintain a global presence, but in modified form; some of the seventeen vessels that sailed that year to Hudson's Bay, the Atlantic, the North and South Pacific, the Indian Ocean and 'Japan and Okhotsk' were no longer expected to bring their own oil home with them. The *Charles W Morgan* and the *Ohio* were sent around the Americas to whale in the Arctic but took that season's fare into San Francisco. The last whaler sent into the Pacific from New Bedford sailed in 1891.

From year to year in the Arctic it was not a question of whether ships would be lost, but how many. On 3 August 1888 five of the fleet were caught in a gale off Point Barrow. Four sank and the *Jane Gray* was abandoned, but by the late 1880s some provision had been made for rescue. The *Bear* was technically a revenue cutter but often found herself taking home wrecked whalemen, on this occasion 114 of them. The USS *Thetis* recovered the *Jane Gray* and returned the schooner to her owners in San Francisco.

By the late 1890s there was a permanent shore whaling station at Cape Smyth near Point Barrow and most of the fleet was steam-powered. A government refuge station capable of accommodating 100 wrecked whalers, set up to meet contingencies of the kind foreseen by Roys half a century earlier, had done so little business that it had been sold off. The mass disasters of the 1870s and 1880s seemed like ancient history. Then in the autumn of 1897 eight whalers were trapped east of Point Barrow. The steamers among them tried to break through under their own power but failed. They had been provisioned only for the season and were already scraping their bread barrels. It was known that there were also two sailing vessels in the ice. One was hard to miss. Off the Point, with hull crushed but masts standing, the *Rosario* was held aloft on display as if the ice were proud of its handiwork. Where the *Wanderer* was no-one knew.

Ships that had got out early raised the alarm. Four hundred men stranded in the Arctic was sufficiently alarming to engage the personal attention of President McKinley and the *Bear* was hastily turned around in Seattle. She had only just returned after finding a way through to the *Navarch*, which had been crushed by ice 25 miles north of Point Barrow in August. Captain Whiteside, his wife and two of the mates had been taken from the whaler and nine crewmen were picked up after three days on the ice. Of the other 30, fourteen perished of starvation and exposure while trying to walk ashore. They had been twelve days on the ice before the whaler *Thrasher* found them. Disaster enough for one year, and now it might be multiplied eightfold.

The *Bear* was an auxiliary steamer, not an ice-breaker, but it was hoped that she would be able to penetrate as far as Cape Prince of Wales on Bering Strait where there were government herds of domesticated reindeer. As it was not possible to carry enough food for 400 men by dog-sled, their winter provisions would have to be taken to them on the hoof. In the event, the land parties had to go ashore at Cape Vancouver, which added 700 miles to their overland journey. They started out at the end of December and were still 1000 miles from Point Barrow when they encountered a lone white man sledding south with two Inuit. George Fred Tilton, third mate on the *Belvedere*, had volunteered to walk across Alaska to find help, and here it was. Tilton could see no point in walking back to Barrow, and he could not stay where he was, so he continued his epic journey, sledding, rafting and rowing to Portland. He reached San Francisco on 17 April 1898 and had difficulty persuading his owner in Boston that he had not deserted before the *Belvedere* had sailed the previous year. Even when satisfied on that point, William Lewis was less than helpful. Tilton wrote to find out what he should do next. He was told to rejoin his ship. He respectfully asked if he was expected to walk. There was no reply.

In the meantime the *Bear*'s officers had requisitioned 400 reindeer and persuaded their Inuit herders to drive them north. When they arrived near Cape Smyth on 29 March 1898, they found the sojourners in reasonable condition. Hygiene had been poor for the 78 men who had been crammed into 'Kelley's old house', but there had been little scurvy and the rations had held out, thanks to the local Inuit. The natives had been sent 150–200 miles south to hunt wild deer and had brought in over a thousand. It was 28 July before the *Bear* could force her way through to Cape Smyth and there she was promptly frozen in. Lieutenant Bertholf, who had just finished one of the longest sled journeys yet made in an Alaskan winter, thought he too might be walking home.

> On August 3 the wind chopped around to the south west, disturbed the pack, and brought on a pressure, so that our port side was pushed in a few inches. The snapping, cracking and grinding of the timbers is a frightful sound, and for a few minutes it looked as if the staunch old *Bear*, that had seen so many cruises to the Arctic, was at last to leave her bones there, but fortunately the pressure ceased before any real damage was done.[10]

The four surviving steam whalers were able to free themselves by mid-August and started south with the *Bear*. And the *Wanderer*? Unable to repass Point Barrow the previous autumn, she had retreated eastwards to Herschel Island near the mouth of the Mackenzie River and there snuggled down with the steamer *Mary D Hume*, which had two years' provisions aboard. They were the last of a fleet of fifteen that had been overwintering there since 1894. The whalers had pursued the bowheads to the inshore limits of their summer grounds and could now lie in wait for them from one year to the next, if not without risk. There were no casualties at Point Barrow, but seven men from the Herschel Island ships were lost in a blizzard and found dead the following day.

The simple fact that it was necessary to endure the Arctic winter to make a successful voyage is evidence enough that the whale stock was being seriously over-exploited. The average whale oil take for the years 1896–1900 was only one-tenth of what it had been 25 years earlier, but the amount of whalebone taken had fallen by only one-third. The discrepancy is accounted for by the relative price of the two products; oil had remained stable over the period but bone prices had risen fivefold. The bowheads were now being killed mainly for their baleen, and for the time being the practice was paying handsomely for owners that had persisted. Between 1896 and 1900, the $99.28 average annual return on each ton of whaleship employed was just off its all-time high and double what it had been when sperm was king half a century earlier.[11]

Craft

or The Instruments

of Destruction

*Now the Harping-Irons are like those, which are usual
in England in striking porpoises; but singular good
metal, that will not break, but wind, as they say, about
a man's hand.*

Richard Norwood, Bermuda, 1667

Craft had nothing to do with boats, but much to do with what
was used in them. The term referred to the tools of the
trade, particularly those used for killing and cutting in. At the
business end, whalecraft was a harpoon to fasten and a lance to
kill. The harpoons were wrought iron and designed to bend under
strain so that, pulled sideways rather than back along the line of
entry, they would be less likely to draw. The fantastic shapes into
which the whales could twist them weakened the metal and,
although a harpoon could be reused, it would only be as the
second iron. The soft blades could not hold an edge, but as they
had only to make a single cut into the whale this was no disadvantage.

The early lances also had wrought-iron shanks and many a
headsman cursed the soft metal as he sweated to straighten a
lance that had struck bone. Heads had to be made of steel to
withstand repeated use, but it was only when the Bessemer

process brought the price down after 1864 that the all-steel lance became an economic proposition. A 2-foot shank was long enough for the harpoon, which only needed to find flesh beneath the blubber, but to plumb the life of a whale a lance had to be 5½ or 6 feet long. Both weapons had long poles slotted into them, but that on the harpoon was expendable once the whale had been struck. Hickory was preferred, and a canny skipper might try to recover the shafts by having a loop that held them to the whale line after separation from the iron.

A means of identifying craft was necessary if the owners of loose whales were to have their property restored to them, and branding was one of the earliest legal requirements that Massachusetts laid on its whalemen, 'to ye prevention of strife'. The mark could take the form of the ship's name, abbreviated or in full, or its initials, cold-chiselled or point-punched on the head. Sometimes there were other initials, as WB for waist boat. In addition to their primary function, the brands haphazardly provided data on the ages to which whales lived and their movements. In 1802 Peter Paddack was on the *Leo* when she lost an iron in a whale in the Pacific. Thirteen years later he was captain of the *Lady Adams* when she took the same whale and recovered the iron. In the early 1840s, the *Howard* of Nantucket likewise parted with an iron in 30° 30' north and 154° west. Five years later, in the same latitude but 14° further west, the ship found whale and iron again. In 1870 the *Cornelius Howland* took a bowhead off Point Barrow that yielded an iron marked AG. The *Ansel Gibbs* had been working Cumberland Inlet and Davis Straits on the other side of the continent for the previous ten years, but before that she had cruised in the North Pacific. Was this a young whale that had navigated the North-West Passage, or an old whale clever enough to escape for ten years the annual slaughter north of Bering Strait? The *Honolulu Commercial Advertiser* had no doubts.

> We have heard before of instances where whales have been caught at Cumberland Inlet with harpoons in them, with which they have been struck in the Arctic Ocean, but we believe this is the first

Frank E. Brown, Manufacturer,
4 South Water St., - New Bedford, Mass., U. S. A.

Pierce Shoulder Gun,
Price $35.00.

Breaks down same as a Breach Loading Shot Gun.
WHALEMEN SAY THE RECOIL IS VERY SLIGHT.
Packed with the Gun are 12 Brass Shells, 50 Wads, Primers,
spare Springs, &c. The shells can be re-loaded the same as
any brass shell.

Pierce Wire Feathered Lance.
Price $1.75.

It is so constructed that it can be discharged from either
Brand's, Pierce's, Eggers' or any other gun of the size, and is
used by Whalemen generally, but more particularly those in the
Arctic, giving perfect satisfaction to all who have given it a
trial. It has greater power than other Lances, the powder being ignited in the centre. It also has great penetration, having
four cuts to the point. It is more convenient in loading the
gun, as it does not require a hole in the wad to fire the fuse.
Leather, Oakum or anything convenient will do for a wad, or
can be used without.
It is the best Lance for Shore Whaling, as it can be kept in
the Gun or withdrawn without injury to the Feathers.

Pierce Rubber Feathered Lance.
Price $1.75.

This Lance has great penetration, having four cuts to the
point. It is more convenient in loading the gun, as it does not
require a hole in the wad to fire the fuse. Leather, Oakum or
anything convenient will do for a wad, or can be used without.

Pierce Darting Gun Lance.
Price $1.60.

This Lance has great penetration, having four cuts to the
point. It is more convenient in loading the gun, as it does not
require a hole in the wad to fire the fuse. Leather, Oakum or
anything convenient will do for a wad, or can be used without.

Pierce Gun Iron, a piece, 80 cents.

Pierce Darting Gun.
Price $16.00.

It is used for Fastening and Shooting a Bomb Lance at the
same time. It is a Breech Loading Gun. I make two kinds,
one a hinge, which breaks down same as a shot gun, and a
screw gun, a few turns of the barrel puts it in place. Packed
with the Gun are 5 Brass Shells, 30 Wads, spare Springs, &c.
The shells can be re-loaded same as shells for shot gun.

Toggle Irons, a piece, 80 cents.

5, 5½ and 6 feet Hand Lances, a piece, $1.10.

Boat Spade, 4 in. wide, a piece, $1.20.

Cutting Spade, a piece, $1.50.

Sliver Spade, 7 to 8 in. wide, a piece, $2.00.

Thick Head Spade, a piece, $3.00.

Flat Shank or Sperm Whale Head Spade, a piece, $1.75.

Blubber Forks, a piece, $1.10.

Long Pike, a piece, 75 cents.

Boarding Knife, a piece, $1.50.

Hand Mincing Knife, $3.50.

Rowlocks, a piece	.30	Marline Spikes, a piece	.50
Coopers' Tools, per lb.	.25	Boat Anchors, per lb.	.08
Boat hooks, a piece	.40	Line Graplings, a piece	.50
Quarter Steering Brace	3.00	Pikes and Gaffs, a piece	.20
Can Hooks, per pair	3.50	Cooper's Hammer	1.25
Drivers	.40	Chisels and Punches	.40
Setts	.50		

Frank E. Brown,
Successor to Eben Pierce,
Manufacturer of the

*PIERCE BOMB LANCES, WHALING
GUNS, &c.,*

No. 4 South Water Street,

NEW BEDFORD, MASS., U. S. A.

Whalecraft: a broadside advertisement, c. 1905 (National Library of Australia)

> authenticated instance of a whale having been caught in the Arctic
> Ocean with a harpoon in it from the Davis Straits side.[1]

The earliest harpoons were double-flued, but the arrowhead
shape had a tendency to cut its way out under tow. The first
attempt to solve this problem involved eliminating one of the
flues. The unbladed side of the head did not hold and the iron
skewed in the wound. The ultimate refinement of the traditional
weapon was the toggle iron, the single flue of which was pinned
nearly flush against the shaft when thrown but, after lodging in
the whale and being pulled back by the line, broke its pin and
pivoted to make a right angle with the shaft, thus locking itself
in place. The most famous variant was called the Temple iron
after its inventor, Lewis Temple, a black smith of New Bedford.
He forged the first of his novelties in 1848 and they quickly
became an industry standard. Such modifications as were made
over the next half-century were only for ease of manufacture. The
idea was a development of the lily-iron used for porpoise hunting,
so Norwood's Bermudan harping-iron may have been as advanced
in its shape and operation as it was in its metallurgy.

The toggle iron, however ingenious, seems but a poor advance
for the century that started with sail and closed with the diesel
engine. It was not for want of experimentation, which focused on
range, accuracy and killing power. Four fathoms on a flat trajec-
tory was considered a long dart with a hand harpoon. Greater
distance was achievable by 'pitch-poling', in which the harpoon
was lobbed in a parabolic curve, but accuracy suffered. Gun-
powder seemed the most obvious route to a quicker kill. Four
years before Temple's invention Albert Moore took out the first
US patent for an explosive harpoon. The barb of his single-flue
iron pivoted to reveal a cavity into which a vial of explosive was
placed, to be held there with a wooden pin.

> As soon as the harpoon is thrown into the whale and fastened to it
> the wooden pin is broken by the power of the whale pulling upon
> the tow-line attached to the harpoon, and the fluke of said harpoon
> will open or turn upon the iron rivet, and in opening or turning upon

Scrimshaw

Whalemen's art and craft were distinct from those of other seamen chiefly because of their unique media, whale teeth and whalebone. The variety of objects that survives testifies to the adaptability of the materials and the ingenuity of the workers, but the amount of labour devoted to them was not peculiar to whalemen; intricate ship models, for example, are universally associated with seamen's leisure hours. What seemed to set the whalemen apart was their almost compulsive need to keep hand and mind usefully occupied; this may have been not merely a proportionate response to the amount of leisure they had, but part of their Nantucket inheritance.

> Idleness is the most heinous sin that can be committed in Nantucket: an idle man would soon be pointed out as an object of compassion: for idleness is considered as another word for want and hunger. This principle is so thoroughly well understood, and is become so universal, so prevailing a prejudice, that literally speaking, they are never idle. Even if they go to the market-place . . . either to transact business, or to converse with their friends; they always have a piece of cedar in their hands, and while they are talking, they will, as it were instinctively, employ themselves in converting it to something useful, either in making bungs or spoyls for their oil casks, or other useful articles. I must confess, that I have never seen more ingenuity in the use of the knife; thus the most idle moments of their lives become usefully employed. In the many hours of leisure which their long cruises afford them, they cut and carve a variety of boxes and pretty toys, in wood, adapted to different uses; which they bring home as testimonies of remembrance to their wives or sweethearts.
> [de Crèvecoeur, *Letters from An American Farmer*]

The engraved whale's tooth is the most familiar and characteristic type of scrimshaw, scrimshander or scrimshoning, as whalemen's art and craft became variously known in the early nineteenth century. The derivation of the word is lost, but it is thought it may be of native American origin. The teeth were exclusively a product of the sperm fishery, as were the elaborately turned and carved walking sticks made from the sperm whale's jawbone, not to mention Ahab's ivory leg. Pieces of this ivory were also carved into a bewildering array of small objects, among the most beautiful and useful of which were jagging wheels for pastry trimming. The pan of the jawbone provided a flat surface for large and minutely detailed engravings. Ivory could be worked into mechanisms as complex as swifts for winding wool and as intricate as birdcages. A more intimate, and slightly risqué use, was as busks to stiffen women's bodices. Many a doggerel engraved on these short lengths of bone suggests that the maker is thinking of where his love gift now lies.

> Accept, dear Girl this busk from me, carved by my
> humble hand.
> I took it from a Sparm Whale's Jaw, one thousand
> miles from land!
> In many a gale has been the Whale in which this
> bone did rest,
> His time is past, his bone at last, must now support
> thy brest.

>   [quoted in Ashley's *Yankee Whaler*]

Few of the articles appear to have been made for sale. They were regarded as gifts and keepsakes of little or no commercial value. When they were disposed of for gain the transactions were characteristically casual, being as often for tobacco or alcohol as for money. Today scrimshaw is so popular with collectors of folk art that the thriving antique market attracts credible fakes. Legitimate copies and plastic imitations are also available.

said rivet will come into contact with the vial and break it, will produce friction, and cause the powder to explode, which will destroy the whale.[2]

Another approach employed explosive to fire the harpoon. William Greener's harpoon gun of 1837, a British invention, was a small cannon mounted in the bows of a whaleboat. Its projectile was a short non-explosive harpoon, double-shanked to accommodate a ring to which the whale line was attached. The ring ran freely so that it could be set outside the muzzle, but would slide to the rear to tow the rope after firing. It was an improvement over earlier swivel guns and like them had greater range than the hand-held harpoon (Greener claimed 14 fathoms), but on the open sea it was still difficult to aim and the recoil strained the boat.

There were attempts to poison the whales with prussic acid (it also poisoned the flensers when they cut in) and to electrocute them (but Sonnenburg & Rechten's machine weighed 350 pounds and needed two additional feet of whaleboat to accommodate it). A more promising line of inquiry explored the potential of the rocket, and sometime around 1805 Francis Rotch took out a patent for an explosive 'whale arrow', to be rocket-propelled from a shoulder-supported tube. Rotch did not intend his rocket to carry the whale line, but experiments with Congreve rockets in the 1820s demonstrated that this was feasible. In 1861 Thomas Roys, the first whaleman through Bering Strait, took out a patent and began manufacturing a rocket harpoon. His patent specification declared that

> To unite in a single gun the means of complete control and the capacity for throwing large rockets weighing as high as eighteen or twenty pounds with accuracy, notwithstanding the motion of the vessel, and without injury to the gunner or anyone standing near him, is the chief object of my invention. To this end I make my gun without stock or carriage, making the barrel of such shape and proportion as to balance on the shoulder of the gunner . . . By this means the gunner is enabled to shoot a much larger and heavier gun with perfect accuracy than he could if the gun were made with a

stock to shoot from against his shoulder and supported by his arms, as is now the practice.[3]

The market niche into which Roys saw his weapon darting was an unexploited resource, the great rorquals. The sulphur-bottom, or blue whale, and the finback were occasionally taken by traditional means, but usually by accident and often to the regret of those who fastened to them. They were too large and powerful for harpoon, lance and open boat. In 1864–65 the *Reindeer* of New Bedford went on an experimental voyage to Iceland carrying Roys rockets, and in 1867 the inventor claimed that 43 sulphur-bottoms, twelve finbacks and seven humpbacks had been taken using his apparatus in the previous season. Roys manufactured only to order, a sure sign that business was slow. Whalemen knew that catching these dangerous beasts was only half the battle: when killed, they sank. Undeterred, Roys patented a whale raiser, a 10-foot, 200-pound harpoon that was to run down the whale line, taking a hawser to the dead whale, which would then be pulled up by the ship's windlass. As boats already practiced line hauling to raise humpbacks and grey whales the raiser should have been successful, at least with those species, but there is no evidence that it was adopted.

Roys progressively refined the rocket harpoon until his death in 1877, but it reached scale production only when his last, posthumous, patent was acquired by Fletcher & Suits of San Francisco. They claimed a range of 30 fathoms for their California Whaling Rocket and published testimonials from the famous captains of the port, including the Williams brothers, Ebenezer Nye and William Kelley, all of whom had 'fitted their vessels with them this present season, and who recommend them to all parties interested in the whaling business'. This was probably a free issue for promotional purposes, as they appear to have been used later only from the decks of a few west coast steam whalers specifically hunting finbacks and humpbacks.

The guns that Roys had wished to supersede were large-bore

muzzle loaders of shotgun lineage. The first was invented by
Captain Robert Brown of New London in the late 1840s. It was
a 34-pound monster with a 1½-inch bore. The amount of powder
necessary to project the harpoon with line attached imparted a
fearsome kick, even to such a heavy weapon. The gunner might
find himself sprawled amidships after a shot, with a broken
collarbone for his trouble. The gun was tied to the boat with a
lanyard so that it would not be lost if the recoil carried it
overboard. Brown claimed great success for the shoulder-gun
harpoon during his 1847–50 cruise on the *Electra*, but the cus-
tomers were not convinced and he had to offer reassurance.

> Brown's whale guns, harpoons and bombs are now warranted, if used
> as directed . . . Formerly the most of my harpoons were too heavy
> and not made in a proper shape, this defect I was only able to
> remedy in part at Honolulu . . . I am now able to furnish Guns,
> Harpoons and Bombs which will be of most effectual service in taking
> whales. My harpoons are much approved in shape and workmanship,
> the heads being of a different pattern, and as they are made half a
> pound lighter there is no recoil now to the Gun in firing them, if the
> Gun is clean and used in conformity with the directions.[4]

More ingenious and a lot safer was the Pierce darting gun. At
first sight it was a conventional hand-held harpoon, but on closer
inspection the harpoon shank was seen to be fixed to the side of
the pole rather than to its end. Instead, the end carried a gun
barrel into which was loaded an explosive projectile called the
bomb lance. When darted, the harpoon would penetrate the
whale far enough for the head to hold. Then a shorter projecting
rod, the bomb lance trigger, arrived against the whale's side and
fired the lance into the animal, where it exploded. The recoil
disengaged the harpoon from the pole, leaving it and the gun to
be retrieved by lanyard. The whale was now held and, all being
well, dead. The main attraction of the darting gun was that
fastening and killing were almost simultaneous, an important
consideration in the Arctic where many conventionally struck
whales escaped by diving under the ice. It also retained the

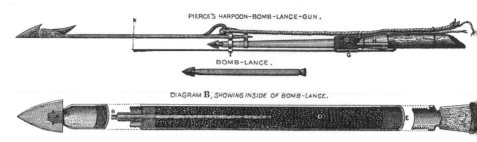

PIERCE'S HARPOON-BOMB-LANCE-GUN.

BOMB-LANCE.

DIAGRAM B, *SHOWING INSIDE OF BOMB-LANCE.*

Struck, held and lanced—instant whaling with Ebenezer Pierce's darting gun (National Library of Australia)

flexibility of the hand-held harpoon while doing away with the need to close with the whale for lancing. Ebenezer Pierce took out his first patent in 1865, and for 30 years he and his competitors refined the concept. It was designed to meet the needs of the bowhead fishery but was so successful that it could be found almost anywhere that whales were hunted. Its only real drawback, one it shared with the explosive harpoon, was that the proximity of the warhead to the barbs at the point of explosion could injure or dislodge them.

A cheaper alternative was to fire the bomb lance from a shoulder gun. As the projectile was smaller than a harpoon and had no line to drag, less powder was needed and the recoil could be reduced to something less of a threat to life and limb. This rapidly became the preferred method of stand-off lancing.

> Guns for driving the harpoon have, we believe, been pretty generally abandoned, but we are assured by a manufacturer of fuse, who has lately contracted for making a quality especially adapted to this sub-marine and blubbery location, that the bomb-lance is now being quite extensively employed by many vessels, and that some have sent home from the Sandwich Islands for further supplies.[5]

Later refinements included the use of metal cartridges and breech-loading mechanisms to replace percussion caps for ignition and black powder for propulsion. The most successful of the older type were the gun and lance designed by Oliver Allen of Norwich,

Connecticut, and improved by Christopher Brand in 1853. Brand's contributions were to shorten the lance to about 2 feet and add rubber fins to stabilise it in flight. He claimed that at ranges up to 23 fathoms it was as accurate as a musket or rifle ball. Muzzle-loaded, percussion cap-ignited and powder-propelled, his gun and lance remained in production for 30 years and Provincetown remained loyal to them throughout. Brand recommended a 3-dram charge of sea-shooting fine-grain powder, whereas Greener had advocated slower-burning large-grain powder for more gradual and smoother acceleration of the harpoon. In the 1870s New Bedford turned to the breech-loading types patented by Pierce (1878) and Chapman (1877). The Pierce & Eggers gun used a Winchester No 8 centre-fire cartridge to propel a muzzle-loaded lance. It could also fire the Brand lance. The Chapman gun was designed to fire Cunningham and Cogan's combination cartridge and lance (1875), and was regarded as a heavy duty weapon particularly suited to Arctic firing conditions.

It might be thought that with all this firepower arrayed against it the whale would have no chance. Captain Martin Malloy of the *Osceola III* would have begged to differ. In December 1866, north-west by north of the Cape Verde Islands, two of his boats got fast to a large sperm whale. One boat was stove and when the other fired a bomb lance it paid for the liberty by having its bottom smashed.

After picking up the crews of the stoven boats, kept the ship for the whale. On seeing the vessel he rushed at her, struck us on the bows, knocking off the cutwater with his head, and at the same time tearing the copper and sheathing from the bow with his jaw. Got into position and ran for the whale; ranged alongside and fired two bomb and two whale [hand] lances into him, but these failed to kill him. He remained on the surface, and in the vicinity of the stoven boats; lowered a boat, and without fastening fired two bomb lances into him without sensible effect. As it was near night, I called the boat aboard, and made sail to hold our position during the night. The whale was occasionally heard fighting the fragments of the boats, oars, etc. Thus through the night he held his ground, although he had two lines

towing on to the harpoons, five bombs exploded in him, and wounds
from lances.[6]

Battle was resumed at first light and the bomb lances prevailed,
but only after 31 of them had been expended. At one to two
dollars each, plus two boats and most of their gear, it was an
expensive whale. Expensive or not, by the late 1880s the bomb
lance had largely superseded the hand lance, even though the
latter was reusable and only half the price. The bomb lance also
rendered the boat spade obsolete, but the hand harpoon retained
its popularity. Thirty years earlier, J Ross Browne had already
concluded that whalemen were very conservative in these matters.

> Many expedients have been resorted to from time to time by the
> ingenious to overcome the hazards and increase the profits of the
> whaling business. It was thought, in the earlier stages of this pursuit,
> that a more safe and expeditious way of killing the whale than by the
> harpoon could be devised. Various inventive geniuses set to work, in
> consequence, and suggested innumerable methods, none of which
> were attended with such success as to insure the expediency of their
> adoption. There was, besides, a repugnance, on the part of old and
> experienced whalemen, to any infringement upon their established
> method of capturing the whale. Its hazards had no terrors for them;
> they had become accustomed to the harpoon and the lance, and
> preferred these instruments to all scientific contrivances . . .
> Experience has sufficiently proved that the old method is the best,
> after all. The dangers to which whalemen are exposed are great, but
> they have learned to regard them as inseparable from their calling. All
> these inventions may do very well in the way of experiment, for it is
> only by experiment that we can hope to arrive at perfection in any
> pursuit; but the probability is, the harpoon and the lance, as they
> have been from time immemorial, will continue to be, in all future
> ages, the most effective instruments in the capture of the whale.[7]

He wrote before the advent of the bomb lance, by which time
the increasing proportion of terrified greenhands in the boat crews
had outweighed the 'repugnance' of the few remaining experienced whalemen. He also misread as conservatism what was,
paradoxically, adaptive regression in response to changed conditions, as indicated by the practice of Captain William Martin of

Provincetown in the 1880s. He was an enthusiastic user of the bomb lance on right whales and humpbacks, but always killed his sperm whales with the hand lance. By then sperm whales were so shy that the use of explosives would improve the whaleman's chances with one whale only at the cost of gallying the remainder of the school. The true craft of the open-boat whaleman was now in the cunning he employed to get within striking distance of the whale.

The technological advances that would finally render open-boat whaling obsolete were not in the means of fastening and killing, for the Americans had experimented vigorously there before discarding most of the possibilities, but in the vehicles of chase. With no capital investment in wooden sailing vessels to protect, and a rorqual population at his door that was beyond them in any case, Sven Foyn of Tönsberg had turned to steam and iron. In 1864 he started a whaling station in Varanger Fjord to hunt blue whales and finbacks off the Norwegian coast. His steamers were tiny; 22–26 metres long and 32 register tons with a 25–35 nominal horsepower engine. Without using the auxiliary schooner-rig, maximum speed was 9 knots. The vessels had no function other than to catch whales; processing was done ashore.

The catcher was armed at the bow with a muzzle-loading swivel gun of 78 millimetre calibre that took a charge of 340 milligrams of powder. The effective range was 10–20 fathoms. Its harpoon was of Foyn's own invention, patented around 1860. The warhead was a 104-millimetre shell filled with half a kilogram of powder. Behind it was a holster that contained the barbs and the whole was attached to a pole, giving an overall length of 2 metres.

> The shell is screwed to the barb-holster, which contains a glass filled with sulphuric acid. To the pole is attached the rope, 143 millimetres in circumference and 733 metres long, with a ring running on the pole . . . When the harpoon is to be used, the barbs, that are pivoting, are secured to the pole by rope-yarn, and the shell screwed on the holster. As the number of barbs are four, the shell and the holster, that turn in the ring at the end of the pole when they are free, now form with the pole a solid mass. When the harpoon

penetrates into the whale the rope-yarn slips off, the barbs turn as to
make an angle with the holster, crushing the glass tube, and the
sulphuric acid, that communicates with the powder in the shell
through a channel in the screw, makes it explode.[8]

The gunner aimed for the spinal cord. The harpoon would
penetrate deeply before exploding; when it did, the warhead
would not only shatter the whale's spine but push the open barbs
backwards, thus embedding them more securely. The noise made
by the guns and the engines was not a drawback. Unlike
whalemen's muscle, the steam engine could just about match the
fastest sustainable speed of a whale and was indefatigable to boot.
Gone was the need for stealth and manoeuvre; whales could be
chased until exhaustion slowed them for the kill. When the
rorqual sank, which it often did, a hemp rope three times the
circumference of that used in the South Sea fishery was able to
winch it up or at least hold it until decomposition gases brought
the corpse to the surface. The rope was not significantly longer
than that of the South Seamen, but its weight was proportionate
to its immense girth. At 1450 kilograms it was heavier than a fully
loaded and manned whaleboat. The balance of advantage in the
contest between man and whale had shifted unequivocally and
irretrievably in favour of the hunter.

It was plain to observers that there would be serious consequences. Other Norwegian firms adopted Foyn's methods and by
1883 the 23 steamers in operation were able to take 506 whales
even though the government insisted on a closed season. In his
summary of the 1881 season the US consul in Christiania reported
that

> During the month of March the Varanger Fiord is said to have offered
> a splendid spectacle; several thousand whales flocked in and carried
> on the wildest antics. The sea was covered with columns of spray,
> and the heavy sound of the whales breathing could be heard as far as
> Vadso. The whale is, however, protected during this month, and the
> fishing could only begin at the end of May, from which time it
> continues through the summer . . . Though it appears that whales are
> abundant on the shores of Finmark, it must be borne in mind from

previous experience that these animals must finally be exterminated. The present fishing grounds are circumscribed, and there may come a time when these giant animals, who propagate but slowly, may disappear from the waters where they resort . . . [9]

The American whalemen did not adopt the new methods. The closest they came to them was the use of Roys' rocket harpoon from the decks of steamers off the Californian coast, an experiment soon abandoned for lack of finbacks to chase. The dead weight of capital already sunk in the wooden whalers and the declining returns were reason enough for owners to keep their hands in their pockets. But among their men there was also contempt for the new ways. Well into the twentieth century Norwegian whalers were extraordinarily sensitive about reference to their vessels as whale chasers. 'Whale catchers', they would insist. To the Americans of the open-boat tradition, whale catching was craft and contest both. In their eyes there was no skill and no sport in running the quarry down until it was as helpless as a bullock in an abattoir.

10

SO ENDS

Some oil will still be used until its perfect substitute is
produced at so low a rate that the expenses of whaling
will entirely absorb its profits.

Alexander Starbuck, 1876

The American whale industry was a long time a-dying, not least because no-one wanted to write its obituary. A bad year might be followed by one that was only indifferent. A really bad year might have one or two bright spots. A disastrous year might yet hold some prospect of revival. The trade reviews published annually by New Bedford's *Whalemen's Shipping List* chronicled a deepening gloom that was occasionally relieved by flashes of defensive optimism. After the minor boom that followed the Civil War it seemed that things were never quite right again.

1868 . . . return of the usual number of whalers, and generally with satisfactory catches, and quite as favourable results as anticipated.

1869 Of the 102 whalers that have arrived during the year, only about one quarter may be said to have made profitable returns; even those, at present prices, would barely have saved their owners from a loss.

1870 Our merchants do not look on the future of whaling with encouragement, and seem disposed to distrust it as to its pecuniary results, induced more by extraneous causes than inherent, having to the list of competitors lard, petroleum, and seal oil, that of cotton-seed oil, said by its advocates to be but in its infancy.

1871 Could present prices be assured for three years to come probably nearly every vessel would go to sea, but with the uncertainty in prices, partly from substitutes and low prices of them, only good prices can be hoped for and not counted upon.

1872 . . . few prizes and many blanks . . . No ground has been abandoned; every sea and ocean is at present explored by our whalers.

1873 . . . a year starting with a small fleet, steadily reducing through the year by sales and losses of vessels, with moderate catches, meager net results, no change of purpose to sell whalers now here, and no new signs of encouragement in the business.

1874 Although the past year has not been one of large profits to our whalemen, we are able to state today that the business wears a more cheerful aspect, with a promise of a brighter future.

1875 . . . quite free from disasters to the fleet at sea . . . Gains and losses have been about equally divided . . . but with a revival of business throughout the country we anticipate better results in the future.

1876 The building of ships for the whaling service marks a new era in the business, and is an encouraging feature . . . the character of the fleet . . . has suffered of late by the adding of worn-out merchant vessels . . .

1877 The present tendency being to cruise on those grounds nearest home, so that the catchings may be shipped at the earliest moment . . . The constant shipments of sperm oil have been largely instrumental in reducing the price to the present figures, which . . . are much below the cost of catching oil, excepting the vessels that are very fortunate.

1878 Of the vessels arriving . . . a majority had taken too small a quantity of oil to reimburse their cost even at higher prices, and those which brought good voyages netted but little profit to their owners.

1879 More than the ordinary number of disasters has occurred, but no serious calamity has overtaken any special portion of the fleet . . . officers and crews are constantly leaving vessels, causing a large expense in replacing them . . . Sperm whaling has not been attended with great success, the whales being scarce on nearly every ground, owing to the size of the fleet.

1880 The year 1880 will be long remembered as a remarkable period in the business enterprises of the country, and although the wave of prosperity that has swept over the United States has not placed whaling interests in a profitable position, we cherish the hope they may yet be benefited.

1881 The incubus of stock that has for so long a time weighed like a wet blanket on our sperm-whaling interests has now been removed, and no mariner returning from a four years' voyage hailed with more satisfaction his home port, than do our merchants the contemplation of the fact that the stock of sperm oil for the whole of the present year will be less in quantity than the consumption of the last.

1882 Sperm oil . . . touching 96 cents at the close of the year . . . The owners, tired of small catches and ridiculously low prices, are changing their vessels to right whaling or withdrawing them from the business . . . As the oil cannot be produced at a less cost than $1.25 per gallon, we cannot blame our merchants for transferring their time and capital to other enterprises.

1883 The past year has been one of loss to those engaged in this business, and its results have been discouraging.[1]

And so on. In their essence, the factors mentioned are among the most adverse to which an industry can be subjected—competition from substitutes, low and fluctuating prices, ageing capital stock, natural disasters, labour turnover, short-term over-exploitation of the resource, over-production. The nearest alternative employment for sperm whalers was the hunt for bowheads in the Arctic, but bowhead whaling had its own limitations, as contemporary observers were only too aware.

The profits in right-whale oil fishing are largely dependent on a freak of fashion . . . If it is the fashion to wear much whalebone in articles of dress, then the demand for that article becomes of such importance that the whale-catcher derives a sufficient profit from its sale to render the price of oil a matter of secondary importance. But it would require an enormous demand for whalebone to do away with the necessity of obtaining something for the oil, and although the fashion in dress for a number of years past has required the use of immense quantities of whalebone, still this has not been sufficient to keep the whaling industry from going into a decline, because a sufficient return could not be had for the oil.[2]

The 'freak of fashion' would undoubtedly have failed the whale-men at some point in time, but in the event corsets outstayed

"THE DUCHESS"
(THOMAS'S PATENT).

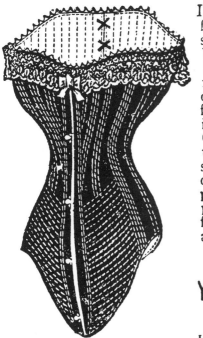

I s constructed on a graceful model for the present style of dress, the shape being permanently retained by a series of narrow whalebones placed diagonally across the front, gradually curving in, and contracting the Corset at the bottom of the busk, whereby the size of the figure is reduced, the outline improved. a permanent support afforded, and a fashionable and elegant appearance secured.

-- --

SOLE PROPRIETORS,

YOUNG, CARTER, AND OVERALL,
117 and 118, WOOD ST.

Busk and bone—women had both sperm and bowhead for support

them. Whalebone was becoming shorter and scarcer as the bowhead were hunted out. Scarcity pushed up the price. At the top of the market, in 1891, whalebone fetched $5.38 per pound, in real terms 60 times what it had been at the end of the War of 1812. Inevitably, a cheaper substitute emerged. Spring steel took over as the support for women's figures. It could have done the same for buggy whips, but there was no need. Soon after the turn of the century the demand for them collapsed so totally that they became a byword for obsolescence. The end for whalebone came with catastrophic suddenness. In 1907 the whalemen could still get $5 a pound: in 1910 there was no market.

Whalebone

Oswald Brierly, explaining whale's bone, wrote that it was 'not to be taken as the same thing as whalebone in the plural—singular as it may sound'. The *Encyclopaedia Britannia* was more helpful.

> Whalebone is the inaccurate name under which the baleen plates of the right whale are popularly known; and the trade-name of whale-fin, which the substance receives in commerce, is equally misleading . . . whalebone usually comes into the market trimmed and clean, with the hairy fringe which edges the plates removed. To prepare whalebone for its economic applications, the blades or plates are boiled for about twelve hours, till the substance is quite soft, in which state it is cut either into narrow strips or into small bristle-like filaments, according to the use to which it is to be devoted. [9th edition, 1888]

By then, spring steel had replaced it for umbrellas and corsets, and although there was continuing demand for women's clothing and millinery its chief use was for brush making. Heavy-duty industrial applications, like street sweeping, chimney sweeping and the cleaning of boiler flues and ships' bottoms, needed fibres stronger than bristle and more durable than vegetable fibre. The great advantage of whalebone for brushes, a use patented by Samuel Crackles in 1808, was that it came in single lengths of up to 14 feet and could be cut to order into strips or filaments. Early in the nineteenth century plentiful supply had driven the price down to as low as £25 per ton, but by the late 1880s it was a very scarce commodity commanding upwards of £1500 per ton on the London market.

And, notwithstanding the brave words of the *Whalemen's Shipping List*, grounds were being abandoned. It was not a deliberate process of withdrawal, and some years would see a speculative return to grounds unvisited for a while, but viewed over time the tide was running one way—out. The famous Japan ground of yesteryear attracted just one whaler in 1869. In 1871 there were no whalers in the Sea of Okhotsk or on the Kodiak ground. In 1874 there was no right whaling at Kerguelen. In 1880 the Indian Ocean and Australian grounds were untroubled by American whalers, although the locals were still active. A chart prepared for the US Fisheries Commission that year made it official; there were more grounds abandoned than current. In the case of the sperm whalers, whose grounds at their furthest extent had encompassed millions of square miles, the story was one of contraction rather than desertion. Of a total fleet of 177 vessels perhaps one-third were still exclusively sperm hunters. With so few ships it was not possible to do more than sample the known grounds and this appeared to be the evidence of the chart. 'On the Line' now only meant the equator east of 130° west. 'On Japan' was now a relatively small area north of the Bonin Islands. Contrary to appearances, the sperm whalers did not maximise their individual prospects by spreading themselves as Charles Enderby had once urged and as the Fisheries Commission map now suggested was the case. In any given year they would gather in just a few of these fragments of once mighty grounds, with predictable results. 'There is a growing tendency of late years for ships to congregate on small grounds, in order to look for the oil which somebody caught the previous year, and a persistence in this course ruins our best opportunities.'[3]

The sperm whales appeared to have a better appreciation of the situation than their pursuers. Gallied in one place, they would simply remove themselves to another part of their range until found again. Every reduction in the size of the fleet decreased the likelihood of early rediscovery of the whales. That they were still to be found, sometimes in large numbers and unexpected places, was apparent from time to time. In 1876, the year of 'ruined opportunity', 13,000 barrels of sperm oil were taken in the North Atlantic, the largest catch in years and in an ocean thought to be all but fished out. On the other side of the world, sperm whales could still be seen during the 1870s in the horizon-to-horizon schools that had greeted the gaze of Thomas Melville and David Porter in the early days. The Solander Ground, at the southern end of New Zealand, outlasted many others. The directions to it given in the log of the *Josephine* confirm the correctness of Wilkes' theory. 'The [Solander] rock 8 to 12 miles distant, bearing any where from N to SE an eddy here on this line which collects the feed No whales to the East of the rock, not much current in vicinity of the rock'.[4]

It was here that Frank Bullen, the author of that second most famous of whaling accounts, *The Cruise of the Cachalot*, did most of his own sperm whaling, although one would not know it from his book, which is an Around-the-World-in-a-Yankee-Whaler epic.

> Now it is evident that no solitary whale is in sight, but a great school, gambolling in the bright spray . . . Around, far as the eye can reach, the bushy spouts are rising. Hundreds of gigantic cetaceans are disporting, apparently not at all gallied by the conflict which has been going on. Some are near enough to the fast boat to be touched by hand. 'Potentialities of wealth beyond the dreams of avarice' are here; but acquisition is impossible for want of steam.[5]

Or want of a profitable price for the product. The first casualties of the decline in trade were the smaller New England ports. Many had never been more than marginal participants, attracted by the boom conditions of 1820–50 but unwilling to absorb losses indefinitely. Providence, Rhode Island, which had entered the business in 1823, did not replace its last whaler when she was lost near Sydney in 1856. Greenport, New York (1833), sold its last whaler in 1860, Holme's Hole, Massachusetts (1816), did the same in 1865, and Salem (1831) in 1872. The following year saw the final exit of Nantucket, but for the different reasons discussed earlier. Nine ports had welcomed returning whalers in 1820, and 41 in 1840. By 1880 only seven were still sending out whalers, with

New Bedford (*c.* 1750) and Provincetown (1820) between them accounting for 44 out of the 63. Decay was palpable.

> It is not astonishing, in view of all the circumstances, that the whale fishery should have ceased to exert an important influence upon the commerce of the country; but it has left many evidences of its former glory behind. Along our coast are a number of ports once teeming with life and activity, their inhabitants nearly all identified, in one way or another, with what was then one of the most remunerative industries of the United States. Now these ports are silent and deserted; their once busy wharves are vacant and fallen into decay; their streets are grass-grown, and most of their inhabitants have long since departed. In place of the numerous harbours affording shelter for the large fleet of whalers, one or two ports now suffice to shelter them all. What possibilities there may be for a revival of the former greatness of the industry remains for the future to show; but so far as the immediate future is concerned there seems to be no good reason to believe that further depreciation in the value of whale or sperm oil will occur. Prices have at last touched 'rock bottom', and there are now indications of improvement.[6]

It was a forlorn hope. The average price for sperm oil in 1881 was 88 cents per gallon. There was an upturn to $1.06 in the following year as exports revived. Domestic demand held as the manufacturers of lubricants sought whale oil to give body and weight to the lighter mineral products, but the reprieve was short-lived. Thereafter the price fell with scarcely an upward glance until 'rock bottom' was found in 1896 to be 40 cents per gallon. Whale oil fell from 48 cents to 35 cents over the same period and did not stop until it reached 31 cents in 1904.

San Francisco appeared to be the one positive in a sea of negatives. The port had promised much, but initially did little after its start in the business in 1868. By 1880 it could still claim only four North Pacific whalers to New Bedford's fourteen. Then the railway tanker and west coast processing reduced costs and shifted the economic balance between east and west. It had long been uneconomic to waste a whaler's time by carrying Arctic oil around Cape Horn, but owners had persisted because the ships were returning anyway, to discharge their crews. In 1881 the *Sea*

Breeze began fitting out and recruiting in San Francisco rather than in New Bedford. Others followed. Both cities also augmented their North Pacific fleets and by 1884 had equal numbers of Arctic whalers. Six of San Francisco's nineteen had previously sailed from eastern ports. Between 1886 and 1890 New Bedford was still the world's premier whaling port with twice the average tonnage of San Francisco. Over the next five years the situation was reversed, but San Francisco had become the biggest fish in what was an ever-diminishing pool. Its decline was as dizzy as its rise, and it surrendered the palm to New Bedford again in the early years of the new century. By then the combined fleets were only half the tonnage they had been in the late 1880s.[7]

It was the same story in Sydney and Hobart. In 1871 nineteen Hobart ships had taken 659 tuns of sperm oil. By the end of the decade there were eleven ships taking 268 tuns. The Sydney whalers withdrew from the Arctic fleet in 1874. In 1895 Henry Kendall's *Waterwitch*, 75 years in the water and most of them a whaler, made her last cruise. Hobart's fleet was reduced to the *Helen*, and she was hulked a few years later. Elsewhere, a small Chilean fleet operated in home waters, sailing out of Talcahuano, and the Azoreans continued to hunt for sperm from the shores of their islands, using the equipment and techniques they had acquired from Nantucket.

The last three Arctic steamers returned in 1914 to hear of the outbreak of World War I, and that was the end of whaling from San Francisco. The sperm whalers were not sorry to see the San Franciscans fade from the scene. Not only did they use steam, and were therefore not proper seamen, but they had taken some of the dignity out of whaling; in 1907, when bone was in demand but whale oil was not, their fleet of ten whalers had brought home 94,000 pounds of baleen but not a single gallon of whale oil. The average bowhead yielded 60 barrels of oil as well as 1000 pounds of bone. Over 700 tuns of oil had been thought not worth the trouble of lighting the trypots. The sharks and the birds ate well that year.

Henry Kendall's school of hard knocks—Waterwitch *near the end of her long career (National Library of Australia)*

As their world contracted, the wooden whalers went home to semi-retirement in their original calling, sperm hunting. In 1904 the *Wanderer* returned to New Bedford after twenty years on the west coast, and over the next few years she was rejoined by the *Alice Knowles* and the *Charles W Morgan*. These three, and another half-dozen assorted barques, brigs and schooners, were all that could sail in 1908 of a New Bedford fleet that 50 years earlier had boasted 320 vessels. Of all the other east coast ports only Provincetown, with three schooners, and Norwich, with a brig, were still putting whalers to sea. New Bedford had not sent a whaler into the Pacific since 1891 and the east coast fleet was largely confined to the Atlantic and the southern Indian Ocean. Three-year cruises were the maximum. Good catches were still possible in 1908; the schooner *Bertha D Nickerson* filled ship in ten months and the *Wanderer* brought back 2250 barrels after eighteen months out. The *Wanderer* did as well on her 1913–16 cruise, averaging 130 barrels a month, but she returned to find that the business was collapsing. In her absence the *Whalemen's Shipping List* had ceased publication. Its last issue, on 29 December 1914, quoted sperm oil at 48 cents the gallon. For bone, 'We are unable to quote any sales—there does not seem to be any demand for the large stock on hand'. Of whale oil there was no mention.

Retirement and attrition continued to take their toll. One owner had his favourite ship towed up-river to be scuttled at the place where she had been launched 50 years earlier. Another ship was given a Viking funeral, all sails set, to celebrate a public holiday. The *Platina* was sold to Cape Verde interests for $1300 in July 1911. The purchasers calculated that by breaking her up in the islands for firewood they could make a profit of $1000. The *Alice Knowles*, with 1600 barrels of sperm aboard, was caught by a hurricane off Cape Hatteras on the night of 2–3 September 1917. There were two survivors. On the following day the same storm claimed the brig *Viola*. Only seven years old, she was the last wooden square-rigger purpose-built for whaling. A month earlier she had put ashore a camera crew that had been filming as she whaled. This, as it happened, was the only documentary footage ever taken of a sailing whaler going about her normal business. The opportunities to record or preserve were slipping away.

The thought had occurred to *Harper's Magazine* as early as 1904. It commissioned a young New Bedford man, Clifford Ashley, to write and illustrate an article that could explain the whaling experience to an unfamiliar audience. Authenticity required a first-hand account and it was arranged that Ashley would ship aboard the *Sunbeam* as a supernumerary. There was no avoiding the fact that his article was about a dead industry—'not that it is extinct, but because it can never recover'—but even this was a particularly brave declaration for a local who would have to go home sometime. The New Bedford of 1904 was in denial—casks of oil had stood dockside for years as the more stubborn owners told each other that they would see a dollar a gallon again. Ashley quickly moved on. He knew that he would be on safer ground celebrating the anachronism.

> Whaling, of all our early industries, has come down to us to-day the least altered in the lapse of years, the least affected by changed conditions, the least trammelled by modern appliances. Of all pursuits, it has preserved to the greatest degree its original picturesqueness. Modern methods have been applied only to the off-shore fishery; deep-sea whaling, Sperm whaling, differs scarcely at all from the whaling of a century ago.[8]

There were seven American-born in the *Sunbeam*'s crew of 38. Only the captain and first mate were 'typical Yankees', but one of the boatsteerers was a full-blood Gay Head Indian. The second mate was a black Portuguese, the third mate a white one. The blacksmith was Pennsylvania Dutch, the cooper Norwegian, the steward Bermudian. There was a St Helena Englishman, a Nova Scotian, two disgruntled farmhands, a fugitive from justice and a cotton-mill striker. After that they were a mixed bunch, but mainly Pacific and Atlantic islanders born with an oar in their hands. The subject matter of the speech they got from Captain Higgins at first day muster would in truth have been familiar to whalemen a century earlier, and if the delivery seems a little tame perhaps reporter Ashley was considering his readers.

> Just remember, I'm boss on this ship. When you get an order, jump. If I catch any one of you wasting grub, I'll put him on bread and water for a month and dock the rations of the whole watch. You greenies have got just a week to box the compass and learn the ropes; after that, no watch below until you do. Let every man work for the ship; I don't mind a little healthy competition between the boats, but if any dirty work goes on, I'll break the rascal who does it. We've got to work together—see? (to the first and second mates) Now go ahead and pick your watches.[9]

As a five-year-old Ashley had tried to stow away in his uncle's sea-chest when he left for a whaling cruise. On the *Sunbeam* he was determined not to be sidelined as a mere observer. He took an oar as often as his 'barked' hands would permit, and had at least one experience on which he could dine out for a lifetime.

> ... the great mossy hump was swimming so close to us I could have reached over and touched it; and bobbing some fifty fathoms astern, with drawn, anxious faces, trailed the other two boats, mere puppets in the drama. Suddenly we heard the sharp suck of the lance, then a hoarse, 'Vast pulling! Stern all! Stern all!' We obeyed just in time! Under us the great flukes lifted with a crash, and we canted off and nearly foundered. I had barely got my oar back in place when the whale broke water again, and with an exhaust like the bellow of a bull, cut across our bows. Instantly the drawn lines trailing behind him to the other boats slipped over our blades with a deadly grip, and began to creep up the looms of our oars. The boat listed and the water rose to the gunwale. We struggled vainly to liberate ourselves. Tony tried to swing her off, but we were being carried broadside with such force that the steering-oar was of no avail. 'Cut the line!', yelled Mr Smith. Kite, the man at my back, dropped his oar, and drew a sheath-knife. The line was whizzing over the oars with a rumble that sounded exactly like a wagon going over a plank bridge. We clung to them for dear life. Kite raised the knife and slashed. Not having allowed for the velocity at which the line was running, his edge turned and the knife buried itself an inch in his thigh. All this while the fast boats were tearing down on us, yet it seemed as if they would never realize our predicament and slacken line. I saw Kite with his knife poised for a second jab. But he had let go his oar in the meantime and the whale-line, pulling over it, brought the handle with a resounding blow against the side of my

Clifford Ashley records cutting-in (New Bedford Whaling Museum)

head, and I lost interest in all immediately subsequent proceedings. I came to a few minutes later to find Alfred, the after-oar, emptying a bucket of sea-water over me, and the boat floating tranquilly on an even keel. The other boats were clustered about in a 'gam', and the lifeless whale was drifting quietly up to windward.[10]

Ashley had been true to his intention to commemorate a living fossil. This episode, in all its particulars, would have been familiar to any whaleman of the previous two centuries, right down to the dead whale's peculiar ability to work to windward, its submerged fin acting as a centreboard. Ashley even retained the traditional whaleman's unreliability about the natural history of his prey; he assures his readers that spermaceti is a fat reserve laid down against lean times. The greenhand/journalist disembarked at the Cape Verde Islands. He would not have been sorry that the editor wanted his story before the cruise was up; he had found the whaleman's diet unattractive but 'ate it without discomfort' and put on 10 pounds. The *Sunbeam* returned a full ship and made two more voyages before being wrecked off the coast of Georgia in 1911.

By 1921 New Bedford was the last American port in the business, with two square-riggers and a handful of schooners making 6–12-month Atlantic voyages. By neglecting their vessels and paring every cent from outfits, owners had been able to make a modest profit during the shortages of World War I, but what was possible at 73 cents a gallon was out of the question at the 30 cents on offer in 1921, and it had long been known that squeezing the seamen could be counter-productive. When the *Sunbeam* had gammed with the *Eleanor B Conwell*, Ashley reported that the steward, the only white man aboard, complained that the captain allowed no molasses for cooking, no yeast for bread, and no butter: 'Why, the damned Gee [Portuguese] eats lard on his bread, and thinks a white man oughter'. Ashley thought the crew looked wild and underfed. He was not surprised when he later heard that they had mutinied a few months after.

For a brief period the ships generated some income for their owners as motion picture sets. The *Charles W Morgan* featured as the *Harpoon* in *Miss Petticoats* in 1916. *Down to the Sea in Ships* was made by the Whaling Film Corporation in 1922. It featured the *Wanderer* under sail in Buzzard's Bay, the *Charles W Morgan* at New Bedford, and boats whaling from the schooner *Gaspe* in the West Indies. The cast included Captain James Tilton, who was said in studio publicity to be treading the same deck on which he had started his whaling career 50 years earlier, and Clara Bow, later the 'It Girl', playing the grand-daughter of Charles W Morgan.[11] Tilton also commanded the *Gaspe* on her filming cruise, which he logged as 'having taken 30,000 feet of whaling film'. In the following year, 1923, Paramount did their best to dress up the *Morgan* as an East Indiaman for *Java Head*, and James Tilton was again employed to get her to Salem for the filming.

Every time one of the square-riggers sailed, the question uppermost in New Bedford minds was whether this voyage would be the last. The *Charles W Morgan* seemed unlikely to whale again, and so the usual rituals of farewell were given particular attention as the other surviving square-rigger, *Wanderer*, prepared for a departure on 25 August 1924. On her last Sunday in port the old custom of blessing an outbound whaler was revived. The barque's decks were crowded with men and women in church-going finery. A portable harmonium provided the music and the chaplain of the Seaman's Bethel gave the benediction. A photograph taken of the crew standing at the gangway as their barque was being towed into the stream shows neatly dressed men with thoughtful expressions on their faces, quite unlike the dishevelled and terminally drunk sailing day reluctants described by most writers. No-one was allowed to spoil the solemnity of the occasion. And if the *Wanderer* were perchance to return? Then obviously the last farewell would have to be repeated until the prophecy was fulfilled.

The *Wanderer* anchored south of Dumpling Rock for the night. By 10 a.m. the following morning a fresh north-easter had turned into a gale with hurricane squalls. The starboard anchor chain parted and the port anchor began to drag. Most of the crew took to the boats. At noon the barque was ashore on the west side of Cuttyhunk Island. Her back broke at the foremast step.

If ever a ship had the fates tempted on her behalf, it was the *Wanderer*. Right down to the name, she seemed to provide a wholly appropriate finale to a wonderful story, but it was not to be. In the following year another whaler sailed. The *John R Manta* was not one of the barques that had dominated the industry in its heyday, nor was she owned by one of the great Yankee whaling families. She was a schooner, 98 register tons, and owned by a member of New Bedford's sizeable Portuguese community. So

The Wanderer lies wrecked on Cuttyhunk Island, 26 August 1924 (by A C Church, New Bedford Whaling Museum)

convinced were William Tripp and Don Waters that this really was the last voyage that they shipped as passengers before being allowed to sign on as unpaid crew.[12] There was an omen before sailing, but mate John Lopes thought that it was for him rather than the ship: '30 April 1925 This Day I Waus Standtheng on bord Dache About 3PM One Bird Cam and Stand on my head And then Flhy Whay I Whander Whaut Tocheng es et for me Pray es Not My Wife trost en God Not'.[13]

The schooner stalked across the Hatteras ground from May to August 1925 and took 300 barrels, which was about half a cargo. Apart from having two masts rather than one, she and her Provincetown kind were reminiscent of the early Nantucket sloops and even more like the early sealers in that their size was no impediment to distant voyages. Peleg Folger would have been quite at home in her, and glad to be returning home before winter.

In the event, American whaling finished with neither disaster nor partial success. The *John R Manta* sailed again in 1927 with a skeleton crew of six, including Captain Joseph Edwards and second mate Peder Martin, clearly intending to recruit in the Azores. On the day after sailing, the foresail ripped. There was no spare. On the next day they saw a school of whales but were too undermanned to lower. By day four the crew were pumping seven minutes every hour. The repaired foresail was set on day six and ripped again the next. On day nine, one pump had to be worked fifteen minutes each hour; on day ten, it was both pumps for twenty minutes of every half hour. The forerigging on the starboard side parted and the schooner was put on port tack to ease the strain on the foremast. The port rigging then gave way and the boom guy parted. Things were no better two days later, as Martin recorded.

> *3 July 1927* Wind is going down left a heavy swell ship still leaking very bad pump every hour 2 pump 45 Minutes start to repair foresail and it a hell of a Job. Decided to go home its very bad but its the only way. I can see Vessel is not in condition to stay out a year. it had bin a very bad day for the Captian When he had to Decided to go

home. I do no know What the Owner Will thing of Me. this day ship
340 Mils E of Nantucket shoals light ship. end this day.[14]

They reached safety on 16 July, exhausted after three weeks at
the pumps. Inglorious perhaps, but without casualties and
defeated only by lack of money for maintenance and enough
Americans willing to work for the lay. The price of sperm oil was
so low that anything other than 'a short and greasy voyage' left
owners without the resources to outfit properly for the next.
Starbuck to the contrary, it was the advance on the next voyage
rather than failure to cover the expenses of the last that deterred
owners. One by one they came to the voyage that did not leave
them enough to try again.

The Norwegian-style whalers produced enough sperm oil to
satisfy what was a limited demand until after World War II, when
shortages of all kinds again put a premium on this 'unique
inedible industrial oil'. As a result, the sperm whale catch rose
from 10 per cent of the total whale catch in 1949/50 to 56 per
cent in 1969/70.[15] When the perfect substitute for sperm oil was
found, in the 1970s, it was jojoba oil rather than a mineral product.

EPILOGUE:
DEAD WHALES AND
STOVE BOATS

Death to the Living, Long live the Killers,
Success to Sailor's wives, and Greasy Luck to Whalers.

Scrimshaw couplet, 1829

When news of the *Wanderer*'s end reached New Bedford, all eyes turned to the *Charles W Morgan*, indisputably, unambiguously the last survivor of the era of square-rigged whalers. But only just. She was lying across the Acushnet River at Fairhaven, alongside the burnt-out hull of the steamer *Sankaty*, which a month earlier had caught fire, burnt through her moorings and drifted against the whaler's port quarter. More permanent protection than that provided by the Fairhaven Fire Department seemed necessary. There was polite interest, but no money until a grandson of the *Morgan*'s principal owner in the 1850s was approached. Colonel Edward Green had enthusiasm, money and a home for the *Morgan*. Under the command of George Fred Tilton, the man who had walked home from the Arctic, the old vessel was towed across to Round Hills, the colonel's waterfront estate at South Dartmouth.

The *Morgan* was brought to rest in a purpose-built gravel bed and no expense was spared to restore her. Tilton assembled a

crew to hoist new yards and sails, re-rig and re-paint. The ship
(her original rig had been restored) had 40,000 visitors in her first
year at Round Hills. George Tilton, as a steam whaleman, was
not quite the genuine article for the *Morgan*, but the distinction
would have been lost on the delighted audiences with whom he
shared his tales of harpoon and lance. His death in 1932 was a
blow, but its impact was as nothing compared with that of Colonel
Green in 1935. For all his money, the colonel's will left nothing
for the upkeep of the *Morgan*. Whaling Enshrined, the management body of which he was treasurer, had little in the way of
other resources.

Left to herself the old lady might have imperceptibly rotted
away to nothing, but the very forces that had destroyed the
Wanderer now came to her assistance. The great hurricane of
21 September 1938, which was long remembered along the New
England coast, all but moved the *Morgan* from her bed. It stripped
her of sails and bottom copper. The carved sternboard had gone.
She probably looked no worse than she had coming out of a dozen
such storms in her sailing days, but her custodians were shocked
and impotent. They could see that her days were numbered
unless she were given attention that they could not afford. At this
juncture the Marine Historical Association offered to remove the
Morgan to Mystic, Connecticut, formerly a whaling port but now
the scene of the association's ambition to commemorate America's
maritime heritage. The offer was accepted and in late 1941 the
whaler was dug from her berth, caulked and towed to Mystic
where, restored to her workaday glory, she rests to this day. It
was a close run thing: Pearl Harbor dragged the United States
into war a month later. It is doubtful that removal would have
been possible in wartime, and who knows whether the *Morgan*
would still have been in restorable condition by 1945. The captain
for her last voyage was William Tripp, a curator of the Old
Dartmouth Whaling Museum at New Bedford and erstwhile
passenger/crewman on the 1925 voyage of the *John R Manta*.

Tripp was foremost among a band of enthusiasts that devoted

whole lifetimes to saving reminders of the great days. Artefacts of all kinds, in abundance and super-abundance, were bought, begged and borrowed from private hands, abandoned wharves, derelict warehouses and deserted offices. Ships' logs in their thousands were retrieved from chests, attics, paper merchants (at so much per pound) and from under the paste of scrapbooks. One was brought to Tripp's attention in 1948 by a bookseller, who had bought it along with some unsaleable rubbish. It was a volume of the *Manta*'s logs, but it did not include the 1925 voyage because twenty years earlier Tripp had already taken the precaution of buying that volume from the widow of his former captain. But Tripp knew where this 1917–23 volume came from. He remembered that in 1940 he had seen it in John Lopes' home. The whaleman had subsequently lost the beloved wife for whom he had expressed such concern in 1925. In his grief he had sold up their home and most of their possessions. Tripp was not particularly interested in post-1900 logs (and the $20 being asked was a bit steep) but the two volumes were eventually reunited in the museum's collection. By such devious courses did the records of the Yankee whalers find their way to safe berths.

Today there are few of the former whaling ports along the eastern seaboard of the United States that do not have a display, a library collection or a monument to mark their participation in this industry that more than any other compelled Americans to continue looking out on the world even while they were busy conquering a continent. Apart from the *Charles W Morgan*, the most striking of these reminders is the larger-than-life bronze that stands outside the New Bedford Public Library. Tagged with the whaleman's war-cry, 'a dead whale or a stove boat', Bela Pratt's boatsteerer stands forever poised, thigh braced in the clumsy cleat, harpoon in hand, ready to 'give it to him'. The model was not a Yankee, nor even a naturalised Portuguese; Richard McLachlan was a New Zealander who had been fourth mate on the *Morgan* in 1903–4. The second mate on that cruise, and on many others, was another Pacific Islander. George Parkin

Christian, great-grandson of Fletcher and grandson of Thursday October Christian, the man who had hailed the *Topaz* at Pitcairn in 1808, had made his career with the people who had found his people.

Trumpo survived the South Seamen. The right, the bowhead, the grey, even the humpback were all threatened with extinction by the puny men in their tiny boats, but not the sperm whale. The best estimate of the early-nineteenth-century sperm population puts it somewhere in the range of 1.8 to 2.4 million animals. In 1874, when the decline of the industry was far advanced, Charles Scammon attempted to calculate the total number of sperm whales taken by American whalers between 1835 and 1872. He assumed an average of 25 barrels from each whale, which meant that he understood 20-barrel cows to figure more prominently in catches than 'five and forty' bulls or the 100-barrel and more monsters of which whalemen were proudest. Allowing 10 per cent for sinkers and mortally wounded escapees, he came up with an estimate of 4253 sperm whales killed each year over the most productive period of the American industry.[1] This gives an annual whaleman-caused mortality rate of about two animals per thousand of the pre-exploitation population. There are many unknowns in the composition of this catch which would have had a bearing on its sustainability: the ratio of bulls to cows, for instance, and the number of cows accompanied by calves, for the latter invariably starved to death if unweaned when their mothers were killed. What is incontrovertible, however, is that the wooden whalers had little if any impact on overall numbers.

We know this because our century has revisited the sperm population and brought to bear on it the overwhelming weight of its technology and its obsession with statistics. Just as New Bedford finally gave up the ghost, steam whalers of the Norwegian type began taking sperm whales in numbers. It was not a specific assault: the floating factories and their attendant fleets of catchers vacuumed the oceans of anything that came their way in spite of the fact that sperm whales were not popular with factory-ship crews. The spermaceti stuck to the boilers and they had to be cleaned more frequently, but distaste was no real protection against a process that did not discriminate as it stripped, boiled and digested until nothing remained. The sperm catch of the factory-ships rose steadily in the 1920s and 1930s but it was not until after World War II that it reached the levels achieved by the 'primitive' industry at its peak in the 1830s. Thereafter the graph went almost vertical, and in the 1960s some 25,000 sperm whales were being legally taken each year by Japanese and Russian fleets, even though their operations were hedged about with minimum size limits set by international treaty, closed seasons and ground limitations. We have little idea how long a catch of this size could have been sustained, but for once the international community did not wait to find out. Numerical limits were introduced and by 1976 the North Pacific catch was down to 7211 from the 16,320 it had been in 1968.[2] (After the collapse of the Soviet Union it was revealed that there had also been a large illegal catch.)

In 1986 the international community imposed a moratorium on all commercial whaling. There are still reports from time to time of poaching in the Azores, but today trumpo is more at risk from mass strandings like that in Tasmania in 1998 than from human activity. Even our pollution seems to have less impact on the sperm whale than on many other species, although relatively high concentrations of mercury have been found in its meat. We can be no surer of present numbers than we are of the pre-exploitation population, but estimates range from hundreds of thousands to as many as 2 million. If the upper figure, from US official statistics on endangered species, is even near the truth, it presents a dilemma for conservationists. It may be morally wrong to hunt sperm whales, and it is certainly difficult to kill them humanely, but the argument for prohibition that is hardest to sustain is the possibility of extinction. The US administration implicitly queries the Congressional designation of sperm whales as endangered by pointing out that there are eight times as many of them as there are of all the other six endangered whale species put together. We have already done our worst and there may be as many sperm whales swimming the oceans today as ever there were. Mobility and dispersal have been their salvation and would be again were commercial pelagic whaling to be resumed. Once the larger and now more desirable whales like the blue and the fin had been exterminated, it would no longer be commercially worthwhile to pursue the remnant sperm population, dispersed as it would be over half the Earth's surface. There has been advantage in being relegated to the status of by-catch.

Were we to devote all of our technology to the extermination of the sperm whale, without thought of cost or benefit, we might do so. But if cost/benefit is added to the equation, humankind's food budget would have to be in a parlous state indeed for harvesting to be worthwhile to the point of species extinction. The oil is unsuitable for margarine and we would certainly not be dining on the meat from choice: of all the cetacea—and the old-timers tried most of them, from dolphins up—the sperm whale was thought to be about the poorest eating.

In 1926 Clifford Ashley, later to become modestly famous in Boy Scout and weekend sailor circles as the author of *Ashley's Book of Knots*, wrote in all seriousness that if sperm whales were not hunted they would become a hazard to navigation. He stopped short of claiming that the prey enjoyed the hunt, as fox-hunters have been known to do, but he saw it as glorious sport, claiming that 'if ever there is to be fairer and better hunting than the chase of the Sperm Whale, man will have to go to other worlds to find it'.[3] With similar disingenuity, the Japanese hunt minke whales for 'scientific purposes', but the whale meat so taken sells very well at home as a traditional food. Likewise, some native Americans of Alaska claim the right to hunt the endangered bowhead as part of their cultural heritage, but they use power boats and modern firearms.

But Ashley was right about fairness. The balance of capabilities between sperm whales and open-boat whalemen in terms of speed, endurance, manoeuvrability and armament ensured that every encounter was a contest—a contest without a foregone conclusion. We would be spared much hypocrisy today were all would-be sportsmen, whale-meat eaters and cultural traditionalists allowed to resume the hunt for sperm whales. A single condition would suffice. Let them emulate the Indonesian whalemen of Lamalera, who are still prepared to take their chances from an open wooden boat, trusting in strong arms, an iron harpoon and a few hundred feet of line.

GLOSSARY

abaft rearwards of

ambergris intestinal secretion of the sperm whale, used as a perfume enhancer

barque three-masted vessel, square-rigged on two and fore-and-aft on aftermost

batten thin strip of wood used to reinforce the internal seam between flush planks

bend, to to tie

bible page-sized slices of blubber held together by the adhering whale skin

blanket piece strip of blubber as peeled from the whale at the start of flensing

boarding knife sword-like implement used for severing one blanket piece from the next

boat spade wide-bladed implement used to disable flukes and cut towing holes

boatsteerer harpooner, describing his function after he has harpooned the whale

bomb gun shoulder-held weapon for firing bomb lances

bomb lance explosive, gun-fired projectile used to kill the whale after harpooning

bow box decked area at bow of whaleboat boxed to contain the first few fathoms of whale line

bow chocks channel at the top of the bow through which the whale line runs

bowline type of knot used to make a loop at the end of a rope

box warp part of the whale line nearest the harpoons, coiled in the bow box

breach, to of a whale, to throw the body clear of the water

bulwark side planking above the gunwale

caboose deck structure containing the tryworks, also a name for the galley

capstan upright cylindrical winch hand-turned by horizontal bars inserted in the head

carvel ship-building technique whereby the hull planks are laid flush, edge to edge

case upper half of the forehead of the sperm whale, its reservoir of pure spermaceti

cathead deck-mounted timber that projects over the bow at an angle to hold an anchor

ceiling planking laid over the ribs in the bottom of a boat

chains outboard attachment for the standing rigging that laterally supports the masts

churn, to to work the lance up and down in the whale without removing it

clumsy cleat semi-circular hole cut into the forward thwart to support the harpooner's thigh

crab, to to miss the water with an oar stroke

crackling whale skin after the blubber has been boiled from it, fuel for the tryworks

craft all whaling implements, but particularly harpoons and lances

cranes retractable outboard scaffolds on which the boats are carried

crotch Y-shaped rest for the harpoons at the starboard bow of a whaleboat

cut in, to to flense or flinch the whale

cutting spade flensing implement with a wide cutting edge

cutting stage [-shaped platform on which flensers stand outboard of the starboard gangway

darting gun hand-thrown combination of harpoon and bomb lance

davit small crane for hoisting boats

drogue squares of wood fastened to the whale line to slow the whale

easting down running before the prevailing westerlies in the Roaring Forties

falls ropes by which boats on davits are raised and lowered

fare cargo

fat lean pieces of blubber to which whalemeat is still attached

fin out position in which a dead whale floats

flake a single layer in a multi-layered coil of rope

flemish coil rope coiled so that a free end is in the centre

flense, to to cut blubber from the whale

flip mixture of beer, spirit and sugar heated with a poker

flue harpoon barb

flukes the whale's tail

flurry the last paroxysm of the dying whale

gaff spar to which the head of a four-sided fore-and-aft sail is bent

gally, to to frighten

gam, to to visit, mutually

gangway section of the bulwark open to allow passage

garboard plank nearest the keel

gig tackle small fore-and-aft rope securing a boat to its cranes

glip oil slick left by passage of a whale

goose pen shallow cistern under the tryworks, filled with water when boiling blubber

gripe lateral lashing that holds a boat secure on the cranes

gunwale plank that covers the tops of the frame timbers of a wooden ship

halyard rope for hoisting a sail

headsman commander of a whaleboat, the man who lances the whale

horse piece small piece of blubber cut from the blanket piece, ready for the mincing horse

iron harpoon, sometimes also lance

junk lower half of the sperm whale's forehead, containing both spermaceti and oil

kicking strap rope along the leading edge of the clumsy cleat to hold down the whale line

kid small wooden mess bucket

kreng English whalemen's term for the carcass of a whale after flensing

lance spear-like implement for killing whales after fastening to them

lantern keg a truncated cone, containing signal light and emergency rations

lanyard short length of rope attached to an implement to prevent loss

lapstrake ship-building technique whereby the hull planks overlap

lay share

lay on, to to turn the boat in to the whale at a right angle so that the harpooner can strike, or to bring the boat on to the whale's back

lime-juicer drinker of lime juice (to avoid scurvy); an English practice, whence Limey

lipper piece of fluke or blubber, into which handholds have been cut, to scrape up oil

live iron harpoon attached to the whale line ready for use

loggerhead stout post set in the whaleboat's after deck, about which the line is snubbed

maintop platform at the top of the mainmast, where it doubles against the main topmast

mincing horse waist-high horizontal plank on which horse-pieces are sliced into bibles

miz(z)en aftermost mast of a three-masted vessel

peak, to to keep oar blades clear of the water by placing their handles inboard in cleats

piggin small bailing bucket with one long stave for a handle

plank shear outermost deck plank, or plank covering the top of the bulwark

red flag blood spouting from the whale; also 'fire in the chimney'

recruit, to to obtain fresh food and water, to trade for them

ripsack one of many nicknames for the grey whale

scrap whale skin after the blubber has been boiled from it, fuel for trying out

scrimshaw whalemen's art and craft, particularly that using whalebone, ivory and teeth

scupper draining hole in the bulwarks that allows water to clear from the deck

scuttle entrance or port let into a space between decks

sheer upward curve of the deck from the waist towards bow and stern

sheet rope attached to the foot of a sail to trim it to the wind

shooks bundled staves which the cooper will set up as casks

shrouds standing rigging that provides lateral support for the masts

snow small two-masted sailing vessel with a trysail on the mainmast

soger 'soldier', slacker

soundings waters shallow enough to be plumbed with the ship's lead

spiracle spout hole

squeegee, to to clear the decks of spilt oil using a lipper

sternsheets the bottom of a boat between the after thwart and the after deck

stink rotted fat-lean

stove, to be to have the boat damaged by a whale to the point of taking water

studding sail light weather sail set on a light boom outboard of square sails

thrum, to to cover with matting

thwart transverse timber of a boat, and used as oarsmen's seats

toggle iron harpoon whose head swivels after striking to improve the chances of holding

topmast section of mast above mainmast

tow iron harpoon to which a drogue has been attached

try out, to to boil blubber

trysail fore-and-aft sail set on mast instead of stay

waif flag mounted on a pole, left in dead whale to indicate position and ownership

warp light rope

whalebone the food-filtering plates in the mouth of baleen whales

whitehorse the bloodless part of the sperm whale's forehead above the skull

windlass horizontal winch turned with handspikes, used for heavy lifting

WEIGHTS AND
MEASURES

In the interests of authenticity weights and measures have, by and large, been left as they were found. Where I intrude a figure of my own it reflects the usage of the context rather than modern practice. 'Fathom' is the best example of this, although it may surprise readers to learn that this hoary but venerable relic is still coin of the realm and will remain so in Britain until 31 December 1999. My affection for 'knot', as a terse and salty way of expressing speed at sea, will have to suffice as explanation for my prejudice against miles or kilometres per hour. Besides, the measure from which it derives, the circumference of the globe, is both more majestic and less arbitrary than the length of Henry I's arm, whence the Imperial yard. Whenever I have found myself without an excuse I have used metric measures, if only because the metre embodies the global principle. None of this will help those who would make sense of statistics across two centuries, three systems of weights and measures, and many different usages. To them, with apologies, I offer a rough guide.

Oil

Before 1824, the most common measures of oil in Britain and its former American colonies were the tun and the barrel. The tun was originally a wine measure, divided into 8 barrels of 31½ gallons each, ie 252 gallons altogether. The wine gallon was 231 cubic inches or 3.7731 litres. When Britain adopted Imperial measures and officially abandoned the tun, the oil merchants and Americans who clung to the old measure found that a tun was 210 Imperial gallons 'very nearly', or 953.8036 litres very precisely. The Imperial gallon is 1.2 US gallons. Many US states still use 31½ gallons to the barrel as liquid measure.

Ships

A ship's tonnage was originally the number of tuns it could stow, recorded for taxation purposes and the calculation of harbour dues etc. Register tonnage, that most commonly used, left much to be desired as a measure of volume; length and breadth were actually measured but depth was arbitrarily allowed to be half the breadth. In 1836 Britain revised the formula to include measured depth, and New Measure, as it was known, re-rated most vessels upwards or downwards, sometimes significantly. The *Charles W Morgan*, for example, was remeasured in 1864 to register 313.75 tons, down from 351 tons Old Measure. In Imperial solid measure, one ton of shipping for cargo stowage purposes was 42 cubic feet or 1.1892 cubic metres.

Length

An inch is one-twelfth of a foot is 0.0254 metres.
A foot is 0.3048 metres.
A yard is 3 feet is 0.9144 metres.
A fathom is 6 feet is 1.8288 metres.
A rod is 5.5 yards is 5.0291 metres.
A mile is 1609.3 metres.
A league is 3 miles is 4827.9 metres.
A nautical mile is one-sixtieth of a degree of latitude is 1852 metres.

Velocity

A knot is the velocity at which a body will travel one nautical mile or 1.15078 land miles in one hour, or 0.514444 metres per second. It is named for the equidistant knots in the log line that was run astern of a ship to measure the distance travelled in the time it took for a small sand-glass to empty.

Weights (Imperial avoirdupois)

A dram is one-sixteenth of an ounce is 1.771 grams.
An ounce is 28.346 grams.
A pound is 16 ounces is 453.544 grams.
A ton is 2240 pounds is 1015.92 kilograms.

Money

Before the Revolution the British pound sterling was legal tender in Britain and the American colonies. It divided into 20 shillings which in turn divided into 12 pence. The penny subdivided into 2 halfpence or 4 farthings. The United States adopted the dollar, which divided into 100 cents. For most of the period of this book the gold coin of the two countries converted at $4.50–$5 to the pound, with paper currency discounted. Nineteenth-century British colonies used a variety of currencies as well as sterling, but trade prices were quoted in the latter.

NOTES

1 South for Spermaceti

1 R R Reeves and E Mitchell, 'The Long Island, New York, Right Whale Fishery: 1650–1924' in *Right Whales: Past and Present Status*, International Whaling Commission Special Issue 10, Cambridge, 1986, pp 201, 203.

2 R H Barnes, *Sea Hunters of Indonesia*, Clarendon Press, Oxford, 1996, p 326. The most eloquent testimony to the antiquity of sperm whaling at Lamalera is the awkward configuration—to Western eyes—of the harpooons. Although long since made of iron, they closely resemble in shape and size the antler of the island's deer, which suggests that this was the material from which they were originally made.

3 *Philosophical Transactions of the Royal Society*, vol I, no 8, 8 January 1665/6, p 132.

4 ibid., vol III, no 40, 19 October 1668, p 794.

5 ibid., vol XXXIII, no 387, March & April 1725, p 267. Captain Atkins later pioneered the American Davis Straits whale fishery.

6 A Starbuck, *History of Nantucket* (1924), Charles E Tuttle, Rutland, 1969, p 278.

7 C W Ashley, *The Yankee Whaler*, Martin Hopkinson, London, [1926], pp 35–7 and PMB film 279.

8 J H St J de Crèvecoeur, *Letters from an American Farmer* (1782), H M Dent, London, 1912, pp 114–15.

9 D C Fonda Jnr, *Eighteenth Century Nantucket Whaling*, the author, Nantucket, 1969, pp 5, 12, 21 and E A Stackpole, *The Sea Hunters*, J B Lippincott, Philadelphia, 1953, pp 35–9.

10 A Starbuck, *History of the American Whale Fishery*, the author, Waltham, 1876, p 57.

11 ibid., pp 168–75.

12 E R Barkan (ed), *Edmund Burke on the American Revolution*, Peter Smith, Gloucester, 1972, pp 80–1.

13 G Jackson, *The British Whaling Trade*, Adam & Charles Black, London, 1978, p 52.

Trumpo

1 Quoted by Thomas Beale in *The Natural History of the Sperm Whale*, John van Voorst, London, 1839, p 128.

2 C Lockyer, *Observations on Diving Behaviour of the Sperm Whale*, Pergamon Press, Oxford, 1977, pp 591–6, 600–3.

3 Baron G Cuvier, *The Animal Kingdom*, Geo. B Whittaker, London, 1827, vol 4, pp 464–6, 470.

4 J Colnett, *A Voyage to the South Atlantic and round Cape Horn into the Pacific Ocean*, the author, London, 1798, endplate.

5 T Beale, op. cit., pp 16–17.

6 F D Bennett, *A Whaling Voyage Round the Globe*, Richard Bentley, London, 1840, vol II, pp 157–8.

7 J S Polack, *New Zealand*, Richard Bentley, London, 1838, pp 411–12.

8 Goode, *Fisheries*, section V, vol 2, pp 72–3.

9 Captain Crocker to Lieutenant Maury (c. 1851), quoted in M F Maury, *Explanations and Sailing Directions to Accompany the Wind and Current Charts*, 6th edn, E & C Biddle, Philadelphia, 1854, p 383.

2 The British Are Coming

1 Petition to Treasury, PRO CO 5, vol 146, p 63b, quoted in E A Stackpole, *The Sea Hunters*, J B Lippincott, Philadelphia, 1953, p 75.

2 A Smith, *The Wealth of Nations*, A Strachan and T Cadell, London, 1793, vol II, p 287.

3 W Rotch, *Memorandum Written in the Eightieth Year of His Age*, Houghton Mifflin, Boston, 1916, p 28.

4 J Adams, *Works*, Little Brown, Boston, 1852, vol VII, pp 63–4.

5 References to British whaleship movements in this work are as extracted from Lloyd's List by A G E Jones and published in his

two volumes on *Ships Employed in the South Seas Trade*, Roebuck, Canberra, 1986–91.

6   Rotch, op. cit., p 27.

7   G Bancroft, *History of the United States of America* (1885), reissued Kennikat Press, Port Washington, 1967, vol V, pp 321–4.

8   Adams, op. cit., vol VIII, pp 308–9.

9   Rotch, op. cit., pp 42–5.

10 Letters to son William and Samuel Rodman, 2 August 1785, quoted in Stackpole, op. cit., p 113.

11 Memorial of Enderby and others, 6 January 1786, PRO BT 6/95, p 33, quoted in G Jackson, *The British Whaling Trade*, Adam & Charles Black, London, 1978, p 96.

12 Enderby to George Chalmers, 2 December 1788, Mitchell Library, Sydney, MS A322.

13 Enclosure in a letter to John Jay, 19 November 1788, in S K Padover, *The Complete Jefferson*, Duell, Sloan & Pearce, New York, 1943, p 197.

14 *Report to Congress on Cod and Whale Fisheries*, 1 February 1791, ibid., p 335.

15 Speaker, Nova Scotia Assembly to Governor, 17 August 1791, quoted in Stackpole, op. cit., p 144.

16 *Report to Congress on Cod and Whale Fisheries*, 1 February 1791, in Padover, op. cit., p 337–9.

Lay On, Cut In, Try Out, Stow Down

1   PMB film 393, 820. Quoted by P A Miller, *And the Whale Is Ours*, D R Gondine, Boston, 1979, pp 167–71.

2   H Kendall, 'Sperm Whaling', *Australian Journal*, vol 5, part 54, November 1869.

3   ibid.

4   F Maynard and A Dumas, *The Whalers*, Hutchinson, London, 1937, pp 105–7.

5   C Nordhoff, *Whaling and Fishing*, Dodd, Mead & Co, New York, 1895, pp 130–1.

6   J Ross Browne, *Etchings of a Whale Cruise*, John Murray, London, 1846, pp 63–4.

7   Nordhoff, op. cit., pp 129–30.

8   F A Olmstead, *Incidents of a Whaling Voyage*, D Appleton, New York, 1841, pp 181–2.

9   Goode, *Fisheries*, section 5, vol II, p 239. This technical, asexual

use of one of the strongest taboo words in English is rare, but not unique. It could only occur in exclusively and unselfconsciously male occupations like whaling and stevedoring.

10 W B Whitecar, *Four Years Aboard The Whaleship*, J B Lippincott, Philadelphia, 1864, p 59.

11 W H Macy, *There She Blows! or the Log of the Arethusa*, Lee & Shepard, Boston, 1877, p 87.

12 H Kendall, 'Beyond Kerguelen', in *Poems*, A Sutherland (ed), George Robertson & Co., Melbourne, 1890.

3 Beyond the Capes

1 *Lloyd's List*, 17 August 1787. Enderby subsequently claimed this honour for one of his ships, but gave no particulars.

2 Log, 1786–89, PRO ADM 51/4376, pt 8.

3 Enderby to Chalmers (?), [1788], Mitchell Library, MS A322, p 403.

4 Shields to Samuel Enderby & Sons, 6 March 1790, ibid., p 511.

5 Enderby to Chalmers, Monday [8 March 1790], ibid., p 515. Chalmers, the Chief Clerk to the Privy Council Committee on Trade and Plantations, saw it as an historic communication, noting on it that 'this is the first vessel which ever went into the South Sea for whales'.

6 Enderby to Chalmers, 17 January 1789, ibid., pp 499–501.

7 Melville to Enderby & Sons, 22 November 1791, ibid., pp 520–1.

8 ibid.

9 Phillip to Nepean, 29 March 1792, *HRA* 1 vol II, p 345.

10 O Macy, *History of Nantucket*, reprint of 1880 edn, Augustus M Kelley, Clifton, 1972, pp 143–4.

11 Enderby to Chalmers, nd [1789?], Mitchell Library, MS A322, p 587.

12 ibid.

13 Hussey and Robinson's compilation, listed in A Starbuck, *History of Nantucket*, pp 394–5.

14 Enderby to Chalmers (?), 14 November 1797, Mitchell Library, MS A322, p 527.

15 *Gentleman's Magazine*, March 1798, p 254.

16 Quested to King, 25 September 1800, Mitchell Library, MS A322, p 595.

17 E A Stackpole, *The Sea Hunters*, J B Lippincott, Philadelphia, 1953, pp 194–206.

18 E Fanning, *Voyages Round the World*, Collins & Hannay, New York, 1833, p 236.

19 Bristow's log as quoted in A G Findlay's *Directory for the Pacific Ocean*, Part II, R H Laurie, London, 1851, p 681.

20 Folger's recollection as recorded by Amasa Delano in his *Narrative of Voyages and Travels*, self-published in Boston, 1817, p 139.

Fast and Loose

1 E A Stackpole collection, appended to his *Whales and Destiny*, University of Massachusetts Press, Amherst, 1972, pp 388–9.

2 F D Bennett, *A Whaling Voyage Round the Globe*, Richard Bentley, London, 1840, pp 206–7.

3 Tasmanian Acts, 5 William IV, c 13, p 2.

4 C M Scammon, *Marine Mammals of the North-Western Coast of North America*, John H Carmany, San Francisco, 1874, p 267.

5 J F Hogan, MP, 'What May Happen to a British Captain', *Westminster Review*, vol 141, April 1894, p 362.

6 Whitecar, *Four Years*, p 125.

7 F M Ringgold to Assistant Secretary of State J Appleton, 1 September 1858, appended to E P Hohman, *The American Whaleman*, Longmans, Green & Co, London, 1928, p 312.

4 Free Trade and Sailors' Rights

1 Jefferson to Kosciusko, 28 June 1812, *Writings*, Library of America, New York, 1984, p 1265.

2 Republican Citizens of Nantucket to President Madison, 21 November 1812, quoted in Starbuck, *History of Nantucket*, pp 279–80.

3 Porter to crew, 30 April 1813, quoted in B Shepard (ed), *Bound for Battle*, Harcourt Brace & World, New York, 1967, p 82.

4 D Porter, *A Voyage in the South Seas*, Sir Richard Phillips & Co, London, 1823, p 52.

5 Shepard, op. cit., p 96.

6 Porter, op. cit., p 65.

7 Shepard, op. cit., pp 106–7.

8 *HRA* 1 vol VIII, p 353.

9 O Macy, *History of Nantucket* (reprint of 1880 edition), Augustus M Kelley, Clifton, 1972, p 214.

10   T Beale, *The Natural History of the Sperm Whale*, John van Voorst, London, 1839, p 152.

11   Palmer was not the first to see this coast, part of which had been charted and named Trinity Land by Edward Bransfield, RN, in the *Williams* a year earlier.

Rope's End

1   H Melville, *Omoo*, John Murray, London, 1847, pp 8, 12–13.

2   ibid., pp 75–6.

3   ibid., pp 150–1.

4   W Lay and C M Hussey, *A Narrative of the Mutiny on Board the Ship Globe of Nantucket*, the authors, New London, 1828, p 39.

5   William Lay as reported by Lieut. H Paulding in his *Journal of a Cruise of the United States Schooner Dolphin* (1831), Australia & New Zealand Book Co, Sydney, 1970, p 145.

6   Stackpole, *Sea Hunters*, pp 432–3.

7   J Ross Browne, *Etchings of a Whale Cruise*, John Murray, London, 1846, p 497.

8   ibid., p 496.

9   Sampson, *Three Times*, p 122.

10   Log of the *Junior*, 1857–58, PMB film 340.

5   Honour without Profit

1   Quoted by G Jackson, *The British Whaling Trade*, Adam & Charles Black, London, 1978, p 123.

2   W C Wentworth, *Description of the Colony of New South Wales*, G & W B Whittaker, London, 1819, p 292.

3   ibid., p. 243.

4   ibid., p. 244.

5   J T Bigge, *Report on the State of Agriculture and Trade in New South Wales*, HMSO, London, 1822, p 56.

6   *Sydney Gazette*, 28 April 1825.

7   T W Smith, *A Narrative of Life, Travels and Sufferings*, W C Hill, New Bedford, 1844, pp 200–1. Smith subsequently heard that the *Alfred*'s second mate had survived and was being held in the mountains as a slave.

8   *Australian Quarterly Journal*, no 1, Sydney, January 1828, p 88.

9   ibid., p 90 and *BPP* 690 (?) 1833, p 512. The bracketed figures are not Enderby's. They assume comparable whaling success,

identical crew numbers and lays, and depreciation pro rata for tonnage. They probably understate British manning expenses. The *Quarterly* overestimated the amount of oil that a full ship could carry, which was about 70 per cent of register tonnage.

10 R McNab, *The Old Whaling Days* (1913), Golden Press, Auckland, 1975 reprint, p 130.

11 C H & G Enderby to Treasury, 11 February 1833, PRO ADM 1/4308.

12 Biscoe's description in the *Journal of the Royal Geographical Society*, vol III, 1833, pp 108–9. Edmund Burke had called the aurora, first reported by Cook, as 'the frozen serpent of the south'.

13 ibid., p 112.

14 Diary of A B Spark, 2 April 1838 in G Abbott and G Little (eds), *The Respectable Sydney Merchant*, Sydney University Press, Sydney, 1976, p 92.

15 Extract from Balleny's journal, *Journal of the Royal Geographical Society*, vol IX, 1839, p 521.

16 *Australian*, 12 May 1829.

17 Monthly Supplement of the *Penny Magazine of the Society for the Diffusion of Useful Knowledge*, no 74, 31 May 1833, p 208.

18 Evidence before the Select Committee on British Shipping, *BPP* 545, vol VIII, 1844, p 37.

19 ibid., p 17.

Melting Pots

1 Whitecar, *Four Years*, pp 163–4.

2 H T Cheever, *The Whaleman's Adventures in the Southern Ocean*, Sampson Low, London, 1850, p 303.

3 Whitecar, op. cit., p 42.

4 Browne, *Etchings*, pp 43, 191.

5 ibid., p 326.

6 Sampson, *Three Times*, p 15.

7 W M Davis, *Nimrod of the Sea* (1874), Christopher Publishing, North Quincy, 1972, p 284.

8 F A Olmstead, *Incidents of a Whaling Voyage*, D Appleton, New York, 1841, p 151.

9 R Coffin, *The Last of the Logan*, Cornell University Press, Ithaca, 1941, pp 40–1.

10 Olmstead, op. cit., p 152.

11 ibid.

12 F Maynard and A Dumas, *The Whalers*, Hutchinson, London, 1937, p 273.

13 ibid., p 128.
14 A Delano, *Narrative of Voyages and Travels*, the author, Boston, 1817, pp 377–8.
15 Davis, op. cit., p 113.
16 J Ward, *Perils, Pastimes and Pleasures of an Emigrant*, T C Newby, London, 1849, p 133.
17 Coffin, op. cit., pp 39–40.
18 Windlass chanty aboard the *Bruce*, 1842, in Browne, op. cit., pp 133–4.
19 N C Haley, *Whale Hunt*, Ives Washburn, New York, 1948, pp 135–6.
20 Olmstead, op. cit., pp 45–6.

6 Of Currents and Backwaters

1 Macy, *History of Nantucket*, p 138.
2 *Nantucket Inquirer*, 1836, quoted in Stackpole, *Sea Hunters*, p 471.
3 L E Davis, R E Gallman & T D Hutchins in P Kilby (ed), *Quantity and Quiddity*, Wesleyan University Press, Middletown, 1987, p 390.
4 Derived from Starbuck, *American Whale Fishery*, p 660.
5 Memorial of the citizens of Nantucket to Congress, November 1828, in J N Reynolds, *Address on the Subject of a Surveying and Exploring Expedition*, Harper & Brothers, New York, 1836, pp 165–6.
6 E Fanning, *Voyages Around the World*, Collins & Hannay, New York, 1833, p 487.
7 J N Reynolds, *Voyage of the US Frigate Potomac*, Harper & Brothers, New York, 1835, p 471.
8 H Holden, *A Narrative of the Shipwreck, Captivity and Sufferings of Horace Holden and Benj H Nute*, Russell, Shattuck & Co, Boston, 1836, pp 101–2.
9 Reynolds, *Address*, pp 67–8.
10 ibid., pp 97–8.
11 C Wilkes, *Narrative of the United States Exploring Expedition*, Wiley & Putnam, London, 1845, vol III, p 357.
12 ibid., vol I, p 134.
13 ibid., vol II, pp 271–2.
14 ibid., vol V, pp 494–5.
15 ibid., p 486.
16 ibid., p 493.
17 ibid., p 502.

Clouds

1 J C Hart, *Miriam Coffin*, Whittaker, London, 1834, vol I, p 55.
2 ibid., vol III, p 221.
3 H Melville, *Moby Dick* (1851), Penguin, New York, 1992, p 82.
4 P Folger, *Dominum Collaudamus*, quoted by O Macy, *History of Nantucket* (1880 edn), Augustus M Kelly, Clifton, 1972 reprint, pp 280–1.
5 J N Reynolds, 'Mocha Dick', in *The Oxford Book of Sea Stories*, T Tanner (ed), Oxford University Press, Oxford, 1994, p 64.
6 O Chase, *Narrative of the Most Extraordinary and Distressing Shipwreck of the Whaleship Essex* (1821), Corinth, New York, 1963, p 20.
7 ibid., pp 34–5.
8 ibid., pp 86–7.
9 ibid., p 89.
10 D Tyerman and G Bennet, *Journal of Voyages and Travels*, Frederick Westley & A H Davis, London, 1831, p 28.
11 *Time*, vol 117, no 26, 29 June 1981, p 47.
12 H Melville, *Clarel*, pt I, canto 37, quoted by Stackpole, *Sea-Hunters*, p 337.
13 Quoted in J Leyda, *The Melville Log*, Harcourt, Brace & Co, New York, 1951, p 432.
14 ibid., p 607.

7 The Princes of Whales

1 O Brierly, *Journal*, 1843–44, as quoted in M Diamond, *Ben Boyd of Boydtown*, Melbourne University Press, Carlton, 1995, pp 100–1.
2 B Boyd to J W Sutherland, PRO J90/1446/B147, as quoted in Diamond, op. cit., p 155.
3 J C Ross, *A Voyage of Discovery and Research in the Southern and Antarctic Regions*, John Murray, London, 1847, vol I, p 140.
4 T R Preston to C Enderby, 2 July 1846, published in C Enderby, *Proposal for Re-establishing the British Southern Whale Fishery*, Effingham Wilson, London, 1847, p 2.
5 ibid., p 7.
6 ibid., p 61.
7 Appendix to C Enderby, *The Auckland Islands*, Pelham Richardson, London, 1849, p 56.
8 *The Times*, 23 October 1849.

9   F B McLaren, *The Auckland Islands*, A H & A W Reed, Wellington, 1948, p 59.
10   *The Times*, 18 July 1855.
11   A G E Jones, *Ships Employed in the South Seas Trade*, Roebuck, Canberra, 1986–91, vol I, p 269.
12   Quoted in W J Dakin, *Whalemen Adventurers*, Angus & Robertson, Sydney, 1977, p 137.
13   H Melville, *Moby Dick* (1851), Penguin, New York, 1992, p 483–4.
14   R Towns to R Brooks, 15 February 1853, quoted in Dakin, op. cit., p 118.

Boat and Barque

1   W M Davis, *Nimrod of the Sea* (1874), Christopher Publishing, North Quincy, 1972.
2   T W Smith, *A Narrative of Life, Travels and Sufferings*, W C Hill, New Bedford, 1844, p 167.
3   H Melville, *Omoo*, John Murray, London, 1847, pp 6–7.

8   Seas Aflame

1   Attachment to a letter from Captain Daniel Mackenzie to Lieut. Maury, 8 June 1849, in M F Maury, *Explanations and Sailing Directions to Accompany the Wind and Current Charts*, 6th edn, E & C Biddle, Philadelphia, 1854, pp 373–4.
2   ibid., p 363.
3   ibid., p 390.
4   ibid.
5   ibid., p 382.
6   R Semmes, *My Adventures Afloat*, Richard Bentley, London, 1869, p 424.
7   J T Scharf, *History of the Confederate States Navy*, Joseph McDonough, Albany, 1894, pp 345–6.
8   Journal of the *America*, 1861, PMB microfilm 573.
9   J D Horan (ed), *CSS Shenandoah: The Memoirs of James I Waddell*, Crown, New York, 1960, p 106.
10   ibid., pp 114–15.
11   ibid., p 145.
12   ibid., p 158.
13   Narrative of J C Hawes, *Report of the Court of Commissioners of*

Alabama Claims, Executive Document 21, 44th US Congress, Government Printing Office, Washington, 1877.

14 C E Hunt, *The Shenandoah*, quoted in C C Beaman, *The National and Private Alabama Claims*, W H Moore, Washington, 1871, p 142.

Spun Yarn

1 W M Davis, *Nimrod of the Sea* (1874), Christopher Publishing, North Quincy, 1972, pp 384–5, 196–7.

2 ibid., pp 385–7.

3 Huntting to J T Brown, 2 October 1881, quoted in Goode, *Fisheries*, section V, vol II, p 275.

4 Davis, op. cit., pp 195–6.

5 PMB microfilms 240–1, 365. Also C B Hawes, *Whaling*, William Heinemann, London, 1924, pp 239–50.

6 *Newgate Calendar*, 15 April 1833, pp 393–402, from Folger's story as told by A G E Jones in vol II, pt III of his *Ships Employed in the South Seas Trade*, Roebuck, Canberra, 1986–91.

9 Frozen Fleets

1 F T Bullen, *The Cruise of the Cachalot*, Smith, Elder & Co, London, 1899, p 259.

2 A G Day (ed), *Mark Twain's Letters from Hawaii*, Appleton-Century, New York, 1966, pp 94–5.

3 Quoted in A Starbuck, *History of the American Whale Fishery*, the author, Waltham, 1876, p 107.

4 D Wilkinson, *Whaling in Many Seas*, Henry J Drane, London, [1905], p 290.

5 H Williams (ed), *One Whaling Family*, Victor Gollancz, London, 1964, pp 238–9.

6 *Whalemen's Shipping List*, trade review for 1872, quoted in Goode, *Fisheries*, section V, vol II, p 152.

7 Quoted in a Starbuck, op. cit., p 108–9.

8 ibid., p 110.

9 *New Bedford Evening Standard*, 21 November 1877, quoted in Goode, *Fisheries*, op. cit., vol II, pp 76–7.

10 E P Bertholf, 'The Rescue of the Whalers', *Harper's New Monthly Magazine*, vol 99, June 1899, p 24.

11 Statistics from Davis, Gallman & Hutchins in P Kilby (ed), *Quan-*

tity and Quiddity, Wesleyan University Press, Middleton, 1987, p 340.

Craft

1   Quoted in A Starbuck, *History of the American Whale Fishery*, the author, Waltham, 1876, p 154.

2   US Patent 3490, 16 March 1844, quoted in T G Lytle, *Harpoons and Other Whalecraft*, Old Dartmouth Historical Society, New Bedford, 1984, p 51.

3   US Patent 31190, 22 January 1861, *ibid.*, p 122.

4   Whalemen's Shipping List, 2 January 1855, ibid., p 105.

5   Whalemen's Shipping List, 13 November 1855, ibid.

6   Malloy's journal, as reported by W M Davis in *Nimrod of the Sea* (1874), Christopher Publishing, North Quincy, 1972, pp 233–4.

7   J Ross Browne, *Etchings of a Whale Cruise*, John Murray, London, 1846, pp 574–5.

8   Captain Neils Juel to Professor S F Baird, 22 September 1884, quoted in Goode, *Fisheries*, section V, vol II, pp 195–6.

9   Commercial Report No 16, US State Department, 16 February 1882, ibid., pp 196–7.

10 So Ends

1   *Whalemen's Shipping List* (1868–80) and I H Bartlett & Sons (1881–83) trade reviews, in Goode, *Fisheries*, section V, vol II, pp 146–66.

2   *Oil, Paint and Drug Reporter*, 23 November 1881, ibid., p 162.

3   Whalemen's Shipping List, trade review for 1876, in Goode, section V, vol II, p 159.

4   PMB microfilm 812.

5   F T Bullen, 'A Day on the Solander Whaling Ground', in *Idylls of the Sea*, Grant Richards, London, 1899, pp 239–41.

6   *Oil, Drug and Paint Reporter*, 23 November 1881; Goode, *Fisheries*, p 163.

7   Statistics from L Davis, R E Gallman and T D Hutchins, in Kilby, *Quantity and Quiddity*, p 344.

8   C W Ashley, *The Yankee Whaler*, Martin Hopkinson, London, [1926], p 1.

9   ibid., p 5.

10 ibid., pp 21–2.

11 None of the *Morgan*'s nineteenth-century crew lists includes Tilton, but aliases were common.

12 Tripp published his account of this voyage, with photographs, as *There Goes Flukes*, Reynolds, New Bedford, 1938.

13 Log of the *John R Manta*, 1925, PMB film 409.

14 ibid., 1927.

15 FAO, *Mammals in the Seas*, Rome, 1978–82, vol I, p 82.

Epilogue

1 C M Scammon, *Marine Mammals of the North-Western Coast of North America*, John H Carmany, San Francisco, 1874, p 244.

2 S Ohsumi, 'Catches of Sperm Whales by Modern Whaling in the North Pacific', in *Sperm Whales*, International Whaling Commission Special Issue 2, Cambridge, 1980, p 18.

3 C W Ashley, *The Yankee Whaler*, Martin Hopkinson, London, [1926] p 120.

SOURCES

The main source for whalemen's logs is the New England Microfilming Project undertaken by the Pacific Manuscripts Bureau (PMB) of the Australian National University (ANU), which includes R B Hegarty's continuation of Starbuck's record of American whaling voyages. Abbreviations used in the notes denote the *Historical Records of Australia* (*HRA*), the British Public Records Office (PRO) and the *British Parliamentary Papers* series (*BPP*).

Monographs and Compilations

Abbott, G, and Little, G (eds), *The Respectable Sydney Merchant*, Sydney University Press, Sydney, 1976

Adams, J, *Works*, Little, Brown, Boston, 1852

Ansel, W D, *The Whaleboat*, Mystic Seaport Museum, Mystic, Connecticut, 1983

Ashley, C W, *The Yankee Whaler*, Martin Hopkinson, London, [1926]

Bancroft, G, *History of the United States of America* (1885), Kennikat Press reissue, Port Washington, New York, 1967

Barkan, E R (ed), *Edmund Burke on the American Revolution*, Peter Smith, Gloucester, 1972

Barnes, R H, *Sea Hunters of Indonesia*, Clarendon Press, Oxford, 1996

Beale, T, *The Natural History of the Sperm Whale*, John van Voorst, London, 1839

Beaman, C C, *The National and Private Alabama Claims*, W H Moore, Washington, 1871

Bennett, F D, *A Whaling Voyage Round the Globe*, Richard Bentley, London, 1840

Bigge, J T, *Report on the State of Agriculture and Trade in New South Wales*, HMSO, London, 1822

Blyth, T, *The Oilmen*, the author, London, 1835

Bowden, K M, *Captain James Kelly of Hobart Town*, Melbourne University Press, London and Carlton, 1964

Brande, W T, *A Manual of Chemistry*, J Murray, London, 1819

Broeze, F J A, *Mr Brooks and the Australian Trade*, Melbourne University Press, Carlton, 1993

Browne, J Ross, *Etchings of a Whale Cruise*, John Murray, London, 1846

Bullen, F T, *The Cruise of the Cachalot*, Smith, Elder & Co, London, 1899

——*Idylls of the Sea*, Grant Richards, London, 1899

Chase, O, *Narrative of the Most Extraordinary and Distressing Shipwreck of the Whaleship Essex* (1821), Corinth Books, New York, 1963

Chatterton, E K, *Whalers and Whaling*, T Fisher Unwin, London, 1925

Chatwin, D, '"A Trade So Uncontrollably Uncertain": A Study of the English Southern Whale Fishery from 1815 to 1860', unpublished MA thesis, ANU, Canberra, 1997

Cheever, H T, *The Whaleman's Adventures in the Southern Ocean*, Sampson Low, London, 1850

Church, A C, *Whale Ships and Whaling*, Bonanza Books, New York, 1938

Coffin, R, *The Last of the Logan*, Cornell University Press, Ithaca, 1941

Colnett, J, *A Voyage to the South Atlantic and round Cape Horn into the Pacific Ocean*, the author, London, 1798

Crèvecoeur, J H St J de, *Letters from An American Farmer* (1782), H M Dent, London, 1912

Cuvier, G, *The Animal Kingdom*, Geo. B Whittaker, London, 1827

Dakin, W J, *Whalemen Adventurers*, Angus & Robertson, Sydney, 1977

Davis, W M, *Nimrod of the Sea* (1874), Christopher Publishing reprint, North Quincy, Massachusetts, 1972

Day, A G (ed), *Mark Twain's Letters from Hawaii*, Appleton-Century, New York, 1966

Delano, A, *Narrative of Voyages and Travels*, the author, Boston, 1817

Diamond, M, *Ben Boyd of Boydtown*, Melbourne University Press, Carlton, 1995

Dow, G F, *Whale Ships and Whaling*, Marine Research Society, Salem, 1925

Druett, J, *Petticoat Whalers*, Collins, Auckland, 1991

Dulles, F R, *Lowered Boats*, Harrap, London, 1934

Enderby, C, *The Auckland Islands*, Pelham Richardson, London, 1849

——*Proposal for Re-establishing the British Southern Whale Fishery*, Effingham Wilson, London, 1847

Fanning, E, *Voyages Round the World*, Collins & Hannay, New York, 1833

Findlay, A G, *Directory for the Pacific Ocean*, R H Laurie, London, 1851

Fonda, D C Jr, *Eighteenth Century Nantucket Whaling*, the author, Nantucket, 1969

Food and Agriculture Organisation, *Mammals in the Seas*, Rome, 1978–82

Forbes, A, *Whale Ships and Whaling Scenes*, Second Bank–State Street Trust Co, Boston, 1955

Forster, H, *The South Sea Whaler: An Annotated Bibliography*, Kendall Whaling Museum, Sharon, Massachusetts, 1985

——*More South Sea Whaling*, Research School of Pacific Studies, ANU, Canberra, 1991

Goode, G B (ed), *The Fisheries and Fishing Industries of the United States*, Government Printing Office, Washington, 1884–87

Haley, N C, *Whale Hunt*, Ives Washburn, New York, 1948

Hart, J C, *Miriam Coffin*, Whittaker, London, 1834

Hawes, C B, *Whaling*, William Heinemann, London, 1924

Hodgkinson, R, *Eber Bunker*, Roebuck, Canberra, 1975

Hohman, E P, *The American Whaleman*, Longmans, Green & Co, London, 1928

Holden, H, *A Narrative of the Shipwreck, Captivity and Sufferings of Horace Holden and Benj H Nute*, Russell, Shattuck & Co, Boston, 1836

Holmes, L, *The Arctic Whalemen*, Thayer & Eldridge, Boston, 1861

Horan, J D (ed), *CSS Shenandoah: The Memoirs of James I Waddell*, Crown, New York, 1960

Jackson, G, *The British Whaling Trade*, Adam & Charles Black, London, 1978

Jardine, W, *The Natural History of the Ordinary Cetacea or Whales*, W H Lizars, Edinburgh, 1837

Jarman, R, *Journal of a Voyage to the South Seas in the Japan*, the author, Beccles, Suffolk, 1838

Jefferson, T, *Writings*, Library of America, New York, 1984

Jenkins, J T, *A History of the Whale Fisheries*, Kennikat Press reprint, Port Washington, New York, 1971

Jones, A G E, *Ships Employed in the South Seas Trade*, 2 vols, Roebuck, Canberra, 1986–91

Kilby, P (ed), *Quantity and Quiddity*, Wesleyan University Press, Middletown, Connecticut, 1987

Lance, W, *Address to the Owners of Ships Engaged in the South Sea Fishery*, G M'Kewan, London, 1844

Langdon, R, *American Whalers and Traders in the Pacific: A Guide to Records on Microfilm*, Pacific Manuscripts Bureau, ANU, Canberra, 1978

Lay, W, and Hussey, C M, *A Narrative of the Mutiny on Board the Ship Globe of Nantucket*, the authors, New London, 1828

Leavitt, J F, *The Charles W Morgan*, Mystic Seaport, Mystic, Connecticut, 1973

Leyda, J, *The Melville Log*, Hartcourt, Brace & Co, New York, 1951

Lockyer, C, *Observations on Diving Behaviour of the Sperm Whale*, Pergamon Press, Oxford, 1977

Lytle, T G, *Harpoons and Other Whalecraft*, Old Dartmouth Historical Society, New Bedford, 1984

Macy, O, *History of Nantucket* (1880 edn), Augustus M Kelley reprint, Clifton, New Jersey, 1972

Macy, W H, *There She Blows! or the Log of the Arethusa*, Lee & Shepard, Boston, 1877

McCulloch, J R, *A Dictionary Practical, Theoretical and Historical of Commerce and Commercial Navigation*, Longman, Brown, Green & Longmans, London, 1842

McLaren, F B, *The Auckland Islands*, A H & A W Reed, Wellington, 1948

McNab, R, *The Old Whaling Days* (1913), Golden Press reprint, Auckland, 1975

Martin, R M, *The British Colonies*, J & F Tallis, London, 1850–57

Maury, M F, *Explanations and Sailing Directions to Accompany the Wind and Current Charts*, 6th edn, E & C Biddle, Philadelphia, 1854

Maynard, F, and Dumas, A, *The Whalers*, Hutchinson, London, 1937

Melville, H, *Moby Dick* (1851), Penguin, New York, 1992

——*Omoo*, John Murray, London, 1847

Mill, H R, *The Siege of the South Pole*, Alston Rivers, London, 1905

Miller, P A, *And the Whale Is Ours*, D R Gondine, Boston, 1979

Murray, G (ed), *The Antarctic Manual*, Royal Geographical Society, London, 1901

Nordhoff, C, *Whaling and Fishing*, Dodd, Mead & Co, New York, 1895

Olmstead, F A, *Incidents of a Whaling Voyage*, D Appleton, New York, 1841

Ommanney, F D, *Lost Leviathan*, Hutchinson, London, 1971

Padover, S K, *The Complete Jefferson*, Duell, Sloan & Pearce, New York, 1943

Paulding, H, *Journal of a Cruise of the United States Schooner Dolphin* (1831), Australia & New Zealand Book Co, Sydney, 1970

Philp, J E, *Whaling Ways of Hobart Town*, J Walch & Sons, Hobart, 1936

Polack, J S, *New Zealand*, Richard Bentley, London, 1838

Porter, D, *A Voyage in the South Seas*, Sir Richard Phillips & Co, London, 1823

Report of the Court of Commissioners of Alabama Claims, Executive Document 21, 44th US Congress, Government Printing Office, Washington, 1877

Reynolds, J N, *Address on the Subject of a Surveying and Exploring Expedition*, Harper & Brothers, New York, 1836

——*Voyage of the US Frigate Potomac*, Harper & Brothers, New York, 1835

Richards, R, *Murihiku Re-visited*, Lithographic Services, Wellington, 1995

Ross, J C, *A Voyage of Discovery and Research in the Southern and Antarctic Regions*, John Murray, London, 1847

Rotch, W, *Memorandum Written in the Eightieth Year of His Age*, Houghton Mifflin, Boston, 1916

Sampson, A D, *Three Times Around The World*, Express Printing Co, Buffalo, 1867

Sanderson, I T, *Follow the Whale*, Cassell, London, 1958

Scammon, C M, *Marine Mammals of the North-Western Coast of North America*, John H Carmany, San Francisco, 1874

Scharf, J T, *History of the Confederate States Navy*, Joseph McDonough, Albany, 1894

Scoresby, W, *An Account of the Arctic Regions* (1820), David & Charles reprint, Newton Abbot, 1969

Semmes, R, *My Adventures Afloat*, Richard Bentley, London, 1869

Shepard, B (ed), *Bound for Battle*, Harcourt Brace & World, New York, 1967

Sherman, S C, *The Voice of the Whaleman*, Providence Public Library, Providence, 1965

Smith, A, *The Wealth of Nations*, A Strachan and T Cadell, London, 1793

Smith, T W, *A Narrative of Life, Travels and Sufferings*, W C Hill, New Bedford, 1844

Stackpole, E A, *The Charles W Morgan*, Meredith Press, New York, 1967

——*The Sea Hunters*, J B Lippincott, Philadelphia, 1953

——*Whales and Destiny*, University of Massachusetts Press, Amherst, 1972

Starbuck, A, *History of the American Whale Fishery*, the author, Waltham, 1876

——*History of Nantucket* (1924), Charles E Tuttle, Rutland, 1969

Steven, M, *Trade, Tactics and Territory*, Melbourne University Press, Carlton, 1983

Stones, W, *My First Voyage*, Simpkin, Marshall & Co, London, 1858

Sutherland, A (ed), *Poems of Henry Clarence Kendall*, George Robertson & Co, Melbourne, 1890

Tanner, T (ed), *The Oxford Book of Sea Stories*, Oxford University Press, Oxford, 1994

Taylor, N W, *Life on a Whaler*, New London County Historical Society, New London, 1929

Tillman, M F, and Donovan, G P (eds), *Historical Whaling Records*, International Whaling Commission Special Issue 5, Cambridge, 1983

Tyerman, D and Bennet, G, *Journal of Voyages and Travels*, Frederick Westley & A H Davis, London, 1831

Ward, J, *Perils, Pastimes and Pleasures of an Emigrant*, T C Newby, London, 1849

Wentworth, W C, *Description of the Colony of New South Wales*, G & W B Whittaker, London, 1819

Whipple, A B C, *Yankee Whalers in the South Seas*, Doubleday, New York, 1954

Whitecar, W B, *Four Years Aboard The Whaleship*, J B Lippincott, Philadelphia, 1864

Wilkes, C, *Narrative of the United States Exploring Expedition*, Wiley & Putnam, London, 1845

Wilkinson, D, *Whaling in Many Seas*, Henry J Drane, London, [1905]

Williams, H (ed), *One Whaling Family*, Victor Gollancz, London, 1964

Articles

Bertholf, E P, 'The Rescue of the Whalers', *Harper's New Monthly Magazine*, vol 99, June 1899

Foxton, J G, 'Notes of a Long Forgotten Antarctic Voyage in 1833',

Transactions of the Royal Geographical Society of Australasia (Victorian branch), vol X, 1893

Garnett, R S, 'Moby-Dick and Mocha-Dick', *Blackwood's Magazine*, vol 226, no 1865, December 1929

Hogan, J F, 'What May Happen to a British Captain', *Westminster Review*, vol 141, April 1894

Johnston, G H, 'The Colonial Whalers', *Blue Peter*, vol 13, no 133, April 1933

Jones, A G E, 'John Biscoe', *Mariner's Mirror*, vol 50, no 3, August 1964

Kendall, H, 'Sperm Whaling', *Australian Journal*, vol 5, part 54, November 1869

Ohsumi, S, 'Catches of Sperm Whales by Modern Whaling in the North Pacific', in *Sperm Whales*, International Whaling Commission Special Issue 2, Cambridge, 1980

Pearson, M, 'The Technology of Whaling in Australian Waters in the 19th Century', *Australian Journal of Historical Archaeology*, vol 1, 1983

Reeves, R R, and Mitchell, E, 'The Long Island, New York, Right Whale Fishery: 1650–1924', in *Right Whales: Past and Present Status*, International Whaling Commission Special Issue 10, Cambridge, 1986

Reynolds, J N, 'Mocha Dick or the White Whale of the Pacific', *Knickerbocker Magazine*, May 1839, in *The Oxford Book of Sea Stories*, T Tanner (ed), Oxford University Press, Oxford, 1994

[Rinder, S], 'Black Skin A-head!', *Household Words*, no 146, 8 January 1853

Townsend, C H, 'The Distribution of Certain Whales as Shown by Logbook Records of American Whaleships', *Zoologica*, vol XIX, no 1, 3 April 1935

Newspapers and periodicals

The Australian, Sydney
Australian Journal, Melbourne
Australian Quarterly Journal, Sydney
The Friend, Honolulu
Gentleman's Magazine, London
Journal of the Royal Geographical Society, London
Lloyd's List, London
Penny Magazine of the Society for the Diffusion of Useful Knowledge, London

Philosophical Transactions of the Royal Society, London
South Asian Register, Sydney
Quarterly Review, London
Sydney Gazette and New South Wales Advertiser, Sydney
Time, New York
The Times, London
Westminster Review, London
Whalemen's Shipping List and Merchants' Transcript, New Bedford

INDEX